# FROM ANZAC TO THE HINDENBURG LINE

*Printed for the Publishers*

9th BATTALION A.I.F. ASSOCIATION
BRISBANE

*by*

William Brooks & Co. (Q.) Pty. Ltd.
Wickham St., Valley
Brisbane

Plate 1.

1.—THE 9th BATTALION MEMORIAL,
Anzac Square, Brisbane.
(*N.K.H. photo.*)

# FROM ANZAC TO THE HINDENBURG LINE

*The History of the 9th Battalion, A.I.F.*

By

NORMAN K. HARVEY, B.A., A.A.C.I.

Foreword by

Major-General E. G. Sinclair-MacLagan

•

1941

The Naval & Military Press Ltd

Published by
**The Naval & Military Press Ltd**
5 Riverside, Brambleside, Bellbrook
Industrial Estate, Uckfield, East Sussex,
TN22 1QQ England
Tel: +44 (0) 1825 749494
Fax: +44 (0) 1825 765701
www.naval-military-press.com
www.military-genealogy.com
www.militarymaproom.com

*In reprinting in facsimile from the original, any imperfections are inevitably reproduced and the quality may fall short of modern type and cartographic standards.*

# Preface

The writing of this history was begun in March, 1933, and the first draft of it was completed in May, 1936. Since that time ceaseless revisions and additions have been made until the manuscript went into the press.

An attempt, not over-successful in places, has been made at the three aims of completeness, accuracy and clearness; how far this attempt has succeeded is for the reader to judge.

The dates and places given for each movement of the battalion between April 25th, 1915, and September 26th, 1918, are in most cases taken from the battalion diary. Where there has been a conflict of opinion with regard to dates and times those given in the battalion diary have been adopted, unless overwhelming evidence has been found to the contrary. In some cases incorrect figures or names may be due to clerical errors in copies of documents used.

It may be noticed that a comparatively trivial matter will sometimes be given more space than something of much greater importance. This is owing to the fact that often very little information has been received, in spite of diligent enquiries, on the more important subjects. The fact that the history was being written was well advertised by the press, wireless, and in other ways, and every attempt was made to get into touch with anyone likely to be able to supply information, so any faults of incompleteness cannot in all cases be attributed to the author.

A few minor circumstances, however, have been omitted because it has been found impossible to reach certainty as to the facts, and some others had to be excluded as their publication might cause distress to persons now living.

In some cases it may seem to many readers that unnecessary explanations have been given of matters whose meaning would be obvious to an Australian. The reason of this is that it is hoped that many overseas people, who may not be acquainted with the meaning of the expressions in question, will be found among the readers of this book.

The title "Official History", which occurs many times, refers to "The Official History of Australia in the War of 1914-1918" by Dr. C. E. W. Bean.

Some of the illustrations may be noticed to be of rather indifferent quality, owing to the fact that it was found impossible to obtain satisfactory photographs of the subjects in question. In a few cases, in portraits, there seemed to be only one picture in existence of the person in uniform, and this had to be used, good or bad.

The maps were, with two exceptions, all specially drawn, so as to secure clearness of the essential details and elimination of the unnecessary. The thanks of the author are due to Mr. R. D. Wearne for drawing twenty-one of them, to Mr. L. G. Fraser for five, and to the Australian War Memorial for permission to copy No. 20, also to the proprietors of the Brisbane "Courier-Mail" for permission to use the block for No. 8, which was obtained from them.

Thanks is also due to the following, who have lent or supplied photographs for the illustrations:—Mrs. W. H. Wearne, Miss M. Butler, Miss M. Warham, Major-General H. Gordon Bennett, Brigadier-General J. C. Robertson, Colonel A. G. Butler, Lieutenant-Colonels C. F. Ross and A. G. Salisbury, Major A. R. Knightley, Captains W. A. Collin and L. A. Jones, Lieutenants E. H. Meyers, J. P. Tunn and C. M. Wrench, Dr. C. E. W. Bean, Messrs. R. D. Huish, S. R. C. Lewis, R. Mills, L. S. H. Wilson, the late E. J. Gandy, the late J. H. Harvey, the Equitable Probate and General Insurance Co. Ltd., the Australian War Memorial and the "Omrah" Association.

The history could not have been written without the assistance and co-operation of a large band of ex-members of the battalion and others—if they were all on parade they would amount to considerably more than a platoon—who supplied information and read through and checked portions of the history. For this the author wishes to thank Mrs. J. A. Milne, Mrs. M. W. Neligan, Mrs. C. Pennefather, Monseigneur the Bishop of Amiens, the late Hon. G. A. Street, Brigadier-General C. F. Aspinall-Oglander, Brigadier-General J. Campbell Robertson, Brigadier E. C. Plant, Colonel A. Graham Butler, Lieutenant-Colonels C. Fortescue, W. C. Harvey, N. G. Hatton, F. A. Hughes, L. M. Mullen, W. G. Penrose, C. F. Ross, A. G. Salisbury, R. H. Walsh, Majors P. Adsett, N. G. Armstrong, A. R. Knightley, H. L. Swain, Captains Walter C. Belford, F. J. Biggs, W. A. Collin, T. W. Farmer, L. A. Jones, S. L. McIntyre, J. F. McNaught, C. D. Monteath, J. P. Ramkema, C. H. Ryan, F. U. J. Tinkler, R. M. White, H. T. Young, Lieutenants Leo Alcock, L. W. Butler, J. J. Chapman, F. L. Cheshire, C. N. Chester, J. G. Earwaker, J. W. Giles, the late H. C. Harvey, the late W. C. Henzell, W. S. Mactaggart, E. H. Meyers, B. Nicholls, A. L. Raff, W. A. Shrewsbury, Geo.

*Thomas, J. P. Tunn, W. J. Williams, C. M. Wrench, Associate-Professor A. C. V. Melbourne, Dr. Norman M. Gibson, Dr. C. E. W. Bean, the Rev. E. N. Merrington, Messrs. G. F. Addison, J. D. Allan, W. F. Allan, A. W. Bazley, J. E. Bell, J. D. Bostock, V. Bowman, J. Brown, F. H. Downes, C. W. Fletcher, the late E. J. Gandy, R. G. Ginn, Geo. Harris, A. Higgins, G. P. Hooper, C. T. Hughes, A. Jeays, H. T. Jones, W. D. Jones, W. K. Jones, J. B. Kennedy, W. Knott, J. H. Nash, E. J. Palmer, A. Pitceathly, H. Preston, E. M. Richards, Robinson, J. Sargood, D. L. Suller, H. E. Thorley, A. J. Wagner, Geo. Walker, F. L. Whyte, V. H. Williams, L. S. H. Wilson, F. T. Wotherspoon, and the authorities controlling the monthly journal "Reveille," who sent a complimentary copy of each number of that publication to the author for more than seven years. Several gentlemen, who assisted by supplying information and in other ways, have preferred to remain anonymous, and the author takes this opportunity of publicly expressing his indebtedness and thanks to them.*

*Thanks is also due for assistance received in various ways from Mr. and Mrs. W. B. Rees, Mrs. M. Sheridan, Misses M. Budge, A. E. Clarke, M. Ingham, M. Ordish, H. Petrie, P. Roper, H. F. Todd, M. Warham, M. Wensley, Mr. G. Carroll, the Australian War Memorial, the John Oxley Memorial Library, and the Colonial Business College.*

*Also to Messrs. William Brooks & Co. Pty. Ltd., and individual members of their staff for the great care and attention given to the printing, and to Messrs. S. A. Best Pty. Ltd. and their staff for the excellent quality of the blocks supplied by them.*

*Finally, the author wishes to thank Captain W. A. Collin and the committee of the 9th Battalion Association for giving him the opportunity of writing this history, for the many long evenings they have devoted to discussing the whole history in detail during several months, and for their assistance in other ways, always most freely given.*

N.K.H.

*Brisbane,*
   *9/12/40.*

# CONTENTS

| | | | |
|---|---|---|---|
| Chapter | I. | Enoggera, The "Omrah," Egypt | Page 1 |
| " | II. | Mena. Lemnos | Page 17 |
| " | III. | The Landing at Anzac | Page 34 |
| " | IV. | The First Week at Anzac | Page 54 |
| " | V. | May at Anzac | Page 65 |
| " | VI. | Anzac, June to November | Page 78 |
| " | VII. | Lemnos. Egypt. First Days in France | Page 94 |
| " | VIII. | Sailly and Rouge de Bout | Page 109 |
| " | IX. | Pozieres and Mouquet Farm | Page 123 |
| " | X. | Ypres and Flers | Page 144 |
| " | XI. | The Maze. Lagnicourt. Bullecourt | Page 158 |
| " | XII. | The Third Battle of Ypres | Page 183 |
| " | XIII. | The Enemy's Last Great Effort | Page 200 |
| " | XIV. | Defence of Hazebrouck | Page 216 |
| " | XV. | Victory | Page 230 |
| " | XVI. | The End of the War and of the Battalion | Page 248 |
| " | XVII. | Et Caetera | Page 269 |
| " | XVIII. | Postscript | Page 281 |
| Glossary | | | Page 285 |
| Index | | | Page 289 |

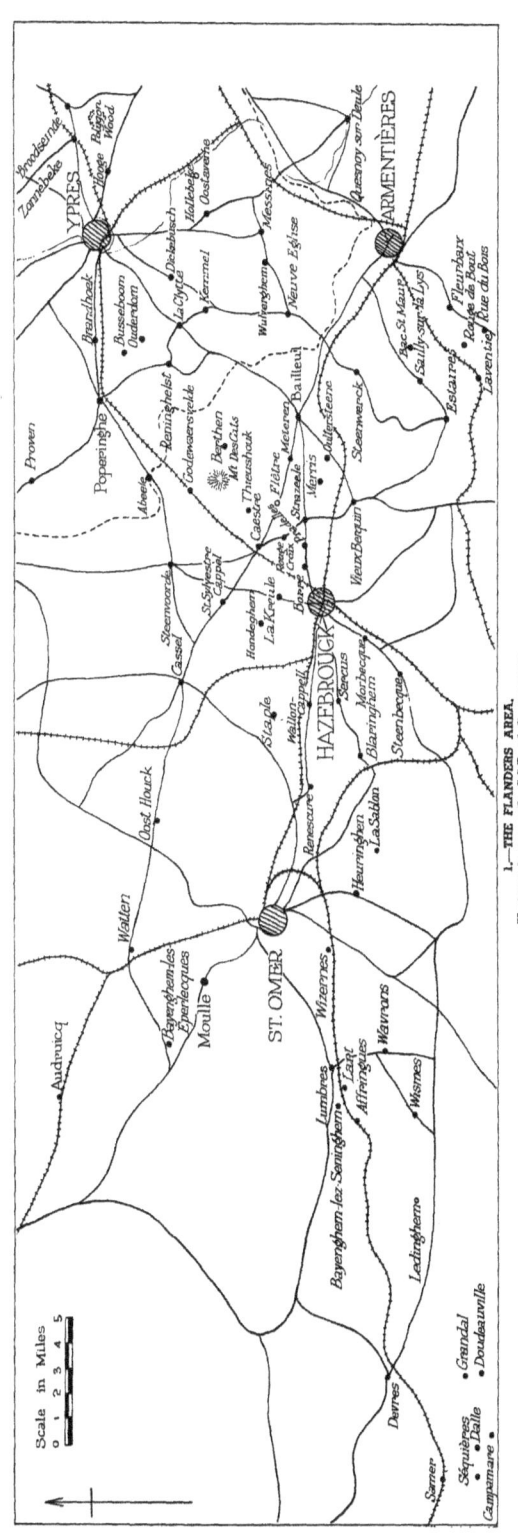

1.—THE FLANDERS AREA.
Herimes is one mile S.S.E. of Campanare.

# ILLUSTRATIONS

| | | Plate | Page |
|---|---|---|---|
| 1. | The 9th Battalion Memorial at Brisbane | I. | Frontispiece |
| 2. | Officers of the Original Battalion | II. | 4 |
| 3. | In Camp at Enoggera | III. | 5 |
| 4. | The "Omrah" | III. | 5 |
| 5. | Prisoners from the "Emden" | IV. | 10 |
| 6. | "Emden" Prisoners Exercising | IV. | 10 |
| 7. | Packing up at Mena | V. | 11 |
| 8. | Captain E. C. Plant in Orderly Room | V. | 11 |
| 9. | Artillery in the Front Line at Anzac | V. | 11 |
| 10. | R.A.P. at Anzac, Showing Lieut. M. Wilder | V. | 11 |
| 11. | Captain D. K. Chapman | VI. | 40 |
| 12. | Lieut.-Col. A. G. Salisbury | VI. | 40 |
| 13. | Colonel A. Graham Butler | VII. | 41 |
| 14. | Major A. R. Knightley | VII. | 41 |
| 15. | F. H. Downes, Blinded at Anzac | VII. | 41 |
| 16. | Captain A. G. Butler at Anzac | VII. | 41 |
| 17. | The First Casualty List, Anzac | VIII. | 60 |
| 18. | General Birdwood at Anzac | IX. | 61 |
| 19. | Four of "The Bearded 9th" | IX. | 61 |
| 20. | The Knife Edge | X. | 80 |
| 21. | Trenches at Gebel Habeita | X. | 80 |
| 22. | Lieut. C. F. Ross in Fire Trench at Anzac | XI. | 81 |
| 23. | Cemetery, Shell Green, Anzac | XI. | 81 |
| 24. | Aid Post and Trench Shelter, Gebel Habeita | XI. | 81 |
| 25. | Drilling a Squad at Sarpi | XI. | 81 |
| 26. | Brigadier-General J. Campbell Robertson | XII. | 154 |
| 27. | Yellow Cut | XIII. | 155 |
| 28. | A Flammenwerfer | XIII. | 155 |
| 29. | Lieut. Col. M. Wilder-Neligan | XIV. | 182 |
| 30. | Westhoek Ridge | XV. | 186 |
| 31. | The Road on Westhoek Ridge | XV. | 186 |
| 32. | Officers at Neuve Eglise | XVI. | 187 |
| 33. | Shelled Out of Billets at Boore | XVII. | 206 |
| 34. | Signallers at Cappy | XVII. | 206 |
| 35. | Lieut. J. P. Tunn | XVIII. | 207 |
| 36. | Machine Gun, Captured near Merris, now at Bulimba | XVIII. | 207 |
| 37. | Lieut.-Col. C. F. Ross | XVIII. | 207 |
| 38. | The Special Anzac Medal | XVIII. | 207 |

| | | | |
|---|---|---|---|
| 39. | Lieut. E. H. Meyers | Plate XIX. | Page 246 |
| 40. | Lieut-Col. L. M. Mullen | ,, XX. | ,, 247 |
| 41. | N.C.O.'s and Men with Decorations | ,, XXI. | ,, 256 |
| 42. | Tug-of-war Team | ,, XXII. | ,, 257 |
| 43. | Presentation of Colours to the 9th/49th Battalion C.M.F. | ,, XXII. | ,, 257 |
| 44. | The Rugby Team | ,, XXIII. | ,, 260 |
| 45. | The Soccer Team | ,, XXIII. | ,, 260 |
| 46. | Officers at Chatelet | ,, XXIV. | ,, 261 |
| 47. | The Band | ,, XXV. | ,, 264 |
| 48. | "Buller" | ,, XXVI. | ,, 265 |
| 49. | Howitzer Captured at Lihons, now at Water Street Drill-hall | ,, XXVI. | ,, 265 |
| 50. | Field Gun Captured at Pozieres, now at Newstead Park | ,, XXVI. | ,, 265 |
| 51. | Machine Gun Captured in Neligan's Fleurbaix Raid, now at Hamilton | ,, XXVI. | ,, 265 |

Some difficulty has been experienced with regard to the names of persons appearing in groups and other illustrations in ascertaining the correct initials and spelling, and in a few cases it is possible that persons in groups may have been incorrectly identified.

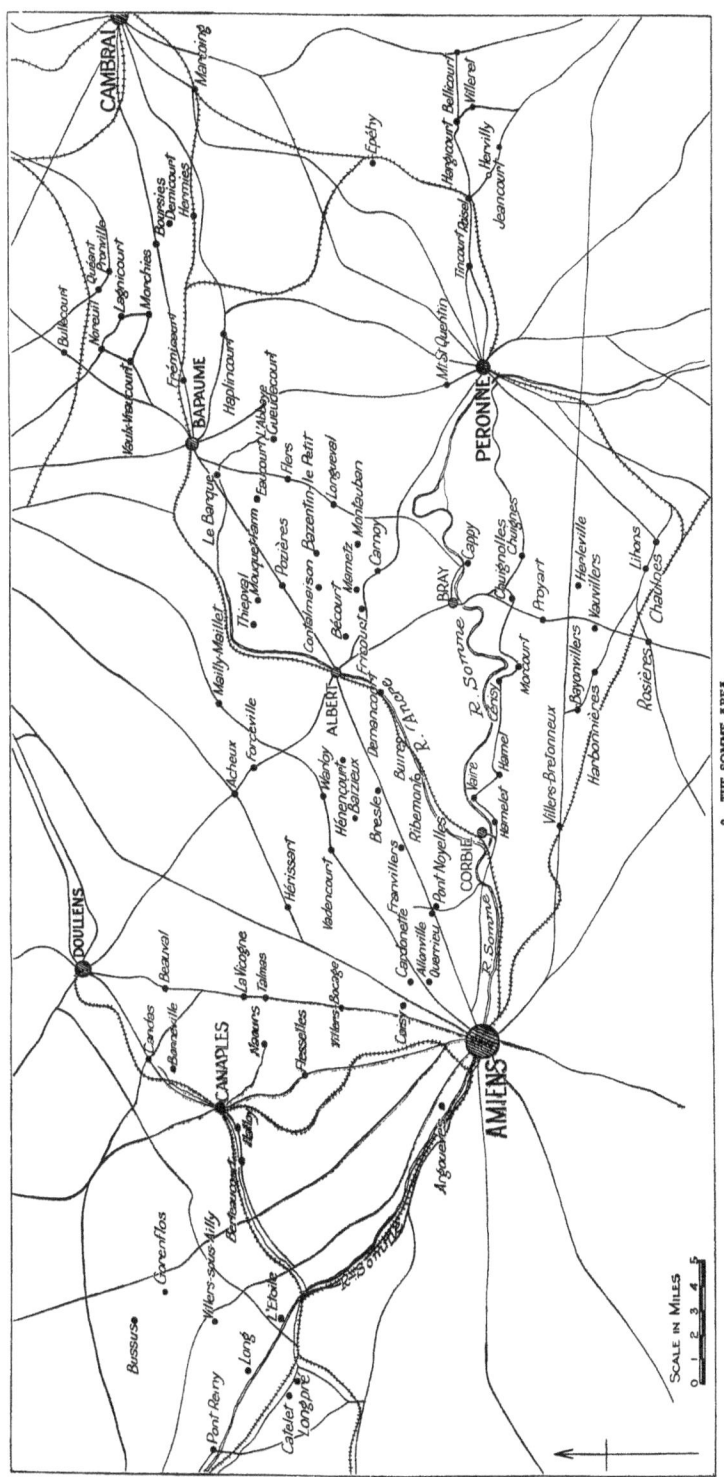

2.—THE SOMME AREA.

# MAPS AND DIAGRAMS

1. The Flanders Area ..... Folding Map
2. The Somme Area ..... Folding Map
3. Egypt and the Suez Canal ..... Page 14
4. Mena Camp ..... Page 22
5. Mudros Harbour ..... Page 25
6. The Aegean Sea and Gallipoli ..... Page 28
7. The Anzac-Suvla Area ..... Page 34
8. The Landing at Anzac ..... Page 36
9. The Anzac Area ..... Page 42
10. Gebel Habeita and Suez Canal ..... Page 98
11. Marseilles to Godewaersvelde ..... Page 104
12. Northern France ..... Page 106
13. The Fleurbaix Area ..... Page 110
14. Neligan's Raid at Fleurbaix ..... Page 115
15. Pozieres and Mouquet Farm ..... Page 124
16. Ypres-Messines Area ..... Page 145
17. Flers Area ..... Page 151
18. The Maze and Le Barque ..... Page 160
19. Lagnicourt ..... Page 169
20. Bullecourt ..... Page 176
21. Polygon Wood ..... Page 188
22. The Area East of Hazebrouck ..... Page 205
23. Meteren ..... Page 208
24. Minor Operation near Merris ..... Page 219
25. Le Waton ..... Page 224
26. Crepey Wood and Lihons ..... Page 232
27. Chuignes, Froissy Beacon and Cappy ..... Page 238
28. Villeret ..... Page 244
29. Gorenflos to Chatelet ..... Page 250

CORRECTIONS.

Map 1.—For **Oostaverne** read **Oosttaverne.**
Map 8.—For **Anderson's Knoll** read **Anderson Knoll.**

# *Foreword*

Although the events in this History took place between 1914 and 1919, more than two decades ago, yet I feel glad that they are to be published, both as a historical record and to bring back to the minds of relatives and descendants of the many thousands of men who served in that fine battalion, the 9th Battalion, A.I.F., their deeds of "derring do," devotion to duty and to their comrades.

Most of the men who sailed in the troopship "Omrah" from Queensland in late 1914 were typical Queenslanders of the tall, lean, wiry type—though in this battalion there was quite a "sprinkling" of ex-soldiers of the British Regular Army.

The battalion took a distinguished part in most of the operations in Gallipoli, France and Flanders in which the Australian Imperial Force was engaged, and part of it was, by a few minutes, the first to land on the hostile shore of Anzac, Gallipoli, on 25th April, 1915. From the ranks of this unit were promoted many leaders of military distinction.

I can truthfully say of this battalion, as of the other battalions of the 3rd Infantry Brigade, A.I.F., that "it never failed to carry out successfully the tasks allotted to it" during the long and arduous campaigns.

When the A.I.F. was expanded early in 1916 the 9th Battalion sent half its officers and other ranks to form the 49th Battalion, A.I.F., and these men instilled into their new unit the splendid traditions of the parent battalion.

To mention only a few of the actions in which the 9th Battalion distinguished itself, there were the Landing at Anzac (Gallipoli), Pozières, Mouquet Farm, Bullecourt, Polygon Wood, Lihons, Villeret and Merris.

I hope this History will not only appeal to the relatives and descendants of men who served in the 9th and 49th Battalions, A.I.F., but that it will be read and studied by present and future members of the Militia Battalions, C. M. Forces, who bear the name and honours of the two A.I.F. battalions and who are entrusted by the Nation to carry on the traditions and soldierly qualities displayed by those battalions, both of whom I had the great honour, and luck, to have under my command during periods of the Great War.

E. G. SINCLAIR-MacLAGAN, Maj.-Gen.,
late commander 3rd Inf. Brigade   A.I.F. 1914-1916
and 4th Aust. Div.                              1917-1919

Glenquiech, by Forfar,
  Scotland, 2nd April, 1939.

# From Anzac to the Hindenberg Line

## CHAPTER I.
### ENOGGERA — THE "OMRAH" — EGYPT.

During the third week in August, 1914,[1] a few military officers in uniform and a number of men in ordinary civilian attire could be seen pitching tents in Bell's Paddock, Enoggera, a pretty spot on the outskirts of Brisbane, five miles north-west of the centre of the city. This was the beginning of the 9th Battalion, A.I.F., Queensland's first contribution of infantry to the Great War; but no one could at that time have foreseen the undying fame which this unit was to achieve by its deeds performed while leading, as a part of the 3rd Brigade, the world-renowned Landing at Anzac, followed by many another fine feat of arms at Gallipoli and in France and Belgium.

When Britain declared war on Germany on August 4th, 1914, Queensland at once decided to play her part in the contest. The Premier, the Hon. D. F. Denham, announced to Parliament on August 5th that he had, at 1 p.m., on that day, received a telegram from the Commonwealth Government informing him that the Empire was at war, and that he had immediately replied that Queensland placed all its resources at the disposal of the Commonwealth and of the Mother Country. Men began at once to offer themselves for active service, and by August 11th some 1400 had volunteered at the Brisbane Town Hall.

In the meantime, particulars were awaited from headquarters at Melbourne as to what contribution would be required from Queensland. By August 8th, Major-General W. T. Bridges, who had been chosen to lead the main Australian expeditionary force overseas,[2] and Major C. B. B. White, his chief-

---
[1] The first men arrived in camp on August 17th or 18th, and on the 21st the C.O. of the proposed infantry battalion and several other officers arrived. This latter date, therefore, can be considered as the birthday of the 9th Battalion.
[2] A small force, known as the "Australian Naval and Military Expeditionary Force," captured and occupied German New Guinea in September, 1914.

of-staff, had completed their scheme of organisation, which included one brigade of infantry (consisting of the 9th, 10th, 11th, and 12th Battalions) from the four less populous States. The 9th Battalion was allotted as Queensland's infantry quota[3].

Thus, about two weeks after war had been declared, the first members of the 9th assembled at their temporary home, and the welding of the raw material into a fighting force commenced. Three days later 300 recruits from the Tweed, Richmond, and Clarence River districts of New South Wales marched into the camp, and a considerable number of them were drafted into the battalion. On August 22nd, 30 volunteers arrived from the Oxley Regiment.[4]

Many of the officers and men had had previous training either in the militia forces of the Commonwealth or the British Army, while a number had seen service in the South African War. Lieutenant-Colonel H. W. Lee, commander of the 4th Infantry (the Wide Bay Regiment) at Maryborough, was selected as commanding officer of the battalion, his appointment dating from August 15th. The troops in camp were at first spoken of as part of the "European Expeditionary Force," but about the end of August the name "Australian Imperial Force" was adopted.

On August 22nd a contingent of 123 men from North Queensland left Townsville by the S.S. *Bombala*. Among them was a certain Maurice Wilder, whose name will appear frequently in this record. Ten more men joined the ship at Mackay, and they reached Brisbane on the 25th. Of this number 77 were included in the 9th Battalion, the remainder joining light horse and other units in the camp.

Meanwhile, enlistment was going on vigorously in the country districts, as well as the city, and by August 28th, three weeks and a half after the declaration of war, 52 officers and 1237 other ranks were in camp at Enoggera. This number had, by September 3rd, increased to 65 officers and 1784 other ranks.

For the first week or two little drill was done, the troops being engaged mainly in preparing the camp site, unloading stores, pitching tents, building cookhouses, and in other necessary work. At first many men had to go on parade in their civilian clothing; suits of dungarees and white cloth hats were issued to them as soon as possible, and uniforms and equipment given out when they came to hand. On one of the early parades,

---

[3] More correctly, the quota of the 1st Military District, which comprised the whole of Queensland and the northern areas of New South Wales.

[4] This regiment had been called up for home service at the outbreak of war and was on duty at Fort Lytton, which at that time defended the entrance to the Brisbane River.

when some hundreds were drawn up, standing at attention, all of them wearing these white hats, an officer noticed a man moving. "Keep still there, that man in the white hat," yelled the officer. It was not easy to know which man was meant, and a loud laugh went up from the assembled troops.

On another occasion a parade included pack animals. The panniers of one of the horses had not been completely strapped on when the animal pulled away from the driver, dispersed men in all directions, and galloped wildly round the paddock, scattering picks and shovels as it went. This method of distributing tools was not according to regulations, but it was very expeditious.

As in all Australian units, there were a number of "hard cases" in the 9th. One of these had a brother in camp, the two resembling one another closely. One of them, having got into trouble, had to appear with other defaulters at the orderly room, and when his turn came to be paraded before the C.O., he was soon proved guilty. The Colonel was about to pronounce sentence on him when he said:

"You can't do anything with me, Sir."

"Why not," replied the C.O.

"You have no jurisdiction," returned the man.

"But aren't you number umpteen umpteen, Private Blank?"

"No, that's my brother."

"Then get to hell out of here," roared the Colonel, and Warrant Officer Pollard was ordered to march him off the 9th Battalion area.

As the camp settled down, squad and company drill was begun, and then battalion drill. Rapid progress was made both in numbers and in training, and on September 12th it was announced that the Queensland quota of the expeditionary force was complete. Further recruits coming in began to train as the nucleus of the 15th Battalion, part of a second contingent, which trained at the Exhibition grounds; others became the first reinforcements of the 9th.

Leave was given very sparingly, but on Sunday afternoons the camp was thrown open to visitors, and relatives and friends of the troops formed many a merry little picnic party, some of these lasting till 10 p.m.

The various articles of equipment were issued as they became available, and each man finally possessed the following: tunic, trousers, singlet, shirt, underpants, cardigan, socks, boots, laces, hat, chin-strap, puttees, braces, suit of dungarees, white hat, cap comforter (Balaclava cap), set of bronze badges, housewife, brush, comb, holdall, razor, shaving-brush, knife, fork, spoon, mess-tin, water-bottle, black kit-bag, sea kit-bag, rifle, bayonet, web equipment, and entrenching tool. There were, of course, more than one item of certain articles of clothing.

About a week before embarkation the battalion was visited by Colonel E. C. Sinclair-MacLagan, a British officer of fine quality, who had been appointed to command the 3rd Brigade. On Saturday, September 19th, the troops who were to leave for overseas marched from Enoggera to the city, in full marching order, and, after traversing the main streets with fixed bayonets, to an accompaniment of tremendous cheering, they returned to camp apparently as fresh as when they started, which was very creditable to men with only a month's training. Experienced officers had expected a few complaints about the long march, but were gratified to hear none. On the 21st, they were inspected at Enoggera by the Governor-General, Sir Ronald Munro Ferguson, and the State Commandant, Colonel G. L. Lee. At this date there were 392 men already in camp for the second expeditionary force.

The battalion band was composed of former members of the Oxley Regiment Band and the Brisbane Excelsior Band, the latter being a civilian organisation. The people of Queensland subscribed money generously for the purchase of band instruments, each of which was engraved with the name of one or more persons who had subscribed an amount equal to its value. One bright Sunday afternoon shortly before embarkation a formal presentation was made of the instruments before the assembled battalion and a number of visitors. Those of the subscribers who were present stepped forward in turn and presented to each bandsman the instrument for which they had subscribed.

The original officers, nearly all of whom were drawn from the militia,[5] were: *Commanding Officer*, Lieutenant-Colonel

---

5 The previous units of the officers were:—

|  |  |
|---|---|
| 3rd Infantry (Port Curtis Regiment) | Lieuts. Pattison and Williams. Lieut.-Col. Lee, Major Harvey. |
| 4th Infantry (Wide Bay Regiment) | Capts. Jackson, Lee and Milne. Lieuts. Harvey, Ross, Thomas and Young. |
| 7th Infantry (Moreton Regiment) | Capts. Brown, Ryder, Salisbury, Lieuts. Adsett, Chapman, Costin Haymen. |
| 8th Infantry (Oxley Regiment) | Lieut. Jones. |
| 9th Infantry (Logan & Albert Regiment) | Lieut. Rigby. |
| 11th Infantry (Darling Downs Regiment) | Major Robertson, Lieuts. Fortescue and Roberts. |
| 14th Battery A.F.A. | Lieut. Chambers. |
| Intelligence Staff | Capt. Robertson. |
| 33rd A.A.M.C. | Capt. Butler. |
| Unattached List | Capt. Melbourne, Lieut. Hinton. |

Hinton and Milne had previously served with the British Army. Dougall, Fisher and Ker were veterans of the South African War. Boase had just graduated from the Royal Military College, Duntroon.

Plate ii.

2.—THE OFFICERS OF THE ORIGINAL 9th BATTALION ON THE "OMRAH"
From left to right.—Back row: Lieuts. H. C. Harvey, Hinton, Capt. Melbourne, Lieuts. Costin. Boase, Capts. Ryder, Jackson, Lieut. Adsett, Capt. Salisbury, Lieut. Ross, Capt. Milne, Lieuts. Chambers, Ker, Williams, Fisher, Thomas, W. McK. G. Young, Capts. S. B. Robertson, H. W. Lee, Lieut. Rigby.
Middle Row: Lieut. Chapman, Majors W. C. Harvey, J. C. Robertson, Lieut.-Col. H. W. Lee, Capts. Brown, Butler, Lieut. Dougall.
Front Row: Lieuts. Haymen, Jones. Fortescue, Roberts.
(Photo. lent by Maj.-Gen. H. Gordon Bennett.)

Plate iii.

3.—IN CAMP AT ENOGGERA
(Block lent by the Omrah Association.)

4.—THE "OMRAH" AT PINKENBA WHARF

H. W. Lee; *Second-in-Command*, Major J. Campbell Robertson; *Adjutant*, Captain T. V. Brown; *Quartermaster*, Major W. C. Harvey; *Company Commanders*, Captains A. G. Salisbury, S. B. Robertson, J. F. Ryder, A. C. V. Melbourne, J. A. Milne, and I. Jackson, and Lieutenants J. L. Fisher and J. M. Dougall; *Signalling Officer*, Lieutenant W. J. Williams; *Medical Officer*, Captain A. Graham Butler, A.A.M.C.; *Transport Officer*, Captain H. W. Lee; *Machine Gun Officer*, Lieutenant J. W. Costin; and also Lieutenants R. W. L. Chambers, P. Adsett, L. A. Jones, W. J. Rigby, D. Chapman, H. G. Ker, J. P. Roberts, C. Fortescue, W. McK. Young, F. G. Haymen, H. C. Harvey, G. Thomas, C. F. Ross, W. B. Pattison, A. C. Hinton, and A. J. Boase. The R.S.M., E. Addy; the R.Q.M.S., W. Aggett; the Machine Gun Sergeant, A. Steel, and the Signal Sergeant, J. Sinclair, were staff sergeant-majors in the permanent forces.

On September 22nd, "H" Company, with the battalion band and drummers at its head, marched to the railway station, about a mile from the camp, and entrained for the short trip to Pinkenba, at the mouth of the Brisbane River, where it boarded the 8,130 ton Orient liner, *Omrah* (then known as transport "A5"). Its task was to prepare the ship for the embarkation of the rest of the battalion. The remainder of the 9th left camp at 4.15 a.m., September 24th, and were on board by 8 o'clock.

All was bustle on board, as the ship was to sail at noon. The time of embarkation not having been noised abroad, there were no relatives and friends at the wharf at first, but later in the morning a number arrived, and there were perhaps a couple of hundred present when the *Omrah* left at mid-day. An hour and a half later she was followed by the *Star of England* (A15). The *Rangatira* (A22) was another transport at the wharf at this time, but she did not leave until the next day. The *Omrah* was thus the first troopship to leave Queensland for the main seat of war, as the *Anglo-Egyptian* (A25), which had sailed the day before, had carried only horses.

The 9th were the only troops on board the *Omrah*, except detachments of the A.M.C. and the A.S.C., and four members of the Australian Army Nursing Service, Staff Nurses B. M. Williams, E. M. Paten, C. M. Keys, and J. M. Hart. It was the ship's first voyage as a transport, but by no means her last; she was on war service for nearly four years, until sunk by a torpedo off Sardinia, in the Mediterranean, on May 12th, 1918.

The officers and nurses, and a section of the N.C.O.'s were provided with cabins, the other N.C.O.'s and the men being accommodated in some of the holds of the ship, which normally were used for the storage of cargo. These, now referred to as "troopdecks," had been fitted with hooks from the ceiling to hold canvas hammocks, and with tables and forms for meals. The hammocks were kept at the sides of the troopdecks in the daytime, and each man hooked up his own when he decided to go to bed. A troopdeck might thus accommodate from 100 to 300 men, according to the size of the hold. Large staircases had been built up the hatchway, and, of course, electric light had to be used all the time, as the only daylight was that which could filter down through the hatchway; in the case of a troopdeck two stories down this was practically nil.

No one knew what was to be the first port of call, but many guessed and hoped that it might be Melbourne. This guess proved to be correct. Arriving in Port Phillip on the 28th, the *Omrah* anchored in Hobson's Bay until the 30th, when it moved alongside the Port Melbourne pier.

The stay at Melbourne lasted three weeks,[6] and during that time a great deal of route-marching and practice in attacking was done ashore at Albert Park, Fisherman's Bend, and Heidelberg. The battalion travelled to Heidelberg by train, and great attention was paid to entraining and detraining quickly and quietly. The column would march straight along beside the waiting train, each section of fours spacing itself so that when it stopped it would be opposite the door of its correct compartment. Detraining was equally systematic.

The uniform adopted for this shore-training, which laid a solid foundation for much of the work afterwards done in Egypt, consisted of dungaree trousers, jerseys, and white cloth hats. A number of musketry practices also took place at the Williamstown range. The 9th Battalion owes a great deal to the ability and energy of Captain A. M. Ross, the Brigade Staff Captain (known at this period as the Brigade Orderly Officer), who directed much of the training here. A great deal of the battalion's progress was also due to the knowledge and driving power of the C.O.

While in Melbourne, the battalion was inspected once more by Colonel MacLagan. Leave to visit the city was granted freely out of parade hours, and one thing in particular which

---

[6] This delay was due to the presence in the Pacific of the German warships *Scharnhorst* and *Gneisenau*. Until an adequate naval escort was provided, the New Zealand Government refused to let its transports leave for Australia to join the "First Convoy."

was enjoyed by all was the opportunity for sea-bathing—"Stubb's Baths" are frequently and favourably mentioned in one man's diary. One of the principal racing events, the Caulfield Cup, was run at this time, and quite a number, at least, of the officers have good cause to remember "Uncle Sam." Another officer, of very "martial" appearance, had good cause to remember the *Omrah* about this period, for one day a number of the subalterns made a combined attack on him, and he emerged with one side of his moustache clipped off.

Although the arrival of other transports and warships, the German vessels detained in the harbour, and the embarkation of some of the Victorian troops provided subjects of interest, the period of waiting became very tedious; "these days of waiting are a hard nut to crack," writes one soldier. All ranks were therefore delighted when, at 3.25 p.m. on the 19th of October, the "A5" slipped away from Port Melbourne. The departure went off without any fuss, very few people being allowed on the wharves; but one incident, not uncommon at the sailing of Australian transports throughout the war, took place. A man was left ashore—"the inevitable chump," someone called him—and had to be raced out to the ship in a motor boat as the *Omrah* steamed down the bay. As the motor boat came close, the "chump" was seen to be "Jerry" Tamblyn, the Colonel's batman.[7]

Many of the men found the cramped accommodation and unusual conditions of troopship life rather trying, especially those from the western districts of Queensland, where there is abundance of space for everybody and everything, in fact, more space than anything else. It was one of these men, probably, who complained in his diary about "the usual scramble for a shave and a bath." However, everyone gradually settled down and soon took all these little troubles as a part of the day's work. More pleasant to remember was the concert held on the night of October 21st, Trafalgar Day.

While passing through the Great Australian Bight, calm but dull and rainy weather was encountered, and except for a little physical drill not much could be done on board.

When the men were called up soon after 6 a.m. on the 24th, they heard the grating of anchor chains, and on reaching the deck they found that the ship, together with a number of other transports, was in a bay surrounded on all sides by low hills. This was King George's Sound, the harbour of the little town of Albany in Western Australia. Immediately after break-

---

[7] Tamblyn died in Toowoomba in 1930, and Colonel Lee attended his funeral.

fast the battalion, taking rations and water-bottles for a midday meal, went ashore in tenders for the purpose of a route march. During the voyage from Melbourne the medical officer (Captain Butler) had recommended that all water-bottles should be sterilised by filling them with a strong solution of Condy's crystals, which, after standing in them for 24 hours, could be poured away, and the bottles rinsed out. Orders were therefore issued that this should be done, and the orders were duly carried out—except, apparently, by the M.O. himself. For on this route-march Captain Butler, after eating a modest lunch, reached for his water-bottle, and took two good gulps before he suddenly began spitting out Condy's fluid, to the great enjoyment of the officers and men sitting along the road.

During the stay at Albany most of the days were wet, so the troops had rather a dull time on board. Only once more, on October 31st, was the 9th given an opportunity of stretching its legs on shore. But one day some sports were organised on the "A5," including tugs-of-war, which combined entertainment with training. Orders were now issued that no more closed letters were to be sent through the post; they were to be left open so that they might be censored, or else postcards were to be used.

On October 28th the battalion was drawn up on its usual 10 a.m. parade, in a mist of drizzling rain. Suddenly the mist lifted, and round the ends of the hills facing the open sea came a long, low warship, a heavy plume of smoke ascending from her funnels. She was seen to be flying the Japanese flag, and turned out to be the *Ibuki*. Next came a four-funnelled British cruiser, the *Minotaur*, and then troopship after troopship—ten in all—rounded the corner and anchored near our fleet. After them came two small cruisers, the *Philomel* and *Pyramus*. It was the New Zealand contingent. There were now some thirty ships in the harbour, among them H.M.A.S.'s *Melbourne* and *Sydney*.

On the 30th an incident occurred which brought the war a little nearer to those on the transports. A steamer entered the harbour, and, as she did not reply to the signal to lay to, a couple of shots were fired across her bows by the warship on duty near the entrance. On this day, too, occurred another break in the monotonous life on the troopships. Because of overcrowding on the next vessel, the *Hororata*, "A" Company of the 6th Battalion was transferred from her to the *Omrah*. To make room for it, "H" Company of the 9th was moved from the lower troop-deck to quarters on the upper deck, which had been used as a guard-room. Unfortunately, the new arrivals brought measles with them, and a number of men on the *Omrah* caught the complaint.

On November 1st, shortly before 7 a.m., the First Convoy began to move off on its long voyage up the Indian Ocean to the seat of war. Those on board the *Omrah*, which was the last but one of the transports to leave, had a good view of the whole proceedings. It was a striking and a stirring sight, this great fleet of 36 troopships with their escorting warships; it took them over two hours to clear the harbour. Once out at sea, the Australian troopships took station in three long lines, the New Zealanders in two lines behind them.

The *Ibuki* had left Albany a couple of days before to escort from Fremantle two transports containing Western Australian troops, who did not embark until the last moment. When, on November 3rd, they joined the convoy, it totalled four warships and 38 transports. The *Minotaur* was in front, the *Sydney* guarding the port (left) side, the *Ibuki* the starboard (right), and the *Melbourne* the rear. For the first two days until the *Ibuki* came up, the *Melbourne* had been on the starboard beam, with the little *Pyramus* following in the rear. The *Pyramus* now left the convoy.

It is worthy of note that on the same day that the convoy left Albany, Britain—following the action of Russia on the previous day—declared war on Turkey. This was not known to those on board the ships, who had no thought that they would ever meet the Turks in battle.

Rough weather occurred during the first few days out from Albany. An attempt was made to hold sports on the *Omrah* on the second day, but the leaping and bounding of the ship gained an easy victory over the running and jumping of the men, so the sports had to be abandoned. That night the motion of the vessel was so rough that some of the men could not stay in their hammocks, so they tried to sleep on the mess-tables, but with each roll of the ship they slid up and down.

One day the cruiser *Minotaur* passed through the fleet to go off to examine a vessel coming up in the rear. It proved to be the *Osterley*, which had left Australia after the convoy, and was on its way to England with passengers and mail. She soon caught up with the transports and left them behind, as they could not travel very fast on account of the necessity for keeping together; the speed of the convoy had to be regulated by the speed of the slowest ship in it, the old horse-boat, *Southern*.

The weather becoming warmer, the ship's officers changed into white uniforms on November 6th, and on the same day a large canvas bath was rigged up on deck and kept filled with sea-water.

At 8 p.m. on November 7th, the troops were ordered to fall in and stand quietly in their company parade places. The lights of the ship then went out one by one until only the red and green side-lights remained aglow. It was noticed that the lights of the other ships were out, too. After half-an-hour of darkness the lights came on again one by one, and the troops were dismissed.

There was much speculation as to the reason for this, and a rumour went round among the men that someone had died on the *Miltiades* and had been buried at 8 o'clock.[8] The real reason was that the convoy was gradually being trained in sailing at night without lights, so as to lessen the danger of an attack by enemy warships, of which two (*Emden* and *Konigsberg*) were suspected to be at large in the Indian Ocean.

On November 8th the *Minotaur* was ordered away on other duty. The *Melbourne* became the flagship of the convoy and took position at the head of the fleet, whose rear was now left unprotected. Shortly before dawn next morning the convoy was passing fifty miles to the east of the Cocos Islands. About 7 a.m. the *Sydney* was seen to swing round and steam away westward at full speed. Later the *Melbourne* and *Ibuki* left their stations and moved over to the port side to put themselves between the transports and the *Emden* (which had now been located), in case she made northwards towards the convoy. During the morning a notice was posted on the deck of the *Omrah* giving news of the naval battle off Coronel, but no word came for some time of what the *Sydney* was doing. Some of the men on the *Omrah* heard a faint sound like the beating of a big drum, but did not pay any particular attention to it. Then, at 11.10 a.m. a wireless message was received from the *Sydney; Emden* beached and done for. The story of that famous action is too well known to need repetition here—how the strange warship appeared off Cocos and landed a party to destroy the wireless station, how the island operator sent out his S.O.S. which brought the *Sydney* at full speed to the scene, and how, little more than an hour later, the *Emden* was a mass of twisted iron.

The news was announced to the troops on the *Omrah* about 11.30 a.m. during a beer parade. There was great rejoicing on board, and the victory was celebrated by the issue of an extra

---

[8] As it happened, a man of the 3rd Battalion died this day on the *Euripides*, and was buried on the next morning.

Plate iv.

**5.—PRISONERS FROM THE "EMDEN"**
(Block lent by the Omrah Association.)

**6.—"EMDEN" PRISONERS EXERCISING**
Lieut. G. Thomas on right, Sgt. W. J. Dewar on left.
(Photo by Lieut Col. W. C. Harvey. Lent by Lance A. Jones, Esq.)

7.—PACKING UP AT MENA, FEBRUARY, 1915.
(See p. 22)
(Aust. War Memorial Official Photograph. No. C 87.
Copyright.)

8.—CAPT. E. C. PLANT IN THE ORDERLY ROOM AT ANZAC.
(Aust. War Memorial Official Photograph. No. C 1458.
Copyright.)

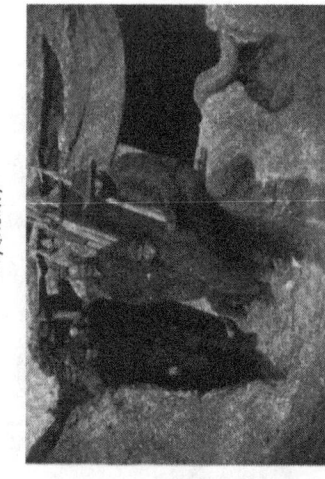

9.—THE 7th BATTERY A.F.A. IN THE FRONT LINE AT ANZAC.
(Photo. lent by Col. A. G. Butler).

10.—R.A.P. AT ANZAC.
Lieut. M. Wilder is third from right.
(Photo. lent by Col. A. G. Butler.)

ration of beer,[9] and the granting of a half-holiday, that is, exemption from parade and fatigues for the afternoon.

On November 11th the *Melbourne* went on ahead to Colombo to coal, leaving the *Ibuki* temporarily in command of the convoy, until later in the day the *Hampshire*—her sides covered with rust from being constantly at sea looking for the *Emden*—arrived to take control. She remained in charge until the convoy reached Suez. Two years later, it will be recalled, the *Hampshire* was lost in the North Sea with Lord Kitchener on board.

On November 12th the convoy crossed the Equator, and the well-known marine comedy of Father Neptune and his attendants was enacted. As most of those on the *Omrah* had never been out of Australia before, there were numbers of "novices" (those who had not previously crossed the Line) to be "initiated." The performance ended with general wild horse-play with hose and water-buckets.

As the *Konigsberg* was now located in the Rufigi River in East Africa, the convoy could proceed without close guarding. Thirteen of the transports, including the "A5," went ahead to coal and water at Colombo, which was reached at midday on the 15th. Next day there were transferred to the "A5" 44 of the survivors from the *Emden*, for whom the 9th Battalion had to provide a guard of 60. Commanded by Captain Melbourne, the guard was drawn up on the deck in two ranks to receive the prisoners—the Chief Engineer, the Torpedo Lieutenant, two petty officers, and 40 seamen. The seamen sat down on deck for a while between the ranks of soldiers, after which they were addressed by their senior officer, and marched forward to their quarters. The bundles they carried having been searched for arms and destructive tools, the first relief of the guard, 12 men, took post to watch over them.

The guard, which was kept permanently on that duty for the remainder of the voyage, was divided into five reliefs, each having two hours on duty and eight off. The prisoners boasted that none of those on the ship would ever reach Aden or England alive. They exchanged with members of the 9th a number of Mexican dollars brought from the *Emden*; some

---

9 On one occasion during the voyage some of the troops broached the ship's beer supply. Entrance was gained through a manhole which was not properly secured. The ship's officers, becoming suspicious, set a watch on the beer, but the trap was sprung prematurely and all escaped except a big man, whose shirt was stuffed full of bottles of beer. He was fined, the fine being entered in his paybook in red ink in the usual way. Towards the end of the war he asked to be paraded before the C.O., and requested that the fine be cancelled, as those who escaped had been just as guilty as he. "I was Jimmy the mug," he said. His request was passed on to higher authority, but the result is unknown.

of these showed signs of the fire which had broken out in the ship. The German officers refused to give their parole, and in consequence they were constantly attended by a sentry, even at their meals and bath.

One evening, while the enemy seamen were up on deck for exercise, under guard, they sang what appeared to be a hymn; and they sang it rather well. At the time all the officers were at dinner. Afterwards, one of the German officers apologised to Colonel Lee, saying that he hoped that the singing had not annoyed them. The Colonel said that, on the contrary, they had rather enjoyed it, and was then informed that it was a ribald song that the men had been singing.

Among the ships in Colombo Harbour at this time was a Russian cruiser, the *Askold*. She had five funnels, which gave her a rather unusual appearance, and earned for her the nickname of "the packet of Woodbines," from a brand of cigarettes, five to a packet, which were much in vogue among the "Tommies."

From Colombo the fleet sailed independently in "divisions," according to speed, the *Omrah* forming part of the "third" and fastest division, leaving at 8 p.m., on November 17th. No shore leave had been granted except to the four nurses, but a couple of officers had gone ashore on duty. At daybreak on the 21st, a collision occurred between two of the troopships, the *Ascanius* ramming the *Shropshire*, with the result that a hole was made in the bows of the former. The heat was now intense, and the guards over the prisoners were allowed to go on duty dressed in singlets and blue trousers.

On the 23rd the island of Socotra was passed, next day the coast of Arabia was sighted, and on the 25th the "third division" arrived at that barren, deserted-looking spot known as Aden. Here the whole convoy was reassembled and next day it put to sea again and was soon in the Red Sea. It is commonly supposed that the weather in this sea is always extremely hot, a view which is not quite correct, as sometimes it is no hotter than one may find in temperate parts of Australia in the summer months; during this voyage, however, it quite kept up its reputation, and all sweltered and perspired while they were in it.

Long before the Red Sea was reached most of the men had preferred to sleep on the decks, but it was a case of the early bird catching the worm; the first-comers captured every available "possy"[10] where a hammock could be slung, and those coming up later had to sleep on the boards of the decks or go

---

10 See Glossary.

back to the troopdeck. It was while the ship was in the Red Sea that a man of "B" Company disappeared, and the only explanation seemed to be that he must have fallen overboard when no one else was by.

Not much could be done on board in the way of training, but parades were held every day, usually with some "physical jerks," under the direction of Lieutenant Boase, and a number of lectures were given on military matters and methods used in warfare. As a rule the men had most of the day to themselves, but in certain respects the same routine went on as in camp. For example, a small guard was detailed for duty every day, and the orderly room functioned all the time. At this period the orderly-room corporal was M. Wilder, of "H" Company, well known afterwards as Lieut.-Colonel Wilder-Neligan, a courageous and distinguished leader from the landing at Anzac onwards.

On November 28th some very unwelcome news was passed round: the battalion was to disembark at Port Said, instead of going on to England, as had been expected. Nothing was known of any fighting or proposed fighting in Egypt, and many of the men in their disappointment expressed their indignation in very ardent language—much of it peculiarly Australian. But as events turned out, the change of plan was to mean to the A.I.F. and to Australia and New Zealand all that is associated with the name "Anzac."

At the outset the 1st Division was to have completed its training on Salisbury Plain, in England, but as sufficient huts could not be provided for them in time, and as the Canadians and the British troops on the Plain were suffering great hardships in the tented camps, Lord Kitchener[11] suggested to the Australian Government that the Australians should train in Egypt, and the suggestion was at once accepted.

On the morning of the 28th was noticed with curiosity a circumstance with which officers and men were later to become very familiar when camped on "the sands of the desert."

Australians had always thought of Egypt as a hot country, and as the troops had been sweltering for some days, and were now off the Egyptian coast, they were surprised early this morning by a cool breeze which made the deck-sleepers draw up their blankets closer round their chins. Next day, according to one diarist, the "dawn was cold, had to curl up to stick it out till reveille."

On December 1st, the *Omrah* dropped anchor at breakfast time at Suez. Here wild rumours were heard of risings

---

[11] The Secretary of State for War.

of Arabs in the desert, and that the *Orvieto*[12] had been fired on in the Canal the night before, so the "A5" and other ships with her had to wait until dark before going through. At 11 a.m. the cruiser *Hampshire* drew near, and sent over boats to take off the *Emden* prisoners; they tramped along the deck with their bundles, and so ended their two weeks' stay on the

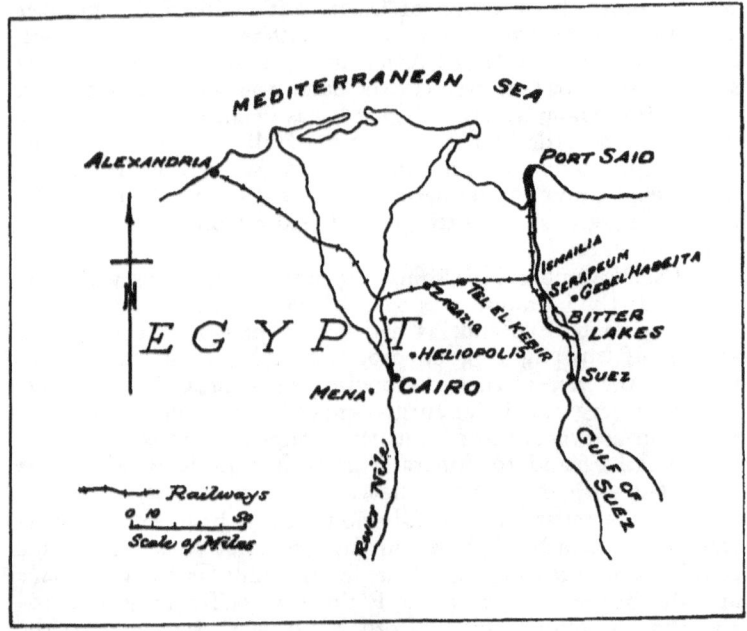

3. Egypt.

*Omrah*. Another important event of this day was the arrival of the battalion's first mail from Australia. On account of the slow speed of the convoy, letters sent from home since it left had arrived in Egypt ahead of it.

At 10 p.m. the *Omrah* left to go through the Canal. It was a glorious moonlight night. A guard of twenty men was posted along the promenade deck, with orders to return any fire directed at the ship from the banks; and emergency beds were prepared in the ship's hospital. However, no shot disturbed the harmony of the passage.

The "A5" was all night passing through the Canal, and all the next morning, too, dropping her anchor at Port Said

---

12 The flagship of the Convoy, carrying Major-General Bridges, commanding the Australian Imperial Force, and his staff.

shortly after midday. Detachments of soldiers were noticed all the way along, as well as a trainload of troops going in the opposite direction to the ship. The men in the train waved, and some of them signalled that they were Manchester Territorials, and that there had been a fight, our side losing 13 killed. At Port Said plenty of rumours were afloat, one being that hosts of Turks were approaching the Canal.

No Turks were seen, but what actually did occur was an invasion of the ship by hosts of native hawkers, selling fruit, cigarettes, silk, and similar goods, which experience had taught them would be likely to tempt the visiting soldier to part with his money.

Next day the *Omrah* left Port Said and by 7 a.m. on the 4th of December she was sailing into Alexandria, past the prominent Fort Marabout, which had put up a strong resistance in 1882 when bombarded by Lord Charles Beresford's fleet. Some of the New Zealand troops could be seen ashore.

Another Australian mail arrived, there was a second invasion of hawkers, and news was received that the 1st Division was to go to Mena camp, near Cairo. The ship moved in to a wharf on the 6th, the first detachment of the 9th disembarking at 9 a.m., and "B," "C," "D," and "E" Companies at 4 p.m. These reached Mena late that night, and were joined next day by the remaining companies, "A" Company, which had been detailed for guards and other duties on the ship, being the last to arrive, about 2 a.m. on the 8th. Four days later Captain Lee arrived with the battalion transport section.

The trip up the Nile flats was full of interest for all ranks, most of whom had never before seen a foreign country. Villages large and small were passed, groves of palms, asses and water buffaloes working in the fields, camels in caravans, and the desert, the famous desert of Egypt. But it was not all desert, and the newcomers were impressed by the great amount of green cultivated land, chiefly growing cotton, which was irrigated from numerous canals carrying water from the Nile.

On detraining at Cairo the troops found refreshments awaiting them—a pint of cocoa, a long roll, and a piece of Dutch cheese for each man. The last stage of the journey to Mena camp was made in open electric tram-cars. Some parties on their arrival were formed up in lines of companies in the dark and issued with two blankets each, and they slept in the open on the sand. Other parties were met by a guide who, after leading them over the desert for about half-an-hour, stopped, pointed to some more sand, and said: "There's your camp." As they settled down for the night, they were thrilled to see the Pyramids showing up clearly in the glorious light of the moon, and apparently quite close.

After a cold night on the open desert, the troops had to be content with the remains of the rations they had brought with them from the *Omrah*, nothing but hot tea being supplied by the cooks. The day was spent in getting the camp into order, and then came the welcome news that 20 per cent. of each company were to be granted leave to Cairo from 4.30 p.m. to 10 p.m.

During the next night rain fell, and it continued, with intervals, for two days. As the troops were still camping on the open ground their plight can be well imagined. On the 10th four bell tents per company were received, but as a military bell tent at best holds no more than twelve men fairly close together, and as a company at that time consisted of a hundred men, this gave only a partial relief. Fortunately it did not rain again all the time the battalion was at Mena. By this time the meals, though they had still to be taken in the open, had become more normal, as the cooks had settled down to the usual routine. Eventually mess-huts were provided for the troops, enabling them to eat in comfort. In the afternoon the battalion was gladdened by the usual parade becoming a bathing parade at the fine swimming-baths at the Mena House Hotel. The hotel itself was turned into a hospital for sick evacuated from the camp lines, and buildings in the rear were converted into offices for the divisional staff.

## CHAPTER II.

### MENA. — LEMNOS.

Military training recommenced on December 10th, for the force was as yet unfit for active service. At first company training was carried out, and when the companies were considered effective, the battalion was exercised together as a whole. On the 11th the troops were addressed by Colonel MacLagan.

On the 14th there began a long series of whole-day parades in the desert. At first these consisted of one-half of the battalion entrenching itself and being attacked by the other half. On returning to camp after the first of these field-days, the men were pleasantly surprised to find that some more tents had arrived and been pitched for them; there were now sufficient to shelter the whole battalion.

One day the trench digging was directed by Major H. O. Clogstoun, a British officer commanding the 3rd Field Company, who was to become a celebrated character in the A.I.F. He always wore a monocle, and on this occasion, after he had passed down the ranks, a number of the men produced their identity discs, and placed them in their eyes. On retracing his steps the major noticed this, and to one of the men he remarked, jokingly: "Yes, old man, but I bet you can't do this," whereon he promptly threw the monocle into the air, and caught it again in his eye with no other help than the muscles surrounding that organ. After this he was acclaimed a "good sport" by all.

Training went on vigorously for the remainder of the year, interrupted only by pleasant interludes of leave to Cairo and visits to the Pyramids. Cairo was ten miles from Mena, and the trip was usually made by tram, although at times the Egyptian gharry drivers seemed to do a brisk business along the route. The cosmopolitan city had many attractions, from picturesque streets and buildings to the varied crowds of people of almost every nation under the sun, from restaurants where one could get a change from the simple fare of the camp to hotel bars where those so disposed could make themselves merry, sometimes too merry, unfortunately, for the peace of their neighbours.

All these new sights—and tastes—were enjoyed to the uttermost by the Australians; everything was so different from what they had been used to—some of the 9th, in fact, had never been in a town in their lives until they passed through Cairns or Townsville or Charleville on their way to Brisbane when they enlisted. The money in circulation caused many a surprise. On changing an Australian pound note, it was not uncommon to receive a mixture of notes and coins belonging to half-a-dozen nationalities, English, Australian, Egyptian, French, Indian, Italian, Greek, or other strange coins.

The "hard cases" of the force sometimes amused themselves in unconventional ways. For example, Sergeant C. R. Heaton, who even before the Anzac landing wore a fair-sized row of ribbons, gained in earlier campaigns with the Imperial Army, was on leave in Cairo, when he passed a ribbonless British colonel. Heaton saluted him, and the salute was, of course, returned. Then the sergeant made it his business to dog the colonel's footsteps, and every now and then to direct his course so that the two should pass again. Each time they met a ceremonious salute was exchanged, but it is said that after a dozen meetings the colonel appeared distinctly annoyed with the performance.

The Arab bootblacks, who were very much in evidence in Egypt, became so enterprising that they would even follow the soldiers on to the trams and, taking advantage of a man's being engaged in conversation, would polish *one* of his boots. The result was that the victim had to pay a piastre to have the other boot polished to match.

The Pyramids were a constant source of interest to men off duty. It was fashionable to be photographed with the pyramids or Sphinx for a background, and it was all the better if one was mounted on a camel. Many, of course, climbed the Great Pyramid, and left a memento of their visit by carving their names on the stones.

During their stay in Egypt, the Australians picked up a number of Arabic words and phrases. Some of these became part of a "digger language" and are still heard in Australia to-day, for example, saida (good-day), walad or walla (boy), bint (girl), tallahena (come here), imshee or imshee yalla (go away), igoree (quickly, hurry up), quaskatia (good), mafeesh (finish, done), mafeesh fooloos (no more money), intermacnoon (mad), and buckshee (alms, charity). The last mentioned words also appeared in a mixed English-Arabic form as "gibbit buckshee" (give me some money).

On Christmas Eve the officers' mess received a festive visit from the 10th Battalion officers. The combined forces then stormed the mess of the 11th, and, after that, reinforced by all the 11th officers, they attacked the 12th Battalion mess, where the brigadier happened to be a guest. A good deal of horseplay took place for some time until Colonel MacLagan mounted a table and asked them to restrain their high spirits. He said that he did not object to a little rowdyism on these occasions, but it would be fitting to put some restraint on their hilarity at this time, as it would be a very sad Christmas in the British Isles, owing to the fact that there had been deaths in so many families.

This period of the battalion's history was not without its share of tragedy. On December 30th, Private S. C. Foster, of "D" Company, died; on January 2nd, Driver N. Matthews, of the transport section, dropped dead, and on the next day Armourer-Sergeant J. W. Moore, who had been injured by a spirit-stove explosion on the *Omrah*, died in hospital in Abbassia. Another death at Mena was that of Private F. J. Gilvarry. About this time, also, Sergeant W. Millward, of "D" Company, was badly hurt by a motor car.

On January 1st, 1915, the Australian battalions, hitherto consisting of eight companies, were reorganised on a four-company basis. The original "A" and "C" Companies became the new "A" Company, "B" and "D" became the new "B," "E" and "G" the new "C," and "F" and "H" the new "D." Each was subdivided into four platoons, a formation previously unknown to Australian troops.

The battalions had now reached the stage at which brigade training could be undertaken. One well remembered part of the field work at this time was the "attack," repeated on many subsequent days, on a pile of jagged rocks in the desert known as the "Tiger's Tooth," more than an hour's march from the camp. Near the Tooth was a rifle range at which musketry exercises were carried out. On these all-day operations the troops had an extensive view on all sides to the horizon, and, although large numbers of soldiers could be seen, no one else was noticed, until the signal was given for a "smoke-oh" or a meal, when "Gyppos" would spring up as if by magic from the sand, and offer everyone (at current prices) oranges and eggs—the "eggs-a-cook," as the natives called them, which later gave the 3rd Australian Division its nickname.[1] These cold hard-boiled eggs were sold everywhere in Egypt, and the troops encountered them later on Lemnos, too.

1 From its oval-shaped colour patches.

The way to the Tiger's Tooth wound along valleys between sandhills, the smoothest track having been selected. It was moderately easy to find the way—in daylight. Early one morning "A" Company had to go along this route in a heavy fog, which blotted out the sight of the Pyramids, and of anything else which was more than 200 yards off. One of the men, on coming out of his tent, caused much laughter by shouting: "Hi, someone shook (*i.e.*, stole) the Pyramids last night." The company commander (Major Salisbury), however, did not join in this merriment. "If we try to follow the track in this fog we'll be lost," he said to Lieutenant Chambers. "We'll have to march on a compass bearing." Accordingly the prismatic compass and a map were laid out, and a bearing taken on Tiger's Tooth.

The company marched off at 7 a.m., through fog which was still thick, and followed the straight line pointed out by the compass over rocky ridges, down hill through heavy sand, and across valleys of coarse gravel which were new to the troops. The company had not gone very far before men were whispering: "He's lost." Salisbury kept his eye glued on the compass, while Chambers looked at his watch every now and then. About ten minutes before they were due at Tiger's Tooth the fog suddenly lifted—and straight ahead, about 300 yards away, appeared the company's destination, the rifle range. Both of these officers had before the war sailed their own boats, sometimes in company, over Moreton Bay on dark nights.

In one attack on the Tiger's Tooth, two men were given a red flag, and were told that they were to represent headquarters, which should always be in a safe position. Carefully following their instructions, they kept so far in rear that they were ultimately found in the canteen. However, when they were paraded to the C.O. next morning, they reminded him of their instructions. Fortunately for them, he saw the point of the joke and dismissed them.

All ranks had a strenuous time on these operations, which took place at night as well as in the daytime—often they returned to camp covered with perspiration and sand and thoroughly tired out. There were also sudden alarms in the early hours of the morning, when all would have to turn out. But the training hardened the men and made them fit for the trying work they were to do later at Anzac.

Rumours were always flying round the camp. One day the 9th was to be sent to Ismailia to fight, the next day it was to go off somewhere else. But the wise soon learned to pay little attention to these "furphies," as they came to be called.

It was still thought by many commanders that the division would go to the Western Front when its training was completed; and one of the last exercises carried out by the 3rd Brigade, on February 23rd, was a billeting scheme at Tiger's Tooth, where an imaginary village was planned, and imaginary streets and houses were marked out with stones. Units and companies were allotted to certain "buildings," and duly marched in. The staff captain who was responsible for erecting the signs, was a humorous individual, and marked "out of bounds" certain buildings, including the convent, and a house marked "Measles."

One day, after a severe sandstorm, "D" Company went for a route-march into the desert west of the camp. After marching for about four miles the troops were enjoying a rest when the wind blew off a man's hat. He did not at once attempt to recover it, but, when finally he did begin to chase it, the hat was bowling along a considerable distance away. Hat and owner disappeared over a sand-hill, and as the man did not return a connecting file was dispatched. He disappeared, too, as did another man who followed him. Eventually their platoon commander, Lieutenant Thomas, took out a section to look for them, returning half-an-hour later with the men, but without the hat.

There was one consolation in the midst of the hard work. Arrangements were made for the use by the division of the swimming-baths at Mena House Hotel, and each unit was able, occasionally, to enjoy an afternoon in the water. These swimming parades were a pleasing variation to the sandstorms which so often disturbed the field-operations.

Although the days were hot, the nights were cold on the desert. Sir John Monash, whose brigade was camped at Heliopolis, on the other side of Cairo, in one of his letters says: "At night it is bitterly cold, cold enough for Balaclava helmets,[2] four blankets, bed socks and rugs."

The 1st Australian Division and a composite division—consisting of the New Zealand Infantry Brigade, the New Zealand Mounted Rifles Brigade, the 4th Australian Infantry Brigade, and the 1st Australian Light Horse Brigade, and designated the "New Zealand and Australian Division"—had by now been organised into the Australian and New Zealand

---

[2] Knitted woollen caps which covered the head entirely except for an opening left for the face. These caps had been issued to all troops.

Army Corps, under General Birdwood. The code name adopted for the corps was "Anzac," a combination of the initial letters of each word in its official title. The suggestion was made on the spur of the moment by a junior officer on corps headquarters, who had become used to seeing "A. & N.Z.A.C." on cases stacked outside his office. Thus the glorious title of Anzac was born.

Mena Camp contained the 1st, 2nd and 3rd Infantry Brigades, together with other troops, and it is still a vivid memory to many, with the long road, bordered with whitewashed stones, stretching for nearly a mile down its centre.

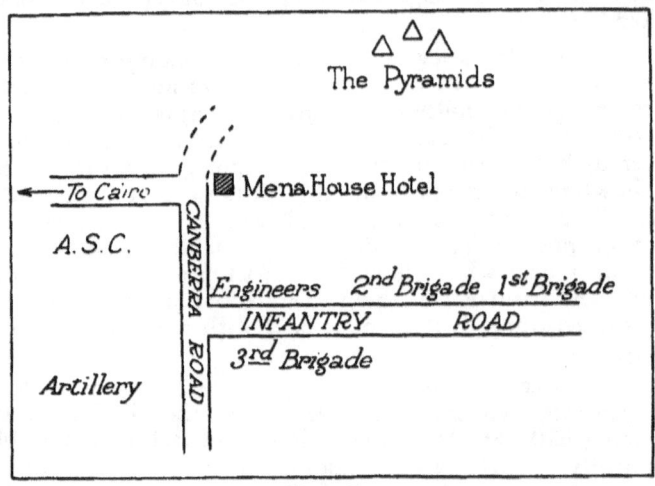

4. Mena Camp.

On February 9th the 1st reinforcements for the 9th arrived at Mena, approximately 100 men under Lieutenant Koch. These were absorbed by the battalion to replace men who had become sick or met with accidents.

Brigade training was completed in the 1st Australian Division by the middle of February. On the 22nd a rumour went round that orders had been received to embark for France, which gave rise to lusty cheering all over the camp. Then there were some busy days, employed by all in renewing articles of kit, packing up stores, and other occupations preparatory to departure. The 25th was a day of rumours: one diary reads: "Rumours are many, some that we move on to Constantinople, some would send us to Marseilles, some *know* we are to reach Southampton."

On February 27th the 3rd Brigade was detailed to move from Egypt to the island of Lemnos, in the Aegean Sea—the battalions were unaware of their destination at the time—and that night, the brigade's last at Mena, was marked by constant outbursts of cheering, which would spread through a battalion, and be taken up by unit after unit till the sound was lost in the distance in the artillery lines. The next afternoon a fierce dust-storm raged through the camp, and at 5 p.m. the 9th marched out to the cheers of the 10th and 11th Battalions, who shortly followed them. On arriving at Cairo the battalion entrained in two divisions, and on reaching Alexandria in the morning they went straight on board a large troopship, the *Ionian*.

As the men settled down on the vessel they noticed that she was loading stores, which included railway sleepers and green firewood. The latter was to be encountered later by the battalion cooks, much to their regret. The 10th Battalion was also detailed to this ship, in which the troops were packed like sardines; at night it was difficult for those retiring late to find a place to lie. One section commander wrote: "My section, 15 men, allotted between decks 6ft. by 12ft., could not stand upright."

The *Ionian* was called by the troops "One-onion," but her smell was much stronger than that of the onion, as she had carried horses on her previous voyage, and had afterwards not been properly cleaned. This ship belonged to the Allan Line, which was sardonically referred to as the "Hungry Allan Line" by many of those on board.

At one period the butter was very rancid. One of the 9th's officers, when talking to the Scotch master of the ship, asked him how long the *Ionian* had been carrying troops, and was proudly informed that the ship had taken troops to and from South Africa fifteen years before. "My word, skipper," said the Australian, "you must have taken on a hell of a supply of butter at the time," and he decamped before that worthy could grasp his meaning.

A remark often passed about this ship was: "Iron boat, iron decks, iron rations, and iron men." The men had to sleep on the hard iron decks, and during the voyage to live on so-called "iron rations"—hard biscuits and tinned corned beef. The vessel was not fitted with mess tables, there was no more than one light for each troop-deck, and very little ventilation, and the only means of access to or from the troop-deck was a narrow upright iron ladder. Soon after the ship left Alexandria, over one-third of the men became seasick.

To understand the reason for the brigade's being sent to Lemnos, we must go back several months to the latter part of 1914. When the fighting on the Western Front had reached such a stage that both sides were well entrenched in positions facing one another stretching from the North Sea to the borders of Switzerland, and it appeared impossible for either to drive the other back, the Allies began to consider whether any new plan could be devised to bring the war nearer to a successful conclusion. In Britain the deadly effects of the German heavy artillery against the strong Belgian fortifications of Liège and Antwerp made some people consider whether the guns of our navy could not be used against enemy fortified positions on the seashore or against their troops where they were placed near the sea.

At this stage, on January 2nd, 1915, Russia asked her allies whether a demonstration could be made by them against Turkey, so as to relieve the Turkish pressure on the Russian armies fighting in the Caucasus; Kitchener thought that an attack might be made at the Dardanelles. As no troops were available at the time, it was suggested that a naval attack might be made. If Constantinople could be captured as well as the Dardanelles, other results would follow besides relieving the pressure on certain Russian armies; munitions could be brought to the south of Russia and grain and oil be sent from there to the other Allies; it would probably be the end of Turkey in the war, and would keep Bulgaria from joining the Central Powers.

Naval bombardments of the forts at the entrance to the Dardanelles were carried out between February 19th and March 4th, and on several occasions parties of marines made temporary landings. On March 18th an attempt which was made to force the passage of the Dardanelles by British and French warships very nearly succeeded.

In the meantime, on February 20th, Lord Kitchener ordered General Maxwell, the Commander-in-Chief of the troops in Egypt, to warn the Anzac Corps to be ready to embark about March 9th to assist the navy, in any way required, to force the Dardanelles and to occupy any captured forts; but plans developed quickly, and an earlier date was fixed for embarkation.

Thus at noon on March 2nd, the *Ionian*, together with other transports carrying the rest of the 3rd Brigade, sailed from Alexandria under sealed orders. Next day the destination was disclosed to the officers. That afternoon land could be seen on both sides, and throughout the 4th the ships steamed slowly with islands on either side. In the evening the *Ionian* reached Lemnos, and anchored in the splendid Mudros Harbour at 8 p.m. The weather was very cold. Only two other ships were in the harbour when the *Ionian* arrived, but next morning it was seen that ten warships had come in during the night.

As the ship was so crowded it was decided that one of the two battalions on board should camp on shore. The C.O.'s tossed up to see which would have the choice. Colonel Lee won, and on Saturday, March 6th, an advance party of the

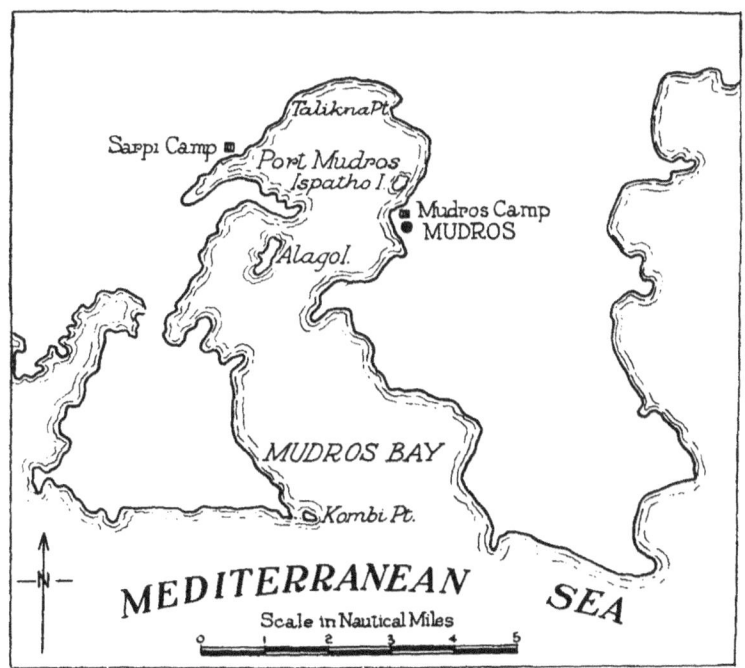

5. **Mudros Harbour, Lemnos.**

9th landed, the rest of the battalion going ashore the next day. During the landing operations, Signaller N. G. Hatton slipped while jumping over a stone wall and broke his ankle, thus becoming the battalion's first "casualty" at Lemnos.

After landing, the troops were taken for a route-march, partly for exercise, partly also for want of other occupation. That night the men had to bivouac in the open, as some of them had done the night before, because no tents had as yet been brought ashore.

The British having decided to occupy part of Lemnos, Rear-Admiral Wester Wemyss, with the title of Governor of Mudros, was sent out to take possession of the village and harbour. This occupation was based on the fact that, although in the possession of Greece, the island was claimed by the Turkish Government as Turkish territory, and thus the British might be said to be occupying enemy territory.

Wemyss landed there on February 24th, and at first had no troops to enforce his occupation, but the landing of the 9th Battalion gave him a force which he could use. Its effect, however, was of a moral nature, and helped Wemyss, who had a very difficult and delicate task to carry out, to gain his ends by tact and "bluff." The disembarkation of the 9th, their march to the camp site and bivouacking there was regarded as the act of occupation. As soon as the battalion was ashore a signal station was established, and it kept in constant touch by flag, heliograph and signal lamp with the *Hussar*, the flagship of Admiral Wemyss.

On the Sunday, a couple of hours after all had settled down in their bivouacs for the night, a terrific storm broke, with bitterly cold wind and sleet. Tentless as the men were, they could only wrap their blankets round them and make the best of it. When dawn broke some were lying in pools of water, and those who suffered no worse mishap than being soaked through were comparatively lucky. Sodden half-loaves of bread were served out for breakfast, but a few men were fortunate enough to be able to purchase some cold boiled eggs from villagers who came up to the camp. At 9 a.m. the tents came ashore and the homeless troops at last had some protection over their heads. However, as a result of these conditions, a number of men contracted pneumonia and a few, including Eric Webster of "A" Company, died of it. Another, named Jones, died on the 8th, the day after the storm.

The site of the camp was a ploughed field a short distance from the landing-place, beyond the village, on a hill between two rows of windmills. As soon as the battalion arrived there, Greeks began to flock around, offering for sale nuts, apples, dates, figs, bread, biscuits and other eatables. These Greeks were very different to the "Gyppos" the Australians had grown used to; one man described them as "the men wild and picturesque, the women fair, and pretty little children." Mudros was a very dirty village of from 60 to 80 houses.

## COMPLETION OF TRAINING. FATIGUES

During the seven weeks the 3rd Brigade spent at Lemnos it put the finishing touches to its training, a great deal of attention being paid to practising landing from boats, followed by hill-climbing. The conditions were quite different from those obtaining in Egypt; rock instead of sand and cold in place of heat. There was no "Tiger's Tooth" to attack here, but a humorous touch was given to one night "raid," when a party received the order: "At the moon five rounds rapid. FIRE."

Mudros Harbour, although a very fine natural harbour, was up to this time quite undeveloped. The first "fatigue" of an engineering nature done by the 9th at Lemnos was the building of a jetty near the camp. Almost the whole battalion was engaged on the work, which was about 200 feet long, 10 or 12 feet wide, and about 3 feet above high water level. It was made of large stones taken from the ground and the hillsides: there was abundance of raw material, as Lemnos is a very stony island. As very few tools were available most of the work had to be done with the bare hands, and two men were needed to carry some of the larger stones. When the stonework was finished a T-head of wood was built on the end by field engineers.

A most arduous and unpleasant task that often fell to the lot of the 9th was the refloating of barges, which were frequently driven ashore by gales. The men had to strip to the bare skin in a cold driving wind, wade into colder water, and work there for perhaps more than an hour. One party was sent to unload a lighter, the cargo of which consisted of large greasy cheeses, coal, numerous 5lb. tins of jam, mostly leaking, and then flour. The condition of the fatigue party when the work was finished can well be imagined.

One night a party was called out of bed at 10 o'clock to unload large sacks of oats, each of which was a good load for one man. Captain Fisher, who with two other officers accompanied the party, noted much grumbling as they were marching down, so he said to the officers: "These men won't work unless we do." When they came to the jetty, Fisher walked straight on to the barge and, lifting a sack of oats, shouted: "Come on," and strode up the gang-plank cracking jokes. The other officers staggered up the plank, each with a sack, and at this the men turned to quite cheerfully and soon had the cargo unloaded.

There was no lack of interest in the life of the troops at Lemnos. Warships of different nations constantly entered or left the bay, and the great *Queen Elizabeth* became familiar to the eyes of all. Another well-known ship was the Russian

*Askold*, the "packet of Woodbines" which had been previously met at Colombo. After bombardments of the Dardanelles forts, ships often returned damaged. One diarist wrote: "One ship had a number of cannon-holes through her," and, in another place, "the ships show signs of batter when they return."

On shore French and Greek sailors, Zouaves, black Senegalese, and other French soldiers, were to be seen and met. These foreign troops and the Australians were very polite to one another. Not far from the Australian lines was a French camp, from which the sound of the trumpets blowing the "Diane" ("reveille") every morning lingered long in the memories of all who heard it. The first French troops had arrived on March 11th, a few days after the landing of the 9th.

6. The Aegean Sea and Gallipoli.

Those who were fond of alcoholic refreshment found every facility for getting it. By the end of March every second shop at Mudros sold cognac, wine and beer. In contrast to this plenty—of liquor—water was scarce, and sea-water had to be used for washing purposes. There was also a great scarcity of wood, and the villagers did their cooking on little braziers of charcoal. Rations were somewhat irregular, sometimes there was bread and sometimes only biscuits, and the meat issue was not sufficient to satisfy the requirements of men in such cold weather. This caused much dissatisfaction. Pay was issued to the men very sparingly, and mails were few and far between. To make up for the small amount of news, rumour was very busy: "Aerial attack expected," "Turks attempted a landing on Lemnos," "A Zeppelin flew over the island last night," are some of the remarks which appear in diaries of this time.

Before the 9th had been long at Lemnos it became known that the battalion was to make a landing at the Dardanelles, and on March 19th, the news passed round of the unsuccessful attack by the navy on the Straits the day before; indeed, on the 18th, just before dark, some had seen a four-funnelled cruiser come into harbour with one mast shot away and three-fourths of a funnel missing, but no particulars of the engagement were heard until next day.

However the troops' thoughts were taken away from warlike matters in the evening by a very heavy gale, which lasted all night and for several days following. A number of tents were blown down during the first night, when it was at its height, and although not so bad after that, it made life unpleasant while it continued. Lemnos is a windy island, and the water in Mudros Harbour is always more or less rough, and often very rough indeed. During the stay here the weather was bitterly cold, broken by a few steamy spring days, and the constant winds were very biting.

On March 21st, a party about 150 strong, under Captain Milne, went across the island to assist in the rescue of the crew of a British torpedo-boat, the "064," *en route* from Port Said, which had been wrecked during the gale which had begun on March 19th. When the party arrived, after a difficult and uncomfortable march, with sleet driving in their faces, it found that the crew had all reached the shore. Later, however, some of the men decided that the day had not been wasted, as they discovered a couple of kegs of rum which had been washed ashore; unfortunately for them, an officer arrived on the scene and ordered the rum to be poured out and let run to waste. A quantity of navy chocolate, in good thick slabs, was also discovered, and was greatly appreciated by the party.

Next day General Birdwood visited the camp, and on the 23rd Sir Ian Hamilton, the commander-in-chief of the Mediterranean Expeditionary Force, came ashore and inspected the 9th. The battalion made a sham attack, including a bayonet charge, and Hamilton's comment on this was that it was very fine, but every man taking part would have been killed on account of not taking cover while advancing.

On the 29th several of the transport men of the 9th reported having seen an enemy aeroplane land at a point six or seven miles in a northerly direction from Mudros. Twenty men from Lieutenant Thomas's platoon therefore left at 10 a.m. under Thomas, each carrying 50 rounds of ammunition. A Greek was taken as guide and interpreter. No sign of an aeroplane could be found, and no one they encountered had heard or seen one, so the party returned to camp at 7 a.m. on the next day, very tired.

On March 31st arrived the first mail (110 bags) since the battalion had come to Lemnos; it took a whole day to sort it. The arrival of a batch of mail was a great event in the life of the troops at any time, especially at this period. One man, in a letter home, said: "You don't know how we look forward to mail day. The men nearly go mad when the mail call is sounded."

April 1st was a very strenuous day for the battalion. Carrying full pack and equipment, officers and men manoeuvred from 8 a.m. till 6 p.m. over various parts of the island, up great hills and boulder-strewn ground. It was on this day that an order was issued that all persons not born or domiciled on the island had to leave it. This was on account of the danger from spies, many of whom were said to be on Lemnos.

The next day was Good Friday. There was a church parade for all the troops, who were very interested in noticing how that day and the next were observed by the Greeks. On Easter Day the villagers made innumerable gifts of dyed Easter eggs to the soldiers.

About this time the first official intimation was received by 3rd Brigade Headquarters that the brigade was to land at the Dardanelles, and would be the covering force for the operation.

M. Venizelos, the Greek Prime Minister, was enthusiastically in favour of the Allies, and especially wished Greece to gain possession of Constantinople. During their early days at Lemnos it had been announced to the officers of the 9th that a force of 40,000 Greeks was to assist in the landing at the Dardanelles. However, a political crisis occurred, in which the Venizelos Government fell; it was then discovered that the other Allies had promised Constantinople to Russia as one of the spoils of war. Greece thereupon became again a neutral nation and the proposed Greek force was cancelled.

These moves accounted for the long stay of the 3rd Brigade at Lemnos while awaiting the arrival of the 29th British Division, the Royal Naval Division and French troops.

On Easter Monday, April 5th, there was another severe gale, in which numerous tents were blown down, and three days later, at 6 p.m., the battalion embarked once more, this time on the *Malda*, a British India Company liner of 7884 tons. She, too, was crowded, as not only was the whole of the 9th on board, but some men of the 11th as well; there were no properly fitted up troop-decks, and conditions were like those experienced in the *Ionian*. As soon as they were on board, men began discussing their hopes of "a speedy run up the Dardanelles for a smack at Constantinople."

By April 9th the ship was full of rumours, but as a matter of fact it was, not known when or where the troopship was to go. However, the part the 9th was to take in the coming operations became known soon after this. Ships were now much more numerous in the bay, and the remainder of the 1st Division began to arrive.

On the 10th the 2nd reinforcements for the 9th arrived under Lieutenant A. Warren. An issue of pay took place on this day, each private receiving £1/15/-. The previous pay (£1 for each private) had been on board the *Ionian*, five weeks before.

Next day the battalion's second mail, another large one, arrived. Another item of special interest to all on this day was the sight of their first seaplane; a good view was had of it ascending, and later when it descended.

At this time disembarkation practice began, at first in the daytime and later at night. This was very strenuous work, as, after landing, the troops had to charge up one hill and then another until they were exhausted. However, these exercises made all ranks quite fit for the work ahead of them. The landings were usually made at Talikna Point, a rugged part of the harbour side a couple of miles from Mudros camp.

Still more troopships were assembling at Mudros. An officer records in his diary: "Apl. 14, ships arriving every hour"; "April 16, harbour full of ships."

On the 15th emergency rations and half-a-pound of tobacco per man were issued. The emergency ration consisted of a tin of "bully beef" (tinned corned beef), a cube of "Oxo," some small biscuits, tea and sugar; these were contained in a small white bag, which was tied on to the equipment and dangled behind the man's back when he was in full marching order. A complete set of equipment, including the rifle, weighed over 80 lbs.

Caps were also issued, and instructions were given that the wire ring which kept the top in shape was to be taken out, so as to make them less noticeable by the enemy. Small rectangular colour patches were issued about this time, too. Worn on the sleeve, just below the shoulder, their object was to distinguish the different units. In the infantry the brigade was denoted by the lower colour and the battalion by the upper; for example, light blue was the basic colour for the 3rd Brigade, and black that for the first battalion in each brigade. Hence black over light blue became the colours of the 9th.

The unit had previously been denoted by a bronze numeral on the shoulder-strap, but when the colour-patches were issued the numerals were taken away.

These colour-patches soon came to have a great sentimental value to Australian soldiers as being the symbol of their unit, like the British regimental badge. There were no "regiments" in the A.I.F. infantry, and the "digger" came to have the same affection for his colour-patch as the British "Tommy" had for his metal badge.

On April 15th there were posted on the decks copies of a letter from General Birdwood, exhorting the troops to do their best in the coming engagement—and many thought that the evening of this day was to witness the expected landing. On the next night a party left the *Malda* to practice landing from battleships, and for two or three nights similar practices were carried out.

On the 18th orders were received to have everything ready to move off, so it was expected to be for the actual landing. However, the time was not yet. The next day the troops began to live on bully-beef and biscuits, no more fresh meat being issued. An engineer party, as well as some navy men for disembarkation and signal work, and one company of the 12th Battalion, were put on board the *Malda*, so everyone was jammed together more than ever.

It was on the 19th that brigade headquarters received some preliminary operation orders from divisional headquarters and battalion C.O.'s were given further verbal instructions by the brigade commander. Some more details of the operation were now given to the troops: they were to be transferred from troopships to destroyers at dusk, and put ashore from them, and on reaching the shore they were to take off their packs before advancing. It will be seen later that some modification was afterwards made in these orders.

On the 20th detailed operation orders were received by brigade headquarters, which passed them on next day to its battalions. The C.O. of the 9th received further verbal orders from the brigade commander. Some of the troops on board had a very uncomfortable time in the rain on the night of the 20th/21st, as owing to the crowded state of the ship, and the necessity for portholes and hatchways to be kept open for air, many got wet.

On April 21st a letter from the brigadier was read to all ranks, urging them to do their best in carrying out "a most difficult operation, landing on an enemy's coast in the face of opposition." It ended with the words: "You now have a chance of making history for Australia."

A couple of days later the troops were all expectation, wondering when the battalion would receive the order to move. Actually the 23rd was the day which had been decided on for the landing (the troops, of course, did not know this at the time), but owing to the gale on the night of the 20th/21st interfering with the preparations, the date of the operation had to be fixed for two days later.

# CHAPTER III.

## THE LANDING AT ANZAC.

In order to understand the Landing at Anzac and the Gallipoli operations, it is necessary to know the main points of the country where the fighting took place, and also to be acquainted with the proposed plan of operations.

The Gallipoli peninsula is roughly the shape of a foot with the toes pointing downwards and the front facing the Straits of the Dardanelles. Suvla Bay is at the heel, Cape Helles at the toe, and Gaba Tepe[1] is a cape on the sole, a little more than half-way from the toe towards the heel, and about 60 miles from Mudros Harbour.

7. The Anzac-Suvla Area.

Nearly the whole of the peninsula is taken up with a series of hills, with separating valleys, running lengthways, with numerous rugged spurs running towards the coast. From the point of Gaba Tepe a beach runs north in a gentle curve about a mile and a half to Little Ari Burnu, then a gently-curved bay running another thousand yards north to Ari Burnu point is the celebrated Anzac Beach or Anzac Cove. North of Ari Burnu is another curving beach which carries the coastline up to Suvla Bay, five miles north of Gaba Tepe.

If we take a point on the coast a mile north of Ari Burnu, and go inland in an easterly direction for two miles, we come to a hilltop known as Koja Chemen Tepe or "Hill 971." From this hill towards Little Ari Burnu runs a succession of hilltops and ridges, about the middle of which is "Baby 700" hill. About six hundred yards further back along this line towards Hill 971 is "Battleship Hill," or "Big 700," and near the beach end is "Plugge's Plateau," overlooking Anzac Cove. From

---

1 The name Kaba Tepe was also used at first.

Plugge's a final ridge ("MacLagan's Ridge") runs towards Little Ari Burnu.

From Baby 700 another succession of ridges runs to the sea at a point a little more than a thousand yards south of Little Ari Burnu. Midway along these ridges is the "400 Plateau," which is continued to the south-west by "Bolton's Ridge."

Running in a nearly southerly direction from Battleship Hill is "Gun Ridge," which ends in Gaba Tepe. On this ridge are two hilltops which will need to be referred to by name, "Scrubby Knoll," east of Anzac Cove, and "Anderson Knoll," east of the end of Bolton's Ridge. Inland from Anderson Knoll, and about $3\frac{1}{2}$ miles back from the coast is another hill-top, Mal Tepe, which is only a mile and a quarter from the Dardanelles, on the other side of the peninsula. The whole range from Hill 971 to Gaba Tepe was known on the War Office maps as Sari Bair; this name, however, meaning "Yellow Slope," was really the Turkish name for a high steep cliff which from the day of the Landing was called by our men the "Sphinx" or the "Cathedral."

The following was the plan for the enterprise: The 29th Division, landing at Cape Helles, was to work its way up the peninsula from the extremity, while Birdwood's Australian and New Zealand Corps would land about ten miles up the side of the peninsula on the beach between Gaba Tepe and a place known as "Fisherman's Hut," three miles further north. After a covering party had occupied a line stretching from Gaba Tepe to Koja Chemen Tepe (Hill 971), the main Australian and New Zealand force was to land and advance beyond it to an objective line running through Mal Tepe. From this position the Turkish communications with Helles could be threatened, and perhaps cut off altogether. The attack was to depend for its success upon surprise, and was to be supported by bombardment from the navy, but this bombardment was not to commence until the operation had come to the knowledge of the enemy. Even the mere threat on this position would, it was thought, prevent the Turks from sending reinforcements to assist in repelling the attack at Cape Helles.

One brigade from the 1st Australian Division was to form the northern covering force, which was to land soon after dawn, an hour before the 29th Division would begin its assault at Helles. General Bridges chose for this purpose the 3rd Brigade. The northern parties of the brigade, immediately on landing near Little Ari Burnu, were to advance and seize Battleship

Hill and extend their line to Hill 971, while the rest of the brigade captured outstanding summits on Gun Ridge, from Scrubby Knoll to Gaba Tepe. The battalion on the extreme right of the advance was to be the 9th; its first two companies were to swing to the right immediately after the landing, about 1,000 yards above Gaba Tepe, and capture and disable the battery believed to be on that promontory. The other two companies, landing at the same point, were to seize Anderson Knoll, about a mile inland.

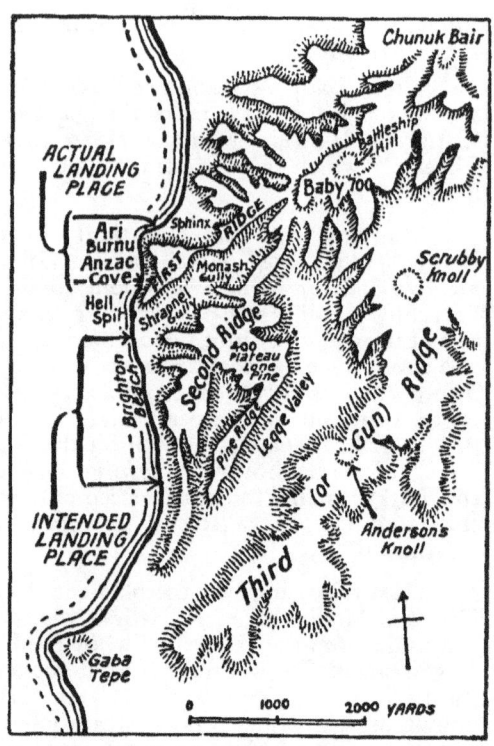

8. The Landing at Anzac.
April 25th, 1915.
(*By courtesy of the "Courier-Mail."*)

Besides the landings at Gaba Tepe and Helles, there was to be a landing by the French on the coast of Asia Minor, at Kum Kale at the southern entrance of the Dardanelles; a demonstration by warships and transports at Besika Bay, south of the French landing; and a pretended landing on the Gulf of Saros, well to the north of Suvla Bay.

The landing at Kum Kale, too, was only intended as a feint, and after having occupied their position for a day or two the French troops were to re-embark and then land at Helles to assist the 29th Division.

The actual landing of the troops was under the control of the naval authorities: the arrangements were worked out in detail, the naval orders for the Anzac landing occupying 27 typed foolscap sheets. The covering force was to be taken from

Lemnos partly in three battleships and partly in transports, those in transports being transferred to destroyers when the fleet had reached Imbros, an island about half-way between Lemnos and the Peninsula. The battleship troops were to be transferred to tows[2] at a sea rendezvous five miles west of Gaba Tepe. The battleships would then proceed with the tows beside them as far as they could go without being seen by the enemy, and would then stop, while the tows made a dash for the beach. The destroyers were to have a number of rowing-boats alongside of them, into which the men would be put when near the shore. Each destroyer would then tow its rowing-boats in as far as the shallowness of the water would allow, and then cast them off, whereupon each boat would row independently to the shore.

On the morning of Saturday, April 24th, everyone was agog with excitement, thinking that the eagerly-desired landing would surely occur on this day, and they were not disappointed. About midday "A" and "B" companies were transferred quickly and quietly to destroyers, which took them over to the battleship *Queen*. Those left on the *Malda* were given a stirring address by Major Brand, the brigade-major. At 2 p.m. the covering force left Mudros harbour, the *Malda* being among the first. It was a fine sight. Ellis Ashmead-Bartlett has said that when he entered the harbour on April 5th he saw "One of the most magnificent spectacles the world has ever seen, the greatest Armada of warships and transports ever assembled together," and on the 24th, when part of this armada was leaving to go into battle, it was indeed an inspiring sight.

During the afternoon final preparations were made, and officers inspected their men to make sure that each had his 200 rounds of ammunition, the full issue of rations, water in his water-bottle, and two sandbags fastened round his entrenching-tool handle. The sandbags were intended to be thrown over any barbed-wire barriers which might be encountered, to make them easy to be climbed over, and later to be filled with earth to help to build a parapet wherever the troops were entrenching.

On the quarter-deck of the *Queen* a service was held during the afternoon by the ship's chaplain. The officers and crew of the ship could not do enough for the Australians. "They gave us," says one account, "tobacco, cigarettes and pipes till we were overloaded." Some of the men were presented with warm clothing.

---

2 A tow is a string of three ship's cutters or other small craft towed by a steam launch or pinnace, and carrying 120 to 130 men.

Later a concert was given, the items being contributed by members of the crew. At the close of the day a good hot meal, given by the ship, was supplied to all the troops, who were invited to eat as much as they liked, after which, for two or three hours, they were able to snatch some sleep.

About midnight the destroyers *Beagle* and *Colne* drew up alongside the *Malda,* and the men of "C" and "D" Companies dropped quietly over the side on to their decks. Two platoons of the 12th Battalion were also on each destroyer, beside which were seen the row-boats in which the troops were to land. For the next five hours the men could do nothing but sit or lie in their crowded quarters and talk or sleep. At 2 a.m. members of the crew came round with buckets of steaming hot cocoa, very welcome by this time, as the night was somewhat sharp.

The men in the *Queen* were awakened about midnight, and, after a drink of hot cocoa had been served out by some of the bluejackets, they began to climb down into the boats. It was then 1.30 a.m. on Sunday, April 25th, St. Mark's Day. "A" Company went into two tows on the starboard side of the ship, "B" Company into two on the port side. Each tow consisted of a cutter and two lifeboats. By 2.35 every man of the covering party from the three battleships was in his tow. Rear-Admiral Thursby, who was in command of the Anzac landing, with his flag in the *Queen,* says:—

> "The embarkation was carried out so quietly and expeditiously that I did not realize it had begun, and sent to know what was the cause of the delay... I would not have believed that the operation could have been carried out so quietly that I could not hear them, although on the bridge only a few yards away."[3]

The troops had not been able to see the coast from the ship, but they were able to see its outline faintly when they were in the tows. It had been a moonlight night, but the moon was now very low, and they had about an hour of absolute darkness ahead of them, as the first streak of dawn was due at five minutes past four, and sunrise at 5.15.

As soon as the men were in the tows, the battleships, which had been stopped since 1 a.m., began to move in slowly through a sea as smooth as glass. The tows advanced with them, each drawn by its picket-boat. About 3 o'clock the moon vanished. Half an hour later, the battleships having arrived as close to the shore as they could without running the risk of being seen, an officer on the bridge of the *Queen* called out in a clear, loud voice, "Go ahead and land." Thereupon the tows quickened their speed, and as they left, the sailors lining the

---

[3] As quoted by Admiral Wester Wemyss in "The Navy in the Dardanelles Campaign."

sides of the *Queen* gave a "silent cheer" by waving their caps and uttering a subdued whisper, which was barely audible to those in the boats.

The naval officer in charge of the most southerly tow, one of those containing 9th Battalion men, was to give the direction, the other tows keeping in line with him at intervals of about 150 yards. It was now very dark, on account of a thick mist, and the men in the boats could hardly distinguish the tows on either side of them. Not a word was spoken above a whisper, and barely heard was the splash of the boats as the little waves lapped their sides. The suspense in the crowded boats was very trying; "I was shaking all over with nervousness and excitement," wrote one man.

Suddenly two searchlights, one after the other, shot their beams out ahead of the tows for a few moments. Fortunately they were on the far side of the peninsula, and so their rays could not reach the boats on account of the intervening hills. On reaching shallow water the steamboats cast off their tows, leaving the troops to row the remainder of the way to the shore. It was about this time that flames and sparks flared out of the funnel of one of the northern pinnaces to the height of at least three feet; this lasted for nearly half-a-minute. Shortly afterwards, at 4.29 a.m., there appeared on the top of a dimly-seen hill to the south a bright yellow light, which lasted for about half-a-minute. A single rifle-shot rang out from the shore, followed a second or two later by several shots. Then a heavier fire began.

At the sound of the firing the feeling of suspense ended. Some began singing in the boats. A voice was heard through a megaphone: "Make your landing, lads, where you can, and hold on." The boats almost immediately began to run aground, and the men climbed over their sides and waded ashore as best they could. This was no easy matter, as the weighty equipment and arms impeded their movements, and underneath the water the bottom was slippery rounded shingle, not very easy to walk on with military boots. Some of the men found themselves in water half-way up their chests, but scrambling to the shore, they ran across a narrow stretch of beach until brought up by a sandy bank about ten feet high. Here they lay on the ground, took off their packs and laid them down, and fixed bayonets. Some had vainly attempted to fix their bayonets while in the water. Orders had been given that no shots were to be fired until daylight.[4]

[4] These orders were for the most part very carefully observed, despite the fact that a few men on first landing lost their heads in the excitement and began to fire into the darkness. It is said that of the men killed or wounded before daylight, none was found with a cartridge in his magazine and every one had the cut-off of his rifle closed, as instructed. This indicates the high state of discipline existing among the troops.

Tradition has it that it was a 9th Battalion boat that was the first to ground at 4.30 a.m., and a number of its men had already reached the bank at the far side of the beach when the first shot was heard. To Lieutenant Duncan Chapman belongs the honour of having been the first Australian soldier to set foot on Anzac. He later reached the rank of major, and was killed in action at Pozières in August, 1916. Among others in his boat were J. D. Bostock, F. C. Coe, E. Coles, W. A. Fisher, L. Hansen, T. A. Hellmuth, J. C. Henderson, C. Holdway, W. Jarrett, B. H. Kendrick, D. Kendrick, W. E. Latimer, R. McN. C. McKenzie, S. A. McKenzie, W. Pollock, B. Rider, and L. Thomas.

In the darkness it was difficult to see what was happening even close by. Many men were hit before they left the boats, some while in the water, and others as they were running across the beach. Some who had dropped into deep water were helpless on account of their heavy kits, and it is probable that not a few were drowned in this way.

At this stage it became apparent that some mistake must have been made in the point of landing. After forming up in the shelter of the bank, the orders were to attack the first ridge across the open ground. However, there was no open ground to be seen. The bank was the lower part of a high steep rugged hill. Some officers thought that this must be Gaba Tepe; others did not think so, but had no idea where they were. To add to the confusion the battalions were found to be mixed up. Men from the 10th were intermingled with those of the 9th.

It is now known that owing to a strong current the tows were carried out of their course, and made the shore at Ari Burnu, about a mile to the north of the intended landing-place. Some of the naval officers, realising they were off their course, had attempted to remedy the mistake at the last moment, and this it was that led to some mixing of the battalions. Major Salisbury, who was in the extreme right-hand tow, says:—

> "The naval officer guiding the tows[5] was in the picket boat of my tow. Apparently he was steering the right course for Gaba Tepe, for somewhat more than half way in to shore the rest of the tows had sagged away to the north and were out of sight. Some of the picket boats were smaller than the others and perhaps could not keep their loads up against the current setting north. Our tow was behind a large picket boat, and when the rest of the tows got out of sight to the north we turned north until we steamed across the sterns of the other tows with the naval officer apparently counting them; we then turned south to get back to our place on the right, but very soon the shore could be seen, so the picket boat drew up into position as third tow instead of first, thus sandwiching half of 'B' Company into 'A'."

5 Lieutenant J. B. Waterlow.

Plate VI.

12.—LIEUT.-COL. A. G. SALISBURY, C.M.G., D.S.O. and bar, Legion d'Honneur.

11.—CAPT. DUNCAN K. CHAPMAN. (See p. 40)

13.—COLONEL A. GRAHAM BUTLER, D.S.O.

14.—MAJOR A. R. KNIGHTLEY, M.C.

15.—F. H. DOWNES IN HOSPITAL IN EGYPT.
(See p. 61.) To his right is W. K. Jones.
(Photo lent by Warrant-officer W. K. Jones.)

16.—CAPTAIN A. GRAHAM BUTLER AT ANZAC.

Instead, therefore, of landing where there was a comparatively easy climb to the first ridge, the troops found themselves facing something which was in places very like a wall. In the meantime they were being met with rifle and machine-gun fire. One man states that, as soon as he reached the bank, he was "shot by a machine-gun through both knees, was spun round, and then fell down." Another, who could not find room at the foot of the bank, lay down a little further back, on the open beach, where he heard a succession of bullets passing just overhead, one of them hitting the man next to him.

However, it had been forcibly impressed on all that on landing they must advance at all costs, so as to clear the way for the main body. Consequently they began to climb the steep hill in front of them. On the southern side of Ari Burnu, where Major J. C. Robertson landed, was a steep bank as high as the wall of a room, and those attempting to climb it slipped back. Then someone found a rough track leading round it, and by this means they reached the top of the knoll.

Besides being very steep, the hillside was covered with scrub. This was mainly composed of small bushes of prickly dwarf oak, about three feet high, with leaves like a small holly: there was also a smaller arbutus, with leaves like those of a laurel. In places this scrub was so close and thorny that even a strong man had difficulty in forcing his way through it. A machine gun was firing from the top of Ari Burnu, but some of the men climbed up to it, quickly drove the Turks away from their gun, and captured a small stretch of trench from which it had been firing.

As they climbed the men cheered, swore, and joked; one of them afterwards said, "the swearing that went on, as well as the jokes, was marvellous." When they encountered any of the Turks they chased the enemy with shouts of "imshee yalla," "eggs-a-cook," "oranngees" (oranges), and other expressions which they had picked up in Egypt.

Some men of various battalions who had lost touch with their officers, cleaned their rifles and began shooting up at the flashes of the Turkish rifles far above on the hills. Captain Graham Butler, the M.O. of the 9th, who was attending to several wounded men on the beach, saw the uselessness of this, and realising that it might endanger the troops who had begun to climb the hills, urged these men to go on with the bayonet alone. He himself led them up a steep hill to Plugge's Plateau. How steep was the slope may be imagined by Dr. Bean's description in the *Official History*:—

"Those who were wounded (he says) rolled or slid down it until caught and supported by some tuft or scrub. Here and there a man hung over a slope so precipitous that Butler, going to his help, had to cut steps in the gravel face with his entrenching tool in order to reach him."

Men from the 9th, 10th, and 11th were now on Plugge's[6], a small triangular plateau with steep approaches on every side. The Turks who had occupied it ran off down a

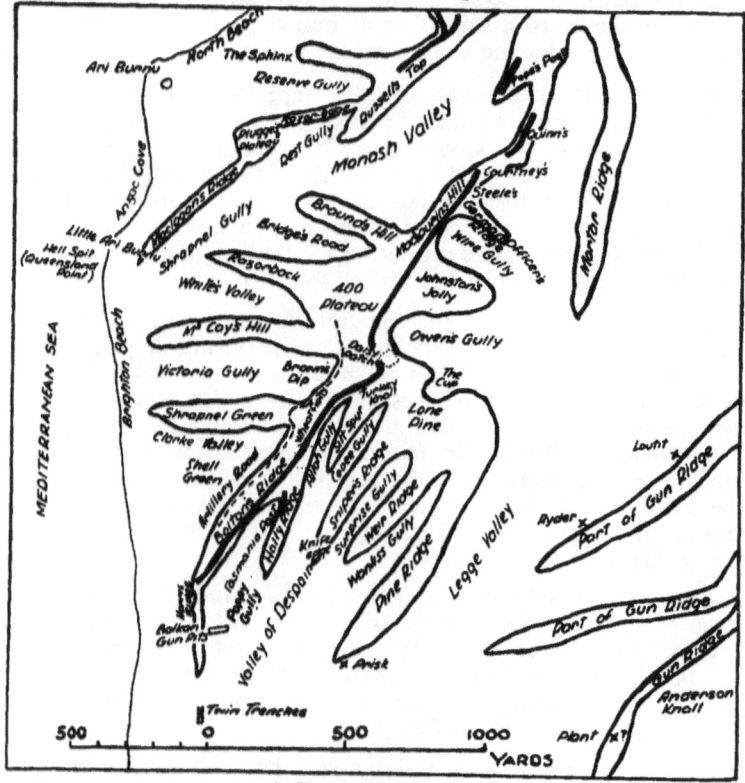

9. The Anzac Area.
The approximate crests of the ridges are shown.

zig-zag path on the far side, while several Australians stood on the edge of the plateau firing at them. A few even went down the zig-zag path in pursuit. Lieutenant Fortescue, who had lost sight of most of his men on the way up to the plateau, "skidded" down a landslide on the far side and lost the rest of his platoon except two, who went down in the same way as he did.

[6] Later in the day, when some New Zealanders were occupying it, Colonel Plugge, of the Auckland Battalion, had his headquarters there, and it was thus named after him.

A few senior officers had now arrived on the plateau. Major E. A. Drake Brockman, of the 11th, sorted out the men of the three battalions, sending those of the 9th to the right, those of the 10th to the centre, and those of the 11th to the left. He also stopped the men from firing at the retreating Turks, leaving them to be dealt with by other parties who were landing further south.

By this time nearly the whole of "A" and "B" Companies of the 9th were on the plateau, but they were without senior officers. The colonel had not reached the plateau. Major J. C. Robertson had received a bullet-wound in the chest; Major S. B. Robertson had gone far to the left with a few of his men, and was killed later in the day on Baby 700. The junior major, A. G. Salisbury, accordingly assumed command of the battalion and led it for the rest of the day. He himself took charge of the right of it, and handed over the left to Captain J. F. Ryder.

Noticing Turks running to the rear down the valley to his right, he ordered the 9th to move into the gully after them. These Turks were fleeing from the second instalment of the covering force, the men in the destroyer tows, whose landing will now be described.

The earlier portion of the trip, in the bright light of the moon, was quite pleasant, "resembling a moonlight river trip," said one man in a letter home. But, after the moon had set, as the hostile shore was approached memories of holiday experiences gave way to the same feeling of suspense as those in the battleship tows had endured, "The suspense was awful," wrote a signaller.

About 4 a.m. or a little later, "C" Company on the *Beagle*, and "D" on the *Colne*, were ordered into the rowing-boats. A wooden staging had been fixed round the side of each ship, and the men stepped on to this and then down into the boats.

The boats from the seven destroyers were better distributed than those from the battleships, having a spread of over a mile from the northernmost to the southernmost, and they landed the battalions in correct order, although all were further to the north than had been planned.

When the destroyers reached a point about 500 yards from the shore, the commander of the *Colne* shouted to the *Beagle* to move south, as they had steered too far north. However, it was too late to rectify the error. As the boats pushed off, the men in them could see the outline of mountains ahead, and the faintest streaks of dawn appeared. After leaving the destroyers the boats spread somewhat, with the result that the several parties of each company reached the shore at different spots. But they landed under similar conditions to their comrades of "A" and "B" Companies, except that for most of them the slope up from the beach was not so steep. Part of "D" Company (Captain Jackson's) landed at Little Ari Burnu (afterwards known as "Queensland Point," or "Hell Spit") and part of "C" Company (Captain Milne's) about 300 yards further south, opposite the mouth of Victoria Gully. Others of "C" Company reached the shore a little farther south still, near the entrance to Clarke's Gully.

Colonel MacLagan, the brigade commander, was in one of "D" Company's boats, and as it approached the land, he looked through his night-glasses to see if the ridge immediately in front was occupied by the enemy. When the boats were about thirty yards from the shore they heard the first shot from in front of them, and then knew that the ridge was occupied; the Turks who were firing were under cover within sixty yards of the beach, some in trenches and some firing from the scrub.

The men landed, dumped their packs on the beach, and rushed the nearest of the enemy. Half-way to the top of the first hill ("M'Cay's Hill") part of Milne's company met a portion of Jackson's coming from the other side. This latter detachment, numbering perhaps half of the company, on landing at the side of Hell Spit, charged, cheering as they ran, over Little Ari Burnu and then began to move south. Going down the far side of the hill through scattered rifle-fire into a valley they found a small stone hut, in which were half-a-dozen Turks sitting by a fire with a pot of coffee on it. These Turks were bayonetted, and the company went on to the top of M'Cay's Hill, a few hundred yards further on, and there joined Milne's company. While some of "D" Company were crossing M'Cay's Hill, Sergeant T. A. Graham was shot in the thigh. "I'm done, boys, I'll never see Constantinople," he said, and soon afterwards he died.

Lieutenant C. F. Ross wrote:—

> "I shall never forget the scene as we reached the top of the hills and could look back on the sea. Huge stabs of flame from the guns of a long line of warships reaching from Anzac to the Straits could be seen as they pelted shells at various points of the enemy positions.
> 
> As the light increased, the flame gave way to smoke, and the noise was terrific. Not only was there the noise of the firing of the guns and bursting of the shells, but the hills of the mainland seemed to take up the echoes and hurl them back to Imbros and Samothrace, whence they were re-echoed back again."

It was still too dark to see a man at 50 yards' distance. The staffs and troops of the main body on the transports could not gain much information of the progress of the landing. They saw the flare and heard the rifle-fire following it, and some heard ·what appeared to be faint cheering—this would be either the shouting of the men in the boats during the actual landing, or else the cheering, swearing, and joking which went on during the charge up the hills.

When daylight came, what was going on ashore could be discerned more clearly, especially by those who had telescopes or field-glasses. The men who were then landing, and those climbing the first ridge of hills, were visible and also the fighting going on along the sides and tops of those hills, but occurrences beyond the first ridge were for the most part out of sight of the ships. Enough of the fighting could be seen, however, to show the sailors and other onlookers what sort of men the Australians were. Admiral Wemyss was very much impressed, and to an Australian officer he afterwards said :—

> "Your men are not soldiers, they are fiends. I have seen many famous regiments charging, but I have never seen fighting like this. Your men will do me. It would give me great pleasure to lead them into action at any time."

Vice-Admiral de Robeck wrote:—

> "At Gaba Tepe the landing and dash of the Australian Brigade for the cliffs was magnificent—nothing could stop such men. The Australian and New Zealand Army Corps in this, their first battle, set a standard as high as that of any army in history, and one of which their countrymen have every reason to be proud."

According to the original plan the troops after landing were to cross the ridge extending from Baby 700 to Bolton's Ridge, and to occupy the next one, Gun Ridge and its extensions. But owing to the mistake in landing too far north, another ridge was found between the beach and the one from Bolton's to Baby 700, with the result that the "first" ridge of the orders actually became the "second" ridge, and the so-called "second" ridge the "third." When daylight came the officers on Plugge's could recognise, from their previous study of the plans, the ridge which had now become the second ridge from a prominent feature on it, half-a-mile to their right front. This was a level-topped hill, a little higher than the rest of the ridge, which has been compared to a heart with its point to the sea. Known as the "400 Plateau," it should have been on the left centre of their landing-place.

At this moment, while the 10th Battalion should have been over the second ridge and on its way to the third, the 9th ought to have been far to the south hurrying to Gaba Tepe, which was two miles away from them when they expected it to be only 1000 yards distant. However, Major Salisbury led "A" and "B" Companies towards the 400 Plateau, moving thither across Shrapnel Gully a little to the south of the 10th, which had also left Plugge's, and was following retreating Turks. The seaward "point" of the 400 Plateau was not exactly a point but was separated into two spurs, the Razorback to the north and M'Cay's Hill to the south, with White's Gully between. Salisbury and his men climbed the steep Razorback, meeting only scattered fire, and reached the far side of the Plateau a little north of the head of Owen's Gully.

In the meantime, Lieutenant Thomas, with a platoon of Jackson's company, had reached the 400 Plateau and was re-organising in the scrub at its edge. One of his sections, under Corporal Harrison, was missing. The rest of the platoon then advanced across the plateau, its 50 men in a line about 300 yards from flank to flank. Reaching Owen's Gully—the valley which divides the northern lobe of the plateau ("Johnston's Jolly") from the southern one ("Lone Pine")—Thomas saw, about 200 yards ahead, some newly-turned mounds of earth which he thought were machine-gun emplacements. He saw, too, some Australians in the scrub to his right going straight in the direction of them.

Thomas tried to warn this party, but each time that his signaller stood up to semaphore the message, an enemy machine-gun fired at him. Thomas then recognised the party. It was Harrison's section, which had reached the plateau some 300 yards south of him. Harrison had for a little while acted under the orders of Captain Milne, and then led his section across the plateau to join Thomas, whom he had seen (or had heard was) making towards Owen's Gully. Harrison, going to the north-east through the scrub, had just caught sight of a cup-shaped depression in front of him, when he came under machine-gun fire from the scrub beyond it. His men fell flat and crawled through the bushes to the edge of the depression, in which, immediately below them, they saw some tents. Other tents were visible further down the valley, while the smoke of camp fires was seen between them.

Harrison at once began to move towards these tents, and it was then that Thomas tried to signal to him. The only word that Harrison could make out was the last—"gun." But at that moment two field-guns fired close above his head. He called together his nine men and all crawled up the steep bank and found the guns just above them. There were seven Turks round the guns and fifty yards behind were others, loading machine-guns on mules. They had not seen Harrison's party, and he told his men each to pick a member of the guns' crews, fire together, and rush the guns. All seven men round the guns fell. A Turkish officer appeared at the entrance of the gun-pit and raised his revolver, but Harrison fired first, with the rifle from the hip, and the officer fell dead. The Australians next fired on the men who were loading the mules, and only one of them seems to have escaped. Then Thomas came up with his platoon and joined Harrison.

There were either two or three guns, and mules had already been harnessed to one of them. In a small roofed shelter was a quartermaster's store, containing books, papers, spare parts for machine-guns, leather equipment, tobacco and cigarettes. Some of our men wheeled one gun round to fire it on the Turks, but found that the breech-blocks had been thrown away. Bugler Maxwell, who was never seen again after that day, knocked off the sights; others, including some of the 10th who had by then come up, tried to burr the screws inside the breeches so as to put the guns out of action. These were the first guns captured at Anzac.[7]

Thomas now placed his men in a line in the scrub about 50 yards beyond the depression which Harrison had stumbled upon and which, for want of a better name, Dr. Bean has called "The Cup." As they were exhausted, they rested for ten minutes, and were allowed to smoke. The fighting hereabouts had temporarily ceased by this time, and there was no noise except a little occasional distant firing. A party of Turks with mules could be seen hurrying over the third ridge, that which was to have been the objective of the covering force.

Major Brand, the brigade-major, now arrived, accompanied by Lieutenant Boase and a platoon of Jackson's company. They crossed the plateau just south of Owen's Gully, passing on their way, near the head of the gully, a level patch of green grass and poppies, about 100 yards square, with the scrub forming a high border all round it. This was afterwards known as the "Daisy Patch." They passed by the south of The Cup without noticing it, and found Thomas's platoon lined out in the scrub.

The first definite orders for a change of plan were now given. The main parties of the 9th and 10th were arriving on the plateau, and the brigadier, Colonel MacLagan, followed them. He ordered that, instead of advancing to the third ridge, they should dig in and reorganise where they were, on the second ridge.

When Major Salisbury reached the plateau he collected the scattered men of the 9th who came up, and carried out the brigadier's instructions to dig in there. Leaving a platoon

[7] These guns did not remain in our possession, as they could not be removed at the time, and during the night they were secured by the enemy and withdrawn.

under Lieutenant Fortescue as an outpost lining the northern side of Owen's Gully, he set the others to dig in to the right of the 10th, making his line face to the south-east.

The line thus formed by the two battalions was not continuous, but had several wide gaps in it. These were to be filled by the 12th Battalion, which was to be in close support according to the plans; and some were soon filled by one company of the 12th which came up. The top of the "plateau" was not flat, but was a succession of ridges and gullies covered for the most part by thick scrub.

Various advanced parties, such as those of Thomas and Boase, remained a few hundred yards in front of the line, and Major Brand decided that the best plan would be for them to act as a screen for the main bodies of the 9th and 10th digging in. He therefore gave temporary orders to this effect to the advanced parties, telling Boase and Thomas to go forward to the far edge of the plateau, where they could get a better view of the third ridge, but to go cautiously and not too far. He then signalled back the suggestion to Colonel MacLagan, who adopted it for the time being and sent the following message to Brand: "Keep advanced companies forward, Second Brigade coming in on our right."

MacLagan's order to dig in on the second ridge did not, however, reach all the advanced parties. A detachment of the 10th, under Lieutenant Loutit, with whom were a few men of the 9th, had been among the first to arrive on the 400 Plateau, and they entered the head of Owen's Gully and passed down it. Then they made their way to the third ridge and, after climbing the greater part of the rise, came upon a large body of Turks, and lay down and opened fire on them. Loutit with two men made a reconnaissance and saw in the distance the waters of the Dardanelles, on the far side of the peninsula.

Then, noticing a party on the inland slope of Lone Pine, he sent over and asked the officer in charge of them to bring his men over to the third ridge and protect his southern flank. This party was a portion of the 9th under Captain Ryder, who had come along with Salisbury from Plugge's. As Brand's order not to advance beyond the edge of the plateau had not yet been made, Ryder at once crossed the valley with his men and took up a position to the right of Loutit.

Lieutenant E. C. Plant led a party of about 20 men from the southern end of the plateau over the spurs which jut out southwards from that end of it. Going very fast, they reached the third ridge, south of the position attained by Ryder's party, at a point which gave a good view over the country behind the ridge. In the distance they could see water, which they took to be the Sea of Marmora. There was danger of being cut off, however, and the party returned.

It was now between 8 and 9 o'clock. The parties of Loutit and Ryder were under very hot fire from a much superior force, and soon they found themselves also under fire from the left. Ryder's party was receiving this fire in their backs, and Ryder sent urgent messages asking for support. One of his sergeants reached the main line on a Turkish horse found in the valley. Some of Ryder's messengers, or wounded men making their way to the rear, met Captain Peck, the adjutant of the 11th, on the northern slope of the 400 Plateau. They said that Ryder was in danger of being cut off, so Peck collected some men and went down Wire Gully, just to the north of Johnston's Jolly, and across the valley to reinforce the advanced party.

It was now nearly 9.30 a.m. and Ryder had already begun to withdraw. His party, together with Plant's and Loutit's, had carried out the whole of the original plan of operations, reaching the nearest point to the Dardanelles which any of our troops ever attained, but, meeting with greatly superior numbers who were about to outflank them, they were forced to retire. After Ryder's and Loutit's parties reached the edge of 400 Plateau, they noticed that a line of entrenchments was being dug about 50 yards further back, but instead of retiring upon it they dug in where they were and remained as an outpost overlooking Wire Gully and German Officer's Ridge beyond it.

In the meantime news began to reach the main line from the advanced parties on the third ridge, first that they were in difficulties, and next that they were retiring. Then word came that it was doubtful if Ryder and his men could get back, but soon afterwards they arrived safely.

Captain Jackson, commanding "D" Company, having been hit on the way up from the beach to the 400 Plateau, Captain Dougall took command of the part of "D," which met men of "C" (as previously mentioned) on the way up to the plateau. Both parties reached the southern or Lone Pine end of the plateau. Victoria Gully on the seaward side, separated it from Bolton's Ridge, and where this ridge joined the plateau there was an enemy trench. Captain Milne was fired on from this position as soon as he arrived at the top of the hill, and was wounded. He sent a section under Corporal Harrison—the same who afterwards attacked the Turkish guns—to work round behind the trench, which was soon taken by this party and by the scouts, the few Turks in it being killed or captured. Milne moved into this trench; he was hit several times, and his second-in-command, Captain Fisher, had been wounded too, whereupon Milne left the trench, and went to the east till he reached the Turkish guns near The Cup.

Dougall, holding a rifle with bayonet fixed, called out, with a broad grin, "Come on, boys," and led his party, now only a handful, at a run along Bolton's Ridge towards Gaba Tepe. Near Bolton's Hill, in which Bolton's Ridge ended, not far from the sea, they found an empty trench. Lieutenant Chambers had now been hit. Occupying the trench, the party soon noticed a large enemy column come on to the third ridge from behind and march along the top of it. As no reinforcements reached Dougall, he withdrew his men to the place where Salisbury was digging in on the 400 Plateau. Here he found the brigadier, to whom he reported the news of the approaching Turks, and soon afterwards they were seen like ants coming over the sky-line. By this time Salisbury, assisted by the orderly-room sergeant, Maurice Wilder, who was doing the work of adjutant, had collected about half of the battalion, and he was under the impression that the line he occupied was being definitely taken up. It was now about 9 a.m.

MacLagan could see the 2nd Brigade, which had landed between 5 a.m. and 7 a.m., advancing towards the plateau. Very heavy firing broke out on the left front. He thereupon went to Salisbury and told him that a serious counter-attack was developing, and that he would have to send men forward by sections to meet it. This action was carried out between 10 a.m. and noon, the trenches which the 9th had been digging being left empty, and no settled line was formed there during the remainder of the day.

As section after section moved off through the scrub, they met with a tremendous fire, both from rifles and machine-guns, and became scattered and hopelessly mixed. Advancing south of Owen's Gully towards The Cup, they overtook about fifty men of various companies of the 9th, among whom were Milne and Lieutenant Young, advancing through the scrub. About this time Major Salisbury was hit in the hand, and losses were heavy.

The enemy had driven in Loutit's and Ryder's parties. Those under Boase and Thomas, still in advance of most of the troops on the plateau, had advanced down two of the spurs leading into Legge Valley, from which they had observed Turkish reinforcements passing along the third ridge. They sniped at them, and also sent back messengers with word of the enemy movements. A fierce fire from rifles and machine-guns began to play on the plateau, but it passed for the most part over the heads of these two advanced parties. Thomas's, however, moving nearly to the foot of the spur, came under fire and lost heavily.

Soon afterwards the Turks, who so far had been advancing northwards along the third ridge, deployed and began to come down towards 400 Plateau in extended order. Both flanks of the 9th's advanced parties were unsupported, and the Turks appeared about to pass them on the left in order to cut them off, so Boase and Thomas decided to withdraw alternately by stages of about fifty yards, each party covering the retirement of the other by its fire.

Corporal Harrison and his section were on the extreme right of Thomas's platoon, and isolated, and they did not see the Turkish attack. Not hearing of the withdrawal, they stayed on. In the meantime the others had retired to a position about fifty yards in front of the Turkish guns at The Cup. Thomas sent Lance-Corporal Harman to Major Brand to report the situation and to ask for support. Harman was hit, but the message seems to have got through, for Lieutenant Haymen with some fifty men was ordered by Brand to reinforce the advanced party. They reached Thomas about half-an-hour after the retirement to The Cup, and then Milne and afterwards Salisbury reached the position with remnants of the 9th and 10th.

By this time heavy loss was being caused by the enemy fire. It was impossible to organise the line, or even to keep communication along it. At some little distance to the right of this position were the two machine-guns of the 9th, under Lieutenant Costin, but he knew nothing of the whereabouts of the rest of the 9th nor of the existence of any firing-line.

Haymen and about fifteen men occupied the trenches near the captured guns. Fortescue, who had been stationed on Johnston's Jolly as a covering party while Salisbury was digging in there, came under severe fire from an invisible machine-gun, and crossed Owen's Gully to avoid it. As his party lay on the southern edge of the gully, it was joined by some men of the 2nd Brigade under a captain whose orders were to reinforce the firing-line. According to the original plan, the 2nd Brigade, when it landed, was to have gone in to the right of the 3rd Brigade, to occupy new ground and extend the front, but owing to the tactical situation it had to be used for reinforcing. The captain sharply asked Fortescue what he was doing there, and not being satisfied with the latter's explanation, ordered Fortescue to go on with his men to the firing-line, towards which he himself thought he was going.

Fortescue therefore went forward, to the south, and soon saw ahead some Australians who proved to be Costin and his machine-gunners. Costin knew nothing of the rest of the 9th, except that he believed that Haymen with a few men was in some gun position down the hill. Fortescue, who had now only seven men left, continued in that direction, and duly found Haymen with fifteen of his men in a somewhat sheltered position. Fortescue asked whether the firing-line was ahead, but Haymen replied that he was sure that there were no Australians in front of them, for he was being fired on from the front at short range.

Between 11 a.m. and noon, a battery of enemy mountain-guns established near Scrubby Knoll opened a deadly fire on the 400 Plateau. The Turks were advancing on to Johnston's Jolly and to the bottom of Owen's Gully. Some of them even tried to steal across the gully into their old trenches on Lone Pine, but they were stopped by fire from a party of the 12th on the northern side.

Salisbury had sent back for reinforcements, but as his messengers did not return and no reinforcements came, he consulted with Milne and they decided to retire to the summit of Lone Pine, about 300 yards in rear. Milne had already been wounded three times, and he now received two more wounds under circumstances which he himself described in a letter as follows:—

> "A man lying next to me got killed, and I put out my left hand to take his rifle and have a shot, and just as I did so a shell burst right overhead and hit me across the fingers, smashing the stock of the rifle to splinters, so I didn't have a shot that time. I got out my field dressing and tied them up and carried on, but very soon after a six-inch shell got to business and a piece of it ripped through the back of my upper left arm."

Nevertheless he continued to lead his men, but finally was only able to crawl about encouraging them. When they went farther forward they noticed him lying down, and thought he was dead. Some men dragged him out and carried him down to the beach, and it was not till they reached there that he was found to be still alive.

Salisbury again advanced a little, close to Costin's position, and remained there for the greater part of the day. The fire was now almost unbearable. Captain Melbourne was badly wounded in the head; Lieutenant Chambers also was hit, and Costin was killed by a shell which destroyed one of his machine-guns. He and his sergeant, Steele, when the rest of the section became casualties, had continued to work one of his guns, and when Costin fell, Steele carried the remaining gun to Haymen's party in the gun-pits.[8] Salisbury returned two or three times for reinforcements to "Brown's Dip," behind the crest, at the head of Victoria Gully, and each time he took forward men of the 2nd Brigade. Most of his own men had now fallen and his line thus became gradually held by the 2nd Brigade, as did Thomas's position fifty yards in front of the gun-pits.

Other parties from the 2nd Brigade now began to arrive on the plateau, but so thick was the scrub and so difficult the communications that they did not get into touch with the Australians already there; in fact, the newcomers had no real idea of their whereabouts or of where they were going. At this time those on the plateau looking back could see men—perhaps a platoon or what was left of it—moving through the bushes. On reaching the edge of a small clearing, their officers apparently ordered a charge, for they rushed, cheering, across the open space, shot at from every side except the direct rear, with their bayonets flashing in the sunlight, before disappearing in the undergrowth again.

At 10.30 the first of our artillery, an Indian mountain battery, began to land. It took up a position just behind the crest, on the north side of the 400 Plateau, and at 11.55 directed its fire on to the third ridge. The sound of these guns brought fresh heart to our men, but the Turks fired heavily on the battery, and at 2.25 its guns had to be withdrawn to shelter.

By about 1 p.m. the tide of battle definitely turned in favour of the enemy, and by 2 o'clock the Australians were gradually falling back to what was to become their permanent line until the August offensive. It seemed to many that "the game was up," and that none of them would be able to withdraw from the Peninsula. But very few of the Turks reached the plateau, those who did being swept off by a fire nearly as deadly as their own had been. Lieutenant Haymen was killed during the afternoon; at 3.30 p.m. Thomas's shoulder was smashed by shrapnel, and he handed over his part of the line to a 2nd Brigade officer. Salisbury, dazed, exhausted and wounded, retired to a dressing station, and later joined a part of the 9th in reserve.

Some more guns were landed during the afternoon, and came into action at 4.45 p.m. Up to this time the only artillery support which the Australians had received was that from the Indian mountain battery and the naval guns, but the latter could only fire at those parts of the battlefield which could be seen from the sea. When the 18-pounders landed, they found it difficult to secure positions in which they could not be enfiladed by the enemy. During the whole campaign, in fact, it was no easy matter to find such positions.

[8] For his work this day Steele was awarded the D.C.M.

# CHAPTER IV.

### THE FIRST WEEK AT ANZAC.

As it is well nigh impossible to write a connected story of the fighting on the first day, since so many detached parties were carrying on independently, it must suffice to give an account of the adventures of some of those of the 9th. When the 2nd Brigade was sent to the help of the 3rd, a company of the 6th Battalion, and also a separate platoon under Lieutenant Prisk, was sent to guard the right flank. They were soon recalled, but Prisk's platoon had gone too far for the order to reach him. Going south along the beach, he turned east and up to the top of Bolton's Ridge, along which he moved southwards, being joined by a few men of the 9th. "Grand lads," he said, "eager for anything—it was a job to keep them back." Leaving Bolton's they went to "Pine Ridge," but finding themselves in front of other Australians, whose fire they were receiving in their backs, they retired to "Allah Gully."

In the morning, when Salisbury advanced to meet the counter-attack, a party about twenty strong, under Sergeant A. R. Knightley, had gone southward immediately after Dougall. They ran until they could run no longer, and, not seeing any sign of the enemy ahead, had to drop from sheer exhaustion. Knightley himself began to move about stealthily in the scrub to see if he could discover anything of the enemy or make contact with any other Australians on the right. He seemed to have got a little ahead of Dougall's party, but it was very difficult to keep touch, as the bush was so thick. Two runners, sent to either flank, reported that there did not seem to be any other troops about, but as the party was being shelled and shot at from all directions, Knightley decided to withdraw it to Lone Pine plateau, from which they might see something to shoot at.

As they were retiring, a strange officer jumped up from the scrub. "What are you doing?" he shouted, "you mustn't retire, go forward." The order was obeyed, but one of the men sarcastically remarked: "Why don't you come yourself?" Knightley felt inclined to make the same remark, but, instead, he led his men forward, still without meeting any more of our men, until he came to a sheer drop, which prevented any further advance.[1] Everything here seemed peaceful, and far away down

---

[1] This was on the edge of Pine Ridge, according to Dr. Bean, but Knightley himself thinks that it was further forward on the next hill, Gun Ridge.

the valley a few horses were grazing. Some of the men fired at these, but apparently without success.

Soon afterwards Knightley observed large numbers of the enemy swarming down the opposite hillside, but, instead of telling his men, he ordered them to lie down and rest while he reconnoitred. One man, Private Gibson, said that he was thoroughly tired, and must sleep. Knightly warned him against this, but as he was never seen again, he may have slept and been left behind when the party retired later. It was during this reconnaissance that Knightley noticed men running from bush to bush behind his party, and firing towards the shore. By their black baggy trousers he realised that they must be Turks.

While returning to his party he met the tall thin sergeant cook, J. R. Irvine, known as "Sergeant Pullthrough." When asked what he was doing there, as a cook had no business in the firing line, Irvine replied, good old soldier as he was, that he just had to be where the boys were. Knightley then went on towards his men, and met an officer with a small party running up from the south. On finding who he was and what he had been doing, this officer ordered him to fetch up his party.

Just as the two parties joined, the enemy between them and the shore saw them and opened a very hot and accurate fire, causing the men to run in all directions.

> "I well remember a sergeant-major of the officer's party (writes Knightley) standing up in the open and calling out 'Don't run, lads, remember you are Australians,' and he said to me 'Don't leave me, sergeant, drop down and give them a lead and fire.' I could not see any enemy, but fired at the flash of a rifle or where I thought they were. One of my men fired just alongside me and slightly to the rear of my head, and the report knocked me sideways. It must have been a close call, for I was practically deaf for some time afterwards. I never knew who that sergeant-major was, but I must say he was a brave and cool soldier."

Although the Australians sustained heavy casualties they drove the Turks away. The survivors then retired to Bolton's Ridge, going very cautiously through the intervening valleys. It was dusk by this time, and the men staggered and stumbled into the trench which had been dug along what was henceforth the Australian front line. Knightley himself arrived half-dazed, and dropping down from sheer exhaustion, fell asleep almost at once.

Many gallant deeds were performed on this day of days. Sergeant C. E. Benson on two occasions rallied and led forward again into the firing line shaken men whose officers had all been killed or wounded. Corporal C. R. Heaton displayed extraordinary bravery when, under shell and heavy rifle fire, he rescued and brought into shelter a wounded man. Earlier in the day, shortly after the Landing, Private G. Robey swam out to a boat under heavy fire and brought back into safety a wounded comrade, its only occupant. Lance-Corporal J. E. Kenyon returned from the firing line under heavy fire, collected reinforcements, and assisted in leading a successful bayonet charge to the top of the hill, which was afterwards held against great odds. At dusk the Turks began to reach Lone Pine in small parties. Corporal Harrison, finding them on all sides, withdrew at 7 p.m. and in the course of this retirement Kenyon stepped upon a group of six Turks lying in a depression of the ground, but escaped unhurt.

Prisk's party was ordered after nightfall to retire to Bolton's Ridge. The right of our line now rested on Bolton's Ridge and the rear slope of the 400 Plateau. During the night, although the enemy made some counter-attacks, these were not of a serious nature and were easily beaten off. Sniping, however, was continuous, and the Turks removed the guns from The Cup. This night was bitterly cold, with drizzling rain, but the men kept on digging through it all.

The stretcher-bearers had a strenuous time all day, and by nightfall they were all thoroughly exhausted, but the work had still to be carried on, and they were organised into squads, which were so arranged that each man was able to have an hour's sleep. The difficulty of their work may be gauged from the following description by one of them, V. H. Williams, who wrote of one of his trips on the following day:

> "The Turks had the position in which we were well marked, and a machine-gun and a small mountain gun just poured shrapnel and bullets into everything that moved. A lad got a smack in the thigh, and I managed to get it dressed, and with him gripping on to my boots I dragged myself along to the slope of the hill on my stomach and then was going to give him a roll down the side and chance what happened, when we saw the gun that was firing at us.
>
> "We saw them load the gun, and the next thing I knew was that the lad had some more wounds. That put the wind up us properly, and we absolutely fell down the side of the hill to safety. I came through with a few torn clothes and a few scratches, but my man was not so well off; he had fallen into a small stream in the valley and was knee-deep in mud. I reached him, and with the aid of another man we struggled down the middle of the muddy stream until we reached a suitable place to land our man. After much struggling we managed to land him, my mate secured a stretcher, and we dressed his wounds and made for the C.C.S.[2]
>
> "Everything went well until we were nearly at the beach, near the mouth of Shrapnel Gully, when shrapnel began to burst all round us, and just as we rounded a corner one burst over us, one piece passing between

[2] See Glossary.

my mate's back and the wounded man's head, and another piece just missing the side of the stretcher. We moved on more quickly, and were turning round the next corner when we heard another shell coming. We dropped down to the ground, stretcher and all, and the shell buried itself in the soft earth not six feet away from us. Fortunately it was a 'dud' and did not burst."

During the night, says Admiral Thursby,

"the beach was crowded with men; some, exhausted after the strenuous day, had just thrown themselves down and slept like logs; some were getting food and drink for the first time for many hours, others were being collected by officers and N.C.O.'s and being formed into organised units."

About 200 of the 9th were "collected."

After dark the two divisional commanders, Generals Bridges and Godley, came to the conclusion that it was doubtful whether the troops could withstand a determined counter-attack by the enemy if made the next day. They were therefore of opinion that the operation should be abandoned and the force withdrawn from the Anzac area, and about 9 p.m. they sent to General Birdwood, who had landed that afternoon but had returned to the *Queen,* a message to come ashore. He arrived on the beach before 10 o'clock and conferred with them. He, too, thought evacuation desirable, but decided to refer the matter to Sir Ian Hamilton and leave the decision to him. When Hamilton received the message he consulted with the naval staff, and as they stated that it was then too late for the troops to be re-embarked that night he decided to continue with the operation.

Next day, Monday, April 26th, the troops of the 9th and 10th who were resting were called for at 4 p.m. to go forward to help in the firing-line, which in this sector was near the actual pine tree which later gave the name "Lone Pine" to this part of the plateau. A slight general advance of the front line was made between 4.30 and 5.30, but it was checked by an enemy counter-attack in which machine-gun fire was very heavy; the Turks were, however, driven off. Sergeant Wilder distinguished himself by rescuing a wounded man. Wilder, assisted by another N.C.O., carried the man under a very heavy fire into a place of safety, and later on he did much useful work in collecting stragglers and leading them back to the firing-line.

The 3rd Brigade Headquarters was relieved on this day by that of the 1st Brigade, and the details of the 3rd Brigade who were still in the front line came under the orders of the 1st Brigade. Like the first, the second night was a cold one, and heavy rain fell. A message from General Birdwood which found its way to the battalion on the 27th read as follows:—

"Well done, Third Bde., you have done magnificently, we are all proud of you; open helio communication as soon as possible, Birdwood."

On Tuesday, the 27th, there were a number of details of the 9th still in the line, and these, with the other troops there, had to face several disconnected enemy attacks on different parts of the line. Although it was not realised by the Australians at the time, these attacks represented an attempt by Mustapha Kemal, the local Turkish commander (who after the war was ruler of Turkey for many years) to launch a simultaneous assault along the whole line. In his written orders for this attack, Kemal said:

> "We must drive those in front of us into the sea. There is no need to scheme much to make the enemy run."

Our men, tired as they were, must have laughed if they had known of these brave words at the time. New enemy troops were used in these attacks, and they did not know the area. Units lost their way and were late in reaching their destinations; their nerves were shaken by the fire from the warships, and delay was also caused by the demoralised condition of the troops already in the line.[3]

Sergeant Knightley gives some particulars of this engagement. He was ordered to occupy a certain hill, but the men in his party were so weak that they could only advance in short rushes. However, they made some progress, although fired on with shrapnel, across ground which was strewn with the bodies of men of the 15th Battalion, killed in fierce fighting on the 25th; they were to be seen lying about everywhere behind the bushes.

As Knightley approached the top of the hill, which was very bare, the shrapnel became more intense, and, as only Lance-Corporal Lynch was now left with him, he decided that it would be foolhardy to go further. So they lay down, while the shrapnel burst above them and pellets and nose-caps fell all round. Fortunately, neither was hit although one nose-cap, whistling down closer than the others, struck the barrel of Lynch's rifle. Remaining here until darkness set in, they saw figures moving about near by, and on making certain that they were Australians, Knightley and Lynch reported to the officer in charge of them.[4] The party dug in and occupied their position; there was to be no retiring, said the officer. Knightley was put in charge of them, twenty-five in number, and here they remained from Monday until the following Saturday. During the nights Knightley would gather water-bottles, rations,

---

[3] It is interesting to note that on April 30th, Liman von Sanders, the enemy army commander, received a peremptory order from Enver Pasha, the Turkish Minister for War, to "drive the invaders into the sea." This was just what he had been trying to do all along, but he could not succeed. By the evening of the 27th there were twenty Australian and New Zealand Corps battalions on the Anzac front, facing eighteen battalions of Turks.

[4] Said to have been Lieutenant L. W. Street. 3rd Battalion.

and ammunition from the dead lying about, and these, issued very sparingly to the party, kept them supplied during the five days.

The whereabouts of the party was evidently not known to headquarters, as no one came near it until the Saturday, when early in the morning an officer arrived. "Anyone who has not been relieved step out," he said, and was greatly surprised when he heard how long they had been there. When Knightley and Lynch reached the 9th Battalion they found that they had been posted as missing.

On April 27th the 3rd Brigade had been ordered into reserve at the southern end of the beach, and its members who were still in the trenches were gradually relieved. They made dugouts for themselves near a spot where the first dead were buried; this place, which afterwards became quite a large cemetery, was in a dangerous spot, at the entrance to Shrapnel Gully, near a turning known as Hell Fire Corner. It was here that Sergeant Sinclair, one of the four staff sergeant-majors who left Brisbane with the original battalion, was killed. He and Stretcher-bearer V. H. Williams were excavating dugouts, when the latter handed his entrenching-tool to Sinclair, who wished to take a turn at the work, and stepped aside. The sergeant had just taken his place, when he suddenly fell forward with a shrapnel bullet through the forehead.

On this day fatigue parties went along the beach to collect the packs of the battalion which had been dropped immediately after the troops had landed on the first day, but very few could be found. On Wednesday, April 28th, as more details kept coming in, another reorganisation of the brigade was made on the beach. By this time the men were bearded and their uniforms were ragged. The officers had taken off their metal badges, and stars and crowns marked in indelible pencil on their shoulder-straps now became the recognised badges of rank. All were in the last stages of exhaustion.

A further roll-call took place at 8 a.m., and the 9th, with a muster of four officers and 251 other ranks left out of a battalion which had gone into action about 1000 strong, proved to be somewhat stronger than the other battalions of the brigade. Major Salisbury took command of the battalion, and the companies were reformed. As there were very few N.C.O.'s left, a number of temporary appointments had to be made.

Two battalions of Royal Marines landed at 4 p.m. on the Wednesday, and some of them relieved the men of the 9th who were still in the line. One private wrote:

"We reached the beach, staggering with weariness, some crawling on hands and knees, others unable to move without the help of their mates. When we arrived at the beach we threw ourselves down and slept for hours."

The marines were raw recruits and most of them were lads, some being only 16 years old. Late that night Captain Butler, still working at his aid-post on Bridges' Road, suddenly found marines rushing back through his station. Having lost a post some of them had retired, so parties from the 3rd Brigade had to go back into the line. Captain Dougall, with Lieutenants Fortescue and Ross and 100 men of the 9th, being sent to MacLaurin's Hill. Most of them returned to the beach the next morning, but twenty under Ross had a longer tour in the line.[5]

Ross's orders were to report to a Lieutenant Street[6] and act as support to him, so he and his men set off along the face of the sloping cliff. Whenever they encountered a communication trench leading towards the firing line Ross passed the word along for Mr. Street, and finally, after a long ramble, they located him at a point which Ross thinks must have been near "Steele's Post." As they stumbled along the cliff during their progress to this spot they often dislodged clods of earth which rolled down the steep slope to their left, and judging by the choice remarks that came up out of the darkness beneath them, it would appear that some of the clods found a mark.

Ross's party remained in this position for three days, when they were relieved by marines. It was here that Private Payne of "A" Company had the misfortune to be killed by a "short"[7] from one of our own mountain guns.

By Thursday, April 29th, the survivors of the 3rd Brigade were resting in "bivvies"[8] and they needed a rest too. Beginning with but little sleep on board the warships and transports on the night of the 24th, they were awake from before midnight on that night; the whole of the next day they were engaged in hard fighting; some had a little rest on the night of the 25th, while others had to continue in the firing line until relieved, a proportion putting in four days and nights in this way with scarcely any sleep. The earlier ones to be relieved had to turn out twice and go back to the firing line when their comrades were hard pressed; then, when they should have been resting they had to dig bivouacs. On the 26th the battalion diary remarks "all busy digging in under fire."

5 See Glossary.
6 Probably Lieut. L. W. Street.
7 A "short" is a shell falling short or bursting short of its proper objective.
8 "Bivvies," a contraction for bivouacs, sleeping places for soldiers. This name was given both to dugouts and also to any other kind of shelter for sleeping purposes, although, strictly speaking, a bivouac is not a shelter but a sleeping-place in the open.

Plate viii.

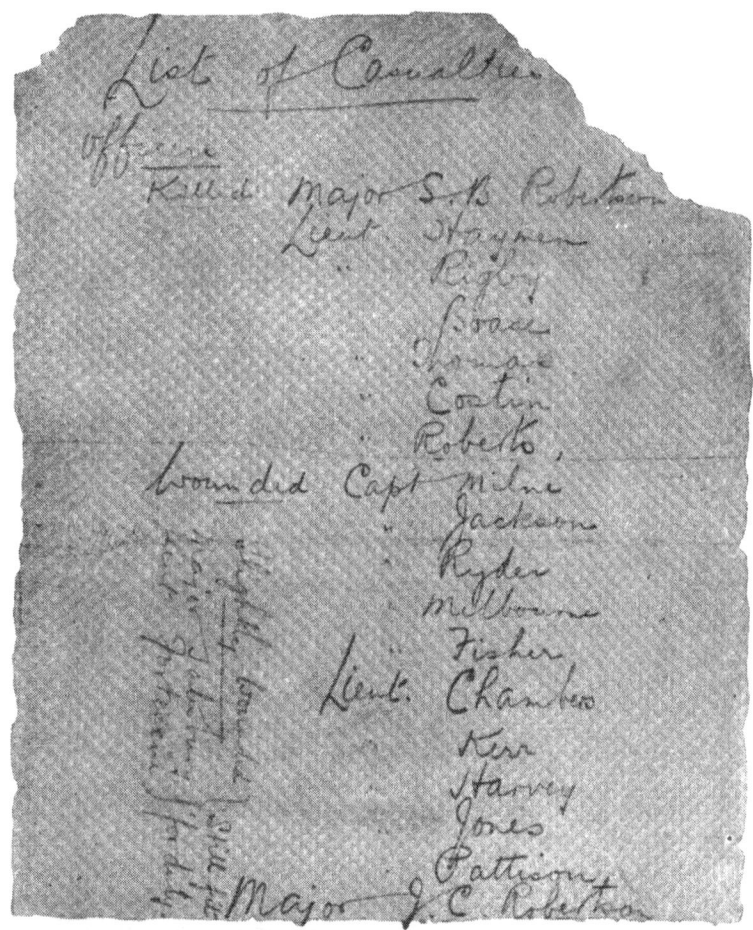

17.—Portion of casualty list sent by the signal officer to the medical officer during the first few days at Anzac. See list of casualties on p. 61. Lieutenants Boase and Thomas had been wounded, but not killed, as thought at first.
(Original lent by Mr. R. Mills, and now in the John Oxley Memorial Library, Brisbane.)

Plate ix.

18.—GENERAL BIRDWOOD AT ANZAC
(Aust. War Memorial Official Photograph. No. G 1222 Copyright. Taken 6th October, 1915. From the Official History).

19.—FOUR OF "THE BEARDED 9th." (See p. 95.)
Left to right.—Standing: L. H. S. Wilson, J. W. Short. Sitting: C. Holdway, B. H. Kendrick.
(Photo. lent by L. H. S. Wilson, Esq.).

Now at last they were able to have some real rest, but not for long. On the 30th, the brigade had to go into the line again to relieve the 4th and 8th Battalions in the trenches at the southern end of the line, the 9th occupying the extreme right flank. Fifty men were detailed under Lieutenant Plant to collect gear and equipment lying about.

> "Part of this job (says Plant) was stripping dead men of their ammunition and gear. Some of the sights were most gruesome, as many of the bodies had been lying in the sun for five days. Some of the bodies were as black as niggers."

The parade state of the battalion at 9 a.m. on this day shows 10 officers and 419 other ranks, and the total casualties up to noon were (as stated at the time) 19 officers, 496 other ranks.[9] The officers killed were Major S. B. Robertson and Lieutenants Costin, Haymen, Rigby, and Roberts; those wounded being Major J. C. Robertson, Captains Fisher, Jackson, Melbourne, Milne, and Ryder, and Lieutenants Boase, Chambers, Harvey, Jones, Ker, Pattison and Thomas. Besides these Major Salisbury and Lieutenant Fortescue had been wounded but were fit for duty. The original statement that seven officers were killed appears to have been incorrect. Among the wounded was Private F. H. Downes. He was carrying a wounded man to the beach about noon when he was shot through the left temple; the bullet shattered both optic nerves and came out of the right eye, destroying the sight of both eyes. Downes, who died last year, is said to have been the first blinded soldier to return to Australia.

The machine-gun section lost over 80 per cent. of its personnel; by the second day only two were left of its original fourteen. On Thursday, however, a new machine-gun section had been organised, and, going into action next day, it put in some good work. E. K. Bedwell was the sergeant of this new section.

The military attack on the Gallipoli Peninsula did not meet with the success which had been hoped for; on the other hand, it was by no means a failure, as some have said. The main reasons why the original plan was not carried through, and the whole southern end of the Peninsula captured on the first day, were the lack of proper preparations beforehand and inability to keep the proposed operations from the knowledge of the enemy. Very little thought seems to have been given by

---

[9] Killed, 7 officers, 25 other ranks; wounded, 11 officers 229 other ranks; missing, 1 officer, 242 other ranks. Of the missing, some were afterwards found to have been sent away wounded without any record being kept; the rest were dead.

the War Office to the possibility of military operations being undertaken in that area; there was not even a good map of the Peninsula available to the M.E.F. at the time of the Landing, and satisfactory maps, as every soldier knows, are of the utmost importance in warfare.

As regards the failure to keep the secret of the proposed operations, it is obvious that the success of such an attack depended entirely upon a surprise. Yet our intentions had been well advertised beforehand by the naval attacks on the Dardanelles, one of which had been accompanied by landing-parties, and also by the sudden buying of small boats in every port in the Mediterranean, which was duly noted and reported by enemy spies. In addition, news of the movements of transports was common property in Alexandria and Port Said, and military units were freely mentioned by name in the Egyptian press, a circumstance which led to their movements and dispositions becoming known to some extent. The fact, also, that a large force of soldiers had for some time been assembled at Lemnos, very close to the Peninsula, could hardly have been expected to remain unknown to the enemy.

The Turks expected an attack, but they did not know exactly where or when it would occur, so the actual landings thus caught them by surprise.

The date originally fixed for the Landing, April 23rd, appears to have been known, approximately at any rate, to the enemy, judging by some false reports of landings. A wireless message from Berlin reached London on April 22nd, stating that 20,000 English and French had landed at Enos, northwest of the Gulf of Saros, and that there was a heavy bombardment by Allied ships. This rumour was cabled to Australia and appeared in the newspapers, and was followed next day by another, stating that the first news had been confirmed by a report from Sofia, capital of Bulgaria, which was at that time a neutral country. Enos was one of the places which had been considered as a landing place, but it had been dropped from the plans finally adopted. Unofficial reports from Athens dated April 24th stated that the Dardanelles had been bombarded, and three landings effected, at Suvla, Bulair, and Enos. Again this is very close to what really did occur a couple of days later.

Notwithstanding the lack of sufficient preparation, and the leakage of information, the Australians and New Zealanders and the 29th Division effected landings under very difficult conditions, captured territory, and held on to what they had captured, defying every effort that the Turks made to dislodge them. The only circumstance which interfered with the Anzac landing was the strong current which carried the boats too far to the north. Owing to the derangement of the operations caused by this, time was given for sufficient Turkish reinforcements to be brought up to prevent our troops from advancing beyond the position, at its furthest point about half-a-mile from the coast, which they had reached within a few hours of landing.

However, the fact of the landing's having been made in the wrong place had one redeeming feature, as the beach near Gaba Tepe, which had been selected for the attack, was found later to be strongly defended by barbed wire, some of which had been laid under the water. The strong Turkish post there would have rendered a landing at that spot very difficult and perhaps impossible; it certainly would have resulted in a very heavy roll of casualties.

Enver Pasha is said to have remarked that Sir Ian Hamilton, in being ordered to capture Gallipoli, had been set to thread a needle with his toes. Nevertheless he succeeded in threading the needle, thanks to the magnificent fighting of all ranks on the 25th, although he did not get the thread as far through the eye as he had hoped to do.

At the time of the landing the German General Liman von Sanders was in charge of the Turkish Fifth Army, totalling about 60,000 men, which had been specially formed for the defence of the Dardanelles. As the peninsula was 50 miles long, he decided on a system of patrols and small detachments along his front, with supports and reserves at strategic points in the rear. One company, consisting of about 200 infantrymen, held the coast between Gaba Tepe and Anzac Beach, and one company from Anzac Beach to a stream (the Aghyl Dere) about a mile and a half further north, with a company in close reserve about a mile inland from Gaba Tepe. There were also larger reserves at divisional headquarters at Maidos, on the other side of the peninsula, six miles from Anzac, and a general reserve at Boghali, almost directly inland from Anzac, five miles away.

So at dawn on April 25th there were about 400 Turks guarding the coast between Gaba Tepe and the Aghyl Dere, and in the whole Anzac area, that is, within five or six miles of Anzac Beach, about 13,000. Sir Ian Hamilton expected to find 20,000 there, and to oppose them he was to land 24,000.[10]

---

[10] At the time of the Landing there were 75,000 men in the Mediterranean Expeditionary Force, made up as follows:—Australian and New Zealand Army Corps, 30,000; British troops, 29,000; French, 16,000.

Colonel Sami Bey, commanding the 9th Turkish Division, which was responsible for the defence of the Peninsula south of Suvla Bay, was at Maidos at the time, but heard nothing of the Anzac landing until an hour afterwards, 5.30 a.m. He thereupon ordered his two reserve battalions and a machine-gun company to drive the invaders into the sea, but it was 7.30 before they were ready to march. These were the troops who were seen from Bolton's Ridge by Dougall's party, from Gun Ridge by some of the advanced parties there, and, about 9 a.m., from the 400 Plateau, as they came along Gun Ridge from the south.

By 6 p.m. on the 25th, 15,000 men had been landed at Anzac. If more troops had been available for reinforcements during the first few days, both for Anzac and Helles, the seizing of the Peninsula might have been achieved in a very short time. Sir Ian Hamilton did not ask for reinforcements soon enough. After the landings had been effected, the home authorities were willing to send adequate reinforcements, and some were sent, but it was then too late for the situation to be affected.

It is a curious fact that in the Commonwealth nothing was known of Australia's participation in the operations until several days afterwards. On the 26th, Australian newspapers announced that a successful Allied attack had been made on the Dardanelles, and troops had been landed there, but it was not until the morning of the 30th that the papers contained the news that the 1st Australian Division had taken part in this attack. At length, on Saturday, May 1st, the evening newspapers published a cable giving the first brief details of the Landing.

The Landing at Gallipoli, although only a small portion of the territory originally aimed at was seized, was a wonderful success, if we consider the results actually achieved. General Birdwood made the following statement, which was published in divisional orders, and reached the 3rd Brigade Headquarters on April 28th:

> "It is an almost unprecedented feat for a landing to be effected on a hostile shore in the face of determined opposition. . . . The manner in which the covering force carried out their landing and at once advanced against a large hostile force through a most difficult and jungle covered mountainous country is a feat of which any army might be justly proud."

## CHAPTER V.

**MAY AT ANZAC.**

From the beginning of May until it left the Peninsula in November the 9th Battalion was not engaged in further major operations. For it the period was one of stationary trench-warfare, varied by a few engagements and raids. The 9th spent its time either manning the trenches on the forward slope of Bolton's Ridge, or resting in the support trenches slightly in rear of the crest, or in "bivvies" cut into the hillside. The back wall of the "bivvies" was the hill, the side walls the sloping hillside, made to an even height with sandbags, while the roof consisted of waterproof groundsheets, or, very occasionally, corrugated iron. The sides of the trenches were cut into to make dugouts for shelter, but this often caused the parapets to fall in, so orders were received to discontinue the practice. The brigadier visited the trenches daily.

After the first few days there were sufficient rations, but water was always scarce. Wells were dug and shallow bores put down, but after the first week or two these could supply only a portion of what was needed. To augment the supply, water was brought by ship and pumped into tanks on and around the beach; rough weather, which interfered with this work, was a source of anxiety whenever it occurred. Towards the end of the campaign condensers were installed on the beach to make fresh water out of salt.

The 9th secured its water from a shallow well situated behind its position, and, whenever possible, from the tanks on the beach. At one period a fatigue party, each man carrying a couple of two-gallon petrol tins, used to leave the battalion daily late in the afternoon to procure water from the wells in Shrapnel Gully. This party invariably came under observation from Gaba Tepe when rounding a point just prior to crossing Shrapnel Green, and more often than not had to run the gauntlet of half-a-dozen shells.

Little or no water could be spared for washing purposes, but the sea was always available for bathing, being distant not more than half-a-mile from the most forward position. Sea-bathing at Anzac, it is true, was liable to be interrupted by shrapnel fire, but that did not trouble anyone unless it came very close, in which case there would be a hurried exit from the water. Later on sea-bathing was forbidden on account of the danger from shelling.

The rations and supplies when landed were sorted out by the A.S.C. on the beach during the daytime. Thither at night the battalion quartermaster would send a party, which loaded the stores on to mules and brought them to the battalion, and then led the animals back to the beach. Very often mules were not available, and rations had to be carried up by a fatigue party. On May 14th the battalion diary records the rations as being "excellent, potatoes, bacon, onions, cheese and jam daily." This was in addition to "bully-beef" and biscuits. The men did their own cooking. Bully-beef was eaten cold, or made into stew, curry or rissoles, and porridge was sometimes made of ground biscuits; however, this proved a very monotonous diet.

All parts of the Anzac area were under artillery fire, but this varied a good deal in intensity. In the battalion diary there appear such remarks as "very little artillery fire," "quiet night," "very severe shelling," "burst of heavy shelling 3.30-4 a.m., otherwise quiet day." In the middle of May it was noted in the brigade diary that there were a few casualties from shell-fire daily among the whole of the brigade troops.

"Beachy Bill" was a well-known enemy gun which paid particular attention to the beach. At first no one knew for certain the location from which it fired, but it is now known that it used various alternative positions in and near the Olive Grove, actually a grove of stunted oaks inland from Gaba Tepe. There were two guns which fired 11-inch shells that could be seen coming: these were from the Turkish battleship *Torgat Reiss*, in the Dardanelles, though at the time it was supposed that she was the German battle-cruiser *Goeben*, which (with the light cruiser *Breslau*) had taken refuge there in the early days of the war and been "sold" to Turkey. Fortunately, for the first eight weeks the enemy refrained from shelling the beach at night.

Patrols were sent out every night along the seaward spur of Bolton's Ridge, sometimes as far as the barbed wire defending Gaba Tepe, or through the valleys south of Lone Pine. They often saw Turkish patrols, but, as their object was reconnaissance, they avoided firing on them whenever possible. Sometimes the patrols were hampered by the searchlights from destroyers which came in close to the shore near Gaba Tepe, and threw their beams up the valleys running down from Lone Pine to help in keeping the Turks under observation.

The weather for the first fortnight was perfect, and after that it continued good throughout May, becoming warmer, although there were some wet days in the latter part of the month. For some weeks the nights were very cold.

During May there were three divisions of Turks at Anzac. which was held by only two divisions of the A. & N.Z.A.C. For a fortnight two brigades—the New Zealand and the 2nd Australian—were lent to the British at Helles during the second Battle of Krithia, two brigades of the Royal Naval Division taking their place at Anzac. Later in the month the infantry was reinforced by the arrival, dismounted, of three light horse brigades and the New Zealand Mounted Rifles; by the 28th General Birdwood had 25,000 troops (19,395 rifles) under his control. These troops had not only to fight but also to dig trenches and dugouts, build roads, cut paths, and carry food, water and ammunition.

On May 4th the first mail was received since the Landing, the second one arriving three weeks later. The mails were always irregular at Gallipoli; one might, for instance, receive letters dated March two or three weeks after those dated April. The 3rd Brigade's diarist mentions on June 14th that brigade headquarters had complained of the delay and the bad sorting of correspondence, ending with the plaintive remark "Mails hopelessly irregular. Are there any postal *officers* at the bases?" When answering their letters the troops often found themselves in difficulties owing to the shortage of paper. Cigarette packets were used as postcards, and also the envelopes in which letters were received, and some men even tried to persuade the Q.M.S. to let them have the side or bottom of a cardboard box to write on.

On May 6th an Arab captain surrendered to some 9th Battalion men on the beach, and was taken by them to headquarters. He was mentioned by one of the brigade staff as being a "queer-looking bird, with long flowing robes." Many of the Arabs in the Turkish Army had no enthusiasm for the war; they only fought because they had to, being subjects of the Turkish Government, so that it is not surprising that they should have seized opportunities of surrendering.

The next day a batch of 120 reinforcements for the battalion arrived. They were most welcome on account of the heavy casualties, and they brought its strength up to 630. By this time everyone had quite settled down to steady trench warfare, without a great deal of firing at the enemy. The average number of rounds fired at the Turks each night now did not exceed 100 per battalion.

On the 8th gaps in the battalion's personnel were repaired by the appointment of seven new officers, Lieutenants M. Wilder, E. Addy, C. E. Benson, S. R. Jordan, C. Morse, F. B. Scougall, and A. Steele, the commissions being dated April 26th. Of these officers it is to be regretted that Addy did not survive the Anzac period, dying as the result of illness. Some have considered this promotion, without previous examination, to be the highest honour that could be conferred on an N.C.O. Later on further commissions were given in this way to a few N.C.O.'s including W. Aggett, W. J. Dewar, G. R. Harrington, A. R. Knightley, J. M. Perrier and N. L. Weynand.

On this day a shell burst directly in front of the door of the dressing station at the head of Clarke Valley. Everyone expected that the M.O. would be found killed, but when those near by reached the spot, they found Captain Butler attending to his less fortunate stretcher-bearers, seven of whom were wounded, three mortally. One, named Tyrrell, was so badly smashed up that the doctor did not know where to begin on him. Tyrrell asked if he was the worst of the wounded, and when told that he was, he suggested that the M.O. should attend to the others first. Soon afterwards he died. Corporal A. Kirby, the medical orderly corporal, also died. He was a splendid N.C.O., and had done wonderful service on the day of the Landing.

At dusk on the same day, just after the men had had their tea, a time at which they would collect into small groups and talk, a tremendous explosion occurred in the lines. Some thought that the enemy had exploded a mine under the front line, but this was not the case. It is said that even the Turks were seen to look over the top of their parapet to see what had happened. Three men[1] were killed by the explosion.

There was much speculation as to the cause of this explosion. Some thought that it was a heavy naval shell which had fallen short on April 25th and had not exploded, and that someone digging had struck the nosecap with a pick. Officers of the 7th Battery, A.F.A., who had a gun in the 9th Battalion sector near the spot where the explosion occurred, examined a fragment of the shell, and were of the opinion that it had been fired from a large Turkish or German gun on the Asiatic shore of the Dardanelles at very long range, and had fallen almost perpendicularly into our front line, exploding immediately on percussion.

On May 9th the first blankets were issued; for the preceding $2\frac{1}{2}$ weeks all ranks had to sleep with only their

---

[1] One was Private J. Oman.

greatcoats for covering. Next day three periscopes were issued to the battalion. The first of these instruments had come on May 2nd, when four arrived for use in the whole brigade. It was now possible to observe the enemy position without exposing oneself to hostile fire. On the 11th a system was adopted throughout the brigade of dividing each company into four reliefs, one platoon being in the firing line, one in the support trench, one in reserve, and one on fatigue, changing about in regular rotation.

On May 12th a patrol found the enemy entrenching on Weir and Pine Ridges; up to this time the spurs running south from Lone Pine had not been occupied, except for scouts and snipers. On this day also a shell came through the parapet and killed two men who were sitting against the back wall of the trench, pinning them to the wall just as they sat.

On the 14th, 100 N.C.O.'s and men from the 3rd Brigade, 25 from each battalion, under Lieutenants Darnell (11th Battalion) and Adsett (9th), were constituted into a beach fatigue party. Camping on the hillside near the spot where stores were landed, the party, besides doing fatigue work on the beach, carried tools, ammunition and other supplies to whatever part of the line they were required. It also dug a sunken road into Shrapnel Gully from near the beach. The details of this party returned to their battalions on June 1st.

On Sunday, May 16th, the first church parade was held, at 6 a.m. There was another on the 30th, in the support trenches.

On May 19th the Turks launched a great attack along the whole of the Anzac front with the object of throwing the invaders into the sea. Early on the evening before word had been received from brigade headquarters that three Turkish transports had landed troops on the far side of the Peninsula, and that they were marching towards the Anzac position, so Birdwood's men were ready for them. Soon after dark the whole of the 3rd Brigade "stood to" with all four battalions in the line, the 9th on the extreme right of Anzac, with its four companies, "A," "B," "C," and "D" in that order from left to right, "D" being posted on the end of Bolton's Ridge and down the slope to the beach.

The battalion's two machine-guns, under Lieutenant Steele, were placed at the seaward end of the ridge; one was the original Maxim gun which had come ashore with Lieutenant Costin, and the other a .45 machine-gun converted to fire .303 ammunition, lent by the navy to replace Costin's second gun, which had been destroyed on the day of the Landing.

The sector from the end of the ridge down to the beach was held by a series of posts only, each—except that on the beach, which was garrisoned by an officer and twenty-five men—consisting of an N.C.O. and from half-a-dozen to a dozen men. This method of defence had to be adopted as there were not enough men to man this part in a continuous line; the battalion was now less than 600 strong, and the only reserve available was one section of the 3rd Field Company, Engineers, which was standing by close to "D" Company's front, the weakest part of the battalion's line. Nearly the whole of the trenches were well sandbagged and loop-holed, but very little barbed wire had been available for putting out in front.

About midnight the Turks opened intense rifle-fire, which was at once met by equally intense rifle and machine-gun fire from the Australians. The attack was pressed almost without pause until just before daylight. Major Salisbury, who was in command of the battalion, writes:

> "In the 9th Battalion the fire was so rapid and continuous that the hot rifle bolts began to jam and had to be well oiled. When rifle oil ran short bacon fat was used. Sometimes the man on the fire-step would borrow the rifle of the support man standing behind him and hand his own rifle down for it to cool, but this did not always suit the support man, for in a number of cases he said to his mate 'No, you get down and let me have a go.'"

A charge was made at 3 a.m. by the 77th (Arab) Regiment, which advanced in two lines in close order, only to be mown down by our rifle and machine-gun fire; a few got as far as our barbed wire entanglements. They were supported by rifle and machine-gun fire, most of which enfiladed our trenches from the north-east. The artillery did much damage to the enemy, one gun of the 7th Battery firing from the front line with "zero" shrapnel, that is, with the shells timed to burst as soon as they left the gun.

Major Salisbury gives the following account of the further course of the battle:

> "In one stage of the attack Turks were seen massing behind a stone building in Poppy Valley, close in front of the 9th. Lieutenant Plant, the adjutant, was sent to ask Major Hughes, of the 7th Battery, to burst shrapnel over the building. On the way to the gun-pit where Hughes was, Plant arranged for two platoons of 'C' Company to fire, one on each side of the building, so as to catch the Turks with rifle fire as they ran away from the shrapnel-bursts, and the Turks were caught by the fire as Plant had anticipated. There were many calls on battalion headquarters for more ammunition, and the last box had gone to 'D' Company before a fresh supply arrived from brigade headquarters. Just before daylight the attack ceased, having failed badly, and the Turkish infantry withdrew, but soon after daylight their artillery heavily shelled the whole front and the 9th Battalion sector in particular."

The enemy artillery fire came from all possible directions; the shells fell on the reserve slopes as well as in the trenches, and lasted till noon, but there was more shelling later in the day, and also a considerable amount of sniping, which caused some losses.

The casualties of the 9th in the action[2] were 16 killed and 25 wounded, those for the brigade amounting to 36 killed and 71 wounded. About 600 enemy dead lay in front of the 3rd Brigade sector, 200 being counted in front of the 9th. The losses of the battalion were chiefly due to the enemy artillery, which completely dominated our guns after the attack had subsided. The Indian mountain battery was useful, however, in keeping the Gaba Tepe gun subdued.

Late in the afternoon of the 19th reports were received that Turks were collecting in front of the trenches, evidently preparing to renew the attack. They did not, however, attempt any advance. On our side it was not considered advisable to counter-attack, owing to the enemy shell-fire.

Next day the battalion's trenches, which had been damaged in the bombardment, were reconstructed, and, as the Turks were very quiet, those of their dead who could easily be reached were buried. About 3 p.m. it was noticed that enemy parties under the Red Crescent flag (the Turkish equivalent to the Red Cross) came out to bury their dead. An informal armistice had been arranged at other parts of the line for burial purposes, and for bringing in the wounded, but the 9th had heard nothing of this, and about 6.30 p.m. the enemy movements seemed very suspicious, as behind the stretcher parties in No-Man's Land the enemy trenches could be seen bristling with bayonets.

Major Salisbury rang up the brigade commander and informed him of this. Colonel MacLagan said that the same thing appeared to be going on all along the divisional front, and he ordered the brigade to man its trenches and be ready for an attack, but not to fire unless ordered or unless the Turks attacked. About 7 p.m. a man in "C" Company called out to Lieutenant Young, the company commander: "The whole ridge is alive with them, sir." Soon afterwards a body of Turks, about a company strong, rushed forward, and "C" Company fired on them. Almost immediately firing broke out along the whole front of the brigade. The attack lasted until 8 p.m., but was beaten off by our fire. The enemy shelled the 3rd Brigade trenches severely during this attack.

2 Called officially the Battle of 'the Defence of Anzac.

Before this General Birdwood had ordered that the armistice should be stopped, and by his instructions a written message was handed to a Turkish officer, which read as follows:—

> "If you want a truce to bury your dead, send a staff officer, under a flag of truce, to our headquarters via the Gaba Tepe road, between 10 a.m. and 12 noon to-morrow, 21st May."

The 9th Battalion was informed of this, as it was to its portion of the line that the envoy would come first.

On the morning of the 21st a large white flag was seen flying on Gaba Tepe, and shortly afterwards the envoy and his party were seen coming along the beach on horseback. Their progress being stopped by their own wire on the beach, they had to make a détour inland to get round the obstacle. Major Salisbury, Corporal Sizer, and a man from "D" Company, carrying a white signal flag with a blue line through it, as they had no plain white flag, went forward to meet them.

The enemy party, which consisted of the envoy with a German officer and two or three more, was held up about 500 yards in front of the battalion's beach post until a staff officer and an interpreter (an Englishman) from corps headquarters came out. Captain A. M. Ross, of brigade headquarters, and Lieutenant-Colonel A. Skeen, of the corps staff, arrived later. The envoy was blindfolded and led in to corps headquarters, and our interpreter, also blindfolded, was taken over to the Turkish lines to be held as a hostage. The request for the armistice was wirelessed to Sir Ian Hamilton at his headquarters at Imbros, and all that could be done further was to entertain the envoy with whisky and send him back to his own lines, telling him to return on the next morning.

The party from the 9th stayed out with two or three of the Turks until about 4 p.m., when the parley was over for the day. While there they exchanged cigarettes and rations, but were unable to converse in one another's language. However, one Turk kept drawing his finger across his throat and then pointing to the battleships—perhaps he was trying to say that submarines would soon arrive and sink them.

On the 22nd, the envoy came back, and was met by General Braithwaite, Hamilton's chief-of-staff. Hamilton had to cable to Whitehall for the necessary permission, but arrangements were made, satisfactory to both parties, for an armistice on the 24th.

The day for the armistice came, and from 7.30 a.m. to 4.30 p.m. firing ceased along the whole of the front. Fifty men of the 9th Battalion were sent out as a demarcation party, to keep the Turks from approaching too close to our parapet, while 200 from the brigade either buried the bodies on the spot or handed them over to the enemy for burial behind their own lines.

In places the dead were so thick that it was impossible to step over them, and the parties had to walk round them to get past. Nearly all the bodies were those of Turks, but the Australians buried or brought back a few of their own dead whom they found, mainly men killed on the day of the Landing or shortly afterwards. The burial of such a great number of dead was most desirable, as the weather was becoming hot, and the odour, particularly from the bodies which had been lying out previous to the attack of the 19th, was another of the many discomforts of trench life.

The Australians were most interested in seeing some of their enemies at close quarters and of exchanging little souvenirs with them. Two Armenians took the opportunity of surrendering. They made a dash for our lines; an officer tried to stop them, but they pushed him aside and ran on. On reaching our trenches they expressed their joy by kissing two officers and trying to shake hands with everybody.

The demarcation parties occupied a line along the middle of No-Man's Land, and consisted of alternate Australian and Turkish sentries. Here occurred a delightful incident, which illustrates the camaraderie existing between soldiers. John Smith,[3] of the 9th, on the beach, was the extreme right-hand man of the line. During the afternoon, as he was on a quiet sector where no burying was to be done, Smith lay down and went to sleep. On waking, he found that the Turk next to him had put two sticks in the sand beside his head and had arranged his greatcoat over them so as to keep the sun from his face. "Abdul"[4] now rolled a cigarette for him, as soon as he noticed that Smith was awake. In return, John gave him some jam, a delicacy which the Turk enjoyed thoroughly. Soon after the armistice stopped, rain began to fall.

Just before the armistice a most welcome issue of clothing and boots had been made to those in need of new articles. Soon afterwards came another pleasant surprise, when fresh meat was issued for the first time since the Landing, the only meat before this having been bully-beef and bacon. About the same time a squadron of the newly arrived light horse[5] was sent to strengthen our right flank, and before the end of the month the

---

[3] This is not the real name of the soldier concerned.
[4] "Abdul" was a name used to denote a Turk as "a Fritz" was used for a German.
[5] These were being temporarily used as dismounted troops.

battalion's 4th reinforcements, together with some men who had recovered from their wounds, about 140 in all, had joined up.

On May 25th the battleship *Triumph*, which had been stationed off Gaba Tepe ever since the Landing, was torpedoed by a submarine. It happened about 12.30 p.m., in full view of the 9th Battalion bivouacs. After eight minutes she capsized, lay bottom up for half-an-hour, then slowly went down stern first. Lieutenant W. J. Williams writes in his diary:

> "It was a shock to see our faithful friend, the 'Triumph,' which was quite close, take a heavy list and sink. She was firing as she sank. No one who witnessed the scene could forget the dash of the destroyers steaming at full speed from Helles. We could see the crew standing on deck which was at an almost impossible angle. Later they dived into the sea, to be picked up by the destroyers."

About this time Lieutenant Wilder, who had noticed signs of new enemy entrenchments being made at a position, known as "Twin Trenches," about 1,400 yards south of our lines, asked permission of the brigadier to make a raid on them at night to "stalk" them, as if "stalking kangaroos." Colonel MacLagan at first refused, but finally gave permission. Wilder called his company together and asked for volunteers; as all volunteered, he had to exercise a choice, and picked out 50 of them. Eventually the party consisted of about 60, mostly from "D" Company, including W. B. Bruns, T. Cooper, H. G. Cornford, F. Dibble, H. Forrister, A. Gardiner, A. S. Hamilton, J. E. Kenyon, J. McDonald, McKenzie, P. Morrison, Robey, G. Walker, and White, and two engineers with explosive charges to destroy any gun emplacements found. Arrangements were made for the destroyer *Rattlesnake* to co-operate, and Lieutenant Plant went on board to direct her fire.

At 9 p.m. on the 28th, the destroyer began to traverse her searchlights slowly along Harris Ridge, which faced the sea beyond Bolton's Ridge, and poured into the enemy trench 20 rounds of high explosive shell and shrapnel. Fifty yards behind the beam went Wilder and his men. Immediately after shelling the trench, the destroyer swung her searchlight on to the enemy communications in rear and shelled them; at once Wilder, a dashing leader, leaving a small party to watch for any attempted counter-attack, led the remainder up the slope over the rough ground and obstacles, and quickly captured the position, in which were about a dozen Turks, somewhat dazed by the shelling.

"Darkie" Kenyon, a man who could see unusually well in the dark, was the first to enter the trench, and, taking hold of one of the Turks cowering in a covered section, he slung him back to those who were following him, saying: "Here, look after this one." Someone, however, misunderstanding the position, and thinking, no doubt, that it was one of the enemy attacking, immediately put his bayonet through the prisoner. In the meantime Kenyon had bayonetted six others and captured a seventh, while the remainder, fleeing in disorder, came under the fire of the destroyer as they passed up the communication sap.

The Turks were taken quite by surprise, and the whole plan arranged by Wilder was successfully carried out without a single casualty to his party. The brigade diary states that it "reflects great credit on this officer for his careful organisation, followed by skilful and gallant leading." Not a rifle-shot was fired during the raid, as it was desired to avoid drawing any enemy artillery fire on the party.

At this time steel plates with loopholes in them were issued for building into fire positions in the trenches, and also iron tubes for use in building loopholes. The Turkish loopholes were made of sun-dried bricks, and if not more than 400 yards distant they were easily seen by our snipers, who would fire at them and often smash the bricks to pieces.

On the last day of May, Major J. C. Robertson, who had been wounded on the day of the Landing, returned to duty and took over the command of the battalion from Major Salisbury.

During the latter part of the month a great deal of sapping was done, saps and trenches being made forward of our front line; throughout June and July life with the 9th, as with the rest of the troops at Anzac, consisted in trench-digging, tunnelling and mining, patrolling, and "demonstrations" to keep the enemy in the Anzac area from sending reinforcements south during battles at Helles. Digging was done by day whenever possible, but it usually had to be done at night, as the work more often than not was under enemy observation.

The regular front-line work consisted of observation of the enemy by day, post duty, patrols and sniping at night. The erection of wire entanglements, called "wiring," and fatigue work already mentioned, such as ration-carrying, was done by the battalions or companies in support or in reserve.

Night-post duty consisted in being on the watch at certain points in the fire-trench, listening for any movement of the enemy, and giving the alarm if he attacked. Each post consisted usually of three men under an N.C.O. Watchfulness was most important at night as the country was covered with stunted vegetation right up to our trenches. All ranks were ordered to sleep in their clothes and boots, and this order was strictly enforced. However, men could take off their boots in the daytime to ease their feet whenever they had an opportunity.

The whole of the battalion "stood to" an hour before dawn, the time when an enemy attack was most likely. After daylight, the signal to "stand down" was given, and the night posts went off duty, only a few men being kept at work in the front-line trench during the day to keep observation. The same men were employed on observation work as far as possible, so that they would grow accustomed to the appearance of No-Man's Land, and thus be able to notice anything unusual.

A transport officer (Captain A. J. P. Crawford) visiting the front line graphically describes everyday life as he saw it there:—

> "Men lay about on the firing-step close to the sentries. Some men were reading papers, and others were dozing in the sunshine. Now and again one emerged from a tunnel which was being dug."

General Birdwood, G.O.C. of the A. & N.Z.A.C., was the right man in the right place. Certain British officers, otherwise very capable, found it impossible to understand Australian troops, but "Birdie," as he was nicknamed, had the wisdom to see that talking to and joking with the rank and file whenever he met them did not lose him their respect. Actually it gained for him their confidence. He saw, too, that the Australians could be more easily led than driven, and that (as with most men) a little flattery and praise combined with a "fair deal" would induce them to do almost anything. Sir John Monash said of Birdwood:

> "There is no mistaking his perfectly wonderful grasp of the whole business of soldiering. He talks a good deal, but every word he says is worth listening to, and his knowledge of the inside working of every department is simply astonishing. I have been around with him for hours, and heard him talking to privates, drivers, gunners, colonels, signallers and generals, and every time he has left the man with a better knowledge of his business than he had before."

Sir Ian Hamilton, in a despatch to Lord Kitchener, said:

> "Lieutenant-General Sir W. R. Birdwood has been the soul of Anzac. Not for one single day has he ever quitted his post. Cheery and full of human sympathy, he has spent many hours of each twenty-four inspiring the defenders of the front trenches."

On May 29th the enemy made a determined attempt to break into Quinn's Post, towards the northern end of the Anzac position, after having exploded a mine beneath the trenches there. On account of this it was decided to undertake countermining activities, and General Birdwood made enquiries throughout the 1st Division for officers and men experienced in mining. The request was made during the morning, immediately after the attack on Quinn's; before the close of the morning, lists of all the miners in the 3rd Brigade had been collected, and by 3 p.m. a hundred men had been sent and began mining from Quinn's, Pope's and Courtney's Posts.

On May 30th the strength of the battalion was 17 officers and 813 other ranks.

# CHAPTER VI.

### ANZAC, JUNE TO NOVEMBER.

On June 3rd arrived news of the decorations which had been awarded to the 9th Battalion. Captain Graham Butler received the D.S.O., Lieutenant Fortescue the M.C., and Sergeant-Major Steele,[1] Lance-Corporal Kenyon and Private Robey each the D.C.M. The decoration bestowed on Captain Butler was thoroughly deserved, but Butler himself for a long time refused to wear the ribbon, and he has always maintained that it should not have been conferred on him personally but as an honour to the whole of the Australian Army Medical Corps at the Landing. It is true that it was a recognition of the work not only of the medical officer himself but of the whole medical establishment of the battalion, but nevertheless it was a source of great satisfaction to the 9th that its medical officer should have been selected for this signal distinction.

The 3rd of June was also notable for a slight enemy attack on our trenches, but the few Turks who made it were easily driven off. More serious, in the evening, was the premature burst of a shell from a gun of the 9th Battery, which was firing over the 9th Battalion trenches. The shell exploded over battalion headquarters and wounded Major Salisbury, Captain Melbourne, Lieutenants Plant, Williams and Wilder and nine others. There were said to be casualties from this burst also among the 7th Battery, whose position was immediately behind the 9th Battalion lines.

On June 5th some respirators were issued, as gas had been used on the Western Front, and it was thought that the Turks might employ it too. However, no gas was ever used on the Peninsula. These respirators were of a very elementary type, being merely pads of gauze and cotton wool to be tied round the mouth and nose. Before being used they were to be dipped in a liquid supplied for the purpose.

By this time almost all the water used had to be drawn from the beach, and the ration was consequently rather low. This was causing a good deal of anxiety, especially as the weather was becoming hotter: June 5th is noted in the battalion diary as being hot, and the next day as "very hot." On

---

[1] Promoted to lieutenant in the meantime.

the 5th the jam ration was increased to 8 ounces per day for each man, and the meat ration was somewhat reduced. About the middle of June bread was first issued to the troops in place of biscuits. This was baked at Imbros, and it arrived every second day.

Flies made their first appearance soon after the Landing, and rapidly increased in numbers. As the weather became hotter they made the men's lives at times almost unbearable with their persistent settling on and crawling over the skin. At meal times they were most unpleasant. When a tin of jam was opened they would swarm on the top of the lid and crowd along the narrow opening left by the tin-opener like horses at a trough. Once opened, the tin had immediately to be covered with paper. Fortunately, there were no mosquitoes, and the nights were cool.

The forward galleries in front of the fire-trench were now nearly finished, and an artillery road had been made so that guns and ammunition could be brought up practically to the line. Our artillery was mainly 18-pounder field-guns, with two mountain batteries, one 4.7 gun and a few howitzers, none larger than 6-inch. The Turks on the other hand had an abundance of guns up to 8-inch in bore, and, in addition, good gun positions, which we had not. It was only shortage of ammunition which prevented the enemy from making our positions untenable.

On June 16th a party from the 9th made a raid on a trench to the south of Bolton's, assisted, as in Wilder's raid, by H.M.S. *Rattlesnake*. This time the enemy fled on the first alarm. Two days after this the beach was shelled at night for the first time. There was now less anxiety about the water supply, as a new well sunk in the valley where battalion headquarters was situated eased the situation considerably.

During June the sector held by the 3rd Brigade (No. 1 Section) was subdivided into Northern No. 1 and Southern No. 1. The latter was taken over by the 2nd Light Horse Brigade, and on the 19th the 9th Battalion was withdrawn into brigade reserve, going into "bivvies" which had been made on ledges adjoining Shell Green, the ridge between Victoria Gully and Clarke Valley. No sooner had the men entered the new camp than they sustained a casualty, Corporal Heaton being hit in the arm by a piece of shrapnel. While in brigade reserve the 9th dug a sunken road from Shell Green to Shrapnel Gully, and, by using this road and the one dug by the 3rd Brigade's beach party from the gully to the beach, movement between the

3rd Brigade's sector and the beach became possible with little risk of casualties.

On the 22nd it was possible for the first time for the troops to buy extra supplies at a canteen which was opened on the beach; the prices ruling, however, were rather high. On the same day a change, which proved to be of considerable advantage, was made in the organisation of the battalions, the machine-gun section being increased from two to four guns. On this day also 150 reinforcements came, bringing to 569 the total reinforcements which had reached the 9th since its arrival in Egypt.

These new arrivals, although they considered themselves trained soldiers when they disembarked at Anzac Beach, were not thought so by the battalion, and in consequence they had to go through a further course of training on Shell Green. In this connection the following message was sent to the companies:—

"Coys. will parade 2nd and 3rd and 5th Reinforcements attached to their Coys., together with all reinforcement N.C.O.'s at 9.30 a.m. and 2.30 p.m. These parades will last 1½ hours and will be under supervision of Coy. commanders with a view to training reinforcements and deciding whether N.C.O.'s are to continue in their appointments. The latter portion of above will also apply to such old N.C.O.'s as may be considered unsatisfactory. Coy. commdrs. to select ground and work in small squads. Parades to be dismissed if shelling commences.

A. G. Salisbury, Major
for Adjt. 9th Btn."

On the 23rd C.S.M. Perrier was appointed R.S.M., though without warrant rank. On successive days the brigade entertained distinguished visitors, Vice-Admiral de Robeck and Sir Ian Hamilton inspecting its section of the line.

At 8.30 a.m. on June 28th General Birdwood received a message suggesting that he should make a minor attack at Anzac to prevent the Turks from sending reinforcements to Helles, where the VIII British Corps was attacking at 11.30 a.m. on that day. It was decided that the operation should be carried out on the right flank by the 2nd Light Horse Brigade and the 3rd Infantry Brigade. Orders for the attack were drawn up and sent at 10.30 a.m. to the two brigadiers concerned, and consequently the local arrangements had to be made very hurriedly. In the 3rd Brigade, at 1 p.m. two companies of the 9th were to go out from Holly Ridge and Silt Spur towards Sniper's Ridge and its continuation, the Knife Edge, and two of the 11th were to lie out on Silt Spur and Turkey Knoll to cover them. At the same time the light horse were to advance to the right.

Plate x.

20.—TURKISH TRENCHES ON THE KNIFE EDGE. (See p. 80.)
Looking towards the Australian lines. Gaba Tepe at top left.
(Aust. War Memorial Official Photograph. No. G 2095. Copyright. Taken in 1919. From the Official History).

21.—TRENCHES AT GEBEL HABEITA. (See p. 98.)
(Aust. War Memorial Official Photograph. No. G 1473. Copyright. From the Official History.)

Plate XI.

22.—LIEUT. C. F. ROSS IN FIRE TRENCH AT ANZAC.
(Photo. lent by Col. A. G. Butler).

23.—THE CEMETERY AT SHELL GREEN, ANZAC.
9th Battalion casualties were buried here.
(Photo. lent by Col. A. G. Butler).

24.—AID POST AND TRENCH STRETCHER, GEBEL HABEITA.
(Photo. lent by Col. A. G. Butler).

25.—DRILLING A SQUAD AT SARPI.
Standing in front of squad.—Left to right: Cpl. Gray, Lieut. A. R. Knightley, Major A. G. Salisbury.
(Photo. lent by Col. A. G. Butler).

"B" and "C" Companies, under Major R. H. Walsh and Captain Young respectively, were chosen for the 9th Battalion's task, both being fully up to strength. At 1.5 p.m. they left their trenches at points a quarter of a mile apart. The southern company ("C") on its way to the starting-point had to pass round the shoulder of a hill under enemy observation from Gaba Tepe. This was equivalent to sending the Turk a message that an attack was about to be made, and as soon as the men reached Oratunga Sap, a communication trench leading to the front line, shrapnel and machine-gun fire fell on them, and continued all the time they were in the sap.

Leaving our line by a sap leading southward into the Valley of Despair, the attackers made a left turn and were in line ready to advance. No. 9 Platoon, under Lieutenant S. R. Jordan, and No. 10, under Lieutenant A. Warren, formed the front line, with Nos. 11 and 12, both under Lieutenant C. F. Ross, behind them as supports. The troops proceeded uphill through country very thick with undergrowth, in which it was difficult for an officer to exercise much control over a long line of skirmishers. When the rear platoons reached the crest (part of Holly Ridge), which was now being lashed by shrapnel and machine-gun fire, someone on the left of the front line shouted "Retire!", and the men from this part of the line came running back and crashed into the left of the supports, who began to fall back also. Lieutenant Ross, who was on the right flank, ran across to the left and tried to stop the withdrawal, but the alarm had now spread to the right flank also, and in about a quarter of an hour most of "C" Company was back at the starting-point in the valley.

Meanwhile, five members of Jordan's platoon, which on reaching the top of the first ridge had been ordered by their leader to charge half-left down the steep slope, had reached the bottom of the valley. These men—G. B. King, G. F. Lee, C. Matthews, J. O'Callaghan and W. J. Sullivan—realising that they were now separated from the others, dug themselves in and kept up fire on the enemy. Lieutenant Jordan then joined them. Sullivan was killed, and King and O'Callaghan wounded, and Lee, and later Matthews were sent back for reinforcements; both, however, were wounded before they had gone twenty yards. At the close of the afternoon this party was found and captured by the Turks.

Another man, D. B. Creedon, who had been wounded in both hands while running down the hill, was dazed for a while, and on recovering began to make for our lines when he came under shrapnel fire. Taking cover in a nearby dugout, where he intended to remain until the bombardment stopped, he fell into a doze, and awoke about six o'clock to find himself looking down the muzzles of three Turkish rifles. He also was made a prisoner, as was W. Allan.

Although the attack upon the Knife Edge had failed, that against Sniper's Ridge met with some success. "B" Company debouched from the dump in front of the 11th Battalion's sector; this dump was situated upon the rear slope of Silt Spur, and consisted of earth from new trenches being dug a little higher up that spur. The company extended as soon as it left the shelter of the dump, and was immediately fired on, but the troops dashed across the open bed of Cooee Gully and began to climb towards Sniper's Ridge.

Here they were in shelter, and so they reached the enemy trench, which was a covered one. Their orders were that the trench was not to be entered, so some of them fired into it through the loopholes, and an attempt was made to use jam-tin bombs, but, as the weather was very hot, the perspiration on the men's clothing had soaked into their matches and few would strike. Finally, a few of the bombs were lit and thrown through the loopholes or on to the head-cover of the trenches. The Turks had apparently retreated, so the Australians lay down outside the parapet, where many ate the rations they had with them. A good line was formed within about ten yards of the enemy trenches by 1.25 p.m.

After a while, however, they were observed and fired on from the flank, but despite casualties they held to their position. A stretcher-bearer, Private G. E. Latimer, of the 2nd Field Ambulance, calmly walked about the fire-swept area attending to the wounded and carrying man after man to safety. He was killed later in the afternoon.

Between 1.30 and 2 p.m. the enemy gunners shelled the ridge and the top of Turkey Knoll with H.E. and shrapnel, causing casualties among the 11th Battalion party and driving it in, and at 2 o'clock they opened heavy counter-fire against all the trenches in the area. At this time word was received by the brigade commander that the Turks were preparing for a counter-attack, so, as the object of the whole movement—the holding down of the enemy's local reserve to this area—had been attained, he consulted with General Birdwood and ordered "B" Company to be withdrawn by sections from the left. The withdrawal began at 3.25, after the company had maintained its position for two hours. As the troops made their way back they were shelled from the Olive Grove and fired on from Lone

Pine, but they withdrew in good order, and by 4.30 were again in their own lines.

The two companies lost 37 killed and 62 wounded, including Major Walsh, who had been slightly hit in two places, and Captain L. A. Jones, who was seriously wounded. This operation was, with the exception of the Landing, the most trying the battalion had yet experienced; indeed, by many it was considered the most unfortunate engagement of the 9th during the whole war. It had been so hurriedly arranged that the platoon commanders did not have very full particulars of what they were to do, nor did they know where the enemy trenches were. Worse still, the Turks (as mentioned above) were practically notified that an attack was commencing.

It is interesting to recall that it was on this same day in the previous year that the Archduke Franz Ferdinand of Austria had been assassinated. It was this deed which, although it was not the real "cause" of the war, set in motion the train of events which led to the outbreak of hostilities.

Most of the men knew the reason for the attack, but it evidently puzzled some, to judge by an incident related in the *Official History*. As Walsh's company was returning to its trenches, the brigadier stood watching them. "What sort of —— business is this," growled one, "sending us out there and bringing us back again?" MacLagan here intervened: "I'll tell you why they sent you out, my lad. It was in order to help your mates down south." "Just as well there was some —— reason," said the soldier as he passed on. The man following him, however, explained to MacLagan that the growler had had three bullets through him and had refused to go to the medical officer to have his wounds dressed.

Another, L. H. Bailey, who had already carried in a wounded man, returned to bring in a second. When he reached him, he found him dead, but as he had heard that, according to a standing order, the rifles of the dead should have been brought back, he set about looking for rifles and brought in four. Others, too, went out on their own initiative to bring in rifles. One of these men was hit, but his mates bandaged him and brought him in, together with several rifles. Private R. G. Grey was mentioned in the report of the action for stripping the dead of web equipment and carrying it back to our lines.

According to the written orders for the operation, red and blue flags were to have been carried by the attackers, to mark the line reached by them, for the benefit of the troops in the Australian front line who were covering them with their fire.

Flags, however, were not used by the two companies from the 9th; no reference to them was made in the verbal orders given to the company commanders.

Parties were sent out in the evening to bring in the dead and wounded, and early next morning further parties went out to recover rifles and equipment. This was done not only to prevent their use by the enemy, but also to economise material for ourselves. As the war progressed, more and more attention was paid to salvaging weapons, stores and equipment of all sorts for re-issue to the troops.

On the nights of the 29th and 30th it was intended to send out more parties to bring in the remaining dead, but it was impossible to do so on account of intense rifle fire directed on our position. The bodies which were recovered were buried by padres Dexter and Fahy in the little cemetery near Shell Green on a beautiful calm moonlight night, with the waters of the Aegean Sea lapping at the foot of the cliff on one side and the thud of bursting bombs at Quinn's Post on the other. Lieutenant Ross describes it as "the most solemn funeral I have ever attended."

This attack is described by Brigadier-General Aspinall-Oglander, the British Official Historian of the Gallipoli campaign, as "an extraordinarily difficult task." On the 29th General Birdwood visited the lines and congratulated the battalion on its feat, and on the next day the 9th was congratulated in divisional orders on the success of the operation. However, the results of the action were greater than was suspected at the time, for it is now known from Turkish sources that the demonstration led to the postponement for twenty-four hours of a proposed Turkish attack on Russell's Top, originally intended for the 28th.

On June 29th Major J. C. Robertson was promoted to lieutenant-colonel. Two days later the battalion once more moved into the firing-line from the reserve positions, taking over this time the sector which had been occupied by the 10th Battalion. This was to the left of the sector previously held by the 9th, and the trenches were found better and more comfortable. On July 6th all men were issued with respirators, as information had been received that the enemy had landed new guns for the firing of poison-gas shells. It was on this day, too, that the 10th Battalion went to Imbros for a rest. This was welcome news for the 9th, as its turn for a rest would come later. All ranks looked forward to this respite, as they had now been cooped up for eleven weeks on about one square mile of the Peninsula.

There were now 23 officers and 368 other ranks of the 9th away wounded at "the base"—the base being Imbros or Egypt—and no word had been received of their condition nor any indication as to when they would be likely to return to the battalion.

On July 12th the 12th Battalion and the 6th and 7th Light Horse Regiments made a demonstration in order to hold down Turkish reserves in the Anzac area while a new attack was being made at Cape Helles. In this they were assisted by the 9th Battalion, which formed up in its trench with fixed bayonets, and began to march up it towards the 12th, as if it were going to reinforce that unit. The troops took care to keep their bayonets well above the top of the trench so that they could be seen by the enemy.

In "A" Company's sector, on the right, part of the parados had fallen in, making a mound almost as high as the natural ground. The men ran over the mound in full view of the enemy, then retired down a communication sap and doubled back, re-entering the front line where they had been at first. The manoeuvre was repeated continuously. Thus the one body of men gave the enemy the impression of the movement of a large body of troops about to attack. The ruse was entirely successful, for it drew both rifle and shell fire from the Turks; at least 60 shells landed near the spot, but the 9th suffered no casualty, the only damage done being the destruction of three rifles. This feint was reported by the enemy as a serious attack, which the Turks had succeeded in repelling.

The battalion went back into supports on July 16th, and for the rest of that month was occupied mostly in digging improvements to the forward positions. It was at this time that an acetylene motor headlight was received for use as a sort of searchlight in case of a night attack.

Sickness among the troops was now putting in an appearance, and, as it increased, it became one of the great difficulties with which the men had to contend until they left the Peninsula. The onset of it was due in part to the lack of variety in the food, but largely to the plague of flies throughout the summer months. On July 25th it was noticed that diarrhoea was prevalent, notwithstanding the measures taken to deal with it. This led to a decrease in the efficiency of all units; most of the troops who remained on duty became very weak, and developed sores on the skin which healed very slowly. There was also a good deal of enteric fever, not the dreaded variety known as typhoid, but other forms nevertheless serious.

During July a further list of decorations was issued, among the recipients being Sergeants Benson and Wilder (who were now lieutenants) and Private C. R. Heaton,[2] all of whom were awarded the D.C.M. A few days later the R.S.M., Sergeant Perrier, was gazetted 2nd-lieutenant; Sergeant Dewar received a commission about the same time, and Sergeant Knightley was appointed C.S.M. It was during this month also that Colonel MacLagan was gazetted brigadier-general. On the 16th Lieutenant H. G. Ker was wounded by a shrapnel bullet, and died at 10 p.m.

A new post (Tasmania Post) had been established on Holly Ridge some time before, and an attack on the enemy trenches in front of it was ordered on July 31st. A party of 200 men of the 11th Battalion, under Captain Leane, was to attack at moonrise, and the 9th had to man some new trenches to the left of Tasmania Post to defeat any counter-attack made by the enemy. The attack was successful, the enemy being driven out of his trenches at 10.15 p.m. About midnight Turks were reported by a patrol to be massing in front of the 9th, as if for a counter-attack, but rifle and machine-gun fire was opened on them, and they made no further attempt. The only casualties in the 9th Battalion were two wounded. One platoon from each company of the 9th had been detailed for this operation; the platoon from "C" Company, under Lieutenant Ross, owing to a misunderstanding of orders, did not reach its destination, and so took no part in the action. The captured trench was afterwards called "Leane's Trench."

At the beginning of August a great change occurred in the Gallipoli operations. The Australians and New Zealanders had been able to advance their lines only a short distance, and it seemed impossible to make any substantial advance in this area alone. It was therefore decided to make a landing at Suvla Bay, four miles to the north of Anzac, with fresh British troops, while the Anzac Corps, heavily reinforced by British and Indian troops, broke out from the north of Anzac and seized the hills as far as Hill 971, one of the original objectives at the Anzac Landing.

In an attempt to deceive the enemy as to our real intentions, the minor enterprises on the southern flank of Anzac during the last couple of months had been undertaken, since they diverted his attention from the northern flank. For the same reason a large scale attack was to be delivered against the

---

[2] Heaton was one of the "hard cases" of the battalion, and for his escapades when off duty was more than once reduced to the ranks, but he always earned promotion to N.C.O. rank again.

Turkish defences at Lone Pine in the late afternoon of August 6th, a few hours before the main operation began, and this, it was hoped, would pin down the local reserves which otherwise would be sent to Hill 971 and Suvla.

The role of the 9th Battalion was to open heavy rifle fire on the opposing trenches while Lone Pine was being assaulted by the 1st Infantry Brigade. This attack, supported by a bombardment from warships and field guns, occurred at 5.30 p.m. After supporting the charge, the men of the 9th, as also the Turks opposite to them, sat on the parapet and watched the attack. They could do nothing to help, on account of the danger of hitting their own comrades. One Turk was seen to hold up a white flag, but his mates immediately bayonetted him. The night began quietly, but at 1.45 a.m. all were warned to be ready for a threatened counter-attack against the 3rd Brigade's position, and the warning was repeated at 4 o'clock. The attack, however, was not attempted.

For the next two days there was heavy and desperate fighting at Lone Pine and on the ridges to the north, but the 9th was not called upon to lend a hand. By August 9th matters were sufficiently normal in the sector for the battalion to recommence its work on saps and tunnels, which had been interrupted for the Lone Pine battle. All ranks at Anzac wore white calico patches sewn on the backs of their tunics or shirts throughout the August operations, so that they would be more easily recognisable. These patches were removed in the 9th Battalion on August 27th. The August offensive at Anzac and Suvla failed to achieve its purpose—mainly because of the efforts of Mustapha Kemal. Early in August Sergeant-Major A. R. Knightley was appointed temporary R.S.M., and on the 12th he was gazetted 2nd-lieutenant.

By the middle of August sickness had increased to such an extent that the 3rd Brigade could do little more than hold its line. In the three weeks following August 6th, 1,146 out of a total personnel of 3,622, that is, more than 30 per cent., had to be sent away from the Peninsula. The men evacuated were described by an M.O. as:

> "just skin and bone; hands, arms and legs covered with septic sores; ill with dysentery; had to work in the trenches on bully-beef, bacon and biscuits."

In the battalion diary are the following entries:—

> "Aug. 14. Considerable sickness in battalion." "Aug. 18. Health of troops deteriorating rapidly." "Aug. 19. Rapid increase in sick parade during last fortnight."

Sickness among senior officers led to several changes in the command of the battalion. On September 9th Lieutenant-Colonel Robertson had to be evacuated, and Major Walsh took command. Walsh, who was promoted to temporary lieutenant-colonel on October 10th, fell ill also, and though he tried hard to carry on, staggering round the trenches and often in a state bordering on collapse, he had to be sent off to the hospital ship on the 26th. "Jock" Milne, who had returned from hospital on October 6th and had been appointed temporary major on the 17th, now assumed command, but on November 11th, two days after his promotion to substantive[3] major, he too had to be evacuated, and a 10th Battalion officer, Major Shaw, was appointed temporarily to take charge of the 9th.

The command of the 3rd Brigade was likewise affected, MacLagan going to hospital on August 24th, and first Colonel Price Weir (10th Battalion) and then Brigadier-General Ryrie (2nd L.H. Brigade) temporarily replacing him. In September the 3rd Brigade was placed under the direct control of the divisional commander because of the shortage of senior officers.

Major Milne was one of the original company commanders, and he had played a distinguished part in the Landing. He did not again rejoin the 9th; after leaving hospital he was sent back to Australia for a change, and left again with the 41st Battalion (3rd Division). In March, 1917, he was promoted lieutenant-colonel and given command of the 36th Battalion. He was killed in action on April 12th, 1918, near Villers-Bretonneux, on the Somme.

Other well-known officers evacuated sick during this period were Major Salisbury, on August 24th, and the adjutant, Captain Plant, on September 11th. Salisbury was the last of the original officers who had taken part in the Landing to leave the battalion, and had been doing duty for several days with a temperature of 102 deg. Plant had left Australia as A.D.C. to the divisional commander, and joined the 9th at Mena Camp on the night before it left for Lemnos. Both these officers had been wounded, but neither had been off duty for one day since the Landing. There were some other original officers with the battalion at this time, but they had all been away either wounded or sick and had returned, except Lieutenant Adsett, who did not land with the battalion on April 25th, as just before he had been detailed to take charge of the brigade baggage, and had remained on the *Malda* until May 8th. He then landed, and, although sick on several occasions, remained on the Peninsula for the remainder of the battalion's stay there.

[3] Permanent.

When Plant went on board the hospital ship he was asked where his kit was. He tapped the bulging pocket of his tunic and said: "Here it is." Lieutenant Wilder was now temporarily appointed adjutant; it will be remembered that he had performed the duties of this office on the day of the Landing, while still a sergeant.

One result of the sickness which ravaged Gallipoli was that every battalion had to be constantly on front-line duty. Before this, one battalion had been kept in brigade reserve, so that each in turn could have a rest, if fatigue duty could be called rest. On two occasions during September it was found necessary to relieve the 9th Battalion from front-line duty for 48 hours by parties of 150 men from the 12th Battalion, and on the 30th an officer and 150 men from the 1st and 2nd Brigades were attached to the battalion. The strength of the 9th on this day was 18 officers and 534 men, but the entry in the unit diary does not state whether this number included the attached party. Two days before this, "B" Company contained only 116 of all ranks. Although the remarks by an M.O., quoted above, infer that the rations were responsible, at least in part, for the poor condition of the troops, the battalion diary for September 26th states: "Food satisfactory, except that not enough green vegetables."

On August 18th, owing to all four battalions having to be in the line together, a rearrangement of the battalion sectors had been carried out. This gave to the 9th an additional 250 yards of front to the right, on which 200 yards of new firing line had to be made, so as to obtain better observation than could be got from the line taken over. This trench was finished on the 26th, and on the next day the battalion began building forward bombing pits and wire entanglements. The bombing pits were tunnels pushed out from the front-line trench, with the ends opening upwards to the surface; men could go quietly along these and throw bombs at the enemy trenches from the end of the tunnel. On September 5th General Birdwood inspected the new firing-line, and afterwards congratulated the battalion on its excellent trenches and general arrangements, and on the spirit of the men.

On September 24th a demonstration was made to draw fire from the enemy. Bayonets and dummy figures were shown above the parapet, and, in order to provide a certain amount of noise, burnt tins were thrown well out in front of the trenches. The tins were burnt to ensure that no refuse was left in them which might become offensive later, and also that there would be nothing bright showing afterwards to make a mark for the enemy. Then our artillery opened, and this was followed by bursts of machine-gun and rifle fire from us. This feint succeeded in drawing much enemy fire. On this day 2nd-lieutenant C. C. Oliver, a new arrival with reinforcements, was killed while trying to operate a rifle and telescope together through a rather large loophole in the sandbags, with the sun behind him.

Another demonstration was made against the trenches from Sniper's Ridge southwards on October 6th. Two parachute rockets were issued to each battalion and light horse regiment, and when these burst, a bright flare burnt in the air for some time, being kept up by the parachute attached to it. They lit up the enemy trenches, on which rifle and machine-gun fire was directed, and this succeeded in drawing heavy fire from the Turks. Ten days later a third demonstration was made, one round being fired per rifle, assisted by artillery fire and heavy gun fire from the ships. This time, however, the enemy replied with only a moderate fusillade; he was evidently beginning to see the point of the joke.

On October 5th a Turkish working party was observed in front of the 9th Battalion lines, and Captain Wilder (he had been gazetted temporary captain on September 26th) arranged that some men should throw bombs at them while the ground over which they would have to retire would be covered by rifle-fire by the rest of the battalion. Judging by the cries which came from the valley, the operation appeared to be successful.

Wilder soon afterwards changed his name, a gazette notice appearing on November 9th stating: "Lieutenant (temporary Captain) Maurice Wilder having changed his name will in future be known as Maurice Wilder-Neligan."

About this time a report was circulated that the enemy was using gas. It was found afterwards that the Turks had thrown into Lone Pine inflammable bombs which had not ignited, but had given off dense smoke; this made men cough and caused their eyes to smart.

On October 8th came the first of the severe storms which enlivened the latter part of the British occupation of the Peninsula. It caused serious damage to the piers which had been built at Anzac Beach just after the Landing. There was another storm at the end of October, and two more in the middle and at the end of November. In the meantime all were busily employed in making new shelters to live in, more suitable to cold-weather conditions. The men found that they were greatly hindered in this by an extreme scarcity of wood and iron. They also built a number of sniper's "possies," and they were more successful in this work than with the building of the winter-quarters.

October 25th was a momentous day for the battalion, as it had now completed six months' service in actual warfare. Its total casualties since the Landing were 43 officers and 1337 other ranks; these included sick, and also 9 officers and 142 others killed. Its strength on this day was 19 officers and 536 other ranks.

Just before the end of October the 9th erected some dummy machine-guns in places where the enemy could not fail to see them. This ruse was successful, and on one day the Turkish artillery fired twenty shells at these "guns." During the early part of November sapping and tunnelling were continued, and much sniping was done. On the 3rd, there was another re-arrangement of units in the trenches; the 9th gave up its area to the 1st Brigade, and took over the trenches which had been garrisoned by the 12th Battalion. At this time the new position was very quiet as compared with the trenches just vacated. On the 9th, N. L. Weynand and G. R. Harrington, the latter an original member of Costin's machine-gun section, were appointed 2nd-lieutenants.

Four days later Lord Kitchener paid his visit to the Peninsula. The question of evacuating Gallipoli had been under consideration, but Kitchener would not agree to this. He had sent a telegram to Birdwood on November 3rd, informing him that another naval attempt might be made on the Straits, followed by a landing at Bulair on the Gulf of Saros.

> "I shall come out to you" (he continued). "Examine very carefully the best position for landing near the marsh at the head of the Gulf of Saros. . . . In order to find the troops for this undertaking, we should have to reduce the numbers in the trenches to the lowest possible, and perhaps evacuate positions at Suvla. All the best fighting men that could be spared, including your boys from Anzac . . . . might be concentrated at Mudros ready for this enterprise. . . . As regards the military command, you would have the whole force. . . . Please work out plans. . . . I absolutely refuse to sign orders for evacuation, which I think would be the gravest disaster and would condemn a large percentage of our men to death or imprisonment."

The evacuation he refused to order was that of Anzac, although he was willing to agree to withdrawing from Suvla. But, after personally inspecting the position and conferring with Birdwood, he saw the uselessness of holding on longer, and decided that the whole of the Peninsula would have to be evacuated.

The 9th Battalion had been looking forward for some time to its turn for a rest at Lemnos, and on the day after Kitchener's visit an advance party of the 3rd Brigade left for the island. The 9th was relieved by the 2nd Battalion at 10 a.m. and went into "bivvies" on the hillside on the west of Artillery Road. Orders had been received on the 13th that it would embark next day, but the move had to be postponed on account of the severe storm which began on the 14th. However, on the 16th orders were received at 6 p.m. to be ready to move in 15 minutes. The battalion finally marched out at 7.30, and, although officers and men did not know it at the time, they said good-bye to Anzac when they embarked from No. 8 pier in small boats for the ship *Abbassia*, which they boarded about 10.30 p.m.

The other Anzac troops remained on the Peninsula until the latter part of December, when they carried out the famous Evacuation, the last parties leaving Anzac Beach early on December 20th. Suvla was evacuated the same morning, and Helles on January 8th. The withdrawals were skilfully planned and cleverly executed, and the Turks did not find out until it was too late that the garrisons had stolen away and left them empty trenches.

Many critics have said that the Gallipoli landings should never have been made; some have considered that the operations on the Peninsula were a ghastly failure; but as time goes on, it becomes increasingly plain that the fighting there was a brilliant success, only prevented from becoming a complete triumph by the want of a sufficient force of troops at the beginning, and by the scarcity of artillery ammunition throughout the operations. The official British historian, Aspinall-Oglander, says:—

> "At the expense of a casualty list which was less than double that incurred on the first day of the Battle of the Somme, 1916, the Mediterranean Expeditionary Force in Gallipoli destroyed the flower of the Turkish Army, safeguarded the Suez Canal, and laid the foundation of Turkey's final defeat."

Admiral Wemyss apportions the blame as well as the praise when he remarks that

> "The campaign of the Dardanelles will remain through all ages to come an imperishable monument to the heroism of our race, to the courage and endurance of our soldiers and sailors, to the lack of vision and incapacity of our politicians."

The results of the Landing and the occupation of Anzac for eight months have been of the greatest permanent value to Australia. Anzac put Australia "on the map"; our country was henceforth known throughout the world, and our troops acquired a reputation which at once put them among the best fighting divisions, not only of the British Army but of the armed forces of all the belligerents.

Aspinall-Oglander says:—

"That the A. & N.Z. troops never relinquished their grasp; that they made this apparently hopeless position impregnable; that after waiting three months for reinforcements they attacked, and attacked again, and very nearly won, is a story that will live forever."

# CHAPTER VII.

### LEMNOS, EGYPT, FIRST DAYS IN FRANCE.

On November 17th the battalion arrived at Lemnos and went to Sarpi Camp, on the opposite side of the harbour to Mudros, finding the island very different from what it had been when nearly seven months before the unit had left it to make the Landing. Dotted over the landscape were many more camps, a number of hospitals, and all sorts of workshops and stores. The harbour was still full of ships, but these now included a number of hospital ships.

Next day a reorganisation of the battalion was begun, and the 7th reinforcements, under Captain Andrews, and the 8th, under Lieutenant W. A. Collin[1], which were already waiting at Lemnos, were absorbed. The reinforcements had erected the camp, and after the arrival of the battalion they did all the fatigues for a while, so as to give the men from Anzac an opportunity of resting.

The weather was very rough and cold. A biting stormy wind arose which blew for a fortnight, and the need of warmer clothing was felt, but immediate satisfaction could not be given. Within a few days the shortage of blankets was remedied, and some days afterwards a supply of woollen vests was issued, as well as some old uniforms, to those in most urgent need of them. This made matters easier, but still left much room for improvement.

Some articles of clothing also were received as "comforts," arrangements having been made for the purchase of two hundred pounds' worth from the store ships in harbour. To meet the cost a sum of £150 was transferred from the officers' mess account, the balance being made up from the extra messing allowance allotted to the troops while in this area, and from the battalion's share of the profits from the troopship canteens. Fortunately the weather became milder later on.

On November 24th Lieutenant-Colonel Robertson returned from hospital and once more took command of the battalion. Two days afterwards 3rd Brigade headquarters arrived at Lemnos, and the whole brigade was thus together again. From December 1st to 23rd the brigade was in quarantine on account

---

1 Captain Andrews did not remain in the 9th Battalion.

of an outbreak of diphtheria, and it was during this period that officers and men of the battalion grew beards.

The weather was (as mentioned above) at first extremely cold, there was but little soap available, and half the men had come from Anzac without razors, articles which were unprocurable at Lemnos. It was then expected that the 9th would go back to Anzac after its rest and have to face the severity of a Gallipoli winter, so the C.O. conferred with the medical officer, who said that beards would be a great protection to the throat. For this reason, and also because he desired a "uniform" appearance in the battalion, Colonel Robertson issued an order that all ranks were to cease shaving and allow their beards to grow.

The order was in force for nearly a month, until the evacuation of the Peninsula, whereupon the instruction was cancelled. The unit was nicknamed the "Hairy 9th," or the "Bearded 9th" (later to become corrupted to the "Beery 9th") by other troops at Lemnos who had not been placed under similar restrictions. The most vigorous growth was in most cases not more than half-an-inch. One officer remarks: "Most of us looked a horrible sight, Wilder-Neligan's red whiskers in particular."

All ranks now had a good rest. At the end of November an entertainment committee was formed, and on December 4th a battalion institute, really a canteen managed by the unit itself, was opened. Before this there had been a canteen near the camp, but it was far from satisfactory, as it was in the hands of Greeks, who charged prohibitive prices, and when the men found that, in the British canteen, goods were sold at half and sometimes at one-third the price charged in the one near their camp, they were, to put it mildly, aggrieved. They could not make use of the British canteen, as it was out of bounds to Australians—not that that would have mattered to them, but the canteen staff would not serve them; besides, it was miles away from the Australian lines.

The first entertainment given was a successful variety concert by N.C.O.'s and men of the 9th, who gave items described as being "most original and topical of Anzac and Sarpi Quarantine Camp." A sports committee was also organised, and some heats in brigade sports were run off before the troops went out of quarantine.

About this time an honours list was published in which Lieutenant-Colonel Robertson appeared as having been made a C.M.G. Soon afterwards Robertson left the battalion for a while to become acting brigadier.

One day the 9th was taken for a march of about ten miles over hilly country to the hot springs at Therma, with the intention of having a bathing-parade. But, through an error of organisation, another unit was using the springs, so, with the exception of a fortunate few, the men of the 9th had to go without their bath.

After the brigade had had a good rest, the battalions were given a little work, the length of the parades being increased to three hours per day. On the 23rd, the day on which the 9th Battalion left quarantine, brigade headquarters received orders to be ready to move at short notice, and next day the 9th was ordered to stand by to leave Lemnos by 9 a.m. However, when the morning came, the embarkation orders were cancelled, and Christmas Day was made a holiday.

"Christmas billies" were issued to all. These had been sent from Australia, where arrangements had been made by the various soldiers' welfare organisations that every man at the front should receive one. The billy-cans were filled with various "comforts," usually chocolate, biscuits, and other food, or wearing apparel, such as socks and scarves.

Next day brigade headquarters embarked, and Lieutenant-Colonel Gellibrand (12th Battalion) assumed command of the brigade. On the 30th orders were again received to embark on the morrow, and this time the movement was not postponed. The 9th Battalion went on board the *Grampian*, of the Allan Line, together with various small units and details, amounting in all to about 1700 men. Captain W. Young was in charge of the 9th, as Major Salisbury had been put in command of all the troops on the ship. The strength of the battalion on this day was 22 officers and 689 other ranks.

The ship left at 8 a.m. on January 1st for Alexandria. As enemy submarines were active in the Mediterranean, the captain of the *Grampian* did not leave the bridge for the whole three days of the trip, taking his meals at his post, and having what little sleep he could snatch on the bridge, too.

On January 3rd, 1916, at 8.50 a.m., the *Grampian* passed in through the boom at Alexandria harbour. It was ten months since the original 9th Battalion, together with its first reinforcements, had left for Lemnos. In the early evening the troops disembarked and entrained in two parties for Tel-el-Kebir, in the desert, 35 miles west of the Suez Canal and 70 miles from Cairo. It was here that in 1882 a combined British and Egyptian force under Sir Garnet Wolseley defeated Arabi Pasha and the Egyptian rebels. It had been wet all day, and it was still raining when the first party arrived at Tel-el-Kebir at 1 a.m. on January 4th, followed by the remainder of the battalion at 4 o'clock.

On leaving the trains the troops marched to the camp site not far off and bivouacked in the rain, thus experiencing again conditions similar to those with which they had to contend during the first days at both Mena and Lemnos. After a short sleep the battalion woke to *reveille* at 6 a.m. and occupied itself with making a camp, but tents and other articles of camp equipment were scarce and difficult to obtain. The 9th was the first unit to occupy the Tel-el-Kebir camp at this period.

All ranks were now wondering where and when the next period of active service was to be, but, to the disgust of the whole battalion, when drill commenced on January 5th the men were instructed in what the official record describes as "elementary work in ceremonial," otherwise "saluting by numbers." After the hard fighting on the Peninsula in which the 9th and other units had made their name resound throughout Australia, the men felt humiliated at having to commence all over again the work which had been done in the early days at Enoggera and elsewhere in 1914. It was as though a university student were taken away from his lectures and required to relearn the alphabet or the multiplication table. What irritated the men more was the apparent uselessness of this work for fighting purposes. However, instructions from higher authorities were that it was to be done, so it continued, heartily disliked by all concerned.

However, to compensate for the disgust at the saluting drill, there was the pleasure of receiving news from home. On the 5th, 150 bags of mail, which had been awaiting the unit here, were distributed. Next day the 9th reinforcements, under Lieutenant C. J. Carroll, arrived from Zeitoun, bringing the strength of the battalion up to 26 officers and 910 other ranks. Lieutenant-Colonel Robertson resumed command of the battalion on the 9th.

Besides the ceremonial drill, training of all sorts was now being undertaken, and on January 15th the 1st Division was reviewed by General Sir Archibald Murray, the new commander-in-chief of the troops in this area.

During this period, as also during the stay at Sarpi, R.S.M. Ruddle put in a great deal of very good and strenuous work in reorganising the battalion and smartening it up. He was very strict, but was liked by all ranks, and his work of reorganisation was crowned with great success.

On January 22nd confidential information was received that the battalion was to move to the Suez Canal zone, and about 8 p.m. on the 25th it entrained for Serapeum, about eight miles south of Ismailia. On arrival, about 11 p.m. on a very cold night, it bivouacked till the next morning, and at 6 a.m. crossed the Canal by the ferry and marched to a desert camp a mile farther to the east.

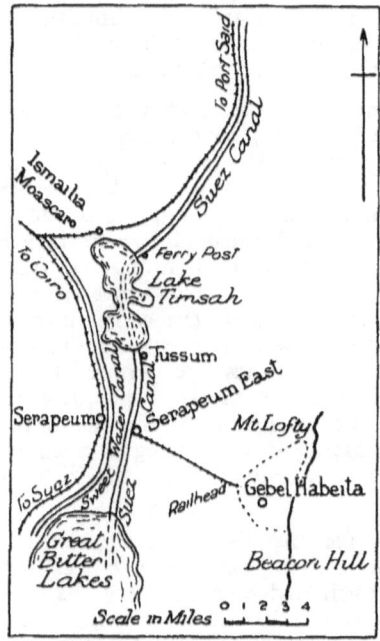

10. Gebel Habeita and Suez Canal.

On the 27th "A" and "B" Companies, under Major Salisbury, moved out at 8.30 a.m., and, after a trying march of nine miles through the soft sand, took up a defensive position at Gebel Habeita at mid-day. Next day the remainder of the battalion arrived at the new position.

The period spent at Gebel Habeita was one of great hardship for all ranks. To guard against the possibility of a Turkish attack on the Canal, trenches were being made, but, since they had to be dug in sand, as soon as some little depth was reached the sides would collapse, resulting in the work having to be done all over again. The only way to counteract this was to line both sides of the trench with bags of sand. Even so, whenever a strong wind sprang up, the trenches would be more than half-filled with sand. Once, indeed, they were so completely submerged that they were not visible. In addition to filling up the trenches, the sand on windy days would cover up the blankets, which were spread out in the sun to air, making it difficult later for them to be found by their owners.

At first the food supply was bad, the main diet being bully-beef and biscuits; the water-ration was supposed to be one gallon per man per day, but only half of this amount arrived. It is not surprising therefore that the men began to grumble. After a week had passed thus, the full ration of water began to arrive daily, and there was an improvement in the food, fresh meat and milk making their appearance. This caused an immediate rise in the spirits of the troops. Firewood, however, was very scarce. Rations and supplies were at first brought every morning by a string of camels from Serapeum, but soon the time of arrival of these supplies was altered to the evening. A light railway and a water-pipe line had been laid to a point about half-way from the Canal.

On February 5th the brigadier visited the posts and gave instructions for ceremonial drill to be carried out for half-an-hour daily; on the 7th the whole battalion was doing these hated exercises from 8.30 to 9 a.m. Next day there was an outbreak of mumps—some might have considered it a judgment on the brigadier for the "saluting drill"—and the sick men were evacuated to hospital, some in "cacolets" (a kind of skeleton invalid-chair) on camels, and some on light sand-carts, which had very broad-tyred wheels.

To supplement the rations, a hundred pounds was spent in Cairo on luxuries by the battalion authorities, who organised a canteen, at which these comforts were sold at cost price. The demand was so great that the stock was sold out in a few hours.

During the stay at Gebel Habeita about a dozen trained Indian soldiers from the Bikanir Camel Corps, with some 40 camels, were attached to the battalion for patrolling purposes. These were under the command of Lieutenant W. A. Collin, the battalion intelligence officer, and patrols went out daily about 30 miles into the desert. Lieutenants Neligan and Knightley led some of these patrols, but very little information was obtained from them except on one occasion, when a captured Bedouin gave some valuable information when interrogated at headquarters.

On February 15th information was received that part of the 9th was to be drafted to a new battalion. It had been decided to increase the A.I.F. by creating two new divisions, and, as only two spare infantry brigades were then in being, General Birdwood ordered that the original sixteen battalions should be halved and each half then brought up to full strength with reinforcements, thus forming thirty-two battalions. One half of them remained with their original brigades, the other half going to the new divisions.

In the 9th Battalion lists were drawn up in each company, and half the strength of each was put on a quota for its daughter battalion, the 49th. It was expected that Major Salisbury would be made C.O. of the 49th, and, so as to be perfectly fair to him, the question as to which officers were to be transferred to his command was settled by the time-honoured method of drawing lots. Major Dougall and Captains Arrell, D. Chapman and Hinton were recommended as company commanders for the four new companies, but eventually Salisbury and Hinton were not transferred. Dougall became second-in-command of the 49th, with Captains Arrell, Fortescue and Plant and Lieutenant Adsett as company commanders, 2nd-Lieutenant H. L. Swain adjutant, and Lieutenant J. L. Gray quartermaster. Chapman was transferred to the 49th, but within a few days he went to the 45th and was promoted major.

On February 26th the quota for the 49th, very depressed at their change of regiment, left for Serapeum, and little more than 400 men remained in the 9th. However, two days later the old battalion was once more brought up to strength, or nearly so, by the arrival of a draft of reinforcements intended originally for the 25th Battalion. There was some trouble over this draft, as, when it reached the 9th, some of its members were found to be medically unfit. Furthermore, it was not fully supplied with rifles and other articles of equipment, and, as there were no supplies on the spot to replace shortages, this was a serious matter. These reinforcements had, on arriving in Egypt, been camped at Heliopolis, about six miles to the north of Cairo. Like their elder brothers of the original battalion, they experienced the delights of sight-seeing in Cairo, but some of them were rather unruly.

There was an electric tram from the camp to Cairo, on which the fare was one piastre ($2\frac{1}{2}$d), but a small proportion of the wilder spirits soon acquired the habit of taking advantage of the helplessness of the conductor in the presence of superior numbers of soldiers, and they either refused to pay at all, or else gave a small coin, and when given their change, they would swear that it was not a 5-piastre but a 20-piastre piece which they had given; they would demand the other fifteen piastres—and usually get them, too, for if the conductor would not give them they would put him off the tram and make the driver go on without him. Instead of using a bell, the conductor blew a little brass horn as a signal to the driver to start the tram; when the Australians put a conductor off the tram, they would seize this horn and blow it, and off would go the tram, with the conductor, wailing loudly, left on the roadway.

It was considered the height of fashion among these lively ones to ride on the roof of a tram, instead of on the seats provided for that purpose, which were left for the less adventurous, or for those who could not find room on the roof. The roof passengers would often amuse themselves by pulling the overhead pole from the electric wire, which of course would stop the tram. It must be understood, however, as mentioned above, that all these pranks were indulged in by only a few of the men.

A fashion, which prevailed among all the "Aussies" at this time, and which amounted to an unwritten law, was that everyone who went into Cairo had to carry a walking-stick. The Australian, often careless about his dress in camp and on parade, was usually particular of his personal appearance when walking the streets of the city.[1] Boots which were sufficiently well polished to wear on parade would not do for town, and the "Gyppo" bootblacks carried on a thriving business. "Boots-a-shine, Mr. Macgregor," was a greeting constantly heard by our men—they were always "Mr. Macgregor" to the bootblacks.

The native café-keepers, being good business men, altered the signs on their cafés so as to attract the new soldiers, who had as a rule more money to spend than Imperial troops, and on one road "Dinki-Di[2] Aussie Meal" appeared on almost every second restaurant encountered.

N.C.O.'s in reinforcements joining the battalion "lost their stripes," and reverted to the condition of private. Many of them, however, gained promotion when a vacancy occurred later.

During February the battalion lost its medical officer, Major A. Graham Butler, who was appointed D.A.D.M.S. of 1. Anzac Corps. Butler had been seconded from the A.A.M.C. to the 9th Battalion in 1914 and had sailed with it on the *Omrah*, remaining with it with scarcely a break through the Mena, Lemnos, Anzac and second Lemnos periods, and during part of the hot sandy stay at Gebel Habeita. He was rather reserved in manner, and at first was not so popular with the rank and file as he became later, but from the moment of the Landing he showed out in a new light to all, and his energy, self-sacrifice and enthusiasm for all ranks of the 9th throughout the campaign endeared him to officers and men alike. At

---

1 This attention to dress when on leave was as marked later on when the troops were in France.

2 Dinki-Di   Australian slang for "genuine."

the conclusion of the war Colonel Butler, as he had then become, was selected by the Minister for Defence to write the Official History of the Army Medical Services in the War.

In March, 1916, Lieutenant Knightley was promoted captain, and Wilder-Neligan, who had been serving as a temporary captain, to the substantive rank. On the 8th, after having been at Gebel Habeita for more than five weeks, the battalion was relieved by the light horse and left for Serapeum. All the battalion gear was taken on camels, and as the troops had not been trained in the loading of these animals many of the loads were badly balanced, so much so that when the awkward creatures rose to their feet, unless the harness gave way, they were dragged over on to their sides, where they lay kicking and bellowing. The lop-sided loads had then to be stripped off and put on again with a more even balance.

The march out was a severe one, being at first through soft sand, which changed to hard gravel about two miles from the Canal. When the troops had come the greater part of the way, and were very fatigued—"just dragging along," as one of them has said—they were cheered by the sight of the band of the 31st Battalion, which had come out to meet them, and played them in to the camp at Serapeum, reaching it at 7 p.m. This thoughtful act was much appreciated by the 9th, which finished its march in fine style.

At Serapeum general training recommenced. Here the Mark III. rifles were handed in and the Mark IV. issued; the latter fired Mark VII. ammunition, having a sharp-nosed bullet. The older form of cartridge had a round-nosed bullet. Lewis gun sections were formed in the battalion at this time, Lieutenant C. J. Carroll being the first Lewis gun officer and L. H. Bailey the first sergeant.

Swimming in the Suez Canal was a popular pastime. Not so popular was a fatigue duty, which fell to the lot of some of the men here, who were detailed to pull the ferry across the Canal. This frequently had to be done at night time, often in pitch darkness. The large flat ferry-boat was filled with a mass of transport vehicles, the horses and mules of which could not and would not keep still, but kept stamping and trampling with their feet, and moving in all directions as far as their harness would let them. The fatigue men, stationed at the side of the ferry, and holding on to a rope which stretched across the Canal, had to walk along the extreme edge of the side of the ferry-boat, from the forward to the rear end, then let go the rope and come forward again, when the process would be repeated. All the while they were in danger either of being trampled under the animals' feet or of being pushed by them over the side into the Canal.

The only incident out of the ordinary which occurred here was a brigade church parade, on March 19th, at which the Prince of Wales and General Birdwood were present. At the conclusion of the service the brigade marched past the Prince, and then General Birdwood, on behalf of His Royal Highness, conveyed to the brigade the thanks of the King for their work at Gallipoli.

When the parade was over the Prince, while stepping backwards, fell over a form, at which a good deal of laughter was heard in the ranks. This no doubt was responsible for the Prince's appearing very embarrassed when he picked himself up. However, when later he rode through the camp, the troops lined the road, and the hearty spontaneous cheering which arose assured him of the goodwill of the Australians.

During the stay at Serapeum there were at first persistent rumours that the Australians were to be sent to France, and in consequence a general "smartening up" of the battalion took place. These rumours gradually crystallised into definite knowledge; on or about the 19th General Birdwood announced that the Australian infantry were to be henceforth employed in France, and would soon be leaving for that country.

A week after this announcement the 9th bade farewell to Egypt. Falling in at 5 p.m. on March 26th, the battalion was spoken to by the C.O. for a few minutes and a prayer was offered by the padre. Three hours later it entrained for Alexandria and, after a very cold night crowded in open trucks almost like sardines in a tin, embarked shortly after dawn in the *Saxonia*, a Cunard liner of 14,000 tons.

The 10th Battalion came on board at 8.30 a.m., and at midday about 800 details from reinforcement camps around Cairo swept on to the wharf like a rabble. Major Salisbury, looking at these reinforcements, remarked to Major Young that he "would not care to command that crowd for all the rice in China." A few minutes afterwards he received from Colonel Price Weir, O.C. troops on the ship, a note which read:

> "You are appointed to command 800 reinforcements for the 2nd Division, which will be quartered in the after part of the ship."

On this ship the troopdecks were fitted up with berths or "bunks" for the rank and file, who in most transports had to sleep in hammocks slung from the ceiling. Certain of the troopdecks were set apart for dining saloons and had been fitted with tables and benches, ship's stewards serving the meals instead of mess orderlies drawn from the ranks of the troops. As rations were not very generous, the ship became commonly known as the "Starvonia."

About 5.30 p.m. the *Saxonia* pulled out from the wharf and anchored in the harbour alongside other troopships, warships and hospital ships. Next morning at 8 o'clock she left Alexandria, escorted by a cruiser and two destroyers. On board also was the staff of the 3rd Brigade.

A watch had to be kept for submarines, and a detachment from the 9th was detailed for this duty. All ranks had to wear lifebelts throughout the voyage, which proved uneventful; a number of sloops passed en route were almost the only objects seen. The usual rumour circulated that the "troopship in front" had been sunk by a submarine, but, as usual, it proved to be untrue.

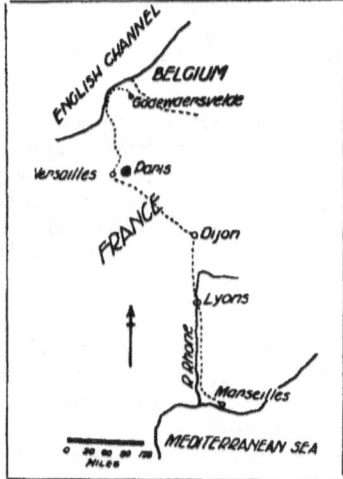

11.—Marseilles to Godewaersvelde.

At 7 a.m. on the 31st the *Saxonia* reached Malta and for a short while anchored about half-a-mile from the coast. Next day first Sardinia was passed and then Corsica, and at 6 a.m. on April 2nd the French coast was in sight. During the morning the *Saxonia* entered Marseilles harbour, passing two hospital ships with wounded "Tommies," who were given a rousing cheer by the Australians. Engaged in various duties in the neighbourhood of the wharves were many French soldiers, some of them guarding German prisoners who were working. The remarkable fact about these French troops was that they were all elderly, having been given this field of service so as to release younger men for work in the front line. They wore very showy uniforms, blue tunics with red trousers and cap.

The battalion disembarked at 7.45 p.m., each man taking rations for 58 hours, and, after a short march to the railway over streets paved with cobble-stones, it began a wonderful journey through the whole length of France from south to north. All the trees and other vegetation wore coats of springtime green, which was especially pleasing to eyes so long used to the desert sand. Spread before them, mile after mile, was a splendid panorama of fruit-trees in blossom, a wonderful sight. The train ran along the valley of the Rhone, and on each side the ground sloped up, with little farmlets cut out of the hillsides and surrounded by stone walls. The destination of the troops was unknown to them. Whenever they stopped at a town or a village, the French people cheered them and asked them for badges and buttons as souvenirs, but through all the novelty and excitement they managed to keep their heads, for the battalion diary records "men wonderfully well-behaved and give no trouble."

Lyons attracted particular attention; from the railway bridge could be seen other bridges spanning the river, seven of them. When the train stopped at Dijon for half-an-hour, many of the men insisted on leaving it, in spite of the efforts of the local police and railway staff, who were powerless against superior numbers. The C.O. had to come to the rescue by detailing one of the platoons as a picquet to keep the rest of the men from leaving the platform.

At one of the stops tea was issued to all, but with an addition not unwelcome to most—a tot of rum in it. The troops were disappointed at finding that they did not pass through Paris but went round it. They stopped, however, at Versailles, and had a good view of the Palace where three years later the peace treaty was to be signed. At Versailles French V.A.D.'s supplied everyone on board with coffee and cake.

As there were no brakes on the French troop-trains, the engine would put on its brake every time the train stopped. Then would be heard clack, clack, clack, clack, as each carriage came to a stop by ramming the one in front of it, and anyone with a head out of the window at such times would risk a broken jaw or at least a bruise on some part of the head when the carriage stopped with a jerk.

Some of the men took the opportunity of airing their French, not always with the most successful results. One of them, on arriving at Dijon, wished to ask for the time, but he mixed two phrases and confused a Frenchman by asking "Quelle heure est le nom de la ville?" ("What time is the name of the town?"). Others were interested in the names of the stations passed through; one "linguist," as the train stopped at a village station, said: "Where's this?" and, looking out of the window, saw a name painted opposite him on the platform. "Oh, it's Sortie. Hey, you blokes, we're at Sortie." It was only later he discovered that "Sortie" was the French for "Way out."

At one place the train stopped beside a stream, and soon a great number of the troops had alighted and were taking the opportunity of having a wash. Suddenly the engine whistle blew, and they made a wild rush to reach the train before it started. Later they became used to the peculiarities of French troop-trains; one could never find out when or where they would stop, nor how long it would be before they would go on again.

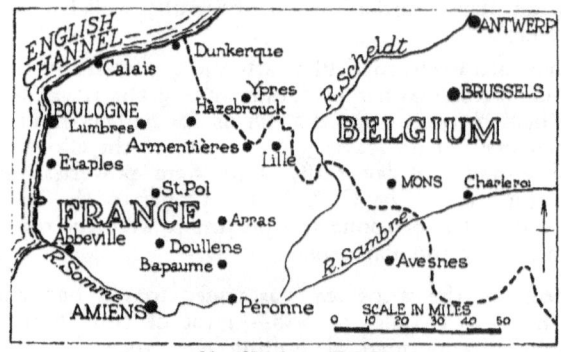

12. Northern France.

At 11 a.m. on April 5th, after meandering for two and a half days, the train arrived at the little Flemish village of Godewaersvelde, not far from Ypres. Leaving the train, the battalion marched five miles to Strazeele, Merris and Meteren, three neighbouring villages, and after a couple of hours of waiting in the cold, they were billeted in adjacent farmhouses. The guns at the front could be heard clearly from here. When the roll was called, it was found that twelve men were missing, but they joined up within the next few days.

Most of the billets consisted of a farmhouse with barns and stables, surrounding or nearly surrounding a large courtyard, much of which was taken up by a large rubbish pit several feet deep. Into this pit was thrown all household refuse as well as stable-manure. The barns and other outbuildings were allotted to N.C.O.'s and men, while one or two officers occupied rooms in the farmhouse. The pathways between the middens and the buildings were often very narrow in places, and more than once men coming in after dark, especially if not quite sober, were known to fall into the pits. On one occasion General Birdwood tried to ride his horse across one of these midden-pits where it looked firm, and the horse sank in it up to the girths.

The battalion remained in this neighbourhood for a fortnight, during which time a great deal of wet weather was encountered. The companies were given further training, including much route-marching over the cobbled roads, which the men found very trying after the soft sand of Egypt. Their Australian-made boots, although most satisfactory hitherto, were found to wear rather quickly in the wet conditions after long service in a very dry climate, and as they wore out the men were issued, at the beginning of May, with the boots worn by the Imperial troops, which were much heavier and clumsier. The combination of sore feet from the hard roads and hard boots on the sore feet caused much discomfort during and after marches, and made necessary frequent foot-inspections which were sometimes made daily. Later Australian boots of a somewhat stouter pattern were issued, and these were found to withstand the conditions in France quite as well as did the English boots, and in addition were much more comfortable to wear.

Gas-helmets, known as "P.H." helmets, were now issued to members of the battalion, who had to don them and test them by walking through a trench filled with gas. The helmet, which consisted of a flannel bag fitted with transparent eye-pieces, was worn over the head, the open end being tucked into the neck of the wearer's tunic. All the air breathed had to come through the pores of the flannel, and this had been soaked in a liquid which "killed" any gas-fumes present, so that they could do no harm when breathed. The air breathed out went through a tube of sheet-iron, which was held in the mouth, and had a rubber valve on the outside to prevent gas-laden air from entering.

Damp and sticky, the P.H. helmet was stuffy and uncomfortable when in use; it could not be worn for any length of time, and very much improved patterns of respirator were used at a later stage of the war. It gave only partial protection against one kind of gas, lachrymatory gas, which rendered a person temporarily blind by causing a flood of tears. For this gas special goggles were issued, as all that was necessary was to keep it from reaching the eyes.

At this stage of the war cloud-gas only was being used. Brought up to the front line in cylinders, it was released at set times when the wind was blowing towards the opposing lines. In our trenches, whenever the wind was blowing from the direction of the German lines, notices containing the words "Wind dangerous" would be displayed at various points. Brass artillery cartridge cases were hung everywhere, for use as gongs, and these were sounded whenever it was thought that an enemy gas attack was being launched. When one was heard, others began to sound, and sometimes the alarm would be passed along for miles. Horns, similar to motor horns, were also used for this purpose.

# CHAPTER VIII.

### SAILLY AND ROUGE DE BOUT.

On their first arrival in France the Australian troops were sent to the Second Army, under General Sir Herbert Plumer, and put into the "nursery" sector south of Armentières to accustom them to the conditions of the Western Front—conditions so different from those which they had experienced at Gallipoli. A scout section was formed in the battalion on April 10th, Lieutenant Frank Page being O.C. and "Sandy" Fraser sergeant. Eight days later the 9th left for Sailly-sur-la-Lys, five miles west of Armentières, a town famous to the Australians owing to the well-known soldier's song concerning a certain "mademoiselle" hailing from there, a lady not quite in the first bloom of her youth, who had somehow avoided being kissed for an exceeding long time, estimated to have been at least forty years. The unit was to be temporarily attached to the 1st Brigade, one of the battalions of which had been isolated on account of the discovery of a case of relapsing fever.

At 4 o'clock next morning the 9th moved to Rouge de Bout, two miles to the south-east of Sailly, relieving the 17th Lancashire Fusiliers. "A" Company was put in close support of the firing line at Rue du Bois, a long road running from north-east to south-west, a mile forward of Rouge de Bout. The other companies were in support and reserve further back.

Everything was quiet except for a little intermittent gunfire. The unit which the 9th relieved was a "bantam" battalion, and it was found that the rampart they had built as a defence line was very low. Work had to be commenced at once to build it up to a height sufficient to give cover to the ordinary tall Australian. On this its first appearance in the forward area in France the battalion numbered 24 officers, 51 sergeants and 885 other ranks. The area was so quiet that the French civilians were still living in their houses as far forward as the support lines.

On April 20th, at 1.15 p.m. "C" Company's billets at Rouge de Bout were heavily bombarded by 5.9-inch howitzers, 50 or 60 high-explosive shells bursting in their vicinity. Early in the bombardment a shell exploded in one of the huts, wounding four men, and others who ran to their assistance were caught

## "C" COMPANY SHELLED

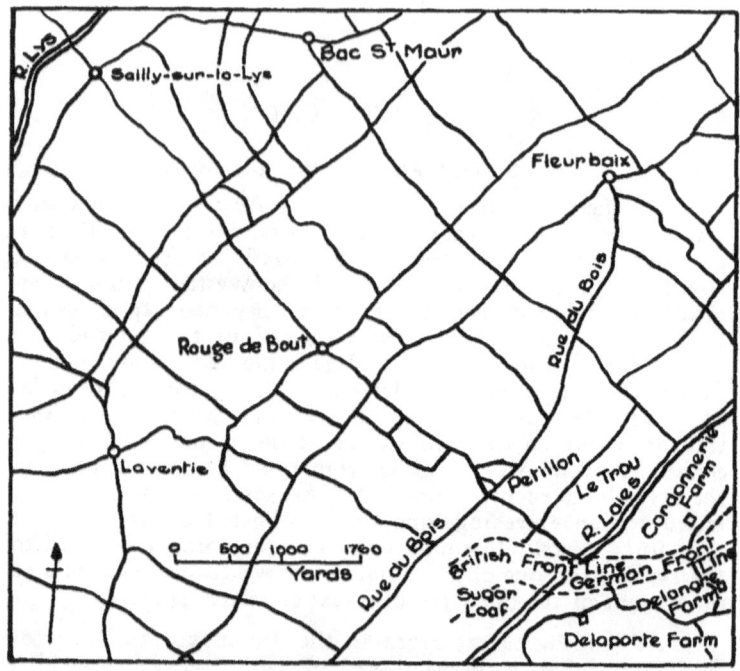

13. The Fleurbaix Area.

by another shell. Later 47 casualties were caused by a shell which struck the wall of a large brick billet, behind which a considerable number of men were sheltering. At the time the medical officer (Captain A. McKillop) was inside the building attending to some of the earlier casualties. Lieutenant A. E. Fothergill, C.S.M. G. T. Phipps, and 23 others were killed, and Captain McKillop and 47 others wounded. All the dead were buried the same evening, Chaplains Fahy (R.C.) and Lundie (Presbyterian) officiating.

"C" Company was relieved at 7.30 p.m. by a company of the 3rd Battalion, and moved out to Sailly. The next day, which was Good Friday, the area was again heavily bombarded, but all the shells landed in an empty field and no damage was done. That evening the remaining companies of the 9th came out to Sailly.

On April 25th the first Anzac Day celebrations took place. The 3rd Brigade was inspected by General Plumer, General Walker, G.O.C., 1st Australian Division, General White, and the brigadier. Plumer and MacLagan spoke to every battalion after the inspection. Company sports were held during the afternoon, £50 in prize money being distributed from regimental funds. A couple of days after this the brigade was inspected by Sir Douglas Haig, Commander-in-Chief of the British Armies in France.

Next day the men received a surprise on being marched into the village to have a hot bath. A tub was provided for each man, with an abundance of hot water. The underclothing taken off was handed in and clean garments issued, and while the men were washing their uniforms were fumigated. These baths were arranged in all the back areas, and sometimes took the form of hot showers, which were often turned on for only a couple of minutes. The result was that the man who was rather slow found that he had just soaped himself nicely all over when the water supply stopped, and he had to wipe the soap off with a towel. At the great base camp at Etaples there was a steam bath something like a Turkish bath.

Just after the middle of May the battalion moved into the Petillon sector, two miles south of Fleurbaix, and here it remained until the end of June. For the first time the 9th was garrisoning part of the front line in France. On becoming responsible for a sector a company had to take over from the company it relieved the trench stores, which remained permanently in the trench. These consisted of ammunition, bombs, periscopes, braziers, gas alarms, Very lights, maps and other equipment.

Life in the line here was comparatively uneventful. The troops were either on guard in the front-line trench, keeping watch for any movement of the enemy, doing fatigue duty, or resting. Fatigues were numerous and varied. Rations and ammunition had to be carried up to the line, and also materials for strengthening the defences; new breastworks had to be built, and damage done by shell-fire to old ones repaired. As a rule this fatigue work had necessarily to be carried out at night time.

A great deal of work was put in in this way, and in laying out barbed wire in front of the breastwork, and some members of the battalion attended a special school of instruction in wiring at Bethune. The country in the Fleurbaix sector being very flat and swampy, there were few trenches. The front line was actually a breastwork of sandbags eight feet high, and in some places ten feet thick; immediately behind this was a parados of similar construction, and the space between them was the "trench." The communication saps too had high walls of sandbags on either side. There were dugouts for the garrison in the back of the parados.

A fatigue duty which was unpopular was that of assisting a battery of 60-pounder trench-mortars known as the "Imshee Battery." Parties from the 9th had to carry these heavy weapons and their half-hundredweight bombs up to the front line, and after their crews had fired them, and immediately retired, the 9th were obliged to "enjoy" the retaliatory bombardment which the enemy sent over in reply. The nickname given to these batteries was derived from the Arabic "imshee" ("go away"), one of the words learnt by the Australians in Egypt.

At times the enemy shelled the 9th's trenches a good deal, and nearly every night there were gas alarms. At first cold weather was experienced, with muddy conditions underfoot, but it soon became more agreeable. When billeted behind the line the troops usually slept on straw, which was often wet or damp, and this made the downy couch less inviting than it should have been after a hard day's work.

When the 9th took over this sector the enemy could be said to be in control of No-Man's Land; they explored it every night as they pleased. But so enterprising were our patrols that they reversed this state of affairs, and when the 3rd Brigade left the sector they were the undoubted "kings" of No-Man's Land. During these excursions No-Man's Land would sometimes be illuminated by a star-shell or a flare thrown up by the enemy, when the patrols would have to lie or stand still. If they moved the enemy might see and fire on them, but if they remained quite still it was difficult at a distance to recognise them as men. If the men of a patrol thought they might be noticed by the enemy when a flare went up they would scatter in different directions immediately it went out, as in the next few seconds of darkness nobody looking in the direction of the flare could see anything.

The British flares were known as Very lights, and were fired from a special pistol with a very wide bore. The Australians seldom used these, leaving it to the enemy to illuminate No-Man's Land. They also looked upon the enemy's flares as a kind of "barometer" to indicate their opponents' intentions. If "Fritz" sent up no flares, this was usually taken as a sign that he probably had patrols out in No-Man's Land, and when he resumed their use, that he had no patrols out and was on the watch.

On one night a patrol went out in charge of Sergeant "Sandy" Fraser. The password was "Whisky." When the patrol was returning towards the front-line trench some nervous individual on duty in a listening post threw a Mills bomb without first challenging. A piece of the bomb hit "Sandy," whereupon the sergeant's yell of "Whisky, you ———, whisky," could be heard a mile away.

By the end of April spring had set in and the weather was quite pleasant. On the 27th it was remarked to be quite hot. The parade ground of "A" Company at Sailly, the yard behind its billet, was a delightful rural spot, with green grass underfoot and numerous apple and plum trees around, all in blossom. The general health of the troops was excellent all the while they were in the Fleurbaix area.

About this time the first "Blighty" leave began. This was the name given by the "Tommies" to furlough to England, and from now onwards it was also given to the Australian troops in France as a matter of routine, small parties of men going in rotation.

On May 5th steel helmets were issued to all ranks. This headgear, which was now worn by all troops in the forward zone, was a most valuable piece of equipment, and resulted in the saving of innumerable lives; it had also a considerable moral effect on troops, as a man wearing a steel helmet knew that one of his vital spots was protected from shell-splinters and shrapnel-pellets, and he was thus able to endure shell-fire with much greater confidence. On May 14 the strength of the battalion was increased by the arrival of a batch of 100 reinforcements. These, after leaving Australia, had first gone to Egypt, and had been for a while in camp at Heliopolis. On the 24th the trenches were inspected by Generals Walker and MacLagan, and on the 26th by General Birdwood, who spent some time in talking with many of the members of the battalion.

On the night of May 30th the Germans raided the trenches of the 11th Battalion, on the left flank of the 9th. This raid was preceded by a sudden and intense bombardment—the first heavy bombardment experienced by the brigade. The 11th suffered heavy loss and had to withdraw to the flanks and rear, but as soon as the bombardment slackened they, assisted by men of the 9th, reoccupied their front line, which was badly battered but empty of the enemy, who had remained only a short time in our line.

For a while in June the rations were very short. One man mentions in his diary that there was neither jam nor butter, and only a quarter of a loaf of bread to each man for a day. On June 14th "summer-time" began, watches being advanced one hour at midnight so as to be in agreement with the time observed all over France.

During June and early July the I Anzac Corps carried out a series of raids on the German line. These, according to Dr. Bean (Official History, Vol. III, p. 243) were "partly necessitated by the fact that, although constant attempts were made to capture Germans in No-Man's Land, it was not until May 28th that a prisoner was so taken." But most of the raids were the result of an order from Sir Douglas Haig to the First, Second and Third British Armies to distract the enemy's attention during the preparation for the great Franco-British attack which was shortly to be launched north and south of the River Somme.

The 3rd Brigade undertook two of these raids—one by the 9th, the other by the 11th Battalion, on successive nights. That of the 9th, which has been described by Dr. Bean as the "most brilliantly executed" of the Australian series, was commanded by Captain Wilder-Neligan. Volunteers were called for, and a large number offered themselves; of these 160 were chosen, detached from the battalion, and billeted in farmhouses between Sailly and Steenwerck in the divisional reserve area. Reaching their billets on June 11th, they began at once to practice for the raid. Trenches were specially made, based on aeroplane photographs of the sector which was to be attacked, and the methods to be followed were worked out in great detail and carefully rehearsed. The numbers were finally fixed at four officers and 151 other ranks of the 9th Battalion, and three sappers from the engineers, divided into three parties. In the operation orders the object of the raid was stated to be not only the gaining of information and the destruction of enemy material, but also the encouragement of *esprit de corps* in the battalion.

The following took part in the raid:—

**In command:** Captain M. Wilder-Neligan (W).

**Left Flank Party:** Lieut. H. T. Young (W), Sgt. L. W. Butler (S.W.), Cpls. W. Jamieson and S. G. Shave, L/Cpls. B. Benjamin (W) and H. G. Young (W), Spr. T. H. E. Miles, Privates G. Buist, J. Calvert, W. G. Campbell, F. Cavers, R. J. Clark, H. J. Coleman, C. H. J. Davis, W. Donaldson, T. Douglas, A. G. Edwards, R. Elliott, J. Ernst (W), J. H. Forde, D. C. Fraser, J. Hall, T. J. Haynes, F. Johnston, P. H. Jurd, J. R. Keane, P. H. Kearney, A. C. Kendrick, G. W. Kennedy, E. Kersley, W. H. Knott, T. W. Lewis, R. McAvoy, A. McDonald (W), W. G. McDonald, F. McMahon, D. Mahoney, A. Miller, J. R. G. Morley, R. J. Noble, A. M. Patterson, J. E. Robinson (K), P. H. Ross, T. Russ, H. E. Thorley, F. C. Titterton, A. Wilson.

THE RAIDING PARTIES 115

**Centre Party:** Lieut. J. P. Ramkema (S.W.), Sgts. H. A. Barry (K), W. H. Carroll (K), G. H. Hirst and J. E. Kenyon, Cpls. A. Lord and B. O'Brien, L/Cpls. T. J. Burton, J. W. Giles, S. T. Lucas and H. Preston, Spr. C. Bethun, Privates H. Allen, C. R. Anstey (W), C. Archer, A. C. Bailey, N. W. T. Black, C. T. Blackman, H. Blakely, P. Boyd, E. Brady, L. Braganza (K), J. H. Campbell, H. Clark, P. R. Collins, A. Crozier, J. Cunningham, F. E. Darchy, H. Dickson, W. Doyle, C. Dungey, O. T. M. Flint (W), P. H. Forbes (W), A. E. Green, T. Horsefield (W), A. James (K), H. G. Jones, R. Kettle, J. Landers, H. G. Limpus, R. G. McKay, J. S. McKean, R. McNeill, R. Morgan, W. Myers, E. O'Brien, E. O'Brien, J. O'Flaherty, A. B. Pratt, J. Richards, L. Semple (W), W. E. Skey (W), C. Smith (W), J. Thomas, F. W. Turner, J. P. Veivers, W. Walker, R. E. White, C. Williams, J. H. C. Williams.

**Right Flank Party:** Capt. C. E. Benson (K), Sgts. S. Brand, J. Hume (D.O.W.), E. H. Meyers (W), and E. F. Little (S.W.), Cpls. R. Penman, E. Teitzel (S.W.), F. Thomas, L/Cpls. A. J. McSewell and E. A. Swayn, Spr. A. Fairhall, Privates W. C. Barlas, H. G. Black (W), J. Bradley, W. J. Bragge, A. Brown, R. D. Brown (W), J. J. Cleary (D.O.W.), P. K. Cox, P. Cromwell, B. J. Dillon, W. E. Donald, G. Dunlop (W), T. W. Foo (W), H. C. Govers (W), A. J. Grand (W), G. Hamilton, J. H. C. Howard, E. Hurley, R. A. P. Jackson, E. James (W), J. G. Jones, B. Kelly (W), J. D. Lewis, J. Mackey, H. McKinnon (W), E. McLune (K), M. O'Connor, J. Ormond, H. Smith, A. Thomas, N. G. Tincknell, C. Tomlinson, H. Turnbull (K), R. J. Whitten (W.), W. Wilkinson, J. Young.

It is possible that two or three names may be missing from this list. K. indicates killed; D.O.W. died of wounds; W. wounded; S.W. slightly wounded.

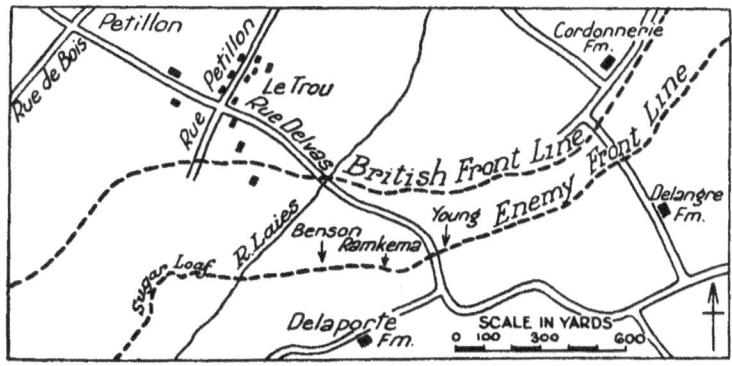

14. **Neligan's Raid at Fleurbaix.**

The point of attack was near the Rue du Bois, north-east of the "Sugar-loaf Salient." No-Man's Land was here 300 yards wide, but the sector was specially chosen because located there was a machine-gun which had been very troublesome to the 9th and to other units. It was decided that the raid itself would not be supported by a preparatory barrage, but that a feint bombardment would be directed on to a neighbouring section of the enemy line, a quarter of a mile to the right, the intention being to deceive the Germans as to the point of entry. In addition, during the days before the operation, the enemy's wire entanglement was methodically cut by our trench-mortars, both in front of the objective and at other points.

Patrols went out into No-Man's Land before the raid to examine the ground over which the advance would be made, and to note the position of the enemy wire. Lieutenant Young, for instance, found that there was some wire blocking the path which his party would have to take, but he also noticed that it was easily possible to get round the obstacle by going to the left, as it did not extend far in that direction. In one of these patrols, on June 18th, Captain A. Warren, who had been picked for the raid, was killed.

The raid was carried out in the early morning of July 2nd while a battalion of the 5th Division was occupying the line. On the evening before, the men, who had been kept in ignorance of the actual date of the raid, were brought up in motor lorries to the ruins of a house some little distance behind our front line. Here preparations were made for what the party had before leaving been told was to be a final rehearsal.

Hands and faces were blackened, as were the bayonets, so that they would not glitter. No identity discs, paybooks, battalion colours or other means by which men could be identified were carried. Chewing gum was given to all to prevent them from coughing. One N.C.O. was wearing a wristlet watch with a luminous dial; this was taken away from him, as being likely to attract the attention of the enemy. White calico armbands, with a stripe of luminous paint around the centre, were issued, to be put on as soon as the men left our parapet, but they were covered over by a strip of hessian.[1]

The parties then proceeded to the parapet, and at 11.50 p.m. they began to leave it by the sally-port. Fortunately it was a dark night. In spite of the chewing-gum, one man of the centre party, F. E. Darchy, developed a cough by the time they had gone fifty yards, and had to be sent back. By 12.40 all three parties were in No-Man's Land opposite their objective, about 200 yards distant from one another and 200 yards from the enemy trenches. Two machine-guns in the Australian line then began to fire in order to drown the noise of the next advance, to within 50 yards' distance. Lieutenant Young, commanding the left flank party, kept his direction by watching

---

[1] It was found that the luminous paint made the arm-bands too conspicuous, so it was not used in future raids.

a tower behind the enemy line. In spite of the darkness this tower could be easily seen against the sky-line when one was crouching down with the head near the ground.

Young's party came to the German wire, but, on turning to the left to pass round the end of it, they could find no end. The enemy had put out new wire, continuing the old entanglement farther still to the left. The wire had therefore to be crossed. It had not been sufficiently broken by the trench-mortars, so the top strands were cut, the wire was beaten down as much as possible, and mats were put over it. These mats, about twelve feet long, were of heavy canvas mounted on a base of wire netting, and special men had been detailed to carry them.

The centre party, under Lieutenant Ramkema, also had some trouble in getting through the wire, but Captain Benson's men, on the right flank, reached the 50 yards' position without hindrance, except that they lost direction and, advancing in a curve, found themselves running into the centre party. This, however, was put right. At 2.3 a.m., all being in position, a code word, "Gallop," was sent by telephone to the artillery and machine-guns. The latter opened fire half-a-minute afterwards, on the flanks, and at 2.5 the artillery put down a barrage beyond the objective.

The raiders thereupon took the hessian coverings from their white arm-bands, and made a wild rush for the German trench. The shells whined and screeched overhead and burst behind the German line in a curtain of fire. Some of the enemy could be seen firing on them from a distance of only a few yards. Lance-Corporal Preston says:

"My gas-helmet was torn from me by barbed wire, and I fell into a deep shell-hole and lost my rifle, but soon recovered it."

When he reached the trench he

"heard somebody call out 'gas'; I reached for my helmet, but it was gone."

By 2.12 all three parties were in the enemy lines. Neligan, while advancing over the last 50 yards of the attack, encountered an enemy observation post just in front of the parapet. It contained three men, two of whom he killed, but the third threw a bomb which wounded him severely in the head and shoulders. However, he went on and superintended the rest of the operation.

The enemy's line consisted of a breastwork eight feet deep. A considerable number of Germans occupied the centre of the objective. They had been driven in from the flank by the feint bombardment, and much hand-to-hand fighting ensued. Private J. Cunningham dropped his rifle and knocked down two of the enemy with his fist, finding that a more expeditious way of dealing with the situation. Lieutenant Ramkema found a large dugout in which were a number of Germans, and he began to fire his revolver into it. Then Lance-Corporal Preston and Private Blackman came up. Preston had an electric torch fastened to his rifle, and he flashed this down the dugout, the light showing up the Germans, who had crowded into one corner when Ramkema had fired down the stairs. One of them jumped forward and threw up his hands, but another behind him fired a revolver shot over his compatriot's shoulder. Preston at once fired several shots in return without putting his rifle to his shoulder, knowing that the bullets would follow the light of the torch. Sergeant Kenyon, arriving at the scene, also fired into the dugout, and Ramkema then ordered the survivors to surrender, which they did. Fifteen of them came out; six had been killed.

Those in this part of the line next heard close to them a burst of song, not in English, nor in German either. It was Kenyon, who, having a few moments to spare before it was time to return to our lines, was sitting on the parados and singing in Hindustani. He was an ex-Imperial soldier and had seen service in India.

Ramkema and Kenyon then drove their prisoners back towards the Australian line, followed by Blackman. Preston joined them a little later. About half-way across No-Man's Land the fifteen prisoners noticed how few in number their guards were, and one of them put up a show of resistance and was at once shot. At this the rest remained quiet, and were brought in without further trouble.

The bombers and bayonet men of Young's party, on the left, encountered but few of the enemy, and these they put to flight. They then found the troublesome machine-gun. It was on a heavy stand, from which it could not be removed, so they carried both stand and gun back to our trenches. Captain Young was helping to carry the trophy when he was wounded in the shoulder. He did not know at the time that he had been shot, but thought that his shoulder had been dislocated, and so he continued to help with the gun. Corporal Jamieson took part in the capture of the machine-gun, and also attacked and killed an enemy signaller, who refused to take a telephone from his ears. Benson's party also killed many of the enemy and captured four of them. Owing to the strenuous opposition encountered very little information was gained.

There were two "tape men" attached to each party. As soon as the raiders reached the enemy breastwork these men laid two tapes back to our own lines, thus marking a lane through which the raiders were to retire. They then returned across No-Man's Land and took position just outside the German parapet, to watch for the signal to return—a rocket fired by the C.O., who was just behind our front-line parapet. When the rocket went up, at 2.17, they began to call out, "This way, this way, imshee!" to guide the raiders to the beginning of the taped lane, and the men in the trench passed on the word "imshee" for the benefit of any who had not noticed the rocket. The actual time of occupation of the German lines was thus five minutes. Captain Benson was almost the last to leave the enemy parapet, and was shot and killed while assisting two wounded men through the wire.

The parties were two-thirds of the way back across No-Man's Land when a German barrage fell on them and between them and our line, quite cutting off the way to the sally-port. It is possible that this barrage was the result of a message sent back by the enemy signaller just before he was killed by Jamieson. There was a ditch or large gutter with water in it[2] running parallel to the Australian line, and all had to take shelter in this. Suddenly to their surprise some of them saw a number of Germans coming straight for them, but it was only the party of prisoners taken by Ramkema, with their custodians; they, too, had to take shelter in the ditch. The majority of the raiders' casualties were sustained when they were caught in this barrage, which died down after a while, and by 2.30 all were back in the Australian lines. A telephone was found to be missing, and Lance-Corporals Lucas and Preston returned to No-Man's Land, found the instrument, and brought it back. Neligan, who, despite his wounds, had carried on in command, was brought back to our lines by Private Hughie Smith.

After the raid the survivors were taken in motor-lorries to the divisional baths at Bac St. Maur, where they removed not only the stains of battle, but also the black with which they had covered their faces and hands. They were then given an issue of coffee and rum and were allowed to sleep for most of the day.

2 Probably the "River" Laies.

The mats for crossing the barbed wire were found to be more useful in the withdrawal than in the advance. Knobkerries—entrenching-tool handles with iron cogwheels on the ends—were carried by some of the men, but these were not found of much use, most of the fighting being with bombs and revolvers.

The casualties suffered by the battalion were 1 officer (Captain Benson) and 7 other ranks (including Sergeants Barry and Carroll) killed, 2 O.R.'s died of wounds, 3 officers and 25 O.R.'s wounded. Three men were missing after the raid; two had been killed in the German trench and the other severely wounded in the legs. The enemy sustained 53 casualties and 21 of them were captured, besides the machine-gun and a quantity of equipment.

A German account of this raid says:
> "After strong artillery preparation an attack was made by about a company of the enemy. . . . . Concealed by thick smoke-clouds, which at first were taken for gas-clouds, the enemy succeeded in passing by surprise the destroyed wire-entanglements, and getting over the breastwork on a broad front. Twenty-five men, including the garrison of a dugout, who had not shown enough toughness or enterprise in defending themselves, were taken prisoner."[3]

Another enemy record states:
> "Through two dead and one badly wounded raider, whom we discovered in the sector, the 9 Bn., 3 Inf. Bde., 1 Aust Div., was identified."[4]

As Neligan was badly wounded in the head, Captain N. M. Gibson, the M.O., arranged for him to be taken direct to the C.C.S. at Neuve Eglise, where he was operated on within two hours of being hit. This probably saved his life. Young's wound in the shoulder proved to be a severe one, and Ramkema was slightly wounded in the leg.

The following decorations were subsequently awarded for this action:—Captain Wilder-Neligan, D.S.O.; Lieutenants H. T. Young and J. P. Ramkema, M.C.; Sergeant L. W. Butler, D.C.M.; Sergeant J. Kenyon and Privates P. Brown, J. Cunningham, B. J. Dillon, D. Mahoney and C. Smith, M.M. The decorations for the other ranks were allotted on the basis of so many for each section, and, as all the officers had become casualties, the survivors of each party were asked to hold a meeting and submit the names of two men to the C.O.

On July 2nd the battalion arrived at Oultersteene, further back from the line, and after a week there, drilling and routemarching to keep the men fit, it was inspected by Generals

---

[3] Diary of the 21st Bavarian Regiment, quoted by Dr. Bean in the *Official History.*
[4] Quoted in the *Official History.*

Plumer, Birdwood and MacLagan on July 9th. Later in the day it marched five miles to Berthen, near the well-known Mont des Cats, a high steep hill rising abruptly from the flatter land around it. Next morning the march was continued to Godewaersvelde, whence the battalion entrained, its destination being unknown. The troops were crowded into trucks, some of them open but the majority covered, and the officers into some very old carriages. The covered trucks, which were in common use for the transport of troops, were branded on the outside "Chevaux 8, hommes 40" (8 horses or 40 men).

Leaving Godewaersvelde at 9 p.m. on July 10th they passed through Hazebrouck and St. Pol to the quaint picturesque town of Doullens, arriving there at 3 o'clock next morning. Then followed a march of 12 miles through Beauval and Bonneville to Halloy-les-Pernois, which was reached about midday. Rather inferior billets were taken over in and near the village, some of them being in the neighbouring hamlet of Canaples.

After a good night's rest they moved on the next morning to Naours, 9 miles north of Amiens and about 19 miles behind the front line. They were now approaching the famous Somme battlefield, where some of the fiercest battles of the war were to take place. The I. Anzac Corps, which now consisted of the 1st, 2nd and 4th Australian Divisions[5], was placed under the orders of General Gough, commanding the Reserve Army.[6]

At Naours on the 13th the P.H. gas-helmets were handed in and the new box-respirators issued. In these a mask went over the face only, and the canvas bag hanging on the chest held a tin container in which were substances to "kill" the poison-gas. The air first passed through the container, then up a rubber tube to the mask, entering the mouth, into which the end of the rubber tube fitted. A wire clip inside the mask held the two nostrils together so that all breathing had to take place through the mouth. The air breathed out escaped through a valve in the rubber tube just outside the mask.

These were less uncomfortable than the P.H. helmets and much safer. They protected against all kinds of gas, and would last for 48 hours continuously, if necessary, before their power of neutralising gas would become exhausted.

In Naours there were caves which were visited by many of the battalion. These were not natural caverns, but were dug

---

[5] The New Zealand Division remained with II. Anzac, which had relieved I. Anzac at Armentieres.
[6] At the end of October it became the "Fifth Army."

by the hand of man at least as early as the second century, and possibly still earlier. They contain about 30 galleries and 300 rooms, a chapel, and six enormous chimneys, and they served for ages as a refuge to the people of the village above whenever the country was overrun by enemies—which occurred very often—and at times also when the region was infested by brigands.

At this period there was experienced a shortage of bread, only one loaf per day being issued for every six men. The troops therefore had recourse to the local baker, who had to bake extra bread to meet the demand, so it was often necessary when coming for bread to wait until the next batch came out of the oven. Although there was an abundance of army biscuit available, so many men still preferred to spend their money on the bread that, as one man stated, "the fight for bread was so strong" that a guard was detailed for duty at the baker's gate and only two men were let in at a time.

After a few days here the battalion marched on July 16th to Hérissart, and left there again on the 18th, part going to Forceville and part to Baizieux. During these marches daily foot inspections were carried out by the company commanders. Where necessary, treatment was given by the M.O. for sore feet, and as a result the troops were kept in first-class marching order. Leaving Forceville and Baizieux on the 19th, after having "dumped" their blankets and packs (a sign that they were going into battle) the companies marched past Albert to Contalmaison, which was reached at 2 a.m. on the 20th. They were quartered in old German trenches in Sausage Valley, and its neighbourhood. The men were welcomed on their arrival by a bombardment of enemy gas shells, and had to stop twice and put on their gas-helmets. This was the first time that they had met with gas shells. These projectiles contained a small amount of explosive, only enough to burst the shell and set free the gas. When they burst the only sound heard was a slight "pop."

When daylight came there could be seen signs of heavy bombardment. Shell-craters, big and small, appeared every few yards. All that was visible of Contalmaison was a part of a house, the remainder of the village being a mere mass of ruins. Great unexploded 9-inch and 12-inch shells were lying about, and enemy equipment was scattered everywhere. From many places came the overpowering smell of the unburied dead.

## CHAPTER IX.

**POZIERES AND MOUQUET FARM.**

A great Anglo-French offensive had been planned for the summer of 1916. It was originally to have been made by 64 divisions on a 45-mile front, but, on account of the heavy losses sustained by the French in the fierce fighting around Verdun, it was modified to an attack on a 23-mile front by 13 British and 5 French divisions, operating north and south of the River Somme.

The attack began on July 1st, 1916, and, while meeting with considerable success in the southern sector, was a comparative failure in the portion of the line opposite Bapaume, a town which was one of the final objectives. By successive attacks, however, the British advanced their line to a position in front of Pozières, a village on the Albert-Bapaume road, on a height commanding the surrounding country in all directions. The next step was to take Pozières, which, together with Thiepval to its north-west, was holding up the left flank of the Allied advance towards Bapaume. Three attempts to capture the village having failed, the 1st Australian Division was selected for a further attempt, while Imperial divisions made an advance on either flank.

Through Pozières, from south-west to north-east, ran the straight Roman road from Albert to Bapaume. A quarter of a mile beyond the village was a formidable double trench-system—known as the O.G. (Old German) lines—which stretched along the ridge running from the Somme to the River Ancre. Behind O.G. 2, on the northern side of the Roman road, were the ruins of an old windmill, which lay on the summit of the ridge. The main approach to the British line in this area was the shallow "Sausage Valley." Two sunken roads led from this towards Pozières village, one from "Casualty Corner" and the other from Contalmaison. That from Casualty Corner ran into "K" Trench, which began at the south-west corner of Pozières, where the road from Albert entered the village, and ran northward past Pozières cemetery, which was to its right.

The 9th Battalion led the Australians into this area when it entered Sausage Valley on July 20th. Early that morning, while the rest of the battalion was settling down in the valley, "B" Company, under Captain Lawrance, went into the line

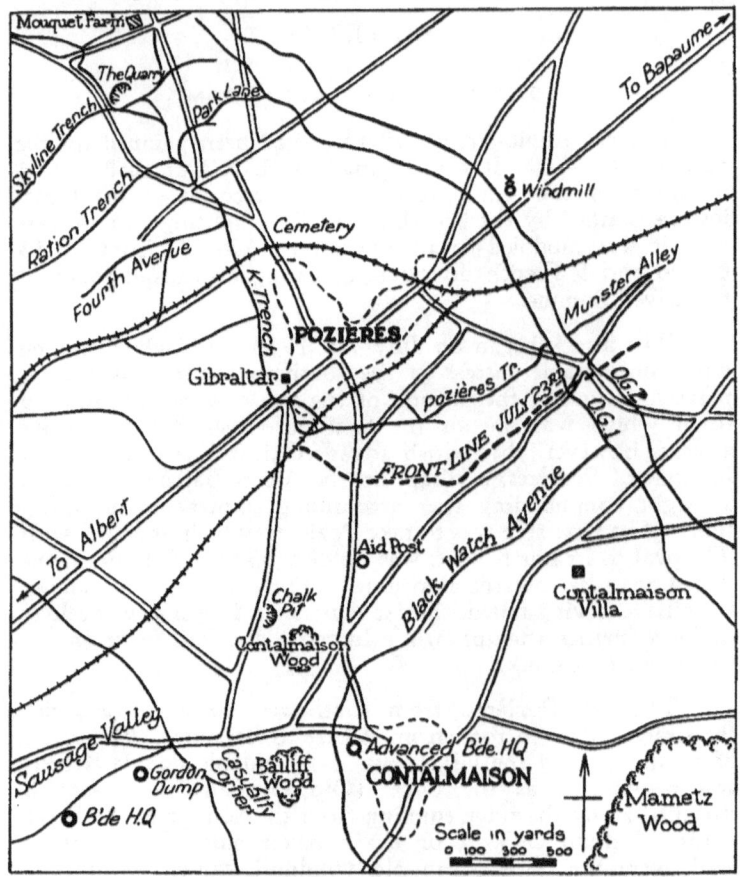

15. Pozieres and Mouquet Farm.

before Pozières, relieving a company of the Staffordshire Regiment in "Black Watch Avenue," which ran up to O.G. 1. During the next night Captain Knightley, with "A" Company, relieved another company of the Staffords.

In the attack, which was planned to commence on July 23rd, Pozières Trench, just outside the village on the south, was the first objective. This was bordered at its eastern end by O.G. 1 and 2, which ran parallel to one another. The northern portion of each of these trenches was in German territory, while the southern sections were occupied by British troops; but the enemy held the junction of O.G. 1 and Pozières Trench, and also the junction of O.G. 2 and "Munster Alley,"[1] a trench which began here in a line with the end of Pozières Trench, and ran further east. Before the general advance was begun, an unsuccessful attempt was made to capture both these junctions, and when the Australians took over from the 1st British Division the 9th Battalion was given the task of taking them.

The battalion's front was 150 yards from either junction, and on the night of July 20th, the scout officer, Lieutenant F. J. Biggs, took about twenty of his men to find if the enemy had put out wire. They sighted a German hurriedly crawling back to his post, and shortly afterwards "hell broke loose" (as one of the party expressed it), the enemy sending up flares and opening on the patrol with bombs and machine-gun fire. The patrol retired, two at a time, crawling from shell-hole to shell-hole, and notwithstanding that it was between the enemy and the rising moon, it suffered no casualty. In spite of the warm reception it had encountered, the party discovered that the German posts had been wired. On the same night a party under Lieutenant Armstrong dug a trench connecting O.G. 1 and O.G. 2 a little way behind our two forward posts.

Early in the morning of July 22nd the preliminary attack began. The plan was to bombard the German posts with two medium trench-mortars, then to attack while a barrage of 18-pounder shells was thrown just beyond the objective. Two parties—one of 51 men, under the battalion bombing officer, Lieutenant Monteath, and one of 31 under Lieutenant Biggs—assembled at the forward posts in O.G. 1 and in O.G. 2, which was 150 yards to the right of O.G. 1. Each sap ended in a small "T"-head. Some brigade bombers participated in this attack as well as the battalion bombers, and some of the battalion Lewis gunners also went forward. The attack was timed to commence at 2.30 a.m., and at 1.55 the trench-mortars began to fire, but they stopped at 2.10, as through some mistake they had only 14 rounds of ammunition on hand. At 2.25 Monteath and Biggs led out their men, and they lay 40 yards in advance, waiting for the 18-pounder barrage. As there was a good deal of artillery activity everywhere

---

[1] Munster Alley was the western end of "Switch Trench."

along the line, the special light barrage which had been arranged could not be distinguished from the other shell-fire and, after waiting till 2.32, Monteath reported that he could see no barrage. Major Salisbury, who was in charge of the attack, then ordered him to advance.

The party went up what was left of the enemy trench, which was in places nearly obliterated; the rising moon was now shining behind them. When they were about half-way up to the point where they expected to meet the enemy, all of a sudden a number of egg-bombs burst among them, causing many casualties. Monteath and Lance-Corporal Ross managed to get far enough forward to see that the trench was blocked by a mound of earth about a bomb's throw ahead. Some of the men, when the bombing commenced, jumped out of the trench into shell-holes on either side and tried to bomb the Germans, but they were driven back into the trench by machine-gun fire sweeping the open at close range.

Monteath, with the survivors, tried to hold on. Their ability to do so depended on their receiving a continuous supply of bombs, but owing to machine-gun fire the task of carrying these forward was almost impossible. Sergeant P. G. Browne, in support, in Black Watch Avenue, left his platoon in charge of his corporal and tried to cross the open with bombs, but was at once killed.

The party attacking O.G. 2, under Biggs, was divided into three groups of about ten men each. They advanced over ground which could not be recognised as a trench, so much had it been cut up by the bombardment, and, although coming under a withering fire, which caused many casualties, they reached bombing distance of the enemy. A bomb fight then took place, but the enemy was reinforced, and the party, under fire from three sides, received further heavy casualties. Biggs had been wounded, and Sergeant Hodgson, who was unwounded, was finally the only other one left of the party. When Biggs became unable to walk, he ordered the sergeant to retire. However, Hodgson remained with him, and although the enemy machine-guns were still firing, he eventually carried Biggs back safely to our lines.

After the withdrawal to our trenches it was noticed that a Lewis gun had been left behind owing to every man in its team having become a casualty. Private Lowe returned to the scene of the fight, through the fire of the machine-guns still sweeping the ground, and recovered the gun. He then went back again to bring in a wounded man.

## THE MAIN ATTACK BEGINS

Both attempts had failed, with heavy casualties to the attackers. Reserves were then brought up and a fresh attempt was organised, but day was now breaking, and, as soon as the leader of the new party climbed out of the trench, the enemy machine-guns opened fire so promptly that the attack was countermanded, as it appeared so hopeless. Our casualties were 8 other ranks killed and 1 officer and 22 O.R.'s wounded.

The attack on the village began the next morning. The objectives were (a) Pozières Trench, (b) the enemy second line, a new trench in a stretch of orchards just outside the village, and (c) the south-eastern side of the Bapaume-Albert road, which ran through the village. The 1st Brigade was to attack on the left, with the 3rd Brigade on its right, the position allotted to the 9th Battalion being a stretch of 450 yards on the extreme right. Battalion Headquarters was in O.G. 1, just south of its junction with Black Watch Avenue. There was an intermittent preliminary bombardment by our artillery which had begun on July 19th and continued up to the time of the attack. At 12.28 a.m. on July 23rd began the barrage accompanying the attack. It was a terrific bombardment, one of the most famous of the whole war, and at 12.30 it lifted and fell on the line of the second objective.

As soon as the barrage lifted, "A" and "B" Companies attacked. The men of "B" Company had been lying out in the jumping-off position beyond the front-line trench. Each man had during the barrage rolled up both his sleeves to the elbow as an aid to identification until daylight. Creeping slowly forward, they rushed the enemy trench the moment the barrage lifted. The first objective was taken immediately, except the strong-points in O.G. 1 and 2, where the attack of the 9th was held up. At 12.45 Captain Lawrance, of "B" Company, reported that he was in possession of his part of the first objective, only moderate opposition having been encountered. Later in the night Lieutenant A. Blair was wounded in endeavouring to save his men from the bursting of a bomb, and Lawrance went out to bring him in to the trench, being himself wounded by a shot through the elbow while doing so. Blair subsequently died from his wounds.

In the O.G. lines, where resistance was being experienced, the attackers formed a line spread out in the open, but owing to the enemy fire they received during their advance, they had to divide into two parties. Monteath, once more in charge of the attack in O.G. 1, reached the junction of that line and Pozières Trench, further on than the point at which he had been stopped in his previous attempt. Both trenches were empty here, but the party, fired on by machine-guns ahead, had to take cover in the trenches. A bombing fight now occurred, but the egg-bombs which the enemy used could be thrown further than ours. Noticing this, one of the party, John Leak, jumped out of the trench and, although fired on by an enemy machine-gun from the right, he ran forward, threw three bombs into the enemy post, then jumped into the post and bayonetted three unwounded Germans who were there. Monteath soon joined him, to find him wiping blood from his bayonet.[2]

By this time it was 12.59. This strong-point was now found to be a deep dugout with the top of its entrance protected by concrete. The trench wall near it had been destroyed, and the concrete, covered with earth, appeared as a mound, in a shallow depression formed by the remains of the trench. The German garrison retired to the dugout whenever there was a bombardment, and afterwards would come up and carry on from behind the mound, using it as a parapet.

A company of the 10th Battalion had been detailed to support the 9th's attack on the O.G. lines, but it was delayed while coming up by an enemy barrage, which included gas shells, and did not arrive until 1.30 a.m.

The attacking party in O.G. 2, under Lieutenants Armstrong and Ramkema, advanced at 12.30, but on reaching the place where the enemy trench should have been, no sign of a trench could be found, the whole ground being churned up and pitted with craters. The attackers lost their way and returned to our trenches. Three separate parties failed to find the trench, and this strong-post remained in enemy hands until the 25th.

During this time our barrage had been falling on the second objective, and was to lie there until 1 a.m. After the first objective had been taken, "C" and "D" Companies came up, passed over the captured trenches, and waited in front of them until the barrage lifted. In these two companies all the officers became casualties except two, Captain Chambers and Lieutenant R. M. White, and the men became somewhat disorganised. When the barrage lifted and they were ordered to advance on to the second objective, they mistook direction in the darkness and, moving to the left, came behind the right of the 11th Battalion. Portion of them under White reached the second objective and held it; the 11th Battalion companies had failed to find or recognise their objectives, and had gone on into

---

[2] Leak was subsequently awarded the Victoria Cross.

Pozières village. On account of the confusion caused by these mistakes officers had great difficulty in reorganising their detachments.

Some men of the 9th and the 11th, however, during the advance to the second objective, had seen by the lights of the flares about thirty Germans running away back towards the village. The Australians, about 140 in number, immediately gave chase, in spite of the shouts of their officers and N.C.O.'s who tried to recall them, and followed the Germans right through our barrage, which had for the time being diminished in intensity. They overtook and killed many of the fugitives, not stopping until they reached the windmill, on the far side of the Albert-Bapaume road. They saw no more Germans to chase, and were becoming tired, so they now took notice of their sergeants, three of whom had followed them: realising the danger of being cut off by the enemy, they began to return, but once more had to go through our barrage, which had again become very heavy. They sustained numerous casualties while passing through the barrage, but finally reached the line they were intended to hold.

During this advance an officer of the 9th called to his men, as he was crossing Pozières Trench, which the first wave had taken, to keep on moving. Hearing this, some men of the first wave followed him in error, to a narrow-gauge railway just outside the village, beyond which was a small plantation. Observing an explosion in this plantation, they went into it and found a battery of 5.9-inch howitzers, which had been abandoned. They threw bombs into some near-by dugouts, and chalked the name of the battalion on some of the guns, so as to establish their claim to having captured them.

The second objective had been reported captured by 1.15 a.m., and the advance to the third objective began at 1.30. In this assault, however, the 9th took no part, having been ordered to remain in its positions, as brigade reserve, after the capture of the second objective. Some of the men under White, however, after the third objective had been taken, advanced and dug themselves in at the front line on the east of the village, just south of the railway, and about 50 yards in front of an old tramway. They did this because they could find no trench at their own objective, and so over-ran it. A platoon of the 12th dug in on the right of White, making the line take a curve towards the place where the remainder of the 9th was in Pozières Trench.

During this time some enemy snipers, in a position behind a wall a short distance ahead, caused many casualties among the 9th. Sergeant Deuchar took a small party to attack them; he himself climbed on to the wall and bombed the enemy out of their position, although he had received a bullet wound in his thigh. Between 12.30 and 1 a.m. Major W. McK. Young and Lieutenants C. A. Wittkopp and J. M. Lukin were wounded and Lieutenant W. Aggett was killed.

While the second and third objectives were being captured, keen fighting, chiefly with bombs, was going on in O.G. 1. Here the second objective could not be reached. The strong-post first attacked had been taken, but the Australians had not been able to force their way far up the trench, and help was asked of the artillery. After a heavy bombardment of the spot the attackers rushed in and pushed the enemy back. Hand-to-hand fighting continued for about fifteen hours, fortune favouring each side in turn, until finally the enemy was pushed back to a second strong-post farther up the trench.

From 1.30 a.m. onwards, the 9th in O.G. 1 was reinforced by a company of the 10th, and at daybreak by a further detachment of that battalion. The South Australians behaved most gallantly in this attack, especially Lieutenant Blackburn, who constantly led his men forward in the most daring manner. He was awarded the Victoria Cross for his exploits on this occasion. In the afternoon the 9th in this part of the field was in the eastern end of Pozières Trench, while the 10th occupied the captured portion of O.G. 1.

After daybreak, as those who were holding the line in Pozières village were sniped at a good deal from the ruins in front of them, small parties of Australians went out through these ruins to catch the snipers. The bombardment on both sides had practically ceased. On finding any cellar or dugout which they thought might contain snipers, they would throw into it a phosphorus bomb (known as a "P" bomb), with which many of the men had been issued before the attack. This filled the dugout with smoke, and perhaps set fire to it, so that any Germans sheltering there had to come out and be killed or captured.

The enemy launched several counter-attacks, but all failed. The first, which took place about 5.30 a.m., was made by several hundred Germans on the trenches occupied by the 9th and 12th, but, on being met by fire from rifles and one Lewis gun, they took cover in shell-holes. A few minutes later they rose up again and ran back under heavy fire. Although the German shelling had nearly stopped by daybreak, it recommenced at 6.25 a.m., and for the greater part of the day the troops had to endure very heavy bombardment.

Many men of "A" and "B" Companies were employed after the first attack as carrier parties. At midday an order given to seize the remainder of Pozières resulted in an advance by nightfall of a few hundred yards to the west and north of the village.

Owing to heavy casualties in the 3rd Brigade, troops of the 2nd Brigade were brought up next day, July 24th, and an attack on the German position in O.G. 2 was arranged by the 5th Battalion and part of the 7th. This was supported by the 9th and the 10th Battalions, who were by now very exhausted—many of the 9th, it must be remembered, had been fighting since the early morning of the 22nd. A jumping-off trench running north from the trench which they occupied, and fronting O.G. 1, had been dug by men of the 9th on the night of July 23rd/24th. This had not been finished by dawn, but was completed during the next night in time for the assault.

The attack began at 2 a.m. on the 25th, after a bombardment of the enemy trenches, the uncaptured portions of both O.G. lines this time being assaulted, not from along the trench, as on previous occasions, but from the front.

The 9th supported the operation with rifle and machine-gun fire while the 5th and 7th Battalions were coming up and until they had crossed the front line trench on their way to the jumping-off position, and also when they were attacking. They came up O.G. 1 and turned to the left into the front-line trench, whence they were helped over the parapet into the end of the jumping-off trench. The enemy's position in O.G. 1 was easily taken; although strong resistance was experienced in O.G. 2, it was captured at 3 a.m., by a detachment of the 5th Battalion, who had to evacuate it, however, at 4.30 since it afforded very little cover, and there appeared great danger of the Australians' being cut off.

In the meantime a party from the 10th and some men of "B" Company[3] of the 9th were engaged in a terrific bomb-fight against the enemy for the possession of two strong-points between O.G.1 and O.G.2, which resulted in alternate occupation of these points with many casualties on both sides. Men of the 5th, 7th, and 8th Battalions also took part in this bombing. Lance-Corporals Larsson and Swayn, in charge of parties carrying up supplies, arrived at the front line at this time, and, though well-nigh exhausted, both straightway lent a hand with the bombing. The supply of grenades was brought along the front-line trench—here the north-eastern end of

Pozières Trench—but between it and O.G. 1 was a tunnel. It was found impossible to get the bombs through this tunnel quickly enough, so Captain Collin called for a volunteer to pass them from one trench to the other over the top. Corporal Slaughter at once responded to the call, and, although aware that he was almost certain to become a casualty, for a quarter of an hour he moved quickly with the bombs backwards and forwards over the top until he was wounded. The Germans then counter-attacked our new line in O.G.1, and the men of "B" Company had to assist in beating them off.

Apart from the fighting around O.G.1, the men of the 9th merely held their part of the line during July 24th and 25th, improving the trenches as much as they could. At 4 a.m. on the 26th they were relieved. Thoroughly tired out, they struggled back to the brickfields at Albert, calling at the Comforts Fund stall in Bécourt Wood by the way for coffee and cigarettes. Some of the men sang and laughed with the reaction from the strain they had been enduring.

In the four days' battle all ranks had little or no sleep; when not engaged in fighting they were occupied in digging in, and all the time, both day and night, were under a heavy enemy bombardment. Some of the men were on duty for as long as six days with very little sleep. The feature most characteristic of this battle was the intense bombardment the troops had to endure, a bombardment which continued for days with hardly any pause.

Great credit is due to the stretcher-bearers, who night and day carried on magnificently with practically no rest, under shell-fire all the time. The evacuation of the wounded was found very difficult to effect, the arrangements made proving unequal to the strain. Aid posts were again and again blown to pieces and the wounded in them killed. Privates Graham and Chandler (known as the "war horses") stood out above all the other stretcher-bearers in the battalion for their gallantry; they kept on their work after other bearers had dropped out exhausted, and at times, when the communication trenches were choked with reinforcements coming up to the line, they climbed with their patients into the open and went on through the shell-fire without the slightest delay. Both subsequently received the D.C.M.

One of the padres[4] had acquired a stretcher on wheels, and going forward as far as he could during the battle, he used this

---

3 "A" Company was supporting the 11th, farther to the left.
4 It is uncertain which of the chaplains this was.

to bring back the wounded. When the battle was over he marched out bereft of great-coat and puttees, which he had handed over for the comfort of the wounded.

The signallers and runners, too, did well. Telephone communication was kept up between battalion headquarters and the forward companies. The telephone line forward of battalion headquarters was cut five or six times, but on each occasion Corporal Wagner travelled across the shell-swept area with new wire, quite disregarding the danger, and three times at least he narrowly escaped being killed.

The line to brigade headquarters, located in a chalk-pit 2,600 yards farther back, was cut so many times by shell-fire that it broke down completely, despite many attempts at repair. All messages back to the brigade staff had accordingly to be sent by runner. Their work required great gallantry, as they had of course to pass through the same bombardment which kept breaking the telephone lines. Company runners and signallers showed equal bravery, two of them being mentioned by name in the report of the action sent to the brigadier —Corporal Bale, who, when the communication trenches were blocked, often had to go through the enemy barrage across the open, and Lance-Corporal Horner who, despite the injuries he received when buried by a shell-burst early in the battle, continued at duty under the constant heavy shell-fire. Not satisfied with his work as runner, when not occupied with this duty, he acted as sentry and assisted in bringing up bombs and ammunition. Other men carrying up supplies of ammunition, rations, and water to the firing-line, also showed great devotion to duty.

Lieutenant Ruddle, the adjutant, a very efficient and popular officer, was mortally wounded in the head in the early hours of July 23rd, when he had gone a little way along the trench near the headquarters dugout to observe the progress of the attack on the strong-posts just ahead of Pozières Trench. Men of the 9th were near Ruddle giving supporting fire when he stood on the fire-step and looked over the parapet. Noticing that the men being fired on were Australians, he called out: "Don't shoot, boys; they're our men," and was hit immediately the words had left his lips; he died in the 9th Battalion aid post. Sergeants "Darky" Kenyon, D.C.M., and "Skinny" Heaton, D.C.M., were also killed on this day. Kenyon, who met his death in the open near the O.G. lines, was a daring soldier, very fierce in action, and he had played a leading part in Wilder-Neligan's raids on the Twin Trenches at Anzac and at Fleurbaix. He was one of the bravest and most adventurous soldiers in the whole A.I.F. Heaton also was a great soldier who had done well at Anzac; both he and Kenyon were old soldiers, having in former days served with the British Army. Their bodies were found by Lieutenant Armstrong and Private V. Bowman, who went out into the open on the afternoon of the 25th to collect water-bottles from the dead. Incidentally, they gathered two bags full of water-bottles.

Captain Knightley was wounded by a bomb but did not leave the line. Corporal Townsend, of "B" Company, was blown up by a shell, but not killed. He was said to be "too tough to kill." An old man, always called "Old Dad," he was never known to be on sick parade, although he would sometimes pay a stealthy visit to the aid post to ask for a pocketful of aspirins.

Instructions had been received from brigade headquarters that not more than twenty officers per battalion were to go into the battle, so as to prevent a shortage of officers in the event of heavy casualties. Some N.C.O.'s were also left out. This was the beginning of the "nucleus battalion," which comprised these reserve officers and N.C.O.'s and, at a later stage of the war, a proportion of privates.

The officers of the 9th who were present at the Battle of Pozières, including the preliminary operation on July 22nd, were:

Headquarters.—Lieutenant-Colonel Robertson, Major Salisbury, Captain Gibson, Lieutenants Ruddle, Page, Monteath and Biggs.

"A" Company.—Captain Knightley, Lieutenants Aggett, Blair, Thompson and Weynand.

"B" Company.—Captain Lawrance, Lieutenants Brennan, Cheshire, Devine and McNaught.

"C" Company.—Captain Chambers, Lieutenants Ramkema, White, and Wittkopp.

"D" Company.—Major W. M. Young, Captain Collin, Lieutenants Armstrong, Ford and Lukin.

During the battle a neighbouring battalion lost all its officers engaged, and a messenger from it reported to Captain Knightley that it badly needed a leader. Knightley thereupon left his company and took command of the other battalion, which was in a very hot corner. After the battle he found himself in trouble with his commanding officer for being absent from his company without leave, but no action was ever taken against him for this.

The casualties suffered by the 9th Battalion were: 3 officers and 54 other ranks killed, 8 officers and 263 O.R.'s wounded, 2 officers and 63 O.R.'s missing. The battalion had gone into action 1,016 strong and came out with 623. The scouts section suffered heavily, losing 22 out of its 28 men.

After the battle congratulations were received by the 1st Division from Sir Douglas Haig, the Army Commander (General Gough), General Birdwood, and the commander of the 1st British Division, which was fighting alongside the Australians. On arriving at Albert on July 26th a hot meal was served out as well as an issue of rum, after which all ranks, completely exhausted, slept for the rest of the morning. A huge mail had arrived at the Brickfields. The letters were given out, but large quantities of papers and magazines had to be burnt, as there was no time to distribute them. The battalion marched on in the afternoon to Warloy, "nestling in its green cup in the hills."[5] It was noticeable that many men were still chattering or laughing loudly, owing to the relaxation of the strain of the preceding days. Nearly everyone had a German cap or spiked helmet, or some other souvenir.

From Warloy the march was continued through La Vicogne to Berteaucourt, which was reached at 4 p.m. on the 29th. Although kits and blankets had been carried by waggons between Warloy and Berteaucourt, the march was very trying, as everyone was very footsore and quite worn out. A sergeant of another battalion,[6] which was passed on the march, described the appearance of the 9th:

> "They looked like men who had been in Hell. Almost without exception each man looked drawn and haggard, and so dazed that they appeared to be walking in a dream, and their eyes looked glassy and starey. . . . . . What they must have looked like before they had a night's sleep and clean-up must have been twice as bad as what we saw."

The men were cheered up on their arrival at Berteaucourt by the sight of the band of the 9th's daughter battalion, the 49th, which played them in to the village.

On the second day in this village the brigadier addressed the assembled troops at church parade. He thanked them for their efforts in taking Pozières, telling them that no troops in the world could have done better. This day the battalion received a welcome addition to its diminished numbers in the shape of 188 reinforcements, 40 more joining up on the following day.

5  3rd Battalion History.
6  Sgt. E. J. Rule, as quoted in the *Official History*.

The 9th remained eleven days at Berteaucourt. After a couple of days of rest, it occupied the time with training. The former battalion Lewis gun section was now divided up into detachments, each of 2 guns, 1 N.C.O. and 12 men, one going to each company. Eight of these light machine-guns were issued to the battalion, and four more were promised. The latter were for two battalion headquarters detachments, making a total personnel of 1 officer, 7 N.C.O.'s and 73 men. Sixteen men were also detailed for duty as rifle grenadiers attached to battalion headquarters; they began practising with the new Mills grenades for firing from rifles.

On August 9th the battalion, on its return journey to the line, left Berteaucourt for Bonneville, where it remained for five days. On the 6-mile march to Bonneville, the 9th, which was very proud of its march discipline, was leading the 3rd Brigade. It was a very hot day—incidentally, there had been a "beano" the night before—and when 32 of the Diggers fell out, the second-in-command shouted out to them angrily, "Call yourselves soldiers!—you ought to be waving flags at the 'Courier' corner." Those who fell out were noticed by R.S.M. Corfield to be almost all newly-joined reinforcements; he paraded them to the C.O., and they were then taken before the R.M.O. Those considered fit by him were ordered two hours' pack-drill.[7]

Bonneville proved a most uncomfortable village for billeting purposes. There was no water obtainable except the small allowance served out daily to each man for drinking purposes; if anyone wished to wash his face or hands or to shave, he had to use some of this allowance. The battalion was paid during the stay here, but as there was not a single shop in the village, there was no way of spending the money.

On arrival at Bonneville the men's blankets were withdrawn from them and they were left with only their greatcoats, as the weather was now warm and blankets were considered unnecessary. Two bootmakers, one being Sergeant Hopper, were now detailed.

On August 14th, the battalion marched nine miles to Hérissart. On this occasion the effect of the pack-drill of a few days before was seen, as no one fell out. The troops reached Hérissart at 4.30 p.m., their pockets full of the money they

---

[7] After fifteen minutes' drill, which was taken by Corfield, they were stood at ease, whereon one of them in an "Irish whisper," remarked, "Ain't he a b——." This was overheard by Corfield, who immediately replied: "I know I'm a b——, but I'm a persistent b——. Party, 'shun, slope arms, about turn, by the right, quick march. Come along, pick 'em up"—and on he carried with the pack-drill. This is said to be the last occasion on which pack-drill was ordered to men of the 9th.

had not been able to spend at Bonneville, but great was their disappointment on learning that they had arrived after the closing hour of the canteen, which had been established in this village. Next day the battalion went on to Vadencourt, where it bivouacked in "Rest Wood." Here the men were addressed by General Birdwood, who also decorated a number with the ribbons of the medals they had won. On August 16th the move was continued to the Albert brickfields, and while here all ranks were able to attend an open-air concert by the "Pierrot Concert Party." Very heavy rain began that night and continued for days, turning the bivouac into a field of soft slushy mud. Ground-sheets kept on sinking into the mud, and sleep was therefore rendered impossible for many.

While the 9th Battalion and the other units of the 1st Division were resting in the back areas, the Pozières heights had been captured, and the line was gradually pushed forward in the direction of Mouquet Farm, a large farmhouse now in ruins, on the crest of a rise about 1500 yards west-south-west of Thiepval and 2000 yards north-north-west of Pozières.

On the 16th Major Salisbury visited the line to inspect the positions opposite Mouquet Farm, returning to the brickfields to receive the news that he had been transferred to the 50th Battalion as its C.O. Thus ended a very distinguished career of two years with the 9th.

Salisbury had gone into camp on 22nd August, 1914, and sailed with the original battalion as O.C. "A" Company with the rank of captain. He was promoted to major at Mena, and within an hour or two after the 9th landed at Anzac he had to assume command, as all its other senior officers had become casualties. He directed its fighting during the critical first day and in the great Turkish counter-attack on May 19th, and continued to act as C.O. until Major Robertson returned on May 31st. Remaining on the Peninsula until compelled to leave on August 24th, owing to sickness, he rejoined the 9th at Lemnos at the beginning of December, and was with it during the Gebel Habeita period, its first days in France, and the heavy fighting at Pozières.

Though quiet and unassuming in manner, Salisbury was a strict disciplinarian, and his services to the 9th Battalion, especially at Anzac, were of the very highest value; it is surprising, indeed, that he was not earlier given a battalion command.

On August 19th the battalion went on to the old British lines at Bécourt Wood and received an issue of rations and water, then it marched through Sausage Valley straight into the line at Mouquet Farm, leaving a number of the officers and 15 per cent. of the sergeants behind in the "nucleus battalion." It had been intended that the troops should go up as far as possible towards the line in daylight. This was because of the poor state of the communication trenches, which were constantly being damaged by enemy bombardment—it seemed to many that there were no communication saps at all—and on account of the absence of well-defined landmarks, which made it difficult to find one's way. The route was through the village of Pozières, and all ranks remarked its thorough destruction, not a house nor even a wall being left standing.

"C" and "D" Companies reached the front line at midnight, relieving the 4th. As they marched in along "K" Trench they could see that the part of the line they were bound for was under heavy shell-fire, and on reaching the last ridge they lost a good many men going down the slope towards the trenches. "D" Company became lost in a sap leading off from "K" Trench, but eventually found the right way again.

The 9th Battalion, in front of Mouquet Farm, was to hold the left of the sector allotted to the 3rd Brigade, with the 12th Battalion in the centre and the 10th on the right. The 11th Battalion was to provide the carrying parties. Facing the 10th and 12th was an enemy trench known as the "Fabeck Graben," which extended from Mouquet Farm eastwards.

The part of the line taken over by the 9th consisted of three disconnected shallow trenches, of which the right-hand one was linked up with the rest of the line, but the troops had to go over the open to reach the other two. The middle trench was just in advance of the top of the Quarry, a large semi-circular chalk-pit, about thirty feet deep, with its open end facing towards our rear. "C" Company held the right flank trench and "D" Company the middle and left flank trenches. From part of "D" Company's lines the farm could be seen 100-150 yards away.

The men who were relieved were in a very bad state. Most of those who had come in with them had been either killed or wounded, and those who remained were so affected by the constant bombardment that they could not give the relieving troops any information, but simply went out of the line as fast as they could go. Owing to the heavy bombardment of the forward area, it was considered advisable that the line should only be thinly held.

"A" and "B" Companies were battalion reserve. "B" Company was stationed in "Fourth Avenue," a trench about 400 yards behind the front line; about 700 yards farther in the rear was a cemetery, and Captain Knightley lined "A" Company out along a footpath leading from it towards "Gibraltar," a concrete strong-post on the western side of Pozières, which had been captured on July 23rd. This footpath was backed by a very shell-torn hedge, little more than the roots of the shrubs remaining; the men huddled near the hedge-roots and kept still, Knightley judging that it would be safer there than in a trench. This was quite a new position for reserves, and was unsuspected by the enemy, with the result that no casualties were received by "A" Company while stationed there. Battalion headquarters was in "Park Lane," a trench about 300 yards behind the front line, while advanced brigade headquarters was in Gibraltar.

Anyone going up to the front line would, after leaving Gibraltar, first of all proceed along "K" Trench, pass "A" Company on the right, and then "B" on the left in Fourth Avenue, before reaching "Park Lane," which branched off to the right. Finally, crossing the top of the ridge and going down the slope towards the farm, one would come to the 9th Battalion's sector of the front line, which began at "K" Trench and went off to the left. Actually, though, a person going up would not continue straight on all the way, as a part of "K" Trench had become so badly damaged that it offered no protection at all. The usual course was to turn down a trench to the right after passing Fourth Avenue, and then again to the left up a sap, which would bring him out near battalion headquarters in Park Lane.

After the front line had been taken over, the remainder of the night was spent in joining up and deepening the disconnected trenches; by daylight they were a little more than knee-deep. In some places the earth was so loose that it would continually fall in under the concussion of the shell-bursts, while in other places it was hard chalk and difficult to dig. Sergeant Preston, of "C" Company, gives a graphic description of his reconnaissance before beginning work on the trenches:—

"I received orders from Captain Chambers that I must have our line connected up with our left flank before daylight, so, as the shell-fire was terrific all the time, and it was pitch dark, I took two men with me and moved out to our left flank where I thought 'D' Company was likely to be. After I had gone about ten or twelve yards I told one man to stay there, and if I did not come back in a reasonable time to go back and report; then I moved out about another ten or twelve yards and posted the other man, but there was still no sign of 'D' Company, so I moved on by myself what seemed to be about 200 yards (but which was really about 80), and after being knocked down several times by bursting 9.2's, I eventually came on 'D' Company's right flank with Corporal W. Bruce in charge of a party of men digging a trench towards 'C' Company, he said. I then gave him our position and started back for our trench, but was knocked down again by the concussion of a big shell and lost my bearings for a time, but eventually found my way back."

There was an open flank on the left of the 9th Battalion. Several patrols attempted to get into touch with the flanking battalion, but they could find no one. Other patrols were sent out with instructions to locate the enemy outposts and, if possible, to bomb them out, but the posts were found to be too strong. From an enemy trench close in front of our line a good deal of shooting and bombing went on.

For the whole of the next day (Sunday, August 20th) the troops in the line were under shell-fire, which became unusually active about 5 p.m., a heavy barrage being then put down between the supports and the front garrison. This barrage was renewed periodically until the morning, when it subsided, but the general enemy bombardment continued. On the 21st, the German shelling was particularly heavy, and in addition the front line of the 9th received shells from one of the British batteries, which was continually firing short. The companies in the front trench were kept busy all day attending to wounded and digging out men who were buried. Badly shell-shocked cases were taken to the Quarry and put in a little lean-to hut which, besides being used as "D" Company headquarters, also accommodated the stretcher-bearers.

The enemy had during the day observed men of the 10th and 12th Battalions coming up to reinforce the firing line, and late in the afternoon his artillery placed a special barrage on "K" Trench.

At 5.30 p.m. an intense bombardment was directed against all our lines, but as the men in the front line, assisted by the reserve companies and some pioneers, had been spending as much time as they could in the past two days in deepening their trenches, casualties were not as heavy as they might otherwise have been.

This day the 3rd Brigade attacked Mouquet Farm and the Fabeck Graben—the first of several attacks in broad daylight made by the Australians on this battlefield. The artillery barrage had been rehearsed beforehand; other preliminary bombardments which had been made were not followed by any attack, so as to confuse the enemy.

It had been the intention originally that the 9th Battalion should take part in the operation, but as it became apparent that there would be no hope of success in an advance in its particular area, the plans were altered, so that it would merely give covering fire to the other battalions which attacked. Arrangements were made for 200 men of the 11th Battalion to occupy the front line between the 10th and the 12th and to join in the attack.

At 4 p.m. orders were received by the 9th Battalion to send two platoons of a reserve company to support the attack of the 11th, in case that battalion was late in arriving at its position and its men were not all there by the time fixed for the assault. These platoons were delayed owing to the congested state of the trenches, and the heavy hostile bombardment, so that they did not reach the 11th Battalion trenches until 5.55, five minutes before "zero" hour. They found the front-line trenches occupied by men from the 11th[8] and by engineers. No one seemed to be in charge, and the senior officer with the two platoons was told that they were not wanted. However, he kept his men where they were and sent another officer back to battalion headquarters for instructions. Colonel Robertson ordered the two platoons to withdraw.

From 1.30 to 2.30 p.m. there had been a bombardment of the enemy by our heavy artillery. The attack itself was accompanied by a creeping barrage resting for two minutes half-way to the Fabeck Graben, then for three minutes on it, then lifting beyond.

At 6 p.m. the 10th Battalion attacked, capturing a part of Fabeck Graben, but it had to retire, as both its flanks were in the air, that is, without any troops continuing the line. "A" Company of the 9th, under Captain Knightley, then joined the 10th, and the two detachments dug in slightly in advance of the jumping-off position. The 12th also advanced at 6 p.m. and captured its objective. Some of the men entered Mouquet Farm, and it was reported captured, but they withdrew from it as it soon came under heavy shell-fire both from the enemy artillery and from our own guns. The enemy later reoccupied the farm.

The 11th Battalion did not attack until midnight. It was not at all to blame for this, the delay being due in the first place to the very short notice that it was required to go into the line, and later to the heavy shelling it received on the way up, as well as to the congestion of the saps and roads

---

[8] An advance party.

it had to use. When the 11th advanced it seized a line joining the positions of the 10th and 12th, and after dawn made a further advance without any assistance from the artillery. Some of the 10th had been cut off by the enemy in Fabeck Graben, but this does not seeem to have been known to the authorities in rear, as at 6 a.m. both corps and division headquarters were under the impression that Fabeck Graben had been captured.

This had been a very difficult operation to carry out. The sap through which "A" Company had gone up to join the 10th was so filled with dead and dying that the men had to leave it several times and walk along the surface to avoid treading on the casualties.

Half-a-dozen men became separated from the others by the time they reached the neighbourhood of Park Lane, where the downward slope began which was under direct observation by the enemy. However, they were in a part of the sap where the sides were as high as the tops of their heads. Suddenly shells from the right flank began to fall directly on the spot at which they had arrived. The wall was blown in beyond and behind them, so they waited for a while where they were in the hope that the shelling would ease down a little. One man found a better position in a dugout on the right-hand side of the sap.

The shells continued to fall, blowing away more and more of each end of the length of sap wall which was sheltering the men. Closer and closer they huddled together behind the gradually diminishing shelter, until one shell registered a bull's-eye, and most of the party were hit. Those who were able began to withdraw further back along the sap, but one, wounded while attempting to crawl into the dugout, fell there, blocking the entrance. As the others retired, an angry voice was heard from inside the dugout: "Hey, you blokes, don't go away and leave me, there's a dead man blocking up the door, I can't get out." Some of the party pulled away the supposed corpse and set free the prisoner.

Next day the front line was continually under shell-fire. Early in the morning it was misty, so supplies could be brought up, and a number of officers from the nucleus battalion arrived to replace those who had become casualties or who were exhausted. At night-time great difficulty was experienced in transporting supplies owing to the ground's being so cut up and to the absence of landmarks. The wants of the troops were not many; none of them ate anything, as they were too shaken by the shell-fire. Cigarettes and drinks of water supported them for the three days they were here.

On the afternoon of the 22nd Captain Monteath was instructed to confer with Major Rafferty and Captain Vowles of the 12th Battalion, with a view to surrounding the farm. The conference, in which Captain Collin also participated, took place to the right of the Quarry and close in front of the farm, and all agreed that the project was impracticable without the assistance of an additional battalion.

Everyone was by now suffering from want of sleep and much shaken by the incessant heavy shell-fire, which was even heavier than that which they had experienced at Pozières at the end of July. Among the casualties were Captain Chambers and Lieutenant Pettigrew, O.C. and second-in-command respectively of "C" Company, who were killed by one shell, and Company-Sergeant-Major J. L. Saunders. The two former were buried just behind the trenches, and Captain Collin had to assume command of both "C" and "D" Companies.

At the close of the afternoon of August 22nd the 24th Battalion, on its way in to relieve the 9th, came under enemy observation as soon as it began to move down the open slope forward of Park Lane. The 24th was in close formation, and a tremendous enemy barrage opened not only on this area but on the communications further back, so for a while, all movement of troops was stopped.

The 24th was badly cut up by this bombardment, and it was not until about 8 p.m. that the relief of the reserve companies was able to be effected. The relief of the front-line companies took place at 3.30 a.m. on the 23rd. Captain Collin handed over his front, which had been held by two companies, to an N.C.O. of the 24th, as all the officers in his relief had become casualties. By this time it was daylight, and now arose the difficulty of getting the men of the 9th back safely. They had to go out in "dribs and drabs," and it was hours before the last of them had left the front line; there were some even who did not come out until the next night.

The casualties during the tour were: 3 officers and 24 other ranks killed, 2 officers and 123 O.R.'s wounded, 12 O.R.'s missing—total, 5 officers and 159 O.R.'s.

# CHAPTER X.

### YPRES AND FLERS.

On coming out of the line the battalion went back to the bivouac at Brickfield Hill, Albert, and left the same afternoon for Warloy. The next day, August 24th, it marched through Hérissart and Talmas to Beauval. The men were much troubled with sore feet through having worn their boots continuously while in the trenches, and at the close of the day's march sixty men reported at sick parade with raw sores on their heels as large as half-crowns.

For this march "D" Company was somewhat late on parade. A written message from battalion headquarters was sent by runner late at night to the companies with orders to move off on the following morning. When the runner reached "D" Company he woke the O.C. from his first real sleep for several days. Captain Collin signed the foot of the message to signify that he had seen it and had noted its contents, and then promptly turned over and went to sleep again. In the morning three companies fell in but no "D" Company appeared. A messenger to the O.C. found him still asleep, and when awakened he protested that he had had no orders to fall in the company. He had quite forgotten his being awakened during the night, and it was not until he was shown his signature on the message that he realised the true facts of the case.

Next day the march was continued to Doullens, where the battalion entrained at midnight for Flanders. Reaching Proven at 8.30 a.m. on the 26th it marched to Poperinghe, to be billeted in a large building with the French word HOUBLONS (hops) painted on its front in large black letters; it had been formerly in use as a warehouse for hops, one of the main products of Flanders. Poperinghe was the largest town that the men of the 9th had been stationed in up to this time. They were now in divisional reserve in the Ypres[1] sector.

"Blighty" leave, which had been stopped during the Pozières and Mouquet Farm operations, was now resumed.

---

1 Ypres was usually pronounced by the Australian troops as "Yeeps," while the "Tommies" called it "Wipers." The correct pronunciation is something very like Eeprer, with the first syllable long and the second cut very short, although many of our men said that they could only distinguish the native pronunciation as "Eep."

About this time Captain Gibson went on leave and Captain W. R. Aspinall took over as R.M.O. while he was away. Aspinall was later detailed to an artillery unit and was killed at Ypres in July, 1917.

On August 29th the battalion left for a camp known as "Connaught Lines," near Reninghelst, a few miles south of Poperinghe. It was on this day that the scout section was re-formed under Lieutenant Brown. On September 1st came

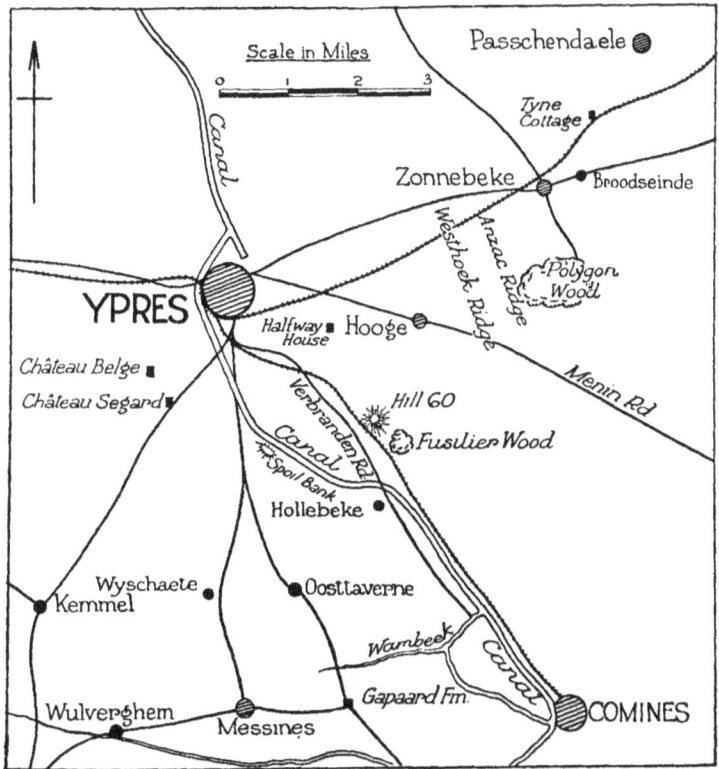

16. The Ypres-Messines Area.

another move, to the "Devonshire Lines," a hutted camp half-a-mile east-south-east of Busseboom. Close by was a divisional variety concert party giving performances. The whole battalion was taken to this at a cost of 120 francs (about £4/5/-), which was paid out of regimental funds.

On Sunday, September 2nd, the divisional commander, General Walker, attended a church parade of the 9th and 12th Battalions. He spoke to the C.O.'s afterwards, telling them that although the Mouquet Farm engagement was not a complete success, the 3rd Brigade had done as well as it was possible for troops to do.

During the next few days officers visited the front line in batches. Battalion sports were held on September 9th with a concert and boxing contest in the evening. The whole day's entertainment was very successful and was much enjoyed by all.

On September 12th the battalion marched to Brandhoek, then went seven miles by rail to Ypres, detraining there and marching three miles to the front line, in the Hill 60 sector W.S.W. of Ypres. Here it relieved the Canadians. The trenches were greatly in want of repair, so much good work was done in improving them; but heavy rain caused parapets to fall in, and on the 18th every available man in the battalion was working at them, using 5000 sandbags. In the actual front-line trench there was slush and water up to the men's knees, and every man had been issued with rubber thigh boots. By this time the weather had become very cold. Summer seemed to have suddenly vanished and to have been replaced by winter.

The Australians had been sent to the Ypres sector for a rest, after the heavy fighting on the Somme. The Germans were employing the area for the same purpose, so that it indeed proved a period of quiet, even if not of physical repose, for both sides. The front line was held much more lightly than usual, by about 200 men to every thousand yards. These men were kept in strong-points, and merely patrolled the trenches between. About 400 men per thousand yards were kept in a support line about 300 yards in rear.

Detachments from the support companies were engaged in building deep dugouts. Some men in the front line were detailed to guard mine-shafts, as in this area several galleries were being driven beneath the enemy trenches; much of the fatigue work consisted in carrying up timber for these mines and explosives for charging them. The enemy also was doing a great deal of mining here.

Patrols were sent out at night to see how much of the opposing trenches was occupied by the enemy, as it was suspected that some of them were empty during the day, being only garrisoned after dark. As soon as darkness set in on September 17th a fighting patrol of five scouts, two bombing teams, and one Lewis gun team went out with the intention of occupying a trench which had been observed by a patrol on the previous night to contain some of the enemy. It had been noticed that this trench was unoccupied during the day, so the patrol hoped to get there first and attack the German garrison when it came to take up its accustomed position.

The patrol was crawling towards the enemy trench, with a bombing team on each flank, when suddenly a shower of stick grenades fell around it, followed by flares and more bombs. In the light of the flares about 50 Germans could be seen advancing. The patrol seemed almost surrounded, so Lieutenant Brown yelled: "Get back for your lives," and the order was carried out at top speed without a single casualty.

The Germans here made much use of the *minenwerfer* (nicknamed the "minnie"), a large trench-mortar throwing a sausage-shaped bomb about two feet long and $9\frac{1}{2}$ inches in diameter.[2] Strangely enough, it was called by us a "rum-jar." Fortunately this could be seen coming through the air, and thus one had a chance of avoiding it. A diary says: "Fritz sent over big bombs the size of oil drums and called rum jars. They make a great noise and a big hole, but are not very deadly." However, these weapons were not at all popular with our men, and the story goes that a "Fritz" prisoner, on being captured, put up his hands and, thinking to soften the hearts of the "fierce Australians," called out: "Me not soldier, me minenwerfer." One can imagine the pleasant welcome this self-styled non-combatant would have received from men who had suffered under the bombardment of the "minnies." The British replied to these bombs with Stokes mortars and the new rifle-grenades; sometimes regular "rum jar" and "Stokes" duels took place. All this added a great deal of zest to life here.

Enemy snipers were very active in this area. The scout section found that periscopes were broken as soon as they were put up. One scout stated that "there is no such thing as looking over the top here, a person wouldn't last one minute." On one occasion, Colonel Robertson went up to try out a new telescopic periscope which was fitted with a large mirror measuring about 8 inches by 6. As soon as this mirror appeared above the parapet it brought a shower of rifle-grenades from the enemy, so the trial of the periscope came to a sudden end.

2 All "minnies," however, were not of so large a bore as this. The name minenwerfer means "mine-thrower."

The rats in this part of the line are worthy of mention. Large and hairy, they swarmed in thousands. The ground here was full of corpses—parties frequently cut through them when digging—and the rats fed on these. The only way to keep food away from them was to put it in tins; even greasy patches were eaten from men's uniforms and equipment while they slept.

The unit spent from the 19th to the 24th of September at "Halifax Camp," two miles east of Busseboom, and from the 24th to the 30th at Château Belge, a mile south-east of Ypres. As the camp at Château Belge had not been kept in a very good state of repair, a party of 50 men was detailed to make the dugouts shell-proof and to repair the bunks—wooden frames with wire netting nailed over them for mattresses. It was arranged that when the 9th left the camp these 50 men would remain under an officer to carry on the work and attempt to make this policy a continuous one.

On October 1st the battalion went into the line for another week, relieving the 10th in the sector stretching from the railway to Verbranden Road, immediately to the right of that which it had previously garrisoned. The trenches here were in what was suspected to be an enemy mine-centre, and because of this they were ordered to be held lightly. They were very close to the enemy lines, being in one place only 25 yards distant. Once more every available man had to work on improving the trenches, and, although they were made much better, one of the officers described the accommodation as "ghastly." There had been a great amount of rain, and mud and wet were more formidable enemies for the time being than the Germans. On October 8th the 7th Battalion took over the line, and the 9th went out to "Dominion Camp," a mile north of Ouderdom and close behind the front.

Four days were spent here, after which the battalion marched to Bayenghem-les-Eperleques by way of Steenvoorde, Oost Houck and Moulle, stopping one night at each place. Between Oost Houck and Moulle it crossed some hilly country near Watten and had fine views of the plains on both sides, with little villages dotted here and there. At Bayenghem the accommodation was very poor, but after some trouble sufficient billets were secured for the whole battalion, some in the neighbouring village of La Commune—called by the troops "Rum Hollow," as rum was the only liquid refreshment which could be bought there.

While here the troops were given an opportunity of voting in the referendum being taken at the same time in Australia to determine whether or not enlistment in the A.I.F. should be made compulsory. The result of the referendum was that conscription was rejected by a majority of 72,476, 1,087,557 voting for it and 1,160,033 against it. The votes of the soldiers on active service, together with those in transports, and in camp in England, Australia and elsewhere, taken separately, gave a majority of 13,505 in favour of conscription, the figures being 72,399 for and 58,894 against.

The weather was now rapidly becoming colder, with heavy frosts in the mornings. On October 19th Captain A. McKillop, the M.O. who had been wounded at Rouge de Bout on April 20th, 1916, returned to the battalion, relieving Captain Gibson. Next day it was learned that the 1st Division was to return to the Somme, and the men had visions of again having to endure the nerve-shattering bombardments and heavy casualty lists of Pozières. The 9th left at midday and marched to Audriucq, a village on the railway to Calais; here it entrained, and, going by way of Calais, Boulogne, Etaples, and Abbeville, arrived at Pont-Remy, near the mouth of the Somme, at 1 a.m. on the 21st.

An accident unfortunately occurred during this journey as a result of which Private C. J. Haines, one of the battalion's original members, lost a leg. The train had stopped near an *estaminet* and a number of men got out. Suddenly the train started without warning, as was the habit of troop-trains, and while trying to board it Haines slipped beneath the wheels.

A march of five miles brought the battalion to Vauchelles-les-Quesnoy, and after a two days' stay it marched six miles to a place where it was picked up by motor-buses and taken to Buire-sous-Corbie, where the night was spent in tents. Fricourt was reached next day, which was very wet, and here the accommodation was in huts. The mud, rain and cold were very trying. When the 9th was last in this area Fricourt was almost in the front line, but now it was five miles in rear. They remained here for a week, the 1st Division being in reserve.

Mud was one of the features of the campaign both on the Somme and Ypres battlefields, but it was at its worst on the Somme. Even the rear areas often became in wet weather a mucky dark-brown or dark-grey sea of mud several inches deep. It was quite common to put one's foot down in the mud and to draw it up again minus the boot; men and horses often stuck and had to be pulled out, the men sometimes leaving their boots and even their trousers behind. The horses, of course, were not in the front line, but these muddy conditions extended a long way back. The boots left in the mud were usually rubber thigh-boots, but even ordinary boots, if they were not tightly laced, were sometimes held in the mud.

Trench feet now began to cause much trouble. This complaint was due to the feet being constantly wet as well as cold; they became swollen and numb, and in bad cases they turned black and had to be amputated. It was found that whale oil helped to prevent it, and this was issued to all ranks now to be rubbed on the feet. In addition, all were provided with three pairs of socks and so were able to keep their feet drier. Dubbin, a greasy preparation, was also issued for rubbing on boots to make them more waterproof.

Later, following the practice in the French Army, French chalk, containing some boracic acid and camphor, was used instead of whale oil, and it seemed to be more effective. However, by the time when it was adopted in the British Army various other preventive methods, such as constant drying of socks, and the provision of hot food and drinks in the front line, were coming into use, and it was probably these methods, and not the French chalk, which brought about the improvement.

On October 30th the battalion went on four miles to Bernafay Wood, 1000 yards east of Montauban. It took six hours for those on foot to travel this distance, and twelve hours for the battalion transport, so great was the congestion of traffic.

The sides of the road were two feet deep in mud, and on the road surface itself there was a double line of wheeled conveyances, one column going forward and one returning; communication was frequently interrupted, and vehicles sometimes had to make long pauses in their progress. Marching infantry had to make their way as well as they could among and through and at the side of this traffic.

On arriving at their destination, $3\frac{1}{2}$ miles behind the front line, the men found the ground a sea of slushy mud, and it began to rain heavily as they entered the canvas shelters in which they were to live. The rain continued all night, but in the morning, as it stopped, all the shelters were taken down and re-erected in a new position not quite so muddy. The clouds cleared away in the afternoon of this day and there was considerable aerial activity. One diary records: "The air was alive with 'planes, counted over twenty observation balloons."

There was a great scarcity of drinking-water. It is true that there were innumerable shell-holes everywhere and that each one was full of water, but the water was very muddy, and one never knew what might lie beneath its yellow surface. Any kind of rubbish might be there, or even a corpse. On November 1st the battalion went a couple of miles further back to Pommier Camp, between Montauban and Mametz, finding it, like Bernafay Wood, a sea of mud. The troops remained here a week,

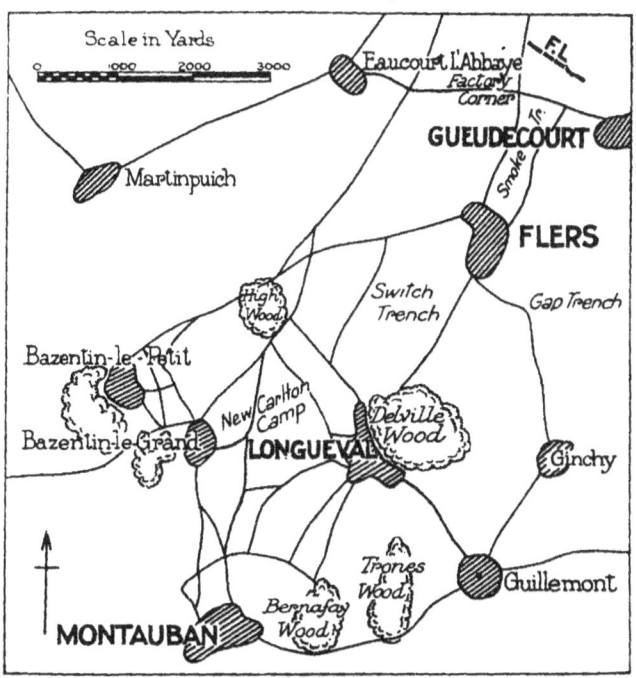

17. The Flers Area.
F.L.—Front line, December 21-30, 1916, according to map locations given in the battalion diary.

and a supply of sheepskin vests and gloves was issued to them. The vests, made of sheepskin tanned with the wool on, were sleeveless and were worn over the tunic. They were a great help to all in the excessively cold weather being experienced. At this time there was also a daily issue of rum.

On November 4th everyone was greatly interested to see one of the new "tanks" passing the rear of the camp, and to the great delight of all it had no difficulty in making its way through mud eighteen inches deep.

Next day the 1st Division took part in an attack, which had several times been postponed on account of the wet weather, the 3rd Brigade being reserve brigade. On November 7th the battalion moved again to Bernafay Wood and still found the mud as much in evidence as before. One man wrote: "Still raining all the time, and water and slush thigh deep everywhere"; and the battalion diary for the 8th stated: "Raining. The whole country is a quagmire."

On November 9th the 9th Battalion went into the line at Flers, relieving the 2nd Battalion about 9 p.m., and coming for the time being under the command of the 1st Brigade. "D" Company occupied the front line, which was not continuous here, there being a gap of 200 yards on our right flank between the 9th and the 10th Battalions, and one of 100 yards farther to the left. The fire-trench was in a fearful condition. The mud in the bottom was twelve inches deep, with occasional small patches going down to a depth of two feet. Most of it was thick and sticky, but some of the deeper patches were thin and watery.

There being no shelter in the front-line trench, men had perforce to stand there exposed to the rain, or to sit on a ledge scooped out of the side of the trench. Happy was he who found protruding from the mud the top of a petrol tin or ammunition case on which he could put his feet. Just as the battles of Pozières and Mouquet Farm were noted for the terrific enemy bombardments, so Flers was remembered by the troops on account of its mud. One Digger grimly described it as "the defunct village that lends its name to the sector of mud and corpses that we guarded for the winter."

Measures were taken to improve these conditions. There was a shortage of duckboards—sections of open-work boarding, composed of short strips of wood nailed across two long beams. However, parties were organised to scoop out the mud and slush and throw it over the sides of the trenches, and by the 12th the front-line trench was clear of mud—at least for the time being, for as the rains returned so did the mud. A new communication sap was dug, as the existing one was so muddy as to be useless, and all traffic to and from the front line had to be over the surface of the ground.

The weather was also very cold, so under these conditions it is not surprising that sickness occurred among the troops. A number of men, most of them suffering from trench-feet, were evacuated during the four days the battalion was here. Officers were instructed to make frequent foot-inspections, and Lieutenant King, with a small party, was specially detailed to attend to the distribution of whale-oil and the treatment of cases of trench-feet not severe enough to justify evacuation.

On the 10th the men had the pleasure of seeing a German aeroplane brought down in front of our line. Next day two Germans came into a sap which had been advanced from our front-line trench, and gave themselves up. The battalion had but few casualties from enemy action while in this position, as there had not been much shelling of our line.

On the 13th an attack was made by the Fifth Army on our left, resulting in the capture of St. Pierre Divion and Beaumont Hamel. The part played by the Fourth Army (of which the I Anzac Corps now formed a part) in this was a feint artillery bombardment on our own front. In view of enemy artillery retaliation, the front-line garrison was reduced to a very small number; no casualties were suffered by the 9th.

About this time the Germans were using a high tower in the distance for observation. It was decided to destroy this, and a large naval gun was brought into action. The artillery observer was in an advanced post on the 9th Battalion sector, and the first shot registered a direct hit on the tower.

By this time the fire-trench had been so much improved that it was possible for men to sit down under cover. A new line had also been dug for the support company, bringing it much more forward. Stew and tea were brought up to the front line in great metal containers about three feet high and eighteen inches wide, strapped to men's backs; each vessel held sufficient for about 40 men. The space between the inner and outer walls of the containers was filled with a non-conducting material which gave to the container more or less of the properties of a vacuum flask and kept the food hot for several hours. The men carrying the hot rations found it very exhausting work ploughing their way through the mud under these heavy loads, especially as they carried also a rifle and ammunition.

The battalion went out of the line on the evening of the 13th, using the new communication sap which had been dug, and returned to its old camp at Bernafay Wood. The next day it moved to Fricourt, to a camp which, although the surroundings were very muddy, was fairly good, as it consisted of iron huts. These buildings were called Nissen huts; the roofs and sides consisted of curved sheets of corrugated iron forming a half-cylinder, with wooden ends and floors. The huts were lined with wood when they were newly built, but most of this lining found its way into braziers. While here, the battalion received a batch of reinforcements.

On November 18th the unit was drawn up in hollow square just off the Montauban road, above the camp, and Lieutenant-Colonel J. C. Robertson addressed them to bid them farewell, as he was leaving to go to the 4th Division to take command of the 12th Infantry Brigade. He had commanded the 9th from the 31st of May, 1915, and as an original officer had landed with it at Anzac, shared its inconveniences during a considerable part of the Gallipoli period and in the desert at Gebel Habeita, led it into France, suffered the anguish of "C" Company's "black day" at Rouge de Bout, enjoyed the glory of Neligan's raid at the same place, and fathered the old battalion at Pozières and Mouquet Farm.

Major Neligan, who now temporarily assumed command of the battalion, ordered all headquarters details to be organised as a company, having its own cooks. As there was not a spare field kitchen available, the cooks had to use the ordinary army dixies for their work.

After four days at Fricourt, the battalion marched to Buire, and, after staying there for one night, went in motor-buses to Cardonette, near Amiens, where eleven days were spent in training. Many of the men took the opportunity of visiting the interesting old town of Amiens, which the Australians were destined to help in saving nearly eighteen months later, when it was threatened with capture by the enemy. Winter had set in thoroughly by this time, and everyone had become quite used to the sight of snow, which most of the Australians now saw for the first time.

On November 30th the 9th left Cardonette to return by stages to the line, spending one night in Franvillers, two days in Dernancourt, and one bitterly cold night in Nissen huts at Fricourt before reaching Bazentin-le-Grand on December 4th. Here were tents which had been newly erected the day before, but when the troops entered them they found the floor to consist of about six inches of mud. For eight days the battalion was quartered at Bazentin, supplying fatigue and working parties, while the 12th Battalion held the line in front of Flers.

Plate xii.

26.—BRIG.-GEN. J. CAMPBELL ROBERTSON, C.B., C.M.G., D.S.O.

Plate xiii.

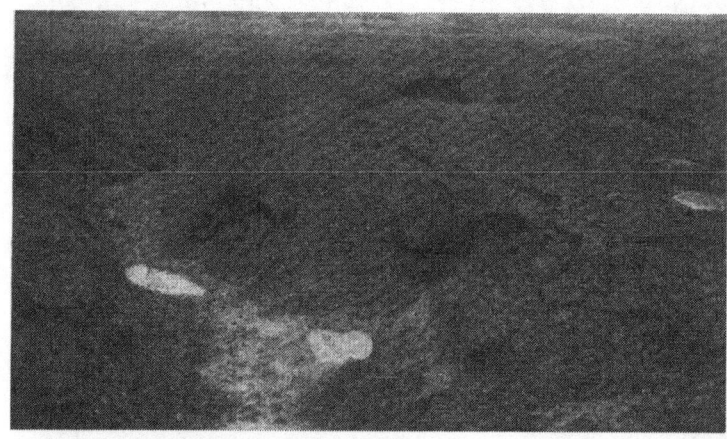

**27.—YELLOW CUT NEAR THE MAZE. (See p. 161.)**
(Aust. War Memorial Official Photograph, No. E 220, Copyright. Taken in February, 1917.
From the Official History).

**28.—A FLAMMENWERFER. (See p. 177.)**
(Aust. War Memorial Official Photograph, No. E 802, Copyright.)

On the day after the arrival at Bazentin, Captain C. F. Ross, Lieutenant C. J. Carroll and Lieutenant S. J. Chapman with his scouts were sent up to the front line so as to become familiar with it. They were ordered to go to "Factory Corner," where the "left battalion" headquarters were supposed to be. However, they found this to be incorrect, as that situation was occupied by the King's Royal Rifle Corps, so they had a look round and returned, Ross and Carroll going straight towards Bazentin, and Chapman more to the right towards High Wood, behind which were some of our 60-pounder guns. As Chapman and the scouts approached these guns enemy shells began to fall close to them.

> "The shells kept getting closer and closer (writes one of the party, Mr. V. A. Bowman, in his diary), and just as we reached High Wood a salvo lobbed all around us. 'Scotty' Boyd was just in front of me. He went down. I grabbed him and with the help of Lieutenant Chapman carried him to a bit of shelter 30 yards away. Poor old 'Scotty' never spoke and passed out in a couple of minutes. Harry Charlton and Vin. Scully were wounded by this same shell."

The next day the padre and two of the men went back to the spot and buried him. On the day after three of his comrades took up a cross which had been made by the pioneers, and placed it on the grave.

On December 8th Major L. M. Mullen (12th Bn.), who had just been promoted to lieutenant-colonel, assumed command of the 9th. On December 12th it became support battalion to the 10th, which on this day relieved the 12th in the front line. The 9th moved to the vicinity of Flers, battalion headquarters being quartered in what remained of the village—mostly mud—"A" Company in "Switch Trench," "B" Company in "Gap Trench," "C" and "D" Companies in "New Carlton Camp." The troops found themselves greeted on their first night here by a fall of snow.

After staying here for nine days, on the 21st the battalion moved into the front line, "A" and "B" Companies occupying the actual front line with "C" and "D" in close support in "Smoke Trench" and its vicinity. "A" Company was in the right sector and was separated from "B" Company by a gap of two hundred yards which could not be crossed in daylight. There was also a gap to the right of "A" Company. These gaps were patrolled during the night, an operation which was most disagreeable. One man described it as:—

> "the worst place I have ever patrolled. Crawling in mud everywhere, and when you stop in a shell-hole for a 'breather,' the cold is unbearable."

Where the trenches were not revetted the sides often fell in. A great deal of work was done in cleaning and repairing these trenches.

The battalion now numbered 36 officers and 877 other ranks. Battalion headquarters was over a mile behind the front line, which in the right sector contained one deep dugout where "C" Company Headquarters and a number of men were sheltered, but in the left sector, where there was no cover, company headquarters consisted of a couple of waterproof sheets laid over some small cross-pieces of wood. The weather during this tour in the line was usually foggy with light misty rain, but at times it would become very cold and ice would begin to form on top of the water and slush.

On December 23 "C" and "D" Companies relieved "A" and "B" in the front-line trench, and hereafter the front-line companies were relieved every day. It had now been raining heavily for two days, and the shell-hole puddles were becoming joined up to form a waist-deep marsh. At half-past three next morning "D" Company noticed a party of six Germans walking towards our line. They were fired on by a Lewis gun and three were wounded, whereupon the others surrendered. One of the wounded men died in our trenches, but the other two were able to walk. They were a carrying party of the 173rd Bavarian Regiment, and had lost themselves.

About the same time a similar mishap nearly occurred to a ration party of eight 9th Battalion men, who fortunately heard voices talking in German when they were close to the enemy trench. Thus warned, they turned back and reached our own lines safely.

Christmas Day was spent in cleaning and repairing the front line. The artillery now had abundant ammunition, and by orders of Sir Douglas Haig every gun in the Fourth and Fifth Armies fired on this day at spots likely to be occupied by the enemy, at a time when it was thought probable that the Germans would be sitting down at their dinner. The enemy replied to this bombardment, and a good many shells fell in "Smoke Trench" while the officers there were having *their* Christmas dinner of tinned plum pudding with a dash of condensed milk.

The shelling was renewed during the afternoon, and Flers and its vicinity were bombarded heavily. One shell burst in a small dugout occupied by Privates Ford and Graham. Graham was killed instantly, but Ford was unhurt.[3]

[3] At the end of February, 1917, Ford was killed instantly by a shell while in the line before The Maze.

119 partially trained reinforcements were sent up at this time, but were not allowed to join the battalion. For the time being they were quartered at the transport lines at Mametz Camp.

To enable the men in the line to withstand the intense cold, two meals a day were sent up to all, even to those who were in the outposts. One meal consisted of hot stew and tea, the other of tea and dry rations (*i.e.*, bread, jam, butter and cheese).

A drying-room had been made at Flers in a brick cellar, where socks and trench-boots were sent to be dried so as to reduce the liability to trench feet. This was found to be a great success, and up to Christmas Day the battalion had had no cases of trench feet since coming into the front-line trenches on December 21st. On the 26th, however, the enemy artillery shelled Flers all day, blowing up the drying-room and killing the R.S.M., S. Corfield, who was coming out of the door at the time. He had been in the room with some of the pioneers drying socks so as to give the men a change, and a good deal of smoke was coming from the cellar, which may have been the cause of the enemy bombardment.

Corfield was a brave, gallant and most efficient sergeant-major. Always cool, calm and collected, in or out of the line he was "on parade" at all times, and did his work without regard either to officer or to man, insisting that duty in the battalion came before anything else. He was, however, very just in his dealings with everyone below him. He was a man of very independent character, but he was rather lonely, as his stern sense of duty and cold efficiency made him rather unapproachable. He was highly respected by all, and his death was a great loss to the battalion.

During the night a dugout fell in and killed four men. On the 29th Flers was again shelled all day. Next day the 9th was relieved by the 11th Battalion and went into huts at Bazentin-le-Grand, being now brigade reserve. The new reinforcements were used for working parties, while the men just out of the line enjoyed some much-needed rest and sleep.

During 1916 the battalion had garrisoned the Suez Canal at Gebel Habeita, and had then been transferred to France. Some of them had participated in Wilder-Neligan's raid at Fleurbaix, then the whole battalion had fought in the Battles of Pozières and Mouquet Farm, had a comparative rest in the Hill 60 sector at Ypres, and had finished the year at Flers by taking part, although not an active part, in the 1st Battle of the Somme.

## CHAPTER XI.

### THE MAZE, LAGNICOURT, BULLECOURT.

From the end of December, 1916, the battalion remained out of the line for nearly two months. During this time a number of schools were held for giving special training to selected officers and men. They were arranged by both corps and divisional headquarters, and gave instruction in trench mortars, Lewis guns, bombing, signalling, observation and other branches of army work; a number of parties from the 9th attended these.

At this period the 9th received several detachments of reinforcements. Troops from Australia for the infantry divisions were no longer sent first to Egypt, but to England, where they underwent further training at various camps, those for the 1st Division being stationed at Perham Downs, near Tidworth, on Salisbury Plain, 13 miles north-east of the city of Salisbury. Perham Downs camp also accommodated those men who, having been discharged from hospital and considered fit for further service, were waiting to be sent back to their units.

When Australian reinforcements left England for France, they went usually by way of Folkestone to Boulogne, staying for the night at a camp outside the town on what the troops called "One Blanket Hill," owing to the amount of bedding provided in winter and summer alike. The next day they went on to the great British base camp at Etaples, usually called by Australian troops, "Eetaps," about fifteen miles further south. Here they stayed for two or three weeks to have the finishing touches put on their training at the "Bull-ring," a training area a couple of miles to the north of the camp. Many men considered the training at the Bull-ring unduly severe, but others took no exception to it. From Etaples reinforcements were sent to join their units.

In the middle of January, 1917, the wet weather, which had been constant since October[1], was brought to an end with a hard frost, and three days later, on the 17th, there was a very heavy fall of snow. Two days after this again it was bitterly cold, with six inches of snow on the ground. Although the

---

1 The whole of this winter had been excessively cold; it was noted as having been the coldest winter in Western Europe for very many years.

cold was felt keenly (on the 24th it was so cold that the band could not play) the change in the weather conditions led to an improvement in the spirits of the troops.

The men were improving in health also. When they came out from the bitterly cold and muddy conditions at Flers, nearly all were more or less ill. They continued to wear the knitted woollen caps and scarves which they had been obliged to use in the trenches to keep warm, but Major Neligan made them discard these, and gave them as much exercise as possible with marches, drills and games. The result was that they rapidly recovered their normal health.

The battalion remained at Bazentin-le-Grand for the first week in January, and then moved by railway to Dernancourt, where it spent another week. Here on January 7th a boxing contest was held for a prize of £10, given by the Town Major, Major Baker. Sergeant Hodgson and Privates Norman and Twomey were prominent in this. Two days later there began a period of three days' relaxation and rest, which the battalion had been ordered to observe by the divisional commander.

The next move was to Bresle, where ten days were spent. Battalion sports were held here in the snow-clad fields on January 20th, followed by a dinner provided from money subscribed by the people of Queensland. This was the troops' Christmas dinner, which was eaten nearly four weeks after the proper date, as on Christmas Day the battalion had been in the line at Flers.

Just as the dinner was about to be served, in came some hungry reinforcements who had just arrived at the camp. The feast had to be stretched out so as to include these, which made rather a short allowance of food for each one, but fortunately there was an ample supply of beer, which held out despite the extra thirsts to quench.

On the 24th the battalion moved back to Fricourt. The roads were frozen and slippery, and the transport animals had great difficulty in keeping their feet on any sloping ground in spite of the fact that frost-cogs were used on their shoes. The camp at Fricourt was now quite comfortable, with duckboards throughout to walk on. Four days later a move was made to Bazentin-le-Petit, to a similar camp, followed on February 2nd by a transfer to Albert, where the battalion enjoyed a stay of nearly three weeks. While there Lewis guns were posted for action against enemy aircraft. A couple of entertainments were arranged for the whole unit, a concert and picture show

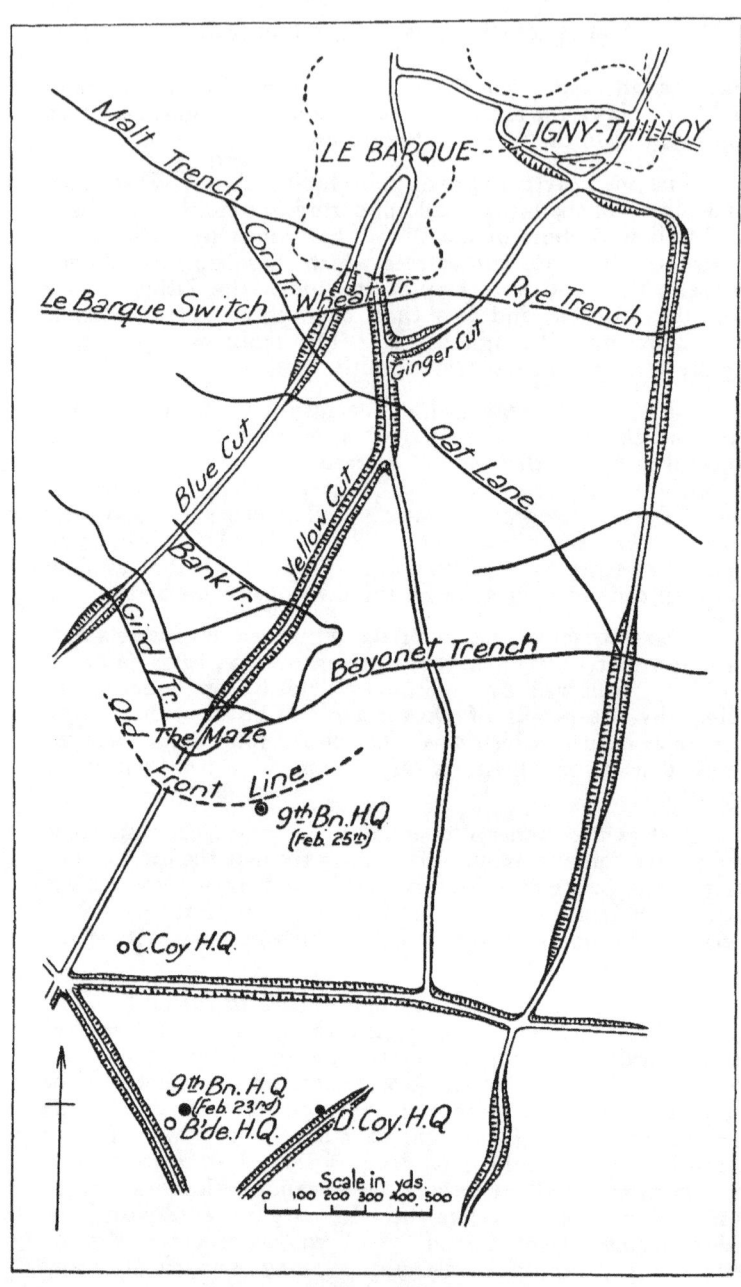

18. "The Maze" and Le Barque.
February 24th, 1917.

on the 14th and a picture show on the 20th. Training was also carried out for an attack which was intended to be made shortly.

On February 16th a thaw began, which ended the long frost. From this time on there was a great deal of fog, most of the days up to the end of the month being more or less foggy. On the 21st the battalion went forward to Bazentin-le-Petit, but, to their disappointment, the men found the camp, which had been a comfortable one when they had left it three weeks before, to be now in a very dirty and muddy condition.

The 3rd Brigade was now in the line again, and next day the 9th relieved the 11th in the front line near Eaucourt l'Abbaye, facing "The Maze." This was the name given to a small local enemy salient, formed by two trenches meeting at an angle, "Gird Trench" from the north-west and "Bayonet Trench" from the east, the point of the angle facing the middle of the battalion's sector of the front line. No-Man's Land here was 150 yards wide. Five hundred yards farther back into enemy territory from the point of The Maze was "Bank Trench."

Five hundred yards to the right of The Maze along Bayonet Trench began "Yellow Cut," a sunken road running towards the rear of the enemy. Five hundred yards to the left of The Maze along Gird Trench a similar sunken road began, "Blue Cut." These converged towards one another, meeting just inside the village of Le Barque, a mile behind The Maze. The two sunken roads were crossed by Bank Trench, and 700 yards farther on by "Oat Lane." "Rye Trench" was about 400 yards still farther, and just behind this on our left front was the village of Le Barque. From the village there ran to the north-west "Malt Trench," while "Barley Trench" was a continuation of Rye Trench to the right. "Wheat Trench" was the name given to Rye Trench where it crossed Blue Cut, 1400 yards beyond The Maze.

At the beginning of February some attacks had been made on trenches near Gueudecourt, and The Maze, which was a little to the left of that village, had been subjected to a feint bombardment; it was intended that the 1st Division should attack here later. On February 10th some troops of this division raided The Maze, and found the trenches stronger than had been expected, so the attack intended to have been made then was postponed until February 22nd, and on the 22nd it was again postponed for a few days.

F

Major Neligan had been training the battalion near Albert for this attack. Extra rations were issued, and the troops were fed on "the fat of the land"; every day they practised attacks on trenches similar to those which they would find at The Maze. The training was very thorough, and in connection with it Neligan gave a number of blackboard lectures.

For several days before the battalion went into the line The Maze had been bombarded by our artillery, and the 9th was to attack, accompanied by a creeping barrage. On the night of February 23rd/24th a patrol[2] went out, but observed no signs of activity in the German trenches; not a sound could be heard. It was remarked, however, that the enemy was sending up flares from trenches farther in rear, and the 10th Battalion, on the flank of the 9th, noticed that the enemy bombardment was falling not only on our front line but on his own also.

At 5 p.m. on the 24th a patrol, consisting of Sergeant Malin, with Lance-Corporal Griffiths, and Privates King and Charlton, went out. It was possible to go out safely in daylight as there were several old saps running from our lines up to the enemy trenches, and it was foggy also. The patrol went up one of the saps to the German line, and, hearing no sound there, entered the trenches. It divided into two parties, which examined the entrance of each dugout, but found no one. The only living thing seen was a black cat which ran from one dugout entrance. The enemy had evacuated his positions.

Two nights before there had been actually only twenty men of each German regiment left in the front line, but the Australians had no suspicion of this. Most of these men had withdrawn at daybreak on the 23rd, so that the enemy had been gone for a day and a-half by the time their absence was noticed.

The patrol returned at 7 p.m. with its news and at 8.28 brigade headquarters issued orders that the 9th Battalion was to occupy The Maze. Patrols from "A" and "B" Companies were then sent out. One of them occupied the objectives proposed for the attack, finding splendid dry trenches, some very good dugouts and large supplies of bombs and flares. The entrances of the dugouts had all been blown in, and many of them had been entirely destroyed. Word was sent back that all was clear, and part of "A" and "B" Companies then advanced, "A" occupying Bayonet Trench and "B" Gird Trench. By 10.30 the proposed second objective, a trench 200 yards beyond the enemy front line, had been occupied.

[2] Corporal Molloy, Lance-Corporal Griffiths and Privates King and Charlton.

A patrol which had left our front line at 9 p.m. reached Bank Trench, 500 yards beyond The Maze, by 10.55, but found only a few snipers there. The patrol easily drove them off and returned at 11 o'clock.

Another patrol of headquarters bombers went out, and it also found the enemy positions evacuated. Sending word back, it then went on further, putting a bomb-stop[3] in a trench which it reached before coming to Bank Trench, and not very far from it. Yet another patrol reached Bank Trench, which had been much damaged by artillery fire, and occupied it without opposition by 1.30 a.m., after which detachments examined Oat Lane and Wheat Trench.

The accounts by different men of this night's operations are very difficult to piece together to make a connected narrative, and often seem to contradict one another, but the night was pitch dark and the area in a very battered condition, so it can easily be understood that many of those who took part had a somewhat confused memory of the events of the advance.

Lieutenant Shrewsbury gives the following account of the operation of his patrol, which was apparently the one that occupied Bank Trench at 1.30 a.m.

> "After holding the front line for 48 hours," he says, "we were to be relieved. I was detailed from the company to go back and take over the trench we were to occupy when relieved. I was waiting for dusk with my batman, Chandler, as it was not very 'healthy' going along the duckboard towards High Wood in daylight. Shortly afterwards I received orders to stand by, and then orders came round for every man to be issued with two bombs and an extra bandolier of ammunition, as we were going over. We went over later and it was very rough going, too, as the place was simply a network of deep shell-holes and broken barbed wire. However, we occupied the Hun front line, and then I was detailed with Lieutenant Barnett to take a party and occupy a trench some distance in front.
>
> "I got about a dozen volunteers and we set out. It was a pitch dark night and we wandered about for some time, but eventually found a sunken road, Yellow Cut I think it was. Barnett took one side of this road with a few men, and I the other with the remainder of the party. We had almost to feel our way along, but an occasional Very light helped a little. We met no opposition and eventually found what we thought might have been a trench, but it had been very much blown in by shell fire. I decided that it must be the trench I had been ordered to occupy, so I posted sentries and we set about strengthening the position. I had a couple of men moving about in front so that we would not be surprised."

During this time the patrols had not succeeded in getting into touch with either of the flank battalions, the 10th on the left and the 7th (2nd Brigade) on the right, but at 1.35 a.m. the 10th joined them at Bank Trench. The progress of the

---

3 A barricade of earth or sandbags erected across a trench to block it.

patrols which had been sent forward was hampered by the shell-torn state of the ground, and by enemy artillery, but at 2 a.m. one of them came into touch with the enemy at a point 800 yards beyond The Maze. A fighting patrol of an officer and 30 men was then set out, but was driven back. Two further patrols went out at 3 a.m., but neither found signs of the enemy.

During the night the remainder of "A" and "B" Companies had occupied the abandoned enemy trenches about The Maze. "C" and "D" had come up to our old front line, some of the men being put to work in the drizzling rain digging a new communication sap to link up the old lines with the newly occupied positions. "C" Company found in a dugout here two old Germans with trench feet who had been left behind to fire off flares and give the impression that the trenches were still being held.

At 6 a.m. the right flank battalion, the 7th, got into touch with the 9th. The patrols of the 2nd Brigade had not advanced at the same time as those of the 3rd Brigade, as Bayonet Trench, in front of them, seemed to be occupied, but finally they reached the same line as the rest of the patrols and made contact with them in thick fog in the morning.

About 9 a.m. Lieutenants Adams and Scrivener and Corporals Green and Martin came up to Shrewsbury's party. The mist was thinning a little by this time, and there was an occasional shot from an enemy sniper. Adams asked Shrewsbury for information, and then he and his party went forward and disappeared in the fog. Soon afterwards shots were heard; Adams, who instead of his steel helmet was wearing a soft cap, had been shot dead by a sniper while attempting to throw a bomb. Private James during a lift in the fog witnessed this, and then saw the sniper advancing on Martin with his bayonet, whereupon James shot the German.

At 9 a.m. Captain Collin, in command of "D" Company, which was then occupying part of the old enemy front line, received orders to take out a patrol and examine the position in front of him. He set off with Sergeants Newbold and Hodgson and six men, and advancing through the heavy fog they had nearly reached Bank Trench when several shots rang out. The patrol halted and spread out. Nothing could be seen on account of the fog, but as Collin knew that there was a patrol somewhere in front of him, and as it was evidently this patrol which had been fired on, he decided to advance to its support. As they went on Collin's men were in turn fired on, and several were wounded, mostly in the stomach. However, they eventually joined the other patrol in Bank Trench, but the whole of Collin's party except Sergeant Hodgson had now been wounded.

Collin, who had been wounded in the leg, sent back Hodgson for assistance. The sergeant crawled away, taking shelter in shell-holes, and got clear, while the two patrols waited for what seemed an interminable time, until finally they were startled by one of the party being hit and killed as he crouched in the bottom of the trench. It appeared from this that they were being surrounded, so Collin decided that the party should withdraw by crawling through the shell-holes, and they succeeded in arriving back at the position where the rest of "D" Company was, to find the men, under Lieutenant White, moving into position to advance.

They all moved forward at once, together with the 7th Battalion on their right, and reaching Bank Trench easily drove off those of the enemy who had been opposing them there. It was still very foggy, and they could only see about ten yards ahead. Picking up Shrewsbury's patrol, they moved into extended order between Yellow and Blue Cuts, when at 12.20 p.m. the fog suddenly lifted.

They were on a long gentle downward slope of open ground between Bank Trench and Le Barque village, in full view of the enemy, who at once opened fire on them with heavy artillery and machine-guns, on what was now a fine sunny Sunday afternoon.

The 10th Battalion was advancing on "D" Company's left, but the 7th, which should have been on its right, was nowhere to be seen. It had evidently been held up farther back, so the line came to a halt and took shelter in shell-holes to wait until the hostile fire died down.

When the report reached Neligan that Collin's company had been held up, he instructed Captain Knightley, in command of "C" Company, now in The Maze, to advance to its assistance. The enemy machine-gunners had the exact range of the trench occupied by "C" Company, and their bullets were ripping the top of the parapet. Knightley called for volunteers to act as runners, to go to battalion headquarters, and he sent off two men to Neligan, reporting that if he moved off immediately there would be heavy casualties.

One of the runners eventually returned with a message from Neligan that the company was to advance at once, so Knightley consulted his second-in-command, Captain

McNaught, and decided that he himself would go ahead with a party, leaving McNaught to follow on with the main body of the company as soon as the machine-gun fire had quietened.

Knightley had no idea where "D" Company was, except that it was somewhere in front of him, but he took his party forward, and soon picked up a telephone line. Considering that this would belong to "D" he followed it up, keeping under cover as well as he could, and eventually found "D" Company in shell-holes. Soon afterwards McNaught came up with the remainder of "C" Company.

The hostile fire had now lessened, so the two companies, under the command of Knightley, advanced, despite many casualties, and occupied Oat Lane at 3.30 p.m. A few small groups of Germans were in the trench, but when the Queenslanders were still 50 yards off these ran away. Two machine-guns were captured, and also two Germans belonging to the 5th Guard Grenadier Regiment; they were chased by Lieutenant White, and when he came to within ten yards of them they dropped on their knees and held up their hands. Reinforcements now came up, and also a ration party under Lieutenant Hilton, but Hilton was killed and the rations were blown up by the enemy bombardment.

At 5 o'clock patrols were sent forward to examine Malt Trench, which had been reported, by air observers and prisoners, to be strongly held. One patrol went up Blue Cut and the other up Ginger Cut, a sunken road branching off from Yellow Cut to the right, between Oat Lane and Wheat Trench. Sniped at a good deal, they met parties of Germans in dugouts on their way, which, the battalion diary records, "were summarily dealt with." In spite of opposition, the patrols occupied parts of Malt Trench.

About 11 p.m. the 9th was ordered by brigade headquarters to occupy Rye Trench and connect up with the 12th Battalion, which was now on the left of the 9th. Therefore at 1 a.m. on the 26th two platoons of "D" Company, under Captain Collin, advanced towards Wheat Trench, where they met with opposition, but captured it at 1.30. They were soon heavily shelled, and suffered a number of casualties, including Lieutenants Barnett and Cameron, who were both killed. Cameron had just joined the battalion.

In the afternoon patrols went out beyond Rye Trench; these were forced back, but they finally dislodged the enemy and established two posts in Rye Trench by 6 p.m. Meanwhile at 4.40 p.m. Malt Trench had been captured by the 12th Battalion and bombing parties of the 9th. These three trenches, Wheat, Rye, and Malt, were all on the outskirts of Le Barque. During the whole of this day enemy snipers and machine-guns had been very active.

Between 8 o'clock and midnight the 9th was relieved by the 11th Battalion. The troops were exhausted, having gone for four days and nights with practically no sleep and for part of the time with no rations. The casualties in these operations included four officers killed, Lieutenants Adams, Barnett, Cameron and Hilton.

Great gallantry had been displayed by all ranks under very difficult conditions. The stretcher-bearers had very heavy work on account of the state of the ground. Eight bearers went with each stretcher, and one of them estimated that the average rate of travel was a mile in about an hour and a-half. One bearer, C. Boyle, was awarded the D.C.M. for bringing in wounded under heavy fire after the fog had lifted.

The German front line between Arras and Soissons formed a salient, which was likely to be attacked by us at any time. As a precautionary measure the enemy had in September, 1916, begun to construct a fortified line along the base of the salient, a distance of about 100 miles; this was known as the "Siegfried Line," but was called by the Allies the "Hindenburg Line." It consisted of two parallel lines of entrenchments protected by wide belts of very thick wire, with a reserve line behind. Early in 1917 the Germans found it an advantage to withdraw to this line, in order to shorten their front so that it could be held by a smaller number of troops, and to exchange for the badly damaged and muddy trenches of the Somme battlefield, a line of good dry trenches. In February the Allies knew of the existence of this new line, but did not suspect that the enemy was about to withdraw to it, although the Fifth British Army intercepted an enemy wireless message which aroused suspicions of the possibility of a retirement.

Patrols had remarked an absence of noise and flares in the enemy front line, but these facts were not reported to divisional headquarters, an oversight which seems rather surprising; and it is also surprising that, although corps headquarters had been informed by Fifth Army of the possibility of withdrawal, it had not forwarded this information on to its divisions. The result of this was that the enemy began his withdrawal under the very noses of the Allies without arousing their suspicions.

The fog was of great help to the enemy. On February 23rd he received several reports that Australian patrols had entered The Maze and part of Bayonet Trench. It was for that reason that his artillery had bombarded the old front line on that night. German patrols went forward on the 24th, and were surprised to find the trenches empty; it was supposed that we had entered and then evacuated them. Further patrols sent out late in the afternoon found that we were actually advancing, and it was they who in places had offered resistance.

On coming out of the line at The Maze, the battalion bivouacked a little to the rear of its former front-line positions, and at 3 p.m. next day, on being relieved by the 2nd Battalion, it went back to Bendigo Camp at Bazentin-le-Grand. Here all ranks bathed, and after resting for a day, furnished working-parties and fatigues for nearly a week, when a move was made to a very insanitary camp at Shelter Wood, near Contalmaison. The battalion remained here for two and a half weeks while it was trained in some new methods.

On February 14th a new organisation had been introduced into the British Army, the specialists (Lewis gunners, bombers, and rifle grenadiers) being distributed among the platoons instead of being attached to battalion or company headquarters; each platoon, with these specialists as well as riflemen, was now a separate little force for attacking "nests" of the enemy. The method of attack was also altered to fit in with this organisation and the different processes employed in attack were standardised.

On March 23rd the battalion moved to Bresle, where the training was continued. Spending twelve days here, it left on April 4th, and after a very wet and cold march arrived at Montauban. This march depressed the spirits of the troops, and they were in a particularly glum mood until at the midday halt the "cookers"[4] moved up and hot tea was served out to all. After that their low spirits left them, and the remainder of the march was found to be more bearable.

By the beginning of April the enemy had finished his withdrawal to the Hindenburg Line with the British and French following close on his heels. On the Anzac Corps front only the villages of Boursies, Demicourt, and Hermies remained to be taken. These places were to be attacked by the

[4] Travelling field cooking ranges, in which the fires were often kept alight during the progress of a march.

1st Division, the capture of Boursies being assigned to the 3rd Brigade.

The day after the 9th arrived at Montauban it went on to Frémicourt and, after resting there all that day and the next, moved up to the front line at Lagnicourt at dusk on April 6th. It had been a very wet day. The line consisted mainly of outposts from 50 to 100 yards apart, with supports in the sunken roads. This method of defence was adopted as the division was holding a very wide front, the battalion being responsible for about 3,000 yards. Nothing of interest happened until April 9th, when Boursies, on the right flank, was attacked and taken by the 12th Battalion. During the after-

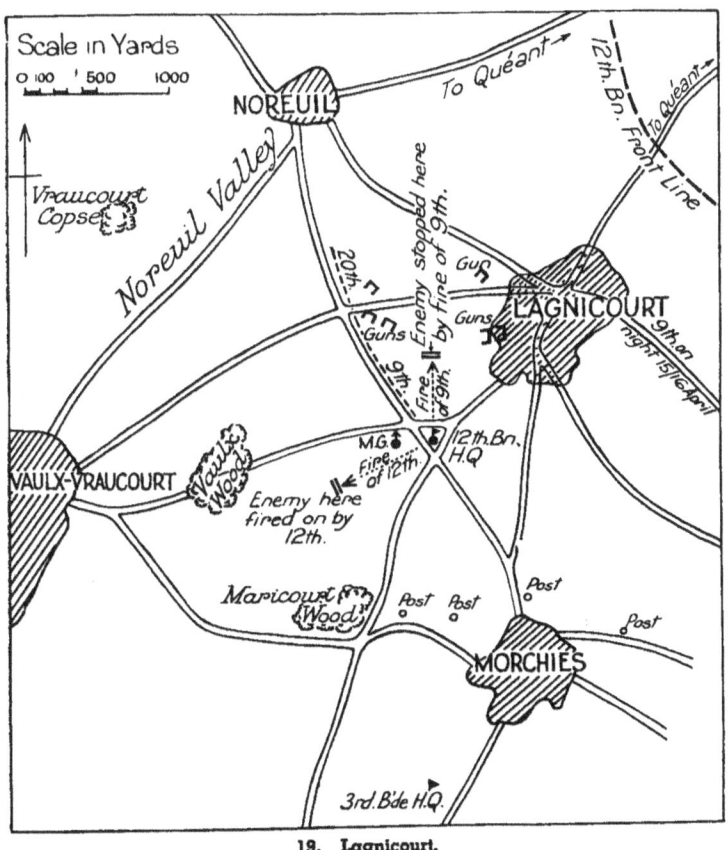

19. **Lagnicourt.**
April 15th, 1917.

noon orders were received to advance 800 yards, so our outpost line was pushed out to that distance.

On the 11th the battalion was still in that position when the ill-fated First Battle of Bullecourt took place on its left flank. Without an artillery barrage, and unaided by tanks, which were to have taken the place of the bombardment, but failed, the 4th Australian Division broke the Hindenburg Line and held on desperately until supplies ran out. The 9th was to have made an attack on Quéant, but owing to the failure at Bullecourt this was cancelled.

The next day an enemy patrol came near one of the battalion's outposts and was fired on by a Lewis gun; two of the patrol were killed. On the 13th a post of a dozen men was advanced 600 yards towards Quéant. On the 14th Lieutenant H. M. Shield was killed and Sgt. Best wounded. The battalion was then relieved by the 12th Battalion, and went back to sunken roads near Morchies; the relief for most of the men was completed by midnight, although it was hours later before all the outposts and front-line posts came in.

"A" and "D" Companies had been ordered to act as supports to the 12th Battalion, coming under the orders of Lieutenant-Colonel Elliott, C.O. of that battalion, whose headquarters were in the bank of a sunken road behind Lagnicourt, near cross-roads. The front line here was some 1,000 yards in front of the village of Lagnicourt. About the same distance behind the village were the headquarters of the 12th Battalion; and another mile and a half further back was Vaulx-Vraucourt. The Lagnicourt valley was to the left of 12th Battalion Headquarters, at a distance of about 1,000 yards, and in it were some of our field artillery. A little over a mile to the left of the headquarters was Noreuil valley, containing some more of our artillery. Morchies was a mile to the south of the headquarters. Brigade headquarters was just behind Morchies.

At 4 a.m. on the 15th, about an hour before dawn, the enemy attacked, and at one point succeeded in entering a gap between posts of the 12th and 17th Battalions. Some of the 12th Battalion posts and their supporting picquets found themselves surrounded and had to retire. By 5.30 the Germans, after reaching some of our field-guns just behind Lagnicourt, were advancing past 12th Battalion Headquarters towards Vaulx-Vraucourt. Colonel Elliott called out his signallers, cooks, batmen, and others at headquarters and stationed them at the side of the sunken road in front of headquarters, from which position they fired into the flank of the enemy, who had now penetrated a mile and a half behind our front line.

About 5.20 a.m. a man of the 12th had arrived at the bivouacs of "D" Company of the 9th, on the road between Morchies and Maricourt Wood, with the startling news that "the Germans have broken through in thousands." Lieutenant Shrewsbury, who was with "D" Company, felt someone hit him on the leg with a stick and yell out: "Get up unless you want to be killed in your beds! The Boche has broken through!" Shrewsbury slipped on his boots (having done that, he was of course fully dressed), and dashed down to Captain Boylan, commanding "D" Company.

Boylan at once brought out his company and ordered it to line the side of the road in front of the bivouacs with fixed bayonets to stop the advancing enemy when they reached that spot.

Sergeant Preston, who had been in an isolated post, was relieved much later than the rest of the battalion. He had just reached Morchies in the rear of his party of a dozen men when he heard someone running behind him.

> "I could see," he writes, "a man coming in my direction; he was running. When he saw me he called out, 'They're through! They're through!' I said, 'Who's through?' and he replied, 'The Hun; they have captured the front line and now they are at Lagnicourt.' I ran along the road shouting, 'Stand to! Stand to!' The first men I saw were my own party at the cookers."

The Germans had advanced very quietly, and owing to this it was difficult for the officers to convince some of the men that there was an attack, as not a few had got into their blankets only a short while before.

"D" Company men, lining the road, soon saw some of our gunners retiring past them carrying the breech-blocks of their guns. This meant that they had been obliged to abandon the guns to the enemy. A messenger then came from Elliott ordering "A" and "D" Companies of the 9th to advance. Boylan led his men forward in artillery formation[5], sending out scouts ahead. These returned with the news that the valley in front of them was full of Germans, who had, they said, captured 12th Battalion Headquarters.

Boylan thereupon determined to counter-attack and recapture it, but when he arrived there at 6.20 he found to his

---

5 Artillery formation. In small scattered parties so as to minimise the danger if they came under artillery fire.

great relief that it had not fallen. The enemy were advancing towards it, however, and Elliott ordered the 9th to line the road where the headquarters' troops had been firing. They did so, and their fire stopped the Germans when they were only a few hundred yards away.

Then a line of troops was seen coming up from the rear; these proved to be one company of the 9th and two companies of the 20th Battalion. They reached a position opposite 12th Battalion Headquarters about 7.5, and after a few minutes' halt they advanced with Boylan's company. Heavy machine-gun fire from Lagnicourt met them, about 20 men of the 9th being wounded, but for the most part not seriously. However, nothing could stop their triumphant advance, the enemy flying before them. By this time the British artillery had placed a barrage between the Germans and their rear.

As the line passed and began to leave Lagnicourt on its right, Lieutenant Wittkopp, with some men of both battalions, entered the village and took many prisoners. Our barrage was still on the far side of the village, so the line had to be halted while the artillery was asked to lengthen its range. Enemy dead were lying in numbers all round the village. During this time a British aeroplane was continually passing up and down the line, directing the artillery fire, harassing the enemy with its machine-gun, and at times flying low over our troops and pointing out to them the position of detachments of Germans.

At 7.30 the barrage lifted and the line resumed its advance. Those Germans who had been caught between the Australian advance and the new line of the barrage began to hold up their hands in token of surrender. A small party of our men went over to them and brought in 147 prisoners, two machine-guns and two converted Lewis guns. Other detachments of Australians were now in action, and whenever they reached a position from which they had a clear view ahead, they could see the enemy streaming back towards the Hindenburg Line. By 8.30 the Australian front was practically re-established where it had been the night before. During this advance the men of the 9th and 20th Battalions had become mixed.

Our artillery shelled for an hour and a-half a section of the enemy wire through which it was thought that the Germans would have to pass, and a rumour was afterwards prevalent that they had been cut to pieces by shell-fire in doing so. This rumour, however, had no foundation; it is true that there were some casualties at the wire, but the German historians say that most of the casualties in the retirement were due to machine-gun fire.

The enemy made this counterstroke to foil an anticipated attack by us, reasoning that the best defence in the circumstances was to thrust while we had not thoroughly dug ourselves in. They had just been reinforced by the 3rd Guard Division, composed of crack regiments. One of the purposes of the attack mentioned in the German operation orders was to show that they "still knew how to attack and how to conquer."

The Germans knew the whereabouts of our guns in the Noreuil valley, but they were not aware, until they found them during the advance, of those in the Lagnicourt valley. They claimed to have destroyed 22 of our guns; actually five only were destroyed, and the remainder were in action again later in the day. Seven villages were intended to be captured and held till nightfall, when the Germans, after doing as much damage as they could within our lines, were to return once more to the Hindenburg Line. It was thus intended to be a raid on an immense scale.

Sixteen thousand Germans had attacked, and we had defeated them with 4000 men[6]. Our artillery fire, 43,000 shells, was the heaviest yet effected in a single day by the Anzac Corps artillery. The total casualties of the 9th on this occasion were only 35, 7 having been killed and 28 wounded.

The battalion remained that night near the front line, just outside Lagnicourt village, along the road to the south-east of it leading to Louverval, and the next night was relieved by the 5th Battalion and went back to positions in the sunken roads between Morchies and Beaumetz-lez-Cambrai. Here it remained for a week, supplying working-parties each night to make strong-posts, as a defence line was now being formed in case the enemy should again break through the forward line. This line, it is true, had been decided on before the events of the 15th, but the "break-through" gave a great impetus to the work on it.

At midday on April 19th instructions were received to stand-to, as a report had been received that the enemy was advancing against the left front. After half-an-hour's waiting the order was cancelled. On the 20th another stand-to was ordered at 5 a.m. Later that day a single shell caused 11 casualties, all in "C" Company. The enemy continued to bombard Morchies and Beaumetz intermittently for the next couple of

---

6 The attack extended further than the 12th Battalion front.

days, and on April 22nd the 9th suffered eight more casualties. During this period a much-desired bath-parade to Frémicourt was greatly appreciated by the troops.

On April 24th the 9th was relieved by a Manchester battalion, and moved back to Haplincourt for the night. Next day a move was made to Bapaume, which had been occupied by the Australians for five weeks. Colonel Mullen now assumed command of the brigade on account of Brigadier-General Bennett's going on leave, Major Neligan taking over command of the battalion during the absence of the C.O. The 9th stayed at Bapaume for a week and a-half, supplying fatigue-parties, who worked 6 hours on and 12 hours off at the railway unloading ammunition and stores.

On one day during this period a car, which bore signs of having travelled a long distance, drew up at one of the 9th Battalion billets. Two French officers and a civilian alighted and hurried into the yard, where, after a quick survey of the position, they began to dig. Soon they unearthed a bag, presumably containing money, and motored off with it in high spirits.

We must now consider the events which led up to the fighting that took place in April and May. At the beginning of 1917 many French politicians were dissatisfied with General Joffre as commander-in-chief, and he was replaced by General Nivelle, who had done good work in repelling the Germans at Verdun. Nivelle, who believed in quick and dashing methods, decided on a large-scale offensive in the French sector, with the British assisting by a subsidiary attack.

The withdrawal of the Germans to the Hindenburg Line interfered with this plan, but in the middle of April Nivelle launched his great attack, at the Chemin-des-Dames, near Laon. It was a failure; the French advanced, but only slowly. Nivelle and Haig then agreed on a "wearing down" offensive; by making constant small attacks they would wear down the enemy's resistance. Bullecourt was again to be attacked as part of this offensive.

The Hindenburg Line was therefore heavily shelled during the latter part of April. The 9th was warned to be ready to move at a moment's notice, orders being given that the men were not to take off their uniforms, even at night. The 1st Division on May 2nd asked that the brigade arrangements for assembling the 9th and 10th Battalions quickly should be tested, so a test alarm was carried out on this day, with the result that the 9th was ready to move from the assembly ground 30 minutes after the alarm had been given.

At 2 a.m. on May 3rd an enemy bombardment broke out, and during the day rumours came through of heavy fighting up in the line. There was a strong presentiment among the members of the battalion that they would soon be in the thick of it again, and this was confirmed at 3.45 p.m. next day, when the order to stand-to was received. At 4.50 the battalion moved off to Vaulx-Vraucourt, leaving behind 200 of its number as a working-party. On arrival at Vaulx further orders directed it to go on to Noreuil and relieve the 12th Battalion. An advance party was therefore sent to Noreuil but, finding the vicinity of that village packed with troops and no accommodation available, it bivouacked near Vaulx. On the 5th the 200 men left behind at Bapaume rejoined the battalion, which was all ready to move off at any time in case of sudden emergency. The wisdom of this state of readiness was made evident next morning, when at 6.30 word was received that the enemy had entered the front line and the battalion was to move forward immediately.

Advancing at 8 a.m. to sunken roads on both the northern and southern outskirts of Noreuil, the companies waited there till 4 p.m., when orders were received that they were to carry out an attack that night on the Hindenburg Line.

The Second Battle of Bullecourt was part of a great attack on a 16-mile front. British troops were to attack Bullecourt village, while the 2nd Australian Division was to capture a section of the Hindenburg Line adjoining the village to the south-east. The attack, which took place on May 3rd, was a failure. In some places the enemy front-line trenches were captured, but by the end of the day the Canadians on the extreme left of the attack and our 2nd Division on its right were the only troops to remain in occupation of the trenches they had taken.

The 2nd Division captured part of the two trenches (known as O.G. 1 and O.G. 2) of the Hindenburg Line after very fierce fighting and held them against several strong counter-attacks. The 1st Division then carried on the fight. A fresh attempt was now to be made to take Bullecourt, orders being issued on May 5th for the village to be attacked by the 7th British Division. At the same time the 1st Australian Division was to capture O.G. 1 and 2 up to the village outskirts, and endeavour to gain touch with the 7th Division.

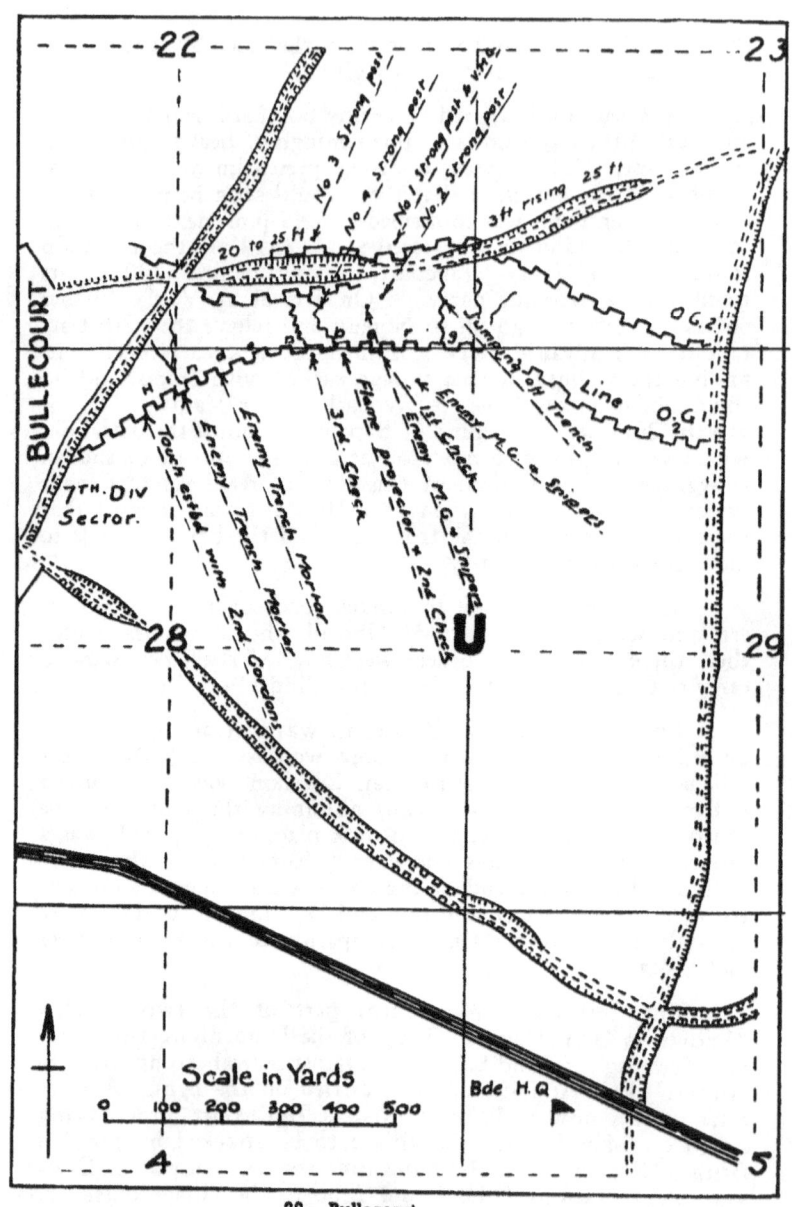

20. Bullecourt,
May 7th, 1917.

The 1st and 3rd Battalions were at the time in O.G. 1 and 2 respectively. The 3rd was very exhausted, and was therefore to be relieved by the 9th, which at 4 p.m. on May 6th was warned that it would be required to attack at 9.30 that night. "Zero hour" was later altered to 4 a.m. on the 7th, a quarter of an hour after the 7th Division would begin its assault on the village. The 9th was to be temporarily attached to the 1st Brigade for the operation.

In the afternoon of the 6th the 1st and 3rd Battalions were relieved by the 4th and 2nd, and at dusk the 9th went into the line and took over the extreme Australian left flank, "A," "B," and "D" Companies (under Captains Carroll and Ross and Lieutenant Norris respectively) in O.G. 1, and "C" Company (Captain Knightley) in O.G. 2. Major Neligan was in charge of the whole operation.

On their way through the communication sap leading to the front, the troops became well aware of the heavy fighting which had been going on. The trench ran along the foot of a steep road bank, which was on its right, while the road itself was just to the left of the sap. In places the sap was choked with dead bodies, so much so that the incoming troops could not help walking over them, while at other spots they had been hastily thrown out of the sap in order to clear it, the corpses lining the top on both sides.

Enemy shells were coming over the top of the bank and bursting close by. Mr. J. D. Allan says:—

> "The Hun shells skimmed the bank and splashed on to the road, and I saw two A.M.C. parties with stretchers on the far side of the road just disappear in smoke."

At 10.30 p.m. working parties commenced to make dumps of wire, stakes, bombs and other material near the end of O.G. 1, and telephone wires were laid to the same point. An hour later the company commanders and the officers in charge of the machine-guns and trench-mortars received their final instructions in Neligan's dugout.

As an apparatus for projecting flame was used by the enemy in this battle, it will be convenient at this point to describe it. The *flammenwerfer* or flame-thrower consisted of a tank carried on a man's back, with a pipe fitted with a nozzle leading from it. The tank contained an inflammable liquid of which the vapour ignited at the nozzle, giving a flame which roared out to a considerable distance. It gave off much smoke, and had a very demoralising effect when it was first used.

*Flammenwerfer* operators when taken prisoner were regarded with as little favour by our men as *minenwerfer* crews were.

At 2 a.m. on the 7th the enemy assaulted the post on the left flank of O.G. 1 which the 4th Battalion was holding, and captured a short length of the trench, the garrison of the post falling back 40 yards to a position near a cross trench.

The barrage for our operation began at 3.45 a.m., and at 3.58 the first attacking platoon climbed over the barrier in O.G. 1 to advance along the trench, but it had only gone seventy yards when it met with opposition from machine-guns, snipers, and bombers, the latter using both egg and stick bombs. It was also bombarded with "pineapple" bombs from a *granatenwerfer*, a small trench-mortar throwing a segmented bomb somewhat resembling a small pineapple. The platoon was driven back to the point from which it had started.

The next platoon, commanded by Lieutenant Henzell, then bombed its way along the trench, but it soon ran out of bombs and was brought to a stop. However, more bombs arriving, it advanced farther along the trench, helped by a couple of Lewis guns, which had been put out into shell-holes in the open, one on each side of the trench. During this advance the *granatenwerfer* already referred to was found abandoned.

Henzell's men were again stopped by a heavy barrage of enemy bombs. They found that an enemy machine-gun and snipers occupied shell-holes in the open on both sides of the trench, and it appeared as if they were being surrounded. However, more men came up to reinforce the platoon, and after subduing the Germans in the open by Lewis guns and rifle-grenades, they continued their advance.

It was at this stage that, to the surprise of the Australians, a great spout of flame went up to a height of 20 or 30 feet when one of our bombs hit a German. When they looked at the body of the fallen man they saw strapped to his back the remains of a *flammenwerfer* which the bomb had exploded. Another *flammenwerfer* was captured at the same place.

After this, little resistance was experienced for a while, till they were brought to a stop by an enemy machine-gun in the trench ahead. A fierce bomb-fight now raged for two or three minutes, and when the enemy resistance died down again they rushed the spot, to find only the lock of the machine-gun and a quantity of ammunition. This was about 400 yards in front of their jumping-off position.

Looking farther along the trench, the Queenslanders could see a body of about 40 of the enemy retiring, their rear being brought up by the machine-gun crew carrying their gun, and also by a small bombing party. Some of the Germans had also retired along two cross-trenches close together leading to O.G. 2. Henzell established small posts with bomb-stops in these cross-trenches to prevent the Germans from returning, and then began to pursue the main body. Attempts to catch up with the party met with no success, owing to the opposition put up by their bombers, but the Australians kept pressing them closely.

Daylight was now coming on, when at 5.15, as the leading men were looking along the trench, and still throwing bombs where they thought the enemy might be, they suddenly perceived a Gordon Highlander standing on the parapet ahead. Then seeing three or four more of the "Jocks," it was realised that they had been bombing men of their own side. They had reached their objective and linked up with the 7th Division, which had captured part of the village. The Highlander first seen was Captain Gordon, who was killed soon afterwards.

Those of the enemy being pursued were now trapped between the Australians and the Highlanders; they went into a dugout in the side of the trench, carrying their gun with them, but the "Jocks" threw "P" bombs down the entrance. The dugout caught fire, but none of the enemy were seen to come out. It was still burning fiercely when Captain Ross passed it over 14 hours afterwards.

"C" Company, in O.G. 2, was to advance with two platoons and establish two strong-posts, one in the trench and the other a little behind it, then the other two platoons were to "leap-frog" over the first two, capture a further length of trench, and establish two similar strong-posts farther along.

The first two platoons, under Lieutenants Brown and Mactaggart went out at 4 a.m. and met with fierce opposition from machine-gunners, snipers, and bombers, but this was soon overcome, and the first objectives were reached and strong-posts established there according to plan. Brown's party had encountered an enemy post, which immediately fell back before his attack. These two posts, as soon as they were established, opened covering fire while the other two platoons, under Lieutenant Ramkema[7] and Sergeant Porter, passed them and continued the attack.

---

[7] Ramkema had been promoted to captain just before this, but word of the promotion had not then reached the battalion.

These platoons came under very heavy fire from a crossroad 250 yards farther on, whence a *granatenwerfer* was firing on them. Ramkema was hit in the elbow, and had to retire; however, when he reached the starting-point he told Knightley where the *granatenwerfer* was, so a Stokes mortar was turned on to it. After about five minutes the Australians attacked again and put the enemy to flight, Porter running along the parapet and throwing bombs at them as hard as he could.

The attacking parties then pushed ahead, and in spite of further heavy bombing from the enemy they established their posts, not exactly on the objectives, at the cross-road, but just short of it. The Gordons had not captured their second objective exactly in this spot, though they had gained it along the greater part of their line.

Although the 7th Division had been bombarded during its attack, there was practically no enemy artillery fire on the Australians until they had gained their objectives, when a heavy bombardment of both their new and their old positions occurred, greatly hindering the work of consolidation. Very little, in fact, could be done besides just sitting down in the trenches and waiting until they were relieved, for, as well as having to endure the enemy fire they had to put up with bombardment from some of their own supporting artillery, which was firing short. In order to make sure that there should be no gap in the line, it was arranged that the Gordons and the Australians should occupy each other's flank post, thus causing their fronts to overlap slightly.

The newly captured trenches were much damaged, and very wide; the portions of them from which the 9th had attacked were also greatly knocked about, and in places the walls were nearly levelled. It was in certain parts of O.G. 1 from behind such traverses as were still left standing that the enemy had been able to hold up for a while the Australian advance.

About 650 yards of trench had been gained in O.G. 1 and 250 yards in O.G. 2. Three trench mortars, three flame-throwers, 250 rifles, and large quantities of egg and stick bombs and flares were captured. The battalion's casualties were 25 other ranks killed and 1 officer and 135 O.R.'s wounded. The weather remained fine until the night of May 7th, when rain set in, thus making the trenches very muddy for the relief of the 9th by the 5th Battalion next morning. The change over was completed by 2.30 a.m. The men of the 9th once more settled in the sunken roads round Noreuil from which they had gone into the line, but their "possies" gave them very little shelter from the rain, which continued to fall steadily. They were relieved from this position at 3 a.m. on May 9th and marched straight back to Bapaume, arriving there at 6.30. Sleeping all day—as well as they might—the next day was spent in resting and bathing and receiving a clean change of underclothes.

During this second stay at Bapaume the 1st Division was in corps reserve, and the fatigues being fewer the men had more rest than on their first visit. Two points of constant interest here were the huge crater which remained after the Germans had mined the town hall with a time fuse that exploded the mine five days after they had evacuated the town, and the exposed vault containing hundreds of human skulls.

On May 11th Lieutenant-Colonel Mullen, who had acted as brigadier since April 25th, resumed command of the battalion, and Major Neligan went on leave. The strength of the battalion was now 41 officers and 800 other ranks. On the 19th an accident occurred, Private Richardson having his hand blown off while examining an old German bomb.

Generals Birdwood and Newton Moore were present at a church parade on May 20th, and on the next day battalion sports were held. After remaining at Bapaume for a fortnight, the battalion marched to Bazentin-le-Petit on May 22nd, moving on to Ribemont on the next day. By the evening of this day the whole brigade was billeted in that village.

This move to the back area was hailed by the troops with a sigh of relief,

> "for while they had stayed in Bapaume there remained the dread of a further tour in the line at Bullecourt. To turn their back definitely on such a place, to hear from the distance the rumble of its thunder, and to see, but no more to approach, the broad band of illuminated sky, constantly lit by the explosion of guns and enemy Very lights, was a circumstance which brought forth expressions of the greatest relief from all ranks."[8]

The 1st, 2nd and 5th Divisions were now beginning the longest and most complete rest they had had since they entered the war. Part of the time they were stationed on the old Somme battlefield and in the neighbourhood of Amiens, and part in Flanders near Hazebrouck.

A brigade competition for the best trained battalion was now organised. There were first inter-company tests from which, after keen competition, "C" Company, under Captain

---
[8] Lieutenant C. M. Wrench.

Knightley, emerged as victor. It represented the battalion in the competition, which was won by the 9th. Most of the final tests were carried out on June 7th.

On Sunday, June 10th, the two-mile run, the final event in the competition, took place. This was a most severe test, as the whole of the company had to run in military boots. Five points were awarded to each man finishing in under 12 minutes, 4 points to those under 15 minutes, 3 to those under 20 minutes, and 1 point to those under 25 minutes. All the 9th Battalion men finished in under 15 minutes, and secured the highest number of points, but the 10th Battalion protested, and a run-off took place next day. Again the 9th proved conquerors.

In the middle of June the battalion went to Hénencourt for the divisional sports, staying there for two nights in a glorious spot in Hénencourt Wood.

On June 22nd Major Wilder-Neligan left the 9th to take temporary command of the 10th Battalion, returning on July 10th. On June 23rd the award of a number of decorations was announced, the M.C. going to Captain C. F. Ross and Lieutenants R. W. Brown, S. J. Chapman, and W. C. Henzell, the D.C.M. to Sergeants W. Greaves and W. A. Porter, Corporal H. J. Bull, and Privates J. R. Atkins and V. Dearden.

Two days later the battalion left Ribemont and went to Mailly-Maillet, and on the 28th they assembled to hear a lecture on the need for physical fitness from their former M.O., Lieutenant-Colonel A. G. Butler, who now commanded the 3rd Field Ambulance.

On June 30th the battalion numbered 34 officers and 964 other ranks, being now nearly up to full strength.

Plate xiv.

29.—LIEUT.-COL. MAURICE WILDER-NELIGAN, C.M.G., D.S.O. and bar, D.C.M., C de G.
(Photo lent by R. D. Huish, Esq., President Queensland Branch, R.S.S.A.I.L.A.)

## CHAPTER XII.

### THE THIRD BATTLE OF YPRES.

On July 6th the battalion went back to Ribemont for a week, and then to Bronfay Farm, near Bray. After eleven days here it moved on to Camp 165, not far from Bray, and stayed there for two days.

On July 8th a memorial which had been erected at Pozières was unveiled, and the 9th sent a detachment to represent the battalion at this ceremony. Soon after this, much to the regret of all ranks in the 9th, who felt the loss of such a fine soldier and outstanding personality, Major Wilder-Neligan left to become C.O. of the 10th Battalion with the rank of lieutenant-colonel. He was succeeded as second-in-command of the 9th by Captain Ross, who was promoted to major.

Neligan was born at Tavistock, Devon, on October 2nd, 1882, and came of a well-connected family. An uncle was formerly Bishop of Auckland, New Zealand, a brother a well-known London surgeon, and two other brothers were naval officers. He had served in the British Army, in one of the "crack" regiments, the Royal Horse Artillery, and subsequently came to Australia. Aged 31 when the war broke out, he enlisted as a private under the name of Wilder. He was in the first draft of men which left Townsville for Brisbane on August 22nd, in the *Bombala,* and left Australia as an original member of the 9th with the rank of lance-corporal. He became orderly-room corporal on the *Omrah* and sergeant at Mena.

On the day of the Landing at Anzac he not only acted as adjutant, although still only a sergeant, but displayed great personal gallantry, for which he received his first decoration. Soon after the Landing he was given a commission, and on May 28th he led a very successful raid on the enemy lines at the "Twin Trenches." In France he planned and carried out the brilliant raid near Fleurbaix, was in charge of the fighting at The Maze when the enemy was retiring in that area, and commanded the successful attack at the Second Battle of Bullecourt.

He had risen rapidly in rank, gaining his lieutenant-colonelcy in little over two years after receiving his commission. He remained in command of the 10th Battalion for eighteen months, until the end of 1918. In February, 1919, when the 9th and 10th Battalions were amalgamated, he became C.O. of the combined unit, and in the following month was appointed to command the 3rd Brigade Group,[1] a post which he retained until the group finally reached Australia. On returning to civilian life he eventually entered the civil service of New Guinea and became district officer at Talasea, near which place he died on October 9th, 1923.

Maurice Wilder-Neligan was a man of great ability, bravery and originality, and, although a strict disciplinarian, who insisted on all his orders being carried out to the letter, he was loved and respected by all ranks. He had a keen sense of humour, and was always able to rise above circumstances and to adopt original methods to meet any emergency, great or small. He always took his valise up to the front line with him, and, whatever the conditions were, he never omitted to take his bath and to shave every day. With the exception of Lieutenant-Colonel H. W. Murray, he was the most decorated officer in the A.I.F., both of them having the C.M.G., D.S.O. (and bar), D.C.M., and C. de G., Murray surpassing him only in the possession of the V.C.

Neligan is said to have made the statement, while on board the *Omrah*, and when still a corporal: "I hope to come back as C.O. of the 9th." Although he did not achieve his wish literally, he nevertheless returned in command of the 3rd Brigade Group, of which the last members of the 9th formed a company—and it must be remembered that he had more than once been temporarily in command of the 9th Battalion.

On July 24th the 9th was selected to provide the guard of honour, of four officers and 100 other ranks, under Captain Knightley, for a presentation of decorations to men of the 1st Division. The presentation, by Lieutenant-General Birdwood, took place at 3rd Brigade Headquarters. This ceremony was noted for the long period, about 35 minutes, during which the men were kept standing at attention. It is possible that this may have been a record for Australian troops.

On July 26th the battalion marched to Albert, and late in the afternoon it entrained for the north, arriving at Steenbecque early next morning. It then marched to Staple, a village about four miles north-west of Hazebrouck, and after three days there went by motor-omnibus to an area near Lumbres, a town 25 miles east of Boulogne. The 9th was billeted in three adjacent

---

[1] See p. 265.

villages, Affringues, Bayenghem[2] and Lart, just outside Lumbres, battalion headquarters being at Affringues. A week was spent here, but it rained nearly all the time. On August 6th the battalion returned in motor-omnibuses to Staple, the week in the Lumbres area having been wasted as far as training was concerned, as on account of the wet weather most of the parades had to be cancelled.

After three days at Staple a move was made to Vieux-Berquin, where five weeks were spent. The four months' training came to an end here, and a series of inspections and tests were made to determine how effective it had been. On August 22nd brigade sports were held, the 9th winning the Brigade Athletic Cup by one point. The event of the day was the 220 yards race, contested by Lieutenants Walsh (9th Battalion), Smith (10th), Vaughan (12th), and a sergeant of the 11th. The competitors arrived at the tape in a bunch, and the judges placed Walsh first and Vaughan second. Before the sports a picked company from each battalion in the 3rd Brigade marched past General Birdwood.

Two days later a detailed inspection of the troops, unit by unit, was begun by the brigadier and the brigade staff. By the 28th the greater part of the units had been thus inspected, and the brigade marched past the G.O.C., Second Army, General Plumer. The army commander also inspected the troops at their field work, lecturing to them afterwards. Next day the brigade inspection of the 9th, which had been delayed by rain, took place. By this time the battalion was well over strength, and was by far the strongest in the Brigade; on August 31st it numbered 53 officers and 1204 other ranks.

Lieutenant-Colonel C. F. Ross afterwards wrote:—

"The battalion was now at its peak in numbers, training and spirit. It was a fine battalion before the Landing and again before the blood-bath of the Somme, but on neither of these occasions was it the splendid fighting instrument which it now was, nor did it rise to the same heights afterwards, though it did some fine work.

"It had been given time to recover from the terrible battering at Pozieres and Mouquet Farm and the chamber of horrors at Flers. The minor actions at The Maze and Lagnicourt had given the men a good opinion of their prowess as fighters, and the heavy and successful fighting at 2nd Bullecourt had served to confirm that opinion."

[2] This was Bayenghem-lez-Seninghem, not to be confused with Bayenghem-les-Eperlecques (mentioned on p. 148).

At the beginning of next month there were signs of a return to the forward area, the intelligence officers of each unit making a visit to the front line to reconnoitre. Two days after this the battalion was taken for a route march of 15 miles, which proved that the men were very fit after their long period of training. On September 6th a drill competition between the battalions of the brigade was won by the 10th. Next day those officers of the 9th who were to go into action went to the Devonshire Lines, near Busseboom, to inspect a large-scale model of the area to be attacked. This model, which was in the open, had been made on the surface of the ground, valleys and trenches being scooped out of the earth, and ridges built from the soil.

On September 12th the C.O. lectured each company in turn on the subject of the forthcoming attack, illustrating his address by a large map of the area. The map, a particularly fine one, painted on calico, had been prepared by Captain S. J. Chapman, the intelligence officer. Next day the 1st Division began to move back to the front line, the 9th Battalion reaching Thieushouk the first night and going on the next day to Abeele, a Belgian village on the frontier. The details who were to be left out of the line went to the 1st Division Reinforcement Camp at Rouge Croix, between Caestre and Pradelles.

Two days were spent at Abeele. Some of the officers visited the new front line, and officers, this time with N.C.O.'s, made another inspection of the large-scale model of the new battlefield. On September 16th the battalion was transferred to Ottawa Camp, half-a-mile north of Ouderdom.

During the two days here, further visits to the front line were made, and rifles, ammunition and gas-helmets were inspected. On the 18th Château Segard Camp, a mile and a half south of Ypres, was reached, and here final preparations were made for the forthcoming operation—the Battle of the Menin Road.

This was the second stage of the great offensive (known as the Third Battle of Ypres) on a 15-mile front, which had opened on July 31st. Several attacks had been made, but the operations were gradually brought to a standstill by wet weather, and Sir Douglas Haig was forced to wait until the battlefield dried before resuming the offensive. The British line was, in the middle of September, on Westhoek Ridge, $3\frac{1}{2}$ miles to the east of Ypres, and an attack was to be made with Anzac Ridge, about a mile further on, as the final objective. There were two intermediate objectives, called, from the colour in

Plate xv.

30.—THE DUCKBOARD TRACK AT WESTHOEK RIDGE.

31.—CORDUROY ROAD ON WESTHOEK RIDGE
Running up towards Idiot Corner. Photograph taken 29th October, 1917.
(Aust. War Memorial Official Photograph. No. E 1197. Copyright.)

Plate xvi.

32.—9th BATTALION OFFICERS

Left to Right.—Back row: Lieuts. Koch, Ryan, Shaw, Forward, J. Young, Raff, Bailey.
Middle row: Lieuts. Nicholls, Russell, Avery, Pumfrey, Knowles, Fraser, Alcock, Gordon, Wilson, Finter, R. B. Salisbury, Meyers, T. W. Cameron.
Front row: Lieuts. Goward, Stenhouse, Captains Biggs, McNaught, McIntyre, S. J. Chapman, Lieut.-Col. Mullen, Capts. Lawrence, Monteath, Lieut. Henzell, Capts. Donaldson, Rae, Lieut. Barcroft.
(Aust. War Memorial Official Photograph, No. E 1762. Copyright. Photographed at Neuve Eglise, 23rd February, 1918.)

which they were marked on the maps issued for use in the attack, the "Red Line" and the "Blue Line," while the final objective was known as the "Green Line." Together with eleven Imperial divisions, the 1st and 2nd Australian Divisions were to attack side by side; this was a source of great satisfaction to our men, as it was the first occasion on which two Australian divisions had attacked together.

The "leap-frog" method of attack was to be used. For example, in the 3rd Brigade, after the 11th Battalion had captured the Red Line, the 12th Battalion would "leap-frog" over the 11th, and occupy the Blue Line, while for the final stages the 9th on the left and 10th on the right were to "leap-frog" over the 12th and take the Green Line.

For seven days before the attack a tremendous bombardment of the enemy positions was carried out by our artillery, with a gun to every five yards of front. No fewer than 3091 British guns of various sizes from 18-pounders upwards took part, and a number of French guns also assisted. This was twice the amount of artillery support employed in the Battle of the Somme, in which 1681 guns were used. This seven days' bombardment included a number of practices of the creeping barrage which was to be used for the attack.

One problem met with in this battle was the bringing forward of the large number of troops necessary through a comparatively small area of communications, bivouacking them for the day before the battle, and bringing out the garrisons which they were to relieve. For this purpose several roads not in the area of the attacking corps were "borrowed" from the corps adjoining on the south, which was not taking part in the fighting.

On September 16th the 1st Brigade took over from British troops the front line on Westhoek Ridge and the edge of Glencorse Wood, and held it until the time fixed for the attack. By order of General Plumer, all troops were given as much rest as possible on the 19th. A quarter of an hour before midnight the 3rd Brigade left Château Segard and proceeded to the area where jumping-off tapes had been laid in No-Man's Land slightly in advance of our front line, the 11th Battalion being placed nearest to the enemy, with the 12th close behind and then the 9th and 10th.

The fine weather had dried the battlefield, but on this evening a drizzle set in, increasing to steady rain by 11 p.m. During the next hour Corps and Army headquarters were considering whether the attack should not be postponed, but the rain stopped about midnight and General Plumer ordered the operation to go on.

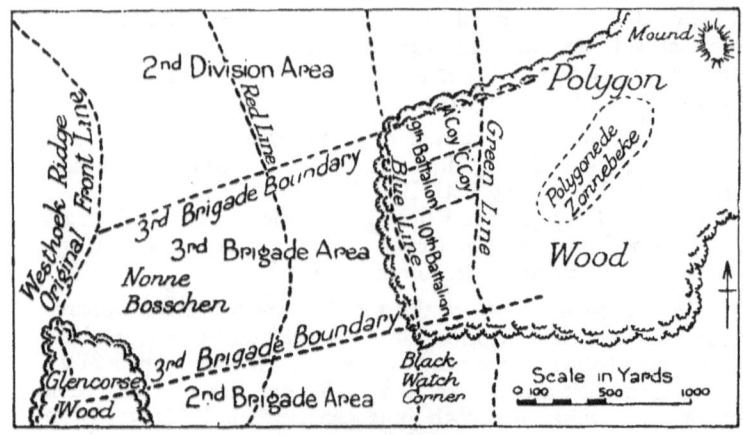

21. Polygon Wood.
September 20th, 1917.

On the way in the 9th passed a little to the south of Ypres, but was delayed somewhat, as the 28th Battalion had got on to the wrong track and held up for half-an-hour the 12th Battalion and those following it. This delay was increased when, at 4.20 a.m., a coloured German flare was seen to go up from the corner of Glencorse Wood, followed in a few minutes by an enemy barrage which fell on the incoming troops and lasted for twenty minutes.

The 9th was passing through Château Wood when this happened, and many were hit. The men were packed as closely as possible to one another, so that they would not lose touch in the dark, and it is surprising that the casualties were not even more numerous. The twenty minutes seemed to the troops more like an hour. At 5 o'clock the German bombardment recommenced, and casualties were again heavy. The men of "B" Company, who were carrying, found that gas-shells were falling on them, so they threw down their loads in order to put on their respirators, and then found difficulty in finding the loads again in the dark.

In these two bombardments the 9th lost all its company commanders and half its junior officers. However, led by Lieutenant Meyers and the other remaining subalterns, "A,"

## NONNE BOSSCHEN AND RED LINE TAKEN

"C," and "D" Companies reached the assembly point in "Jabber Trench" just at zero hour, "B" Company coming up 20 minutes later.

Subsequently, when looked at from the captured territory, the forming-up position was seen to be on the skyline of a rise. The enemy barrage was therefore probably due to our troops having been observed by the Germans while getting into place.

When the three leading companies reached the jumping-off tapes, the advance had to be commenced immediately. Owing to the enemy shelling on the way in, the troops arrived somewhat in confusion, and there was no time to reorganise. "A" Company had been intended to advance on the left, "C" on the right, with "D" behind them, but everyone pressed forward in one dense line to escape the German barrage on the rear, and men of the 9th became mixed with those of the 12th and some of the 10th. All, however, kept perfect silence till our bombardment opened.

At zero hour, 5.40 a.m. on September 20th, just after the first faint light of dawn had appeared, the barrage from over 3000 guns suddenly crashed out, and the line immediately began to move forward. Almost every man, as he rose from the ground, lit a cigarette. The three companies of the 9th advanced behind the troops detailed to take the first and second objectives, having to make their way in a thick mist through the thinly-wooded swamp of Nonne Bosschen. The creeping barrage was advancing at the rate of 100 yards in six minutes, so this had to be the rate of progress of the troops.

The first objective was captured without difficulty by the 11th Battalion at the time decided upon, 6.9 a.m. The Germans in most of the concrete strong-posts ("pill-boxes") surrendered as soon as they were reached, and it was only when an occasional post refused to surrender that there was any fighting. At the beginning of the advance but one enemy machine-gun could be heard firing.

Our barrage was the best that had ever been employed up to this date. Indeed (as Dr. Bean has said[3]) it was the barrage which really captured the ground; the operation might be described as an artillerymen's battle, as the infantry had only to walk behind it and occupy each objective as they came to it.

The barrage was so perfect that it was like a wall in front of the men, so that they could walk close behind it. When the first objective, the Red Line, was taken, the troops had to wait

---

[3] *Official History*, Vol. IV., p. 761.

in that position for an hour, and the battalions were reorganised during this time. Many 1st Division men had become mixed with 2nd Division battalions in the 2nd Division sector, but these were at once collected and returned to their proper frontage.

At 7.8 the 12th Battalion left the Red Line, followed by the 9th and 10th, and attacked the second objective (the Blue Line), which was taken on schedule at 7.40. This line, however, was not occupied, as the ground there was found to be much encumbered with tree-stumps and roots, which made digging very difficult, so a trench was dug by the 12th 100 yards in rear, where a good field of fire was obtained. The situation was fairly high, and commanded a good view to either flank. Nevertheless, the 9th and 10th did not occupy this trench, but remained at the actual Blue Line, where they sat down quite calmly and waited until it was time to advance on to the third objective, some of them taking advantage of the opportunity to eat portion of their rations.

The noise of the bombardment was deafening at this time, and casualties were constantly occurring. Throughout the advance touch was kept with the units on the flanks of the 9th, the 10th on the right and the 28th (2nd Division) on the left. The 9th and 10th Battalions were thoroughly reorganised here, as there was a wait of over two hours, and at 9.59 they began to move forward to attack the Green Line.

The men of the 9th were so eager that they began to advance before the barrage had lifted, and so, running into the fire of their own guns, they had to retire and make a fresh start. The enemy resistance was now stronger, but the objective was reached in a few minutes and occupied by 10.9 a.m. as easily as had been the other two objectives.

Resistance was met with from a machine-gun in a pillbox, but it was easily taken by the party attacking it dividing into two, advancing on either side of the pillbox, and capturing it from the rear. Pillboxes had not before been encountered by the 1st and 2nd Divisions. The troops did not know what they were, and were surprised when they saw Germans step from behind them and fire at the attacking line. There were about half-a-dozen pill-boxes in the 9th Battalion sector.

The 28th Battalion, on the left of the 9th, overran its objective, and so touch with it was lost for a while, but was soon regained. The troops dug in on the edge of Polygon Wood, in full view of the enemy, and were covered by Lewis gunners in shell-holes 50 yards in front. After our barrage stopped the front line sent back word that they were well and happy, and ready for anything that might come along.

Polygon Wood was so called because it contained the Polygone de Zonnebeke, an area of elliptical shape marked out on the ground. It was known to the troops as "the racecourse," but was probably the driving-track of an old Belgian artillery training ground. Beyond this was a prominent mound, which had been the butt of a former Belgian rifle range.

A good supply of ammunition as well as of other stores was on hand, and throughout the night further ammunition, rations, water, and entrenching materials were brought up by carrying parties. A dump of German barbed-wire found just in rear of the trench proved a great convenience.

From 2 p.m. onwards the enemy made attempts at counter-attack, but they were all defeated by the artillery. In fact, the counter-attacks were hardly noticeable, none of them reaching anywhere near our front line.

Next day was quiet. Lieutenant T. W. Cameron, the transport officer, brought up a string of about 30 mules laden with supplies to within a few hundred yards of the front line after day had dawned. Colonel Mullen, when he saw the convoy, said to him: "Cameron, you fool; you'll get blown to hell." Cameron's only reply to this was: "Well, you want your b—— rations, don't you?" The 9th was relieved that night by the 2nd Battalion, the relief being completed by 11 p.m. Just before the arrival of the 2nd there was a heavy enemy bombardment of 5.9-inch shells, and this delayed the change-over for some time.

A few casualties were received while the battalion was coming out after the relief. The total casualties of the 9th during this tour in the line were—killed, 3 officers, 32 other ranks; wounded, 7 officers, 142 O.R.'s; missing, 56 O.R.'s. The officers killed were Lieutenants H. M. Flynn, R. M. C. McKenzie and F. B. Scougall. The total British casualties in the battle were between twenty and twenty-five thousand, including five thousand in the two Australian divisions.

Although the official name given to this stage of the Third Battle of Ypres is the "Battle of Menin Road Ridge," members of the 9th usually referred to it as the "Battle of Polygon Wood," as in it they captured the western edge of that wood. The true Battle of Polygon Wood, however, occurred on September 26th, when the whole of the wood was captured by the 5th Division.

In the Menin Road battle the enemy was taken by surprise. It was only on September 17th that the German high command thought that there would be a resumption of the attack at Ypres; and they were under the impression that the 1st Australian Division had been transferred to Egypt. Early in the morning of September 20th they captured an Australian officer with operation orders on him, but these did not give the date of the attack.

After being relieved the battalion went to billets in the Dickebusch area, and on the afternoon of the 23rd it moved further back by 'bus to Steenvoorde. A week was spent here in reorganisation and training, and on the 29th the battalion returned to Dickebusch. Next day it once more went into the line, relieving the 47th Battalion on Anzac Ridge.

In the attack now projected, four Anzac divisions, the 1st, 2nd, 3rd Australian, and the New Zealand Division, were to attack side by side, with the object of capturing the Broodseinde Ridge. The 3rd Brigade was to act as divisional reserve.

On the second day on Anzac Ridge the 9th's positions were heavily shelled by the enemy, but the casualties sustained were very few. "A" and "C" Companies were detailed as a cable burying party to lay a telegraph line for the 1st Divisional Signal Company. They were shelled heavily, and among the casualties were Captains Knightley and Wittkopp and Lieutenants L. H. Foote and Clay. Knightley was helping to rescue wounded men from the mud when a 5.9-inch shell blew him into the air. His leg was broken in three places (and had subsequently to be amputated), and he received eleven other wounds, being thus rendered incapable of further active service.

A. R. Knightley left Brisbane as a corporal in the original battalion, and took part in the Anzac Landing as a sergeant. He soon rose to company sergeant-major, and on August 10th, 1915, received his commission, promotion to lieutenant following on October 16th, and by the time of the Battle of Pozières he had become a captain.

Knightley had been with the battalion (except for a few weeks of guard duty at Imbros) during the whole of its stay at Anzac, and was with it during every one of its battles in France up to this time. Towards the end of 1916 he attended a course for senior officers at Aldershot, in England, where be obtained a very good pass. He was a very efficient officer and was universally respected.

To return to the cable burying party. The two companies, when they had completed the work, went straight out to

"Halfway House," a big dugout nearly a mile west of Hooge. Roomy enough to hold a whole battalion, it was very deep and therefore safe, but it was also very damp, and water had to be pumped out of it continuously. The other two companies, on being relieved next day, October 2nd, by the 8th Battalion, also went to Halfway House. Some detachments of the 9th, however, apparently were not relieved, but seem to have remained in the line all the time until the night of October 9th/10th. The weather was now becoming much colder.

October 3rd was spent in resting, and at 8 p.m. the battalion went forward again to its reserve positions, two companies on Westhoek Ridge and two on Anzac Ridge, the next rise beyond Westhoek Ridge.

The Battle of Broodseinde took place on October 4th, all the attacking brigades capturing their objectives. Zero hour was at 4.50 a.m., and shortly afterwards prisoners poured in over Anzac and Westhoek Ridges, many of those who were unwounded being used as stretcher-bearers.

Next day, in drizzling rain, which now set in, the 9th relieved the 8th Battalion in the support lines. The rain continuing, the countryside became very boggy. The German artillery had been very quiet after the attack, but on the afternoon of the 5th it recommenced firing, and on the 6th shelled the support lines severely, Lieutenants E. J. Chester and Henzell being among the wounded.

On October 7th it was still wet, the rain falling in heavy squalls. The 9th relieved the 11th in the left sector of the front line at night: moving about was very difficult on account of the boggy state of the ground. On this day Lieutenant Stenhouse was killed. One of the company headquarters was in a captured pill-box, and Stenhouse was just about to enter it when a shell burst in front of the door. He appeared to have been killed by the concussion, as there was no sign of any wound on his body. On the same day Lieutenant Knowles was wounded.

The battalion remained in the front line for three days, on the first of which torrential rain fell during the afternoon. The next morning was fine, but a gale sprang up after midday, and in the evening it again rained heavily. The 9th was relieved on the night of October 9th, the relief being complete about 1 a.m. on the 10th. It was on October 9th that the first attempt was made on Passchendaele (known officially as the Battle of Poelcappelle). The 1st Division was not directly concerned in this, but at zero hour a raid, which turned out disastrously for the attackers, was made by the 10th Battalion against Celtic Wood.

On coming out of the front line the 9th went to huts near Château Belge, halfway between Ypres and Dickebusch, and at mid-day on the 10th moved on again to Dominion Camp. During the march out of the line Lieutenant-Colonel Mullen and Captain Page were wounded, the latter subsequently dying.

Frank Page was an original member of the battalion. At first a signaller, and later orderly-room sergeant, soon after arriving in France he received a commission. After Ruddle's death at Pozières, Page was appointed adjutant, and filled that position with great distinction until mortally wounded. He was a particularly brave soldier, and received both the M.M. and the M.C.

The total casualties during the Battle of Broodseinde and the few succeeding days were: 1 officer and 33 other ranks killed; 1 officer, 5 O.R.'s died of wounds; 2 O.R.'s missing; 7 officers, 101 O.R.'s wounded. Major James now became acting C.O.

A fortnight was passed in the Dominion Lines, the only noteworthy incidents being the arrival of two batches of reinforcements, a combined sports meeting of the 9th and 10th Battalions on the afternoon of October 20th, and a brigade parade on the 22nd, at which General Birdwood presented ribbons to those who had been awarded decorations. On this same day advice was received that the M.C. had been awarded to Lieutenants C. W. C. Bluett, H. Finter, E. H. Meyers, R. B. Salisbury, H. L. Norris, and L. W. Butler.

On October 24th the battalion moved by 'bus to "Esplanade Sap," under the ramparts at Ypres. The dugouts there were very wet and muddy, making it necessary to spend a great deal of time in cleaning them out before they could be used. Battalion Headquarters remained at Dominion Camp.

The first attack at Passchendaele had failed, on account of the wet weather which had set in, and a second attack a few days later also failed. The Canadians were then detailed to make the third attempt, which took place on October 26th, followed by subsequent attacks which finally resulted in the capture of Passchendaele Ridge by the Canadians and the ending of the Third Battle of Ypres. The 3rd Brigade took no part in these attacks.

After six days at Ypres the battalion went, on October 30th, into the support lines on Anzac and Westhoek Ridges, and two days later it relieved a Canadian battalion in the front line on Passchendaele Ridge. The 11th Battalion was on its right, but on November 2nd the 11th was withdrawn and the 9th had the 12th Battalion for neighbours. Battalion Headquarters here were at Tyne Cottage,[4] a position beside the Ypres-Roulers railway about a mile north-east of Zonnebeke.

In the front line the railway ran through a cutting, and "D" Company occupied a line extending from it towards the left. The headquarters of "C" Company was also situated on this side of the railway, but the line occupied by the company was to the right of the cutting. The exact position of the German line was not known, but patrols went out and gained touch with the enemy.

Early in the morning of November 3rd "D" Company's trenches were heavily bombarded by the enemy, who then attacked, but was driven off. There was a swamp in front of the Australian position, and the Germans had to skirt this in order to advance. A little while later, just before daylight, another party of the enemy suddenly rushed "D" Company from the side of the swamp opposite to that from which the previous assault had come. Its men, who had lost heavily and been badly disorganised by the shelling which preceded the first attack, were now probably taken unawares, as they had thought that the swamp was impassable on this side. They were driven out of the right-hand section of the position, adjoining the cutting, some escaping down the cutting and some falling back on shell-holes in rear of the trench.

Soon after daylight "A" Company, which was in support, made an attempt to recapture the trench by a frontal advance with no flank support, but was unsuccessful, and had to take shelter in shell-holes, where it remained trapped for the rest of the morning.

On hearing of this, the acting C.O., Major James, came up to the front line, and ordered Sergeant Porter to take a party of bombers along the cutting and bomb the Germans out of the trench. This plan also failed, as Porter and his men had to throw their bombs over the side of the cutting into the end of a narrow trench running at right angles from it: they dared

---

4. The actual Tyne Cottage (also called Tyne Cot.) was a barn fifty yards west of the level crossing where the Broodseinde-Passchendaele road crossed the railway. This barn, which had become the centre of several pill-boxes, had been captured by the 2nd Division on October 4th.

not show their heads to see where to aim, and possibly not one of their bombs reached the trench. On the other hand the enemy bombs thrown into the cutting caught our men unprotected, and in a few minutes the whole of the party became casualties, one or two subsequently dying.

At this stage Major James was summoned back to his headquarters to speak to the brigadier urgently on the telephone. Before leaving he asked Lieutenant L. W. Butler, the intelligence officer, who had come up with him, whether the latter could retake the trench if the matter were left in his hands. Butler replied that he could if he had Lewis gun and rifle-grenade support. This was arranged for, and a plan was carefully drawn up.

A section with rifle-grenades first opened fire on the Germans from behind "C" Company's position across the cutting. Then three Lewis guns took up an enfilading position in "C" Company's front line and another one in a shell-hole about 200 yards from the enemy's left flank, and shortly after they opened up the Germans were completely silenced.

Some officers and N.C.O's then went out to the men of "A" and "D" Companies who were trapped in the shell-holes and quickly organised them. On a Very light being fired as a signal the rifle-grenadiers ceased fire, and simultaneously the shell-hole parties charged with rifle and bayonet, the Lewis gunners continuing their enfilade fire until the attackers were right on the parapet. The trench was recaptured with practically no resistance and with only one officer and one man of the 9th slightly wounded. The German casualties were ten killed, and two officers and seven men captured.

The chief credit for the success of the counter-attack belongs to Lieutenant Butler, who organised and led it. The Lewis gun and rifle-grenade fire was arranged by Captains Monteath and McNaught, commanding "B" and "C" Companies respectively.

On this day Lieutenant Devine was killed while entering a dugout in the cutting, and Lieutenant D. Bailey was also killed. Lieutenant Bluett was mortally wounded, his lower jaw being shot away, and Lieutenant Wheatley was wounded.

The battalion's positions were shelled all the next day, but November 5th proved to be quiet on its front. On account of the heavy shell-fire here the telephone lines were constantly being broken, and in consequence much of the communication devolved on the runners. In this hazardous work Kevin O'Neill outshone the others. On one occasion he was given a message for all companies. He set off with it, and about an hour afterwards returned, reported that the messages had all been delivered, and then collapsed. He had been wounded in the chest soon after leaving headquarters, but he completed his task before succumbing to the wound.

On the evening of November 5th the battalion was relieved by the 2nd Battalion and went back in small parties, to the Esplanade Sap at Ypres. The total casualties during this tour in the line were 7 officers and 102 other ranks.

The 3rd Brigade now became the support brigade of the division. The next few days were spent in reorganising, and in cleaning mud from arms, equipment and clothing. On November 9th a move was made to Halifax Camp for a couple of days, and then further back to Renescure. On the 13th the unit marched twenty-three miles to Ledinghem, the men's packs being carried by motor-lorry. This was the battalion's longest march. Besides the length of the journey, there was also the disadvantage that the troops were practically just out of the line, and it was only to be expected that everyone arrived at Ledinghem dog-tired. However, not one man had fallen out. The 9th was congratulated later by the brigadier on its fine performance on this march.

While officers and men were settling down after their fatiguing journey, a Canadian staff car arrived at battalion headquarters with the news that there was trouble in a camp of the Chinese Labour Corps[5] some three miles away. Some hundreds of Chinamen had besieged their three or four English officers and a handful of N.C.O.'s in their headquarters. The men's paybooks had all been collected for some reason, and the Chinamen conceived the idea that it was for the purpose of entering fines therein.

Major James, with some other officers and half-a-dozen men who were close by, thereupon crowded into the car and went to the Chinese camp. When they arrived they found that their small numbers were insufficient to deal with the situation; but, as news of the happening had quickly spread among the battalion, "reinforcements" soon began to come up on foot. Most of them were without puttees, which they had taken off to ease their legs after the long march. When a number of them

---

5  China was now one of the Allies, having declared war on Germany in August, 1917, but she took no part in the fighting. The Chinese Labour Corps was a non-combatant body recruited for auxiliary work, such as road making, on the Western Front, and was officered by Europeans.

had arrived at the camp, they were formed up and marched off with fixed bayonets and magazines charged to surround the Chinamen, but it was with difficulty that the "diggers" were restrained from dealing radically with the insurgents there and then.

After the mutineers had been surrounded they were prevailed upon to allow out of the hut the one and only interpreter, an officer. Major James told him to inform the Chinese that the Australians had surrounded them and would shoot them all if they did not submit. This threat brought the mutiny to a sudden end.

A stay of five days was made at Ledinghem. On November 16th General Birdwood presented medal ribbons to a number of members of the 3rd Brigade who had been awarded decorations.

Two days later the 9th marched to the Samer area for a rest. Headquarters were fixed at Doudeauville, but owing to poor accommodation in these parts the remainder of the battalion had to occupy five villages—Campamare, Hérimez, Séquières, Dalle, and Grandal. Nearly a month was spent here in training, and leave was granted to Boulogne for 25 men each day from 2 p.m. to 8 p.m. Early in December a brigade competition in drill was conducted, and was won by the 12th Battalion, the 9th being awarded second place.

On December 5th voting was carried out among the troops for the second referendum as to whether conscription should be introduced in Australia. As in the case of the first referendum the proposal was rejected, this time by a majority of 166,588. 1,015,159 votes were cast in favour of it and 1,181,747 against it; the sailors and soldiers were again in favour of the measure, by 103,789 to 93,910.

On the 13th the rest was over, and the battalion left for Wismes. Next day it marched to Wavrons, and, rising early on the 15th, the troops left their billets at 4 a.m. and marched to Wizernes, where they entrained at 7 a.m. for De Kennebeke siding, between Kemmel and Neuve Eglise. Arriving there at 11 o'clock, they went straight in to the reserve line at Wulverghem, in the Messines sector.

On December 16th the 9th relieved the 29th Battalion in the front line, in the vicinity of Gapaard Farm, having the 10th on its right. Two companies garrisoned the front line, a third was in supports, and the fourth in reserve. Very little accommodation was available for the men in the front line and the supports. Battalion headquarters were in a pill-box in "Huns' Walk," a cobbled road, bordered by shell-torn trees, running towards the front line. It was given this name earlier in the war, while still in enemy hands, and well behind their line, as the Huns (Germans) could be seen walking up and down there.

A quiet time was spent here for nine days, during which a great deal of work was carried out in improving the defences and building more shelters for the troops. On Christmas Day the 9th was relieved by the 11th and went back to dugouts and huts at Gable Farm, 500 yards north-west of Wulverghem.

Next day ample supplies of food and beer could be purchased at Wulverghem by the troops, who proceeded to make the Christmas season as merry as they could, in spite of very cold weather. For the rest of the month the battalion supplied working parties in the forward area, improving the defences and accommodation still further.

It is of interest to note that in December the five Australian infantry divisions came together for the first time in a single command, under General Birdwood, in the I Anzac Corps. On the 1st of January, 1918, I Anzac became the Australian Corps, II Anzac the XXII British Corps.

The battalion had begun the year 1917 resting behind the lines in the Somme area. It had then taken part in the advance at The Maze, following the German withdrawal; had helped to defeat the German sortie at Lagnicourt and fought nobly at Bullecourt; and after enjoying four months' rest, had experienced the successes and trials of the Passchendaele offensive. This was followed by a quiet tour in the lines at Messines.

## CHAPTER XIII.

### THE ENEMY'S LAST GREAT EFFORT.

The battalion began the year 1918 by going into the line on January 1st in the quiet sector at Messines which it had occupied in the previous month. Colonel Mullen, who had been wounded three months before, rejoined the unit on January 4th. Five days later it returned to Gable Farm, and on the 21st, the 3rd Brigade having in the meantime become divisional reserve, to Ramillies Camp, at Kemmel. Here working parties kept the troops occupied.

On January 23rd the 3rd Brigade relieved the 2nd Brigade. On this occasion all four battalions had to go into the line, the 9th to the Oosttaverne sector, near a watercourse called the Wambeek. This sector was very quiet, so much so as to arouse comment. After a week here the battalion was relieved and taken by light railway to Neuve Eglise, reaching there on the 31st.

During the whole of February the 1st Division was out of the line, the 3rd Brigade resting at Neuve Eglise. The time was occupied by training and by sports, in the latter of which the 9th met with a good deal of success, defeating the 1st Field Artillery Brigade and the 1st Field Ambulance at Rugby football and the 3rd Division team at tug-of-war, and winning the brigade soccer competition by remaining undefeated in five matches. The battalion had to submit, however, to the 1st Pioneer Battalion in the final of the divisional tug-of-war competition.

Before these events a special holiday had been granted to the battalion on February 15th, in place of Christmas Day, which had been spent in the line. A sports meeting was held, of which the following results have been preserved:—

      100 yards: 1st, Pte. Steadman; 2nd, Sgt. E. M. Richards.
      200 yards: 1st, Sgt. Richards.
      880 yards: 1st, Lieut. J. Young; 2nd Sgt. Richards.

On the last day of February the battalion left the rest area and went into supports, relieving the 16th Battalion at "Crater Dugouts" in the Spoil Bank at Hollebeke, not far from Hill 60. Next day it moved into the front line, battalion headquarters being situated in a pillbox in a gully in "Fusilier Wood," on the left of the Ypres-Comines Canal.

The German artillery now became more active, and at 4 p.m. on March 6th a heavy bombardment of gas shell, which lasted for four hours, fell around battalion headquarters and on "D" Company's position in the battalion reserve line. As the air was very still, the fumes lay about in the low ground of the gully, and when the men took off their respirators after the shelling had stopped, most of them were gassed. The casualties were heavy, including almost the whole of the battalion staff and a large part of "D" Company. The C.O., eleven other officers, and 150 other ranks were evacuated; of the officers, Lieutenants Bryson and Warneminde died from the effects of the gas a few days later.

Lieutenant Henzell, in describing his brief experience of this bombardment, says that he was sent in with a party to relieve "D" Company. On his way, a gas-shell burst just in front of him. He was wearing his box-respirator and so was not gassed, but he was splashed and burned by the liquid. When he reached the line he found he was unable to carry on and had to go out again.

Henzell had brought with him a supply of whisky which some of the officers had asked for, but they were so sick that they could not drink it. Similarly, the troops were unable to drink the rum issue waiting in the quartermaster's dugout.

At 7 o'clock next morning brigade headquarters sent up Major McPherson, of the 12th Battalion, together with the R.M.O. of the 12th and other necessary personnel, to take temporary command of the 9th. They established a new headquarters in another position, and soon afterwards Lieutenant-Colonel Rafferty, C.O. of the 11th Battalion, moved up with his headquarters and one company of that battalion to take over the sector, relieving what was left of "D" Company of the 9th. The divisional gas officer also came up, cleared the dugouts and pill-boxes of gas, placed the gassed area out of bounds, and removed all the troops from it, posting sentries to keep anyone from wandering into the dangerous locality. At 11 a.m. the enemy resumed the gas bombardment, but there were no further casualties.

On March 8th the remainder of the 9th Battalion was relieved by the 11th Battalion and went back to Tournai Camp, two miles south-west of Dickebusch, arriving about midnight; here it remained for a fortnight. On March 17th the Lewis gun sections, one from each company, were sent up to Crater Dugouts to garrison a line of reserve posts under the 10th Battalion.

On March 21st an intense bombardment began against the fronts of the British Third and Fifth Armies and along the French front in Picardy, and this was followed by Ludendorff's mighty offensive. On the first day of this attack the enemy captured 16,000 prisoners, and before a week was out had regained nearly all the territory captured during the twelve months which began with the Battle of the Somme in July, 1916.

On March 23rd the 9th relieved the 11th Battalion in the line at Hollebeke, remaining there for eleven days. On the 26th Lieutenant Dearden and six other ranks left a post known as "Potsdam Group" at 2.16 a.m. to patrol No-Man's Land. At a certain point three men were left behind and the remaining four were moving towards a locality which had been named "Wet Pond," when suddenly they saw a party of the enemy, about 20 strong, approaching.

Dearden and his men at once withdrew to the point where they had left the other three and took up a defensive position there, allowing the enemy to approach to within forty yards, when they challenged and fired on them. The enemy threw one or two bombs and then retired hurriedly, leaving behind them their officer, who had been wounded. Two men carried this officer back to "Potsdam Group," and when three-quarters of an hour later they returned to Dearden, the patrol went on through "Wet Pond" to "Hessian Wood," where they were attacked from the rear by a party of the enemy about 30 strong. The Queenslanders turned and engaged them, but Dearden and four other men were wounded, and one was killed. The Germans then withdrew a short distance, apparently to the cover of some shell-holes, and this enabled the 9th's patrol to return to its own lines. The body of the dead man could not, however, be brought in.

A counter-patrol of 20 men under Lieutenant Gower, with a Lewis gun, was then detailed. Leaving our lines at 5.30 a.m., it soon encountered the enemy, who retired when fired on. Gower and his men followed, shooting while on the move and inflicting casualties on the Germans, and eventually penetrated the enemy wire, to see the Germans take cover in some pillboxes. Gower then decided to withdraw, but the enemy, noticing the move, came out from the pill-boxes and opened fire with two machine-guns. The Lewis gun had jammed and could not be used, and the enemy machine-gun fire kept the patrol down in the shell-holes in which they had taken shelter, until it was too light to move. Gower found that four of his party had been killed and two wounded.

The right section of the patrol managed to return to our lines by 9 a.m. without casualties, and some hours later Gower made his way back by rolling and crawling, having first hidden the Lewis gun under water in a shell-hole. The remainder of the patrol, however, had to remain out all day and they returned when it had become sufficiently dark. At 8 p.m. a party went out, under cover of artillery fire, to recover the casualties. It succeeded in this task, but two of its number were killed in No-Man's Land.

The battalion was relieved on April 3rd by the Royal Scots and the Cameron Highlanders, who themselves had just been relieved after heavy fighting further south. Marching as far back as Spoil Bank, the 9th entrained and went to "Murrumbidgee Camp," La Clytte, arriving there about 6 o'clock next morning. The same afternoon it moved by 'bus to Caestre, and here Major J. Newman, of the 11th Battalion, assumed command of the 9th with the temporary rank of lieutenant-colonel.

On April 5th the 3rd Brigade began to entrain for the Somme, the 9th leaving next morning at 6.30 a.m., arriving at St. Roch station, Amiens, at 4 p.m. Leaving the train there, the battalion marched about five miles to Argoueves, which they reached at 6 p.m., the officers being billeted in the empty château and the other ranks in the village.

Three days were spent in training and reorganisation, and brigade headquarters noticed that the men were very "soft" after their stay in the trenches in the north. On April 9th the battalion marched five miles to Flesselles, where accommodation was very limited, this being due to the fact that not only was the 12th Battalion billeted here as well, but also the headquarters of the 3rd Brigade and of the 17th British Division.

On April 10th news arrived that the enemy had on the previous day broken through in the north on part of the front held by Portuguese troops, and had taken Laventie, Estaires, Sailly-sur-la-Lys, Bac St. Maur, and Steenwerck, although the Messines Ridge was still held by the British. The 1st was the only Australian division not yet fighting on the Amiens front, so on April 11th it was ordered back to Flanders to defend the important railway junction of Hazebrouck.

The 9th Battalion therefore left Flesselles at 11 o'clock next morning and marched to Amiens, where, together with the rest of the brigade, it bivouacked on the outskirts of the town, near the citadel. The men had received strict instructions to keep out of the city; many of them therefore made it their business to go into Amiens.[1] One party from "C" Company, after looking on the wine when it was very red, gained possession of some civilian overcoats and hats, put on these over their uniforms, and returned bristling with bottles, which stuck out from their clothing in all directions.

"A" Company was detailed as brigade loading party, and began duty at 5 p.m. The station area was shelled at intervals during the day, and at 8 p.m. enemy aeroplanes came over and bombed the neighbourhood of the bivouac for more than three hours, causing, however, only a few casualties, none of which were in the 9th. During this aerial bombardment the troops around the citadel were illuminated for some time by three enemy parachute flares.

Dozens of our searchlights swept the sky looking for the aeroplanes, and whenever one was located all would swing round and converge on it. The resulting pyramid of light was a wonderful spectacle, with the aeroplane at the apex manoeuvring in all sorts of ways to escape from the beams while "archies" (anti-aeroplane guns) concentrated their fire on it.

At 2 a.m. on April 13th the battalion left the bivouac and marched to St. Roch station. On their way the troops found an egg store, which they raided, and almost everyone carried, in addition to his official equipment, a box or a basket of eggs. The train was supposed to leave at 4.47 a.m., but owing to breaks in the railway lines caused by the enemy bombing, congestion of traffic, and disorganisation of the civilian railway personnel by the bombing, trains were not leaving at the times arranged. Every time an enemy aeroplane arrived over the station the railway officials would dive into their shelters and stay there, leaving the loading party to carry on as well as it could without them.

The battalion rested in the boulevard and park near the station and eventually entrained at 11.30 a.m. While they were waiting the men made the engine-driver supply them with hot water from the engine to boil their eggs, and the reduction of

---

[1] Australian troops were always apt to enter places which had been put out of bounds. There was a common saying in the A.I.F. that the best way to end the war would be to put Berlin out of bounds to the Australians.

the engine's steam pressure thus caused may have been an additional reason for the delay in the train's departure.

After a slow journey the 9th arrived at about 3 a.m. on the 14th at Hondeghem, and marched to a position a mile east of Hazebrouck. The battalion was now in divisional reserve. In the evening officers from each company were sent up the line to reconnoitre. By this time the 1st and 2nd Brigades, which had preceded the 3rd, had helped to bring the German attack to a standstill, just after Meteren and Merris had been captured by the enemy. The 1st Division was now back in the Second Army, forming part of the XV British Corps, under General

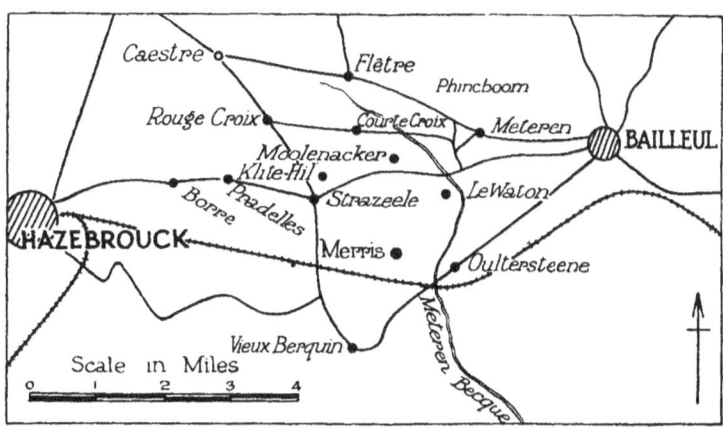

22. The Area East of Hazebrouck.

de Lisle, and in this corps it remained for the next four months. Conditions of living were quite comfortable here, as the troops were billeted in empty farmhouses which had recently been evacuated by the inhabitants. Many of the men were able to sleep in feather beds with the sheets still on them. "D" Company's Headquarters found in their billet a ready set meal which they consumed. In one farmhouse it had evidently been washing day, for a partly-wrung sheet was found hanging over the side of a tub.

The livestock from the farms was made use of to add to the regulation rations, and fresh milk, poultry and other food not usually provided near the front line made life quite enjoyable. *Estaminets* were found fully stocked, and naturally the troops took advantage of this. One company commander, finding that a large proportion of his company was missing, investigated some near-by wine cellars, where he found happy parties enjoying themselves. It required all the eloquence at his command to persuade them to return to their trenches. The same circumstances had occurred with the Germans, and had helped to bring their advance to a stop.

On the day of arrival 12 officers and 92 others went back to Morbecque to the brigade nucleus battalion. The remainder stayed where they were until the 16th, when they moved to Borre, a mile further forward, remaining here for three days and relieving the 12th Battalion. On the 17th the enemy shelled Borre incessantly from 9 a.m. till 2 p.m., and the troops billeted in the village had to leave it, going into the surrounding fields for safety. The casualties were 4 killed and 11 wounded, a small number considering the heaviness of the bombardment, which accompanied an unsuccessful enemy attack. Among the casualties was "A" Company's cook, who had set up his kitchen in a large barn, and was killed just at the troops' dinner-time. He had finished cooking the meal, and at the time he was hit the men were enjoying it in scattered positions all over the adjoining field. Lieutenant J. Young was hit in the eye by a shell-fragment which carried away part of his cheek and a portion of his nose as well; eventually he lost his sight completely.

A number of pigs were casualties in this bombardment, with the result that pork became an addition to the ration list, so much so that finally some became heartily sick of the sight and taste of it. Lieutenant C. M. Wrench writes:—

> "In this shelling the livestock also suffered. It was pitiful to see, in particular, a wounded pig run out into the field and succumb. When the shelling subsided he was solemnly carried off on a stretcher to the cookhouse."

A similar occurrence possibly gave rise to the story of the officer who saluted some stretcher-bearers carrying a "dead hero" under a blanket; the corpse on investigation proved to be that of a porker.

Early in the morning of the 19th the enemy shelled the billets of "A," "B," and "D" Companies, and everyone had to leave them and once more go into the open fields. At dusk on the same day the battalion marched through Rouge Croix and Flêtre to the support trenches at Phincboom, on the Meteren Becque front, so called from Meteren Becque, a watercourse which runs close by the village of Meteren. Here for the first time the 9th relieved French troops, the 321st Regiment. The French did all they could to make the taking over easy, their officers with marked thoroughness giving attention to every

Plate xvii.

**33.—THE BATTALION SHELLED OUT OF ITS BILLETS AT BORRE.
17th April, 1918. (See p. 206.)**
(Aust. War Memorial Official Photograph. No. E 2088. Copyright. From the Official History.)

**34.—SIGNALLERS AT CAPPY.
Connecting telephone line to "A" Company.**
(Aust. War Memorial Official Photograph. No. E 2991. Copyright.)

Plate xviii.

35.—Lieut. J. P. TUNN, Albert Medal. (See page 227.)
(Block lent by The Equitable Probate and General Insurance Coy. Ltd.)

36.—MACHINE GUN AT BULIMBA, BRISBANE.
(See p. 220.)
In front of the School of Arts. The inscription reads:—This machine gun captured by the 9th Battalion A.I.F. during operations near Merris, Flanders, in June, 1918.
(N.K.H. photo.)

37.—LIEUT.-COL. C. F. ROSS.
(From Aust. War Memorial Official Photograph. No. E. 4153. Copyright.)

38.—THE SPECIAL ANZAC MEDAL. (See p. 278.)
(S. R. C. Lewis photo.)

detail. In some cases, though not in all, this resulted in the relief taking longer than usual. For example, one N.C.O., A. Pitceathly, took over an outpost on the crest of a hill, and had all the enemy machine-gun positions pointed out to him, as well as the lay of No-Man's Land.

The "front line" in this sector consisted of outposts, with groups of men occupying trenches and in some cases farmhouses and barns about 200 yards behind. Whenever the buildings were shelled, their "inhabitants" moved into short trenches. All the French earthworks were well made and well wired. The sanitary arrangements, however, were very primitive, and compared badly with those of Australian troops, who were most particular in this respect.

In "A" Company's sector the French guide had failed to notify the position of one of their machine-gun posts, with the result that towards morning a very excited French corporal arrived at company headquarters and treated the O.C., Major Ross, to some voluble language, much hand-waving, and vigorous pointing towards the eastern horizon, which was now showing the first streaks of dawn. The O.C., through an interpreter, told him to go off out of the line, but he would not listen to any suggestion of informal relief, so to appease him Ross sent Sergeant McMaster and a few men to take formal possession of the post. The French machine-gunners then left, and the beat of their heavy boots on the cobble road indicated that they were making a valiant effort to overtake their comrades.

As the position taken over was under the direct observation of the enemy, it was difficult to move about in the daytime, so the men were allowed to sleep then. At night they improved the defences. Hot meals were served from a cookhouse in the rear at 8.30 p.m. and 3.30 a.m., and tea was provided at midnight.

The line ran close to Meteren, a village two miles west of Bailleul, on the road to Cassel. The 3rd Brigade was now ordered to capture this place, which had been taken by the Germans on April 13th. The plan adopted was to advance our lines on either side of the village so as to pass it, and when it was "held in a pair of pincers," to send in parties to mop up[2] the enemy troops in occupation.

The operation was to take place in two phases, without artillery preparation, on successive nights; in the first phase

[2] See Glossary.

the two battalions (11th and 12th) holding the line were to advance, one on either side of the village, to a position about opposite to its centre. The 9th and 10th on the next night would attack with three companies each so as to outflank the village, the 9th to the south-west, the 10th on the north-east.

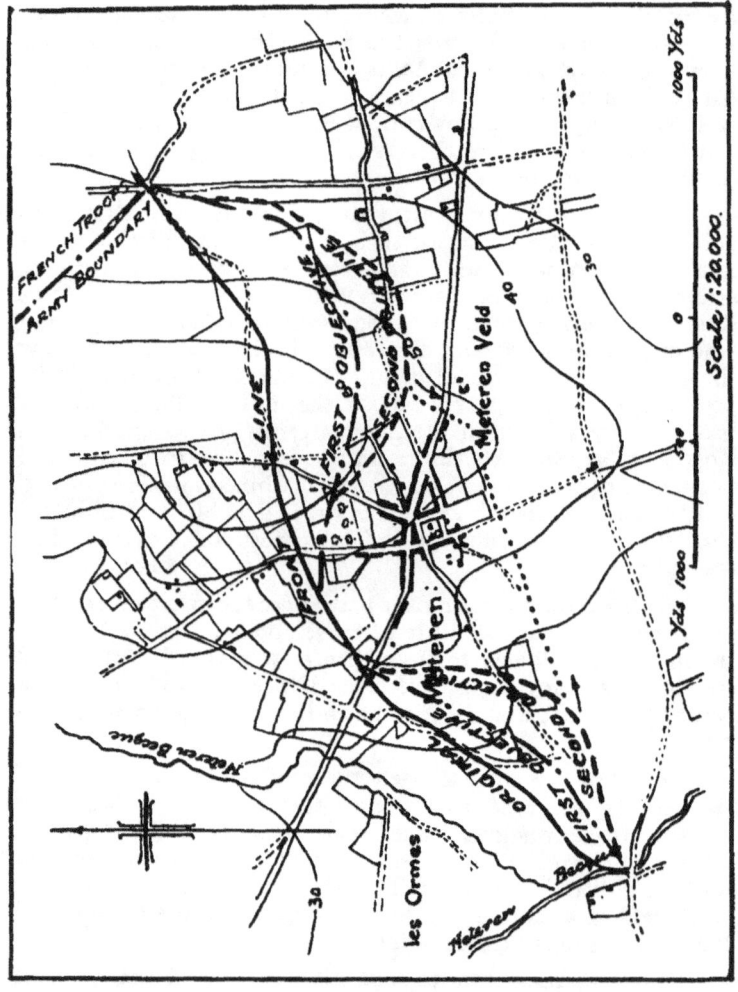

23. Meteren.
April 23rd-24th, 1918.

A party of 100 men from the 11th and 12th Battalions would then enter the village from the west, north and east and capture or drive out the enemy troops. After this the 9th and 10th were to send out their reserve companies to join up the battalions by forming a line just beyond the southern outskirts of Meteren.

The attack began at 1 a.m. on April 23rd, the first phase being carried out without much opposition. Immediately after the hot meal which arrived at 8.30 p.m., "B," "C" and "D" Companies moved forward to relieve the 12th Battalion. During the relief the enemy shelled the front area incessantly, causing eleven casualties in the 9th. The relief was completed at 11.55 p.m., and five minutes later, at midnight, the two flank companies—"D" on the left and "B" Company on the right—left the front-line trench and began their advance in the bright moonlight. They reached their objective without a great deal of opposition; but when "C" Company, in the centre, advanced five minutes after midnight it came under heavy machine-gun fire from behind hedges in front of the village and from a large house (called by the Australians the "château") on its left flank, and could not make much progress. A request was made for artillery support, but this could not be given on account of the danger of hitting our own men. Stokes mortars then fired on the machine-gun positions, but could not subdue them, and a second attack by "C" Company failed. The centre of the company was forced to withdraw, but it kept its flanks in touch with the two neighbouring companies.

The time for the next stage of the operation now arrived, and at 1.30 a.m. the mopping-up parties from the 11th and 12th Battalions advanced. Instead of mopping-up, however, they found that what they had to do was to make a frontal attack on an enemy position which had not been captured. Up to this time, although the line had been advanced on the two flanks, not a single enemy post had been taken.

The parties from the 11th and 12th met with intense machine-gun fire from the edge of the village. Heavy fighting took place among the first outbuildings encountered, and several attempts were made to get within bombing distance of the machine-guns, but without success, and the parties were forced to retire. One enemy post, however, was captured by "D" Company of the 9th soon after 1.30 a.m.

At 2 o'clock "A" Company, which had come up on the extreme right, attempted to advance past Meteren from the south-west, according to orders. Major Ross, the company commander, found a length of trench running from our line towards the enemy, and as there was no other cover in the vicinity, decided to launch his attack from it. However, when the leading section of Lieutenant Avery's platoon jumped out of the trench it was immediately shot down, several men being killed, including Sergeant W. Jamieson, a splendid N.C.O. The other sections, hesitating at the heavy machine-gun fire, blocked the trench and thus prevented the remaining platoons from moving forward. This was no doubt the best thing that could have happened, as any further movement outside the trench would only have resulted in useless loss of life. An attempt later to recover the bodies of the dead failed. After this "A" Company lay out ahead of the new front line, waiting for the village to be captured before it again tried to carry out its orders.

At this stage Lieutenant A. R. Wheatley tried to capture or silence a machine-gun which was causing much trouble to "C" Company, but was unsuccessful. He then essayed to gain touch with "D" Company's post on his left, but was shot dead in the attempt. Another man was killed near the same spot during the night. When dawn broke C.S.M. J. Brown, of "D" Company, and a private went out, and, despite the heavy fire, dragged the bodies in one at a time by means of a rope. They were both buried in one grave about 150 yards behind the front-line positions.

The 10th Battalion had met with even less success than the 9th. At dawn orders were received from brigade headquarters that no further attempts were to be made to advance, and that the positions reached were to be consolidated. Before daylight it could be seen that several fires had been started in Meteren.

It is difficult to understand how the plan could have been decided upon. After the first stage of the advance had taken place it must have been plain to the enemy what our intention was, and it was only to be expected that he would prepare for the next night's attack in the way he did—by reinforcing strongly with machine-guns the outskirts of the village, and so making it almost impossible to capture it without strong artillery support. The only help received from the artillery was that the village was bombarded intermittently until 1.30 a.m., as the attack had been intended to be a surprise one, with no preliminary bombardment and no barrage. In addition, the operation was begun immediately after a relief, in unknown territory, and the junior officers had no opportunity of getting their bearings.

The casualties of the 9th in this minor attack were: Killed, 1 officer and 11 other ranks; wounded, 32 O.R.'s. The strength of the battalion immediately after the battle was: In the line, 29 officers and 484 O.R.'s; detached and with nucleus battalion, 18 officers, 231 O.R.'s.

In the early morning of the 25th "B" and "C" Companies withdrew their forward posts slightly so as to make a continuous line. A further attempt was made to recover the bodies of the men who had been killed in the attack, but it failed owing to heavy enemy fire. While the party was getting ready one man of "B" Company, who had just demolished his rum issue (and apparently that of several other men as well) turned to some of his companions and said: "Ahr, give me another rum and I'll go out and chew the b—— muzzles off their rifles." Dutch courage, indeed!

The morning was very misty, and at 9 o'clock the enemy opened up a heavy bombardment of H.E. and gas on "B" and "C" Companies' front-line posts, but only three men were wounded. At 11 the mist dispersed, and the day became quite clear. On this day, the third anniversary of the Landing at Anzac, a message was received from 1st Divisional Headquarters conveying greetings to all comrades of Peninsula days, and to this a suitable reply was sent.

About 8.30 a.m. next day the O.C. of "B" Company, Lieutenant Gower, was watching from the attic of a house which served as his headquarters when he saw dimly through the mist a man walking behind our lines. When this man came closer, he could be seen to be a German officer. Gower rushed downstairs, picked up a rifle, and, running out to a gate opening on to the road along which the German was walking, halted him and took him prisoner. The captive explained that he had been patrolling in No-Man's Land and had lost his way in the fog. From what he said it seemed likely that he had crossed our front line in the sector of the next brigade, and had then wandered along until stopped by Gower.

Major Ross, commanding "A" Company, was asleep in the cellar of the house. Roused by loud voices, he looked up to see a dandy little German officer walking down the steps, followed by Gower covering him with a rifle. It was a cold morning, but streams of perspiration were running down the German's face. He sat down, and then said: "Are you Highlanders"? but seemed to be quite relieved when he heard that his captors were Australians!

At this time heavy fogs covered the countryside until 10 or 11 o'clock every morning. There was also a good deal of gas lying round in many places; most of the troops in the front line had lost their voices, being able to speak only in hoarse whispers.

A further attempt to take Meteren had been arranged for the evening of April 26th, but it was cancelled. This alteration of plans may have been due to the fact that on April 25th the French had been driven back from Kemmel Hill, seven miles to the north-east of Meteren, necessitating the withdrawal of part of the Allied line in this sector.

On the 27th an enemy aeroplane flew very low over the battalion's lines for about half-an-hour, until driven off by Lewis guns. As it flew away it dropped a single bomb, but unfortunately for the Germans this fell not on our line but about ten yards from one of the enemy's own outposts.

It had been decided to make an attempt to silence Meteren Château, which was a very strong enemy machine-gun post, and on this day a special 4.5 inch howitzer was detailed for the purpose. The shooting was excellent, and, after the "château" had been demolished, a number of shells were dropped on to various parties of Germans who had been driven out of the ruins and were trying to take cover behind hedges in the neighbourhood. While this was going on the snipers of the battalion took full advantage of their opportunities, and had some fine shooting at the enemy parties. One result of this onslaught was a particularly quiet night, especially around the "château."

At 11 p.m. on the 28th the first of the 3rd Battalion companies arrived to relieve the 9th. They were late in coming, as the village of Courte Croix, along the route of their march, had been bombarded by the enemy with incendiary shells and set on fire. The relief was completed twenty minutes after midnight. On going out the battalion had to work its way round well to the north of the burning village, as on the more direct route, on the south, the light from the fire would have shown up the troops as a good target for the enemy artillery. On arrival at the railway camp at South Borre, a welcome hot meal was awaiting them. The last company marched in at 2.30 a.m.

The battalion remained for five days at South Borre in good billets, supplying working parties. On May 3rd volunteers were called for a raid: twelve men were chosen and placed under Lieutenants Gower and Knowles for special training. Next day the battalion, minus the raiding party, went into the reserve line on the right of Pradelles, being billeted in farm-houses. On the 5th it was shelled out of its billets into the open fields by 12-inch shells, the bombardment being similar to those of April 17th and 19th. After four hours here it relieved the 11th Battalion in the front line between Meteren and Strazeele.

On the first night here and for several succeeding nights a party was detailed from "A" Company to round up a number of cows, which had been reported to be straying round the front line, drive the beasts back to St. Sylvestre Cappel and hand them over to the military police. Mr. D. L. Suller writes:—

"These expeditions were the cause of much fluent language by those who took part in them, cows being hard enough to find in daylight without searching deserted farmyards for them in the dead of night. Occasionally one would stumble over a dead beast in the darkness, and if it had been dead for some days—well, the remarks heard were unprintable.

"One evening some ten animals were collected and were being driven to the rear when the enemy began to shell the road and gradually lengthened his range. When the shelling came too close to be comfortable, both men and beasts became restive. Suddenly several 5.9's landed ahead and the cows stampeded amidst a barrage of bad language."

On May 11th, Colonel Mullen, who had been gassed two months before, rejoined the battalion.

In front of our line here were the Meteren baths, which had been erected by the British two or three years before, and which the men of the 9th had used at a time when the area was well behind the front line. A German machine-gun post had been noticed near these baths, and Lieutenant Gower's raiding party set out to capture it after midnight on May 11th/12th.

Trench-mortars shelled the post for eight minutes, after which the raiders advanced on it from the northern and south-western sides, but, finding the trench unoccupied, they returned. Captain McNaught, commanding "C" Company, then sent No. 9 Platoon, which was only 15 strong, to dig in near the enemy trench. They did so, and just before daybreak saw some Germans, on whom they fired with a Lewis gun. A small party then went over to their dugouts and took two prisoners.

When day broke it was seen that a party of the enemy near by had been cut off. They tried to get back to their own line during daylight, but every time they moved they were fired at. Towards the close of the afternoon a party of the 9th moved out into a position from which it could block the withdrawal of the Germans, who thereupon surrendered. They numbered about 18, and all were youths; only one of them had ever been in an outpost before. Their machine-gun having been put out of action, their officer had taken it back for repairs and had left them without a leader.

These events are very well described by Mr. W. F. Allan:—

"Just before daylight the machine-gunner saw a couple of 'Squids'[3] just in front and let fly a couple of rounds. One of them squealed, so Tom Auton, number two on the gun, came back to get someone to go out and collect the squealer. I chucked down the shovel, grabbed my rifle and went off with him. Couldn't see any sign of him, and after a bit I noticed a hole. This proved to be a dugout, and we could hear one moaning and another whispering to him. Gave a prod with the bayonet down the hole and requested them to appear upstairs for a bit. Not exactly in these words, of course, as we had just spotted other dugouts to our right and left, and also half expected to get a bullet or two from the one we were interviewing. No reply, so I pulled the pin out of a bomb and laid it on the doorstep. One, two, three, four, five and bang she went and two Squids shot out like sky rockets. . . .

"Just before dinner time I was looking over the ground when I suddenly saw a big square-head pop up and start shaking the dust out of his blankets barely 100 yards away. Pointed the rifle his way and you could hear him squeal for miles. Corporal Holm jumped up and I put him wise. Another big square-head with eyes full of surprise looked over the top. Holm made him squeal also. After dinner Doug. saw a hand with a tin of water appear and spill the tin, so we periodically drilled the ground about a foot lower down all day with a German rifle and bullets. Charlie Holm asked Lieutenant Knowles if we could get the couple of squids about 5 o'clock. It was still daylight, but he said: 'Yes, take a couple of the old hands with you.' Ern. Dagg, Herb. Bradshaw, Doug., the corporal and I went over for them. Instead of about four as we had expected, we gathered about 18, made them pack up and sent them back for the new chaps to 'rat.'[4]

"Watched them safe across almost to our outpost and then a sniper started to shoot at them and a couple of machine-guns started on us. We dropped flat, and then Doug. heard a bolt being rammed home behind us in a hedge. We ducked into a ditch and scuttled away in water up to our knees, and the devil opened on us at about twenty yards. He did no good, and the corporal nipped behind a tree and opened on him, shutting him up quick."

This last sentence expresses the facts as they seemed to Allan and his companions, but actually, while the German's attention was taken up by Holm, who was firing at him, Private Henry silenced him by Lewis gun fire from our outpost.

On the night of May 12th the platoon dug a new outpost just in front of the baths, and on the next evening it had instructions to set fire to them. Several incendiary rifle-grenades were fired at them, but these proved to be "duds," so some of the men offered to burn the baths if petrol could be obtained.

[3] Germans.
[4] To rat is to pillage. The "new chaps" were newly-joined reinforcements, who were keener on collecting souvenirs than the old soldiers.

Captain McNaught therefore brought up a tin of petrol, and a couple of men went to the right-hand shed and cautiously prepared everything, while two more did the same at the second shed. When all was ready and everyone had got under cover, W. F. Allan and Corporal Holm went out to set the baths alight. Allan struck six matches together and threw them on to the petrol, which at once went up in flames, but Holm struck three matches separately without result. An enemy machine-gun then opened on them and they had to make their way back to their trench.

The fire which had been lit burned for a quarter of an hour and then went out. By this time it was daylight, but Allàn and Holm once more crawled out with the remainder of the petrol and prepared the second shed more thoroughly. After setting light to it they rushed back to their trench; the enemy fired at them, but they reached cover safely. The attempt this time was successful, and all the sheds were destroyed. For this piece of work five Military Medals were subsequently awarded—W. F. Allan, E. Dagg, C. Holm, T. Howard, and C. Lewis.

## CHAPTER XIV.

**DEFENCE OF HAZEBROUCK.**

On the night of May 13th the battalion was relieved by the 5th Battalion and moved back to South Borre, into divisional reserve. After five days here it marched further to the rear through Hazebrouck to Sercus, arriving there about 8.30 p.m. on the 18th, after a trying march in hot weather. The 1st Division was now in reserve, and the unit was quartered in tents under trees in small fields, in delightfully green surroundings.

On May 20th, 21st, and 22nd, battalion sports took place, and on the last mentioned date there was also a parade at 7 a.m., when the 9th was reviewed by the divisional commander, General Walker. Training was being carried out, too. The following is the time-table for May 21st:—

|  | 7.30-8 a.m. | 8-8.30 | 8.45-9.15 | 9.15-9.45 |
|---|---|---|---|---|
| Practice in Rifle-grenades | A | D | C | B |
| Bombing | B | A | D | C |
| Bayonet | C | B | A | D |
| Musketry | D | C | B | A |

Smoke-oh and lecture, 8.30-8.45.

(The initials represent the companies.)

On May 22nd the canteen opened and, although a G.S. waggon went to St. Omer every day and returned full of goods, it was found impossible to keep it sufficiently stocked owing to the abundance of money in the camp.

The stay at Sercus lasted only eight days, and at 8.30 a.m. on May 26th a move was made once more towards the front line. The battalion marched along the St. Omer-Hazebrouck road, and at a point near Hazebrouck General Walker had stationed himself to watch the 3rd Brigade go by. Just as the head of the column reached the general the enemy began shelling, and two high-velocity shells burst in the ranks of the 9th, wounding two men. The battalion at once split up into artillery formation and continued its march, the battalions in rear being diverted to another road. The divisional commander moved further back along the road to continue his inspection undisturbed.

The 9th marched through the outskirts of Hazebrouck to Rouge Croix. Next day it went into the front line, relieving the 1st Battalion at Klite-Hil, half-a-mile north of Strazeele, where nine days were spent. Soon after taking over here Lieutenant C. O. Brown was mortally wounded.

At midday on May 31st Private R. P. Knight, from a post in the centre of the battalion's sector, crawled out through the crops in front of him to reconnoitre an enemy trench which seemed to be unoccupied. Arriving within a few yards of it, he saw no signs of occupation, so decided to go in and examine it. Inside Knight found stick bombs lying about and a rifle, but no men. He walked along the trench to a small shelter cut in the parados, and, lifting a bag hanging in front, found a German lying inside. The man called out in surprise, and Knight at once shot him with the revolver he carried. The report aroused the rest of the garrison, about 25 men, who came running towards him. Knight fired at the nearest of them, then turned and ran out of the trench. He turned again and once more fired at the Germans as one of them was about to throw a bomb. The Lewis gunners in the post on our side had seen the enemy running along the trench after Knight, so they fired, thus preventing them from leaving the trench, and enabling Knight to return unharmed.

Next morning, at 2 a.m., three Portuguese soldiers came into the front line from No-Man's Land. They said that they had been captured by the Germans and kept at Lille, but had escaped two days before, and had made their way through the German lines without being seen. They had been acting as servants for German officers; only one of them could speak English, and he knew only sufficient to make himself understood with difficulty.

The strength of the unit at this date was:—

| | | | | |
|---|---|---|---|---|
| With the unit, | 25 | officers, | 622 | other ranks. |
| Detached | 22 | ,, | 216 | ,, ,, |
| Total | 47 | ,, | 838 | ,, ,, |

On the night of June 1st the enemy shelled battalion headquarters and set fire to the R.A.P., which continued to burn till about midday on the next day. On the afternoon of June 3rd, battalion headquarters was again shelled, as was "A" Company's headquarters in a hop-drying kiln close by. The first shell knocked in the side of the kiln and wounded Major Ross, but there was no other casualty. On the night of June 4th/5th the 9th was relieved by the 5th Battalion and went back to Hondeghem, going on viâ Wallon-Cappel to Sercus on the 7th. Two days later there was an inspection by General Plumer after church parade, and on the 12th brigade sports were held.

The sports were noteworthy for the visit of "General Plumer." Corporal Wilson of "C" Company, who could impersonate this general to perfection, obtained the necessary uniforms and horses and, accompanied by an "orderly officer" and pennant-bearer, he rode on to the sports ground. The brigadier, General Gordon Bennett, was deceived for a while, but when he discovered the impersonation he entered into the joke, and said to "Plumer": "General, I suppose this young staff-officer of yours is a smart young chap." "Oh, dear, no! Oh, dear, no!" said "Plumer," "if he were he would not be on the staff." The "orderly officer" was Private J. Hayward, an original member of the battalion. Unfortunately, Wilson was killed in his next tour in the line.

On June 14th, in glorious weather, the battalion marched to Blaringhem, a beautiful spot, four miles from Sercus, on the Neuf-fosse Canal, for swimming and sports. The sports consisted of boat-races, the boats being mostly bulky pontoons, difficult to propel. No rules were observed in these races, therefore each crew, consisting of about a dozen men, attempted to win by fair means or foul—usually the latter. At 5 p.m. the battalion left to return to Sercus.

On the 15th the battalion went forward to La Kreule, in readiness for a German attack which the higher authorities expected. It bivouacked in open fields in very pleasant weather. The day was very clear, and as the troops were under observation from seven enemy balloons, movement had to be restricted as much as possible. After a while some eighty trench shelters were supplied—just enough to afford cover for all when rain fell in the afternoon. These shelters consisted of light canvas tarpaulins of khaki colour, something like tent flies, which were fixed over shallow holes dug in the ground.

This day was a memorable one for the officers, as there reached the mess a case of whisky which had been on order for some considerable time.

After a very quiet two days, during which scarcely a shell or a gun was heard from either side, the battalion went into the front line opposite Merris, relieving the 5th Battalion. "A" Company held the right section and "B" Company the left; "C" was in support and "D" in reserve. The battalion's right flank reached the Hazebrouck-Armentières railway.

A minor operation was carried out early on June 20th, with the intention of advancing the line about 200 yards. The attack was in charge of Captain F. J. Biggs. At midnight "C" Company took position along a taped line behind "B" Company's outposts, and at 12.30 there opened a hurricane bombardment of artillery, light and medium trench-mortars, and rifle-grenades, which lasted for five minutes.

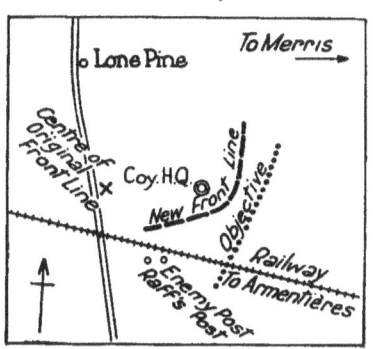

24. Minor Operation near Merris, June 20th, 1918.

At 12.35 the artillery barrage moved forward 100 yards, "C" Company following it, and at 12.36 it moved forward another hundred yards. A minute later the centre and left platoons reached their objective and began digging in, each platoon firing three green Very lights as a signal to battalion headquarters that they had carried out their part of the movement successfully. These platoons had met with hardly any opposition, but No. 12 platoon, on the extreme right, was held up by machine-gun fire and could not advance very far. Its commander, Lieutenant Barcroft, was seriously wounded and the platoon sergeant killed; there were seven or eight other casualties, and the platoon became disorganised.

An attempt was now made, by firing rifle-grenades, to dislodge the enemy from the machine-gun post which was firing on the platoon, but they could not be driven out. The section to the left of the railway reached to within fifty yards of its objective, but the other three sections had to dig in about forty yards from the enemy machine-gun post which was blocking them. About 2 o'clock this party was reinforced by a Lewis gun section.

Captain Biggs then arranged for a platoon of "B" Company, under Lieutenant Raff, to advance along the right of the railway. At 2.30 Raff and his men went out and gradually worked up the railway to a position in line with the troops to the left of the railway and settled down in a shell-hole there.

Dawn was now breaking, and the light was sufficient for the Queenslanders to see a German emerge from an improvised shelter in a hedge which skirted the railway about fifteen yards in front of the shell-hole which had been occupied. Fire was opened on him, and, though he seemed to be wounded, he broke into a run and disappeared. It was quite evident that there were other Germans in the shelter, and during the day rifle-grenades were fired at the post, some of them making direct hits.

In the afternoon Privates A. C. Cauchan and Ward volunteered to crawl up to the post and investigate it. This they did, and, after throwing a bomb into the post were making their way back when Cauchan was shot dead by a sniper from the direction of his right front. Later Lance-Corporal Miller and Private Vance went out, and reached the post without meeting with any resistance. Miller put his head inside the post, to find three Germans, two of whom were dead. The other, who was wounded, surrendered and came out. Miller and Vance returned with their prisoner, and with a machine-gun they had found there, and, although repeatedly fired at from the right front, they arrived back at the shell-hole safely with their booty. As prisoners were urgently required at headquarters for identification purposes, it was decided to take the wounded German back to the rear immediately, although it was still daylight. One man volunteered to take him, and started off, carrying him on his back. On emerging from the shell-hole he was fired at by the enemy, but he was not hit and was soon out of the line of fire. The prisoner belonged to the 4th Bavarian Division.

The total casualties in this action were: Killed, 6 other ranks; wounded, 2 officers and 16 O.R.'s. On the afternoon of the 20th enemy snipers were very active on the right, and five more were wounded, including Lieutenant Bailey.

At 10 o'clock next morning an attempt was made to capture an enemy post to the right of the railway. Two parties, each of an N.C.O. and four men, attacked the post at either end, supported by Lewis gun fire, but both were held up by barbed wire, and suffered casualties while looking for a suitable place to cross it. The left party at length succeeded in finding a narrow gap, and advanced towards the post, but the leader, Sergeant Sutton, was killed, one man was wounded, and another, Private Robertson, who was afterwards missing, was presumed to have been killed.

Next day at 2 a.m. a new post was established by the 9th slightly forward of the right-hand post. It had been evacuated by the enemy probably because he had found it untenable.

At 7.30 p.m. on June 23rd Sergeant G. Goulburn went out to reconnoitre the Plate Becque, the stream running across the battalion's front. Crawling through the grass, he found first an unoccupied enemy trench, which bore signs of having been garrisoned not long before, and going on, reached the stream and crossed it by an improvised footbridge he found there. On the other side were some trenches, and Goulburn observed several dugout entrances with blankets or waterproof sheets hanging over them. He found that they were occupied by sleeping Germans, so decided to return for help to capture them. Unobserved by the enemy, he reached our front line and started out again with Lieutenant Cork and Private McKenzie, but the three were seen as they were crossing the enemy wire on the far side of the stream. The Germans fired on them, McKenzie being killed and Goulburn wounded.

On June 24th, at 1.30 p.m., a badly shaken man came into our lines from No-Man's Land. It was Robertson, who had been posted missing on the 21st. He had taken cover that night, but was unable to move for some time as he was under enemy observation. When the enemy stopped firing flares, Robertson began to crawl through the high crops to what he thought were the Australian lines, but he lost his bearings and did not find his way in till nearly three days later.

At 1 a.m. on June 25th a reconnaissance patrol, accompanied by two Americans who had been sent up to the battalion to gain experience, went out through a wheat crop knee-high, and presently came to a spot from which they observed several Germans working on their barbed-wire. The Americans, not appreciating the difference between a reconnaissance and a fighting patrol, wanted to fire on them, and their excitement was such that they had forcibly to be restrained from doing so.

That night the battalion was relieved by the 12th and went back to Borre, becoming brigade reserve. Here it remained for ten days, occupying its time with two hours' training each day, while working parties were supplied to the front line area at night. The enemy was very quiet at this time.

The unit was fortunate in finding some cricket material, and many enjoyable games were played on a pitch partly protected from observation by some farm buildings. However, enemy observation balloons may have noticed the unusual movement, for one day, in the middle of a game, half-a-dozen long-range shells came over and landed, some on and others near the cricket pitch; half of them, however, were "duds." After a short interruption the game continued.

It may be of interest to give here the method by which the front was now being held in this area. In the line between Strazeele and Merris were two battalions, with half a battalion in the reserve line, each battalion being organised according to the following diagram:

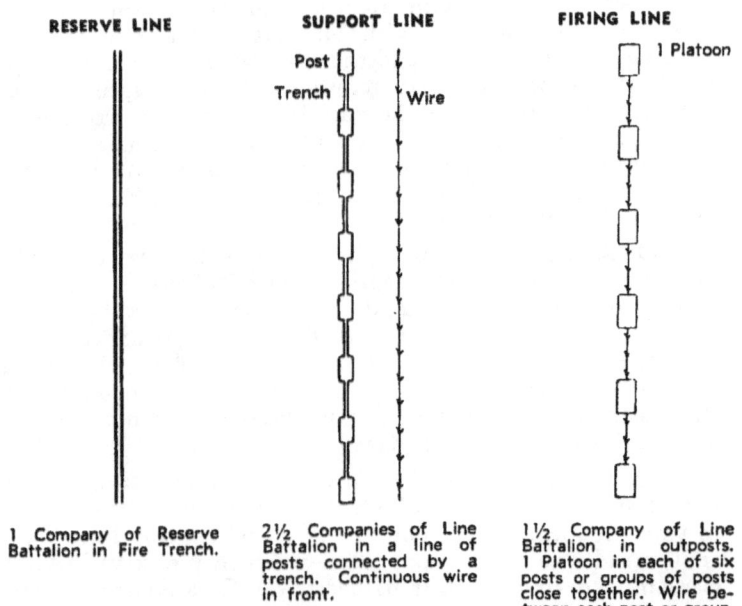

Behind the reserve line there were three villages which were specially defended, Strazeele, Pradelles and Borre.

The battalion moved back to La Kreule on July 5th, as the 3rd Brigade was to be in reserve. On the 7th a brigade church parade was held on the 10th Battalion parade ground at Hondeghem. General Birdwood was present, and after the service he presented medal-ribbons to a number who had been awarded decorations. A party from the 9th attended this parade. Three days later the battalion again visited Blaringhem for aquatic sports and boat races, staying there for the night and returning to La Kreule on the evening of the 11th. A boxing tournament was also held, and the outing was appreciated very much by the troops, although the proceedings were partially spoilt by rain.

On the night of July 13th the battalion left La Kreule for the front line at Le Waton, two miles east of Strazeele, relieving the 5th Battalion at 12.30 a.m. on the 14th. It was now the left battalion on the divisional front, the 11th being on its right. A patrol was sent out immediately the battalion entered the line, and this was followed by many others, but very little was seen of the enemy for a few days. On the night of July 14th/15th a readjustment of the divisional front was made, the 9th taking over two posts from the 11th Battalion.

There was one interesting little patrol action during this period. On the morning of the 16th Lieutenant S. H. Russell, a young officer from the Northern Rivers district of New South Wales, son of a British war correspondent, went out with two men to examine some hedges in No-Man's Land. Some unoccupied enemy posts were entered, and one of them showed signs of recent occupation. In it lay a number of German grenades and some captured British Mills bombs. Russell carefully went through the Mills bombs and after removing the detonators he left them, but took all the German grenades away with him.

It was desirable that some prisoners should be captured for identification purposes, that is, so that the Australians should know what regiments of the enemy were facing them. Accordingly, Russell went out about dusk with Sergeant Preston and five men; they lay near the abovementioned post, waiting for the Germans to come to garrison it for the night. At 10.30, as there was no sign of the enemy, Russell decided to return. While Preston and two men went to look through the hedge to see if all was clear, he himself entered the post for another look around. A few minutes later a party of about ten men became visible, approaching through the darkness from behind. Russell challenged them, and when the answer came back in German he immediately shot the leading man. Since his patrol had been divided, he decided to withdraw, and as his party began to retire they bombed the enemy, causing, it was considered, four casualties. No casualties were received by the patrol.

On July 18th the divisional boundary was again adjusted, and the 9th took over a further post from the 11th. An attack was now to be made along the front in this area; while the 9th (Scottish) Division advanced on Meteren, the 3rd Australian Brigade would capture the tiny hamlet of Le Waton, a mile to the south-west of it. The portion of the attack allotted to the 9th was to be carried out by two platoons of "A" Company and two platoons of "C," reinforced where necessary by further

224  LE WATON TO BE CAPTURED

platoons from "A," "C," and "D" Companies. "B" Company was in reserve. The 11th Battalion, on the right, would advance its left flank so as to conform to the advance of the 9th.

The advance on Meteren was accompanied by a barrage, but that on Le Waton was assisted neither by artillery nor by trench-mortar fire. The troops were in position at 3 a.m. on

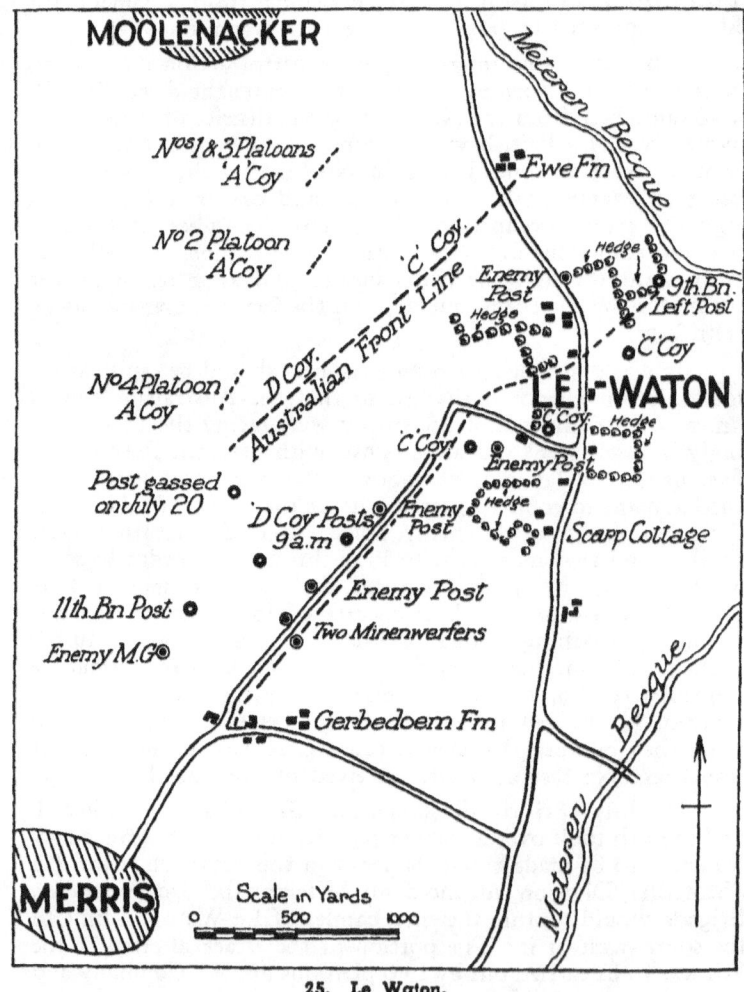

25. Le Waton.
July 19th, 1918.

July 19th, but the attack did not commence for another five hours. "C" Company on the left and "D" on the right occupied the outpost lines, while "A" Company was just behind them. "D" Company advanced its line 150 yards before daylight came.

At 7.55 the barrage commenced for the Meteren operation, and at 8 o'clock Nos. 1 and 3 Platoons of the 9th left their jumping-off positions near "Ewe Farm," one platoon having orders to clear the ground round Le Waton, the other attacking it from the left, to mop up the houses in the village. At the same time the other two platoons of "A" Company, and also "D" Company, supported the attacking platoons by Lewis gun and rifle-grenade fire.

In No. 2 Platoon, according to a statement by its Lewis gun corporal, F. L. Whyte:—

> "Before the attack began the Lewis-gun Section crawled out through the high crop in front of our line (this crop extended from the centre of our position about 150 yards to the left flank and varied in depth from 50 to 100 yards) and when the other platoons started to move up the fire of this gun kept the machine-gunners in the first enemy post under cover; one post which was getting a bit of enfilade fire put up a white flag before the advancing platoons got within 50 yards of it."

No. 1 Platoon, commanded by Lieutenant E. H. Meyers, divided into four fighting patrols, moved out through the crops in No-Man's Land, and was followed immediately by No. 3 Platoon, under Lieutenant C. M. Wrench, in a similar formation. The men had green wheat stalks fastened to their steel helmets and their shoulders, so as to be less easily seen among the wheat, which was in ear, and just turning yellow. As No. 1 moved towards the houses, heavy machine-gun fire was met from an enemy post which harassed the advance until the Australians worked their way through the ruined houses in a semicircle and reached the rear of the post. No. 3 Platoon was forced by the machine-gun fire to take cover in the wheat for a while, but when this abated a little it pushed on through the crop, and, on reaching ground with a more open view, was able to locate the enemy positions and to open fire on them.

Meanwhile two platoons of "C" Company had left their trenches at 8.15 a.m. and advanced, one of them coming to the support of the two "A" Company platoons. When this occurred the Germans saw that they were being surrounded, and fled. The "C" Company men rushed into the post and captured several prisoners, together with five machine-guns. This was about 8.20 a.m.

No. 1 Platoon chased the fleeing enemy, who numbered between 30 and 40, several hundred yards into German territory. The Australians could not catch up with their quarry, to whom fear had lent wings, so the pursuers opened fire with rifles and machine-guns until they disappeared into their support posts. This caused some casualties in the German ranks.

Some smaller enemy posts in this neighbourhood were also mopped up, and No. 3 Platoon then swung to the right and began to "roll up" the enemy front line by attacking it from the flank. A road running south-west into Merris began here, and along it lay the German front line. No 1 Platoon assisted in this movement, advancing in the rear of the enemy posts.

The advance was soon held up by heavy machine-gun and rifle fire from a strong German post near the head of the road. The platoons advanced slowly, supported by the fire of their own Lewis guns, some of which were fired from the hip, some by resting them on other men's shoulders. Supporting fire was also given by rifle-grenades until, sniping as they went, the platoons reached bombing distance. Some of the enemy then made signs that they wished to surrender, but others hurled at the Australians stick grenades; these, however, hurriedly thrown and badly aimed, caused no casualties.

The post was then captured, No. 2 Platoon, which had been sent to reinforce the others, arriving just afterwards and helping to occupy the post. "D" Company then arrived and garrisoned this post, while Nos. 2 and 3 Platoons went forward along the road and captured several smaller posts, which offered little resistance though equipped with machine-guns, several of which were captured.

A strong-post was then encountered. This offered a determined resistance with rifles, machine-guns, and stick grenades, but the platoons moved forward through the tall wheat under covering fire from Lewis guns and rifle-grenades, the latter bursting with deadly effect and causing severe losses to the enemy. "A" Company began to encircle the post, No. 1 Platoon moving to its rear, while Nos. 2 and 3 advanced on flank and front. The Germans continued to throw stick grenades, but our men retaliated with Mills bombs, and, rushing the post, captured the entire garrison. "D" Company now came up, and another enemy post a little farther on was attacked; it resisted for a while but was soon rushed and taken.

The time was now about 9 a.m. "C" and "D" Companies, covered by Nos. 1, 2 and 3 Platoons, then consolidated the whole of the captured position, while harassing long-distance fire was received from enemy machine-guns. "A" Company then withdrew and occupied the original front line under heavy machine-gun fire, which fortunately was not very accurate. Later, however, a bombardment of an hour's duration fell on the front line, and after dark intense artillery fire was directed by the enemy on the roads and tracks leading to the rear.

The battalion's total casualties in the action were 9 killed and 39 wounded, while 98 prisoners, 16 machine-guns, and two *minenwerfer* were captured. One particularly brave deed was performed early in the attack. At this stage of the war Mills bombs were also used as rifle-grenades by being fired from a special cup fixed to the muzzle of the rifle. Lieutenant J. P. Tunn was leading his party out when the man beside him, Corporal P. Norman, who was carrying a grenade in the cup on his rifle, with the pin out[1] just ready for firing, tripped and overbalanced, with the result that the grenade fell out of the cup. Tunn, realising the danger to the party if the explosion were not smothered, at once dived for the bomb. He seized it, but at the same time caught in his hand some long grass or wire, and the grenade was jerked out of his hand. It immediately exploded, blowing off his right forearm and wounding him severely in both legs; a fragment of the bomb also hit him over the right eye. The other men, however, escaped unharmed. Tunn was immediately carried to the R.A.P., where the M.O., Captain Grieve, attended to him, and later he was carried back to the C.C.S. by German prisoners.

In recognition of his self-sacrifice, Tunn received the Albert Medal. He had been recommended for the Victoria Cross, but this could not be granted to him as he was not actively engaging the enemy at the time. However, the award of the Albert Medal was an outstanding distinction; there were only three awarded in the whole A.I.F.

Another casualty was Lieutenant Barclay, who was hit in the knee by a piece of shell. He was in command of No. 2 Platoon, and only a short while before had come to the 9th Battalion from the 1st Divisional Artillery.

The operation was one of the most successful and exciting of those engaged in by the 9th, and after the somewhat doubtful commencement the troops carried on with great enthusiasm and thoroughly enjoyed the attack, the nature of which gave them ample scope for individual initiative. While Nos. 1 and 3 Platoons were the spearhead of the movement it was not long before practically the whole front line was drawn into it.

1 The Mills grenade contained as a safety device a steel pin. While this was in place the grenade could not explode, but when it was removed the bomb, although still quite safe while held in the hand, or in the rifle cup, would explode five seconds after leaving the hand or cup.

The attack of the 9th Division on Meteren was quite successful, and resulted in the capture of this village. These two engagements were fought on the anniversary of the first Australian battle in France, the Battle of Fromelles, two years before, on July 19th, 1916, in which the 5th Division had participated.

On the next afternoon the enemy attempted two counter-attacks, but they were held off by Lewis-gun fire and were finally routed by the artillery. For several days after the capture of Le Waton our troops were very active, going out in daylight patrols in the tall wheat and "stalking" the enemy.

On July 20th Lieutenant Henzell was blown up and seriously wounded by a whizbang, which hit the parados of his post. He had subsequently a long struggle for life, but eventually he recovered. Lieutenant S. H. Russell was killed on the same day.

At midnight on July 20th/21st, a terrific explosion was heard in rear of the battalion frontage, when a thousand gas projectors were fired from Moolenacker, a mile and a half to the north of Merris. These projectors were a species of bomb, a large number of which were fired simultaneously from mortars by electrical means. Some of the projectors, unfortunately, went in the wrong direction, five of them falling in the 9th Battalion's right-hand post, half-a-mile to the west of Le Waton. One dropped on the very edge of the trench occupied by No. 14 Platoon, several of the men being drenched with the liquid.[2] All immediately put on their box respirators, but they were too late to avoid the gas, and the whole platoon had to be evacuated. Two of the men subsequently died. The gas remained in the neighbourhood for hours like a dense fog.

It had been intended to advance the outpost line during this night, but owing to the casualties caused by the mishap just described, the project had to be abandoned.

On July 21st, two of the forward posts were slightly advanced, and at 10.30 p.m. relief by the 12th Battalion began. During the three days after the capture of Le Waton artillery bombardment of our lines had been heavy and continuous, and had caused a number of casualties.

On being relieved, the 9th went back to the vicinity of "Mango Farm," 500 yards north-west of Pradelles, to take over

---

[2] Mustard gas and some other poison gases were in liquid form, but they vaporised very easily. When the small bursting charge which was used blew open the shell or projector, the liquid escaped and immediately began to evaporate. The gas thus formed affected the eyes, throat, and lungs, while the liquid, if it came in contact with the skin, caused painful burns.

the duties of brigade support battalion. Here baths were extemporised by collecting coppers and tubs from demolished farmhouses in the neighbourhood.

A message from the G.O.C. of the 9th Division was received on July 22nd by the 1st Australian Division and communicated to the units, thanking the Australians for their support during the capture of Meteren, and expressing admiration of their fighting qualities. The message ended with the hope that the 1st Australian Division "may be on our flank when active operations are resumed."

While the 9th was at "Mango Farm," Merris was captured on the night of July 29th by the 10th Battalion, under Neligan, who on this account subsequently received the Croix de Guerre from the French authorities.

On the night of July 30th/31st, the battalion moved back to La Kreule.

# CHAPTER XV.

### VICTORY.

On the 15th of July, 1918, General Foch, who since March 26th had been generalissimo of the Allied forces on the Western Front, made his first counter-stroke against the Germans, who were thrown back from the Marne to the Aisne. While this attack was in full swing east of Soissons a general counter-offensive was planned, and the post of honour in it was entrusted to the Australian and Canadian Corps, who would have French troops operating on their right and the III British Corps on their left. The 1st Australian Division was ordered to rejoin the Australian Corps, from which it had been separated since April.

An army corps normally consists of three infantry divisions, but from August, 1918, to the end of the war the Australian Corps comprised all five divisions of the A.I.F. Besides the infantry and other divisional troops, which numbered about 100,000, General Monash had under his command a large number of corps troops, the greater part of whom were not Australians. The numbers of these corps troops varied, and in September, 1918, they brought the total of the corps up to nearly 200,000. The Australian Corps was the largest army corps ever organised in any war, and it is interesting to compare its numbers with those of the British forces at the Battle of Waterloo, where they amounted to only 50,000 in all.

Accordingly, on August 1st, the 9th Battalion went back by motor 'bus to La Sablon, near Heuringhem, and remained there for five days, the first two of which were very wet. During the stay here many of the troops were able to go into St. Omer, a fairly large town and important railway junction five miles away. It was possible to procure here vegetables and other commodities, and mess carts were sent in, cabbage, cauliflowers, beans, peas, tinned fruit, milk and other food being purchased. Moving off again on the afternoon of the 6th, "A," "B," and "D" Companies entrained at St. Omer and "C" Company at Wizernes. The arrangements, for which the 3rd Brigade was not responsible, were bad, as the entraining points did not seem to have been chosen with any regard to the places where the troops were billeted.

Next morning "A," "B," and "D" Companies reached Longpré at 6.15 a.m., and, after breakfasting by the wayside, they marched to Villers-sous-Ailly, arriving there at 12.30 p.m. Here they were joined by "C" Company, which had detrained at Pont-Remy. At 6.30 p.m. the battalion resumed its march, proceeding through Long to Catelet, whence it travelled by 'bus to the neighbourhood of Amiens, reaching at 1.30 next morning a point on the road between Cardonette and Coisy. The air was full of rumours as to what was to be the next move; all that was known definitely was that the battalion was to be ready to go forward into the line (wherever it was) at any moment. However, the unit marched into Coisy and by 2.15 a.m. was settled in billets. The 1st Division was once more in the Fourth Army under General Rawlinson.

At 4.20 a.m. on this day, August 8th, the opening battle (the Battle of Amiens) of the great offensive was begun on a 16-mile front, extending from Morlancourt to Moreuil. Behind a great force of tanks—which took the place of the usual artillery preparation—the Australians and Canadians swiftly penetrated the German defences. 17,000 prisoners and 500 guns were taken on the first day. On the Australian front the 2nd and 3rd Divisions made the initial attack, the 4th and 5th leapfrogging over them and going on to the final objective.

Meanwhile during the morning orders were received by the 9th Battalion to be ready to move at noon, and at 11.30 the time of departure was definitely fixed for 1.30 p.m. The nucleus battalion was detailed and remained behind, while the main body duly left at 1.30 and made a forced march of 13 miles in hot weather, along very dusty roads, through Allonville, Querrieu, Pont Noyelles, and La Neuville-Corbie to Hamel, which was reached at 9.45 p.m. Here the battalion was billeted in trenches between Hamel and Accroche Wood.

Next day battalion headquarters received a message from brigade to advance four miles to a position just south of Bayonvillers. Moving off just after midday in artillery formation, the 9th made a very fine picture as it passed over the countryside. On reaching the position indicated a meal was consumed and a conference of company commanders took place. Late in the afternoon the battalion moved a little further forward, to the south-west of Harbonnières, where it occupied some German huts. There was great aerial activity all the afternoon.

232    FOLLOWING UP THE ENEMY

At 8.30 p.m. another order was sent from brigade that the battalion should take up a defensive position south-east of Harbonnières and towards Vauvillers. About 11 p.m. it marched to the new position, a couple of miles away, and the companies dug themselves in there.

At 2 p.m. that day the 2nd Brigade had attacked a line (known in the operation orders as the "Red Line") between Vauvillers and Lihons. It made good progress, but was brought to a halt 400 yards from its objective. At 2 o'clock next morning, therefore, the 9th and 11th Battalions were ordered to

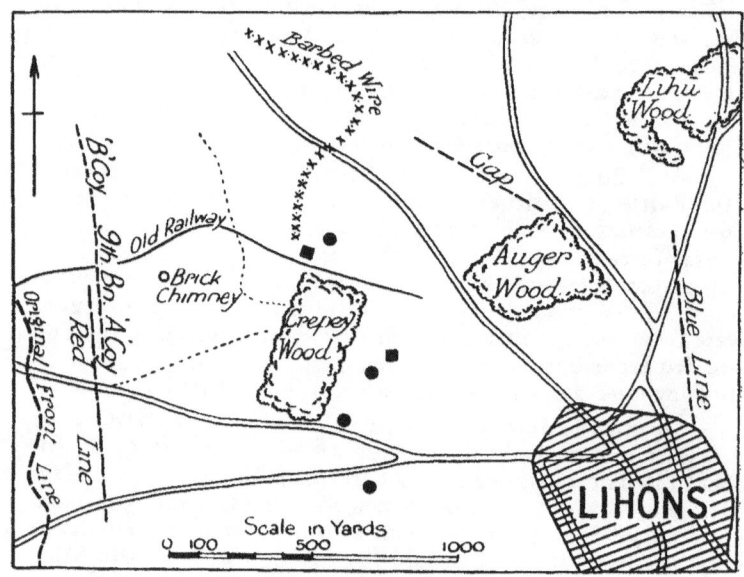

26. **Crepey Wood and Lihons.**
August 10th, 1918.

●● Two posts first established.    ●●●● Four posts established later.

advance over the "Red Line" and capture the "Blue Line," which ran northwards from Lihons for some 600 yards. The troops, who had been busy from midnight to 3.30 a.m. digging themselves in, moved forward at 6.30 in artillery formation, and received no casualties until they reached the Red Line. Here they waited until 8 a.m., when they attacked, the 9th on the right and the 11th on the left, over flat open ground towards Crepy[1] Wood.

---

1  This is the spelling used in the *Official History*, but ordnance maps give "Crepey."

They were at once met by terrific machine-gun fire, and did not receive much support from our own artillery, whose barrage on this occasion was described in one report as "wretched, skimpy and without sting." The 9th received heavy casualties, but reached the western edge of Crepy Wood, where it was held up for a while. The officer in command[2] then ordered three platoons to advance, and in spite of very strong resistance by the enemy, whose machine-gun fire, mostly oblique or in enfilade, continued to be very severe, some platoons of the 9th eventually forced their way through the wood and reached its eastern outskirts.

One platoon from "C" Company had not much difficulty in doing this, and suffered not one casualty. Others, however, met with stout resistance, finding, as they advanced, that German machine-gun fire began to come from the rear. Some platoons now found their flanks in the air, and sent back two men to report the fact to company headquarters, but on their way thither they encountered a couple of Germans on guard over the area through which they had just come. They shot the Germans and reported their discovery to headquarters, and it was accordingly decided to withdraw the advanced parties and to form a line in an old trench running north and south along the western boundary of the wood.

In their advance the troops had lost their direction somewhat, and men of both battalions had become intermingled. In the meantime very heavy casualties had been received, including Captains Penrose and Monteath and Lieutenants E. J. Chester. Gower, Butler and Walker. Penrose, who received a scalp wound right across the top of the head, had a very close shave, Monteath was shot through the lung, Chester had a nasty wound in the thigh, and Walker an ugly one across the shoulder-blade.

Major C. F. Ross was then put in command of the firing line, and arrangements were made for the 9th to be reinforced by "A" Company of the 10th. At 1 p.m. this company was sent forward, under Captain McCann, and on its arrival it attacked with the 9th, and, though the resistance met with was again very heavy, and casualties were many, they drove the enemy out of the wood and established posts on its northern and eastern sides.

A platoon of the 5th Battalion, which arrived shortly after the attack commenced, was used as supports until the new posts were established and was then instructed to report back to its

---

2 Probably Captain Armstrong.

battalion. The establishment of this new line was complete by 4.30 p.m. By this time the 9th Battalion's fighting strength was little over 300. About 4 o'clock a counter-attack had been attempted against the new posts, but only a few Germans (carrying full packs with overcoats) left their trenches, and these were soon driven back by our Lewis gun fire.

It was mistakenly thought that this position was the objective, the "Blue Line." That line, however, was 500 yards farther on, and more to the north, being in front of Auger Wood, whereas the 9th was established in front of Crepy Wood.

In this operation 90 prisoners, eight 4.2-inch howitzers, 30 machine-guns, 2 trench-mortars, and 3 complete telephone installations were captured. The captured machine-guns were made use of with great effect in the later stages of the advance. The howitzers were marked personally by Major Ross, during a lull in the fighting, as having been captured by the 9th Battalion, but after the battle the brigade commander decided that all captured material should be shown as having been taken by the 3rd Brigade, instead of by individual battalions.

At 5.30 p.m. a very heavy barrage was laid down for half-an-hour by the enemy, followed by an assault by a force about 300 strong against the posts occupied by McCann's company of the 10th Battalion. Some of these posts were driven in and the Germans gained a footing in the wood, but the support platoons of the company immediately counter-attacked, and after an hour's severe fighting the enemy was driven out, leaving 90 of his dead in the wood. After this the Germans shelled the outposts and supports and battalion headquarters incessantly.

It was decided by the brigade commander that on the next day, August 11th, the 10th and 12th Battalions should attack the "Blue Line." The morning was very misty, but by 5.15 a.m. they had captured the objective, which included the village of Lihons. Lieutenant C. M. Wrench writes:—

> "The 10th Battalion passed through us very early in the morning, and it was not long before unescorted prisoners came back, each with one hand up and the other full of cheap German smokes. We concluded, accordingly, that the 10th had reached their objective."

A couple of hours later Lieutenant-Colonel Mullen found that there was a gap of about a mile between the 11th and 12th Battalions, extending from the northerly point of Auger Wood towards the north-west. The whole of the 9th Battalion was therefore ordered to advance and close the gap.

To this position Germans also were moving, and as the 9th was making its way forward it came into contact with them. Fierce fighting followed, and the enemy was eventually driven out of the gap. In one place a platoon of the 10th was pursuing about 50 Germans when a small party of the 9th, under Acting C.S.M. George Walker, cut off their retreat. The enemy took refuge in a trench, and Walker, posting J. Young with his Lewis gun and a couple of men near a gap in the trench which the enemy would have to pass, instructed them to keep it covered, while he tried to find some more men. He could find only two men, but the three of them rushed the trench (about 50 feet distant) with the bayonet. One was killed before it was reached, but the other two entered the trench, drove the Germans along it and overtook them. Walker then threw a bomb at them, causing four casualties, whereon the remainder immediately surrendered. Some of them had become casualties and some had escaped before they were surrounded, but 28 were taken prisoner.[3] By 9.30 a.m. the gap had been filled. Lieutenant Meyers describes the part played by his platoon as follows:—

"When the gap in the line was first apparent the extent of it was not actually known. At the time I was in charge of a support platoon in 'A' Company, with Captain Armstrong as company commander. Armstrong came to me and stated that battalion headquarters had advised that there was a gap in the front line and that he was to detail a platoon to move forward and fill it. The direction was indicated to me on Armstrong's map, but no information was available as to the extent of the gap.

"Accordingly I moved up with my platoon, the strength of which would be from 30 to 35 men, with the object of cleaning up Auger Wood and then extending to pick up the flanks in the front line gap. Auger Wood was held by the enemy with machine-gun posts. With the gradual advance of my platoon through the wood, which was difficult for some time owing to being harassed with bursts from machine-guns whenever we presented a target, we were relieved to find the enemy retire with the exception of a heavy machine-gun post with two men, which commanded a good field of fire over our approach. This post was towards the northern end of Auger Wood. Both these gunners were 'picked off' by our men, and we had no further opposition until we cleared the northern edge of the wood.

"When we emerged and moved north-westerly we came on a large body of Germans, about 100 to 150 of them. Some were in the open moving back to their own line and some were occupying a small trench, and packed in as if they had taken cover in surprise. As we were small in numbers and did not know what support we might or might not have following up our work, we had to attack, and we captured 20 to 30 Germans, the remainder having retired. My opinion of the presence of this body of the enemy was that they were some of the number we cleared out of Auger Wood, together with some who had moved up to the gap in our line. They apparently took our appearance from Auger Wood as being of greater strength than it actually was.

3 Walker received the D.C.M. for this action.

> "Immediately after this we were subjected to continuous fire from the German light artillery and 'whizbangs.' The whizbangs fairly rained at us and we suffered a few casualties, including, I remember, Corporal Barney Grimish, who had done splendid work. We then extended north-westerly, establishing small posts at intervals of 100 yards or more, thus making a thin veil in the gap."

As a consequence of the action, Meyers was awarded a bar to his Military Cross.

A continuous fire on the Australian line was kept up by the enemy, some of whom were seen at 1.30 p.m. coming out of Lihu Wood, north-east of Lihons, for another counter-attack. This attack was stopped by our artillery and machine-gun fire.

The casualties of the 9th during the whole of the Lihons operations were 12 officers and 166 other ranks. Lieutenants Smith and Morgan were killed, the latter while visiting one of the platoon posts on his flank on the eastern side of Crepy Wood. C.S.M. Todd was another who lost his life here; in the early stage of the advance from the Red Line he raced along a piece of broken trench to a dead end, and was looking over the top when he was shot through the head. Known as "the little man with the big voice," Todd was highly respected by all ranks. Among the wounded were Major Ross and Lieutenants Cork and Knowles.

There is on record the following list of names of one officer and 18 other ranks who, killed in this battle, were buried in a common grave on August 10th:—Lieutenant W. Morgan, Sgts. C. Archer, D. W. Gordon and G. W. Green, and Ptes. J. Wilson, G. R. Taylor, N. Nelson, G. Armstrong, J. Roache, W. Michin, N. M. Tidyman, H. Caven, L. Harvey, R. C. Markham, J. Clark, C. A. Kerr, V. Cleveland, A. C. Johnson, and T. Cuppy.

Throughout the operation, which was sometimes referred to in the 9th as the Battle of Crepy Wood and sometimes as the Battle of Lihons, the battalion received a hot meal daily, and cigarettes also were issued to the troops.

The 9th was relieved at midnight on August 11th/12th, and went back to trenches just behind battalion headquarters, moving the next afternoon farther back to a position near Vauvillers, where it stayed for two days. The battalion had had a very strenuous time; between the night of the 5th/6th and that of the 12th/13th it had not enjoyed one good night's rest.

Just before the fighting at Lihons, one man had a run of good fortune at the Australian "national" game of two-up, and he went into action carrying in his pocket French bank-notes amounting to 10,000 francs—about £370 in our money. A 5.9 shell burst alongside him and he was blown to pieces, bank-notes and all. After the battle, his mates were loud in their lamentations that so much good money had gone up into the air, but no word of regret was heard for "poor old Blank."

In the afternoon of August 14th reinforcements arrived, but only 31 of them. At dusk the 9th relieved the 10th Battalion in the line a little to the north of Crepy Wood.

On the evening of the 15th the line was advanced about 200 yards, after which the battalion was relieved by the 13th, the relief taking two hours, from 9.30 to 11.30 p.m. The 9th moved back to a bivouac between Lihons and Herleville, and next day marched in artillery formation to Vaire, putting an end to a very trying and fatiguing ten days on arriving there at 5 p.m. Here it remained for five days.

On August 21st the Australian Corps resumed hostilities. The 1st Division was ordered to attack beyond Proyart, with the 3rd Brigade in divisional reserve. Accordingly the 9th left Vaire at 2.50 p.m. on the 21st, and moved across country to a rendezvous a mile south-west of Morcourt. Arriving there at 5 o'clock, a good hot meal was provided and all ranks were ordered to rest. Next day the battalion was instructed to be ready on one hour's notice to move forward and go into action.

The objective laid down for the 1st and 2nd Brigades, the Red Line, was half-way between Chuignolles and Bray; that of the 10th and 11th Battalions, the Blue Line, along the valley between Chuignolles and Chuignes up to the River Somme in the direction of Bray. The support battalion of the 3rd Brigade would make a further advance to an unlimited objective.

The far side of the valley between Chuignolles and Chuignes was formed by a steep bare hill, almost precipitous in places, rising to a height of about 400 feet, of which the northern end, Froissy Beacon, sloped sharply down to the Somme Canal.[4]

On August 23rd reveille was blown in the 9th battalion lines at 1 a.m., and after a hot meal the 9th moved off at 2.30, reaching at 4.20 the rendezvous on the western edge of St. Germain Wood. Here the men were concealed from observation partly in the wood itself and partly along steep banks and in

---

4. The River Somme flows for a great way with very many bends along a swampy valley, and to facilitate navigation a canal has been made, formed in places by the river-channel and in places cut in the swampy valley.

sunken roads near by. At 4.45 the barrage began, and the 1st and 2nd Brigades attacked and duly captured the Red Line. News of this reached the 9th Battalion at 11 a.m., and after a hot meal it moved off at 12.30, but to reach the Red Line it had to pass through a terrific enemy barrage of 8-inch and gas shells, which caused numerous casualties and some disorganisation. The 10th Battalion had been called on to assist the 1st and 2nd Brigades in their advance, so the 9th had to take the place of the 10th in the next attack, being on the left flank, with the 12th on the right and the 11th in support.

At 2 p.m. the second stage of the advance began, the 9th, protected only by a smoke barrage, attacking Luc Wood. Heavy casualties were received from shell-fire, which delayed and somewhat disorganised the battalion, but it pressed on to the main road at Froissy Beacon, meeting with very little individual opposition until it reached the valley in front of the Beacon, where it was temporarily checked by strong machine-gun fire and by field-guns firing at point-blank range. The 12th Battalion had advanced between Froissy Beacon and the village of Chuignes to attack Garenne Wood, and "B" and "D" Companies of the

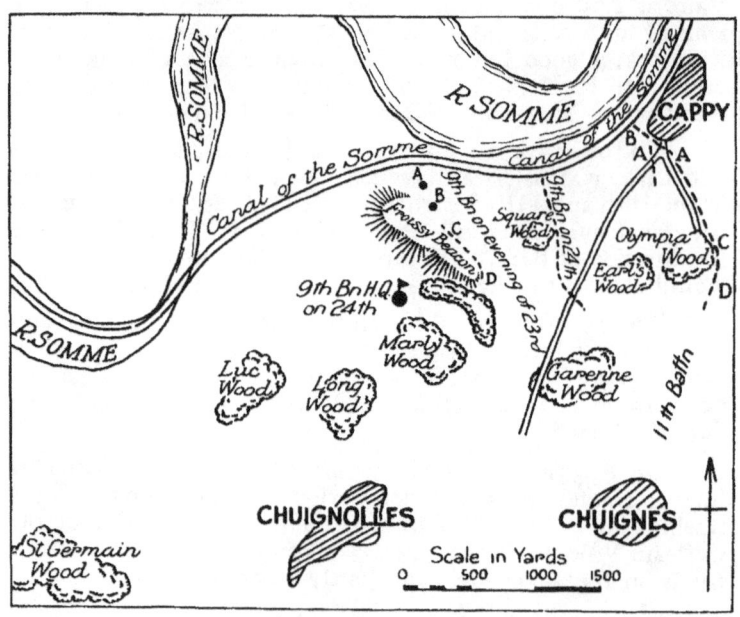

27. Chuignes, Froissy Beacon and Cappy.
August 23rd-25th, 1918.

11th, which had followed the 12th, now swung to the left and enfiladed with Lewis-gun fire two enemy machine-guns posted on the slopes of the Beacon, which were holding up the advance of the 9th. This action enabled the 9th to continue its advance. The 11th then stormed the cliffs of the Beacon, men from "D" Company of that battalion establishing themselves about 3 o'clock on the top where part of "B" Company of the 9th, under Captain Farmer, joined them five minutes later. Farmer had been wounded during the advance, but he continued with his company and did not report to the medical officer until after the Beacon had been captured.

Detachments from other companies of the 9th soon reached the summit. They found themselves, not on a hill-crest, but on the top of a plateau which stretched along towards the village of Cappy.

The 9th and the 11th now mopped up the low ground to the north, between the Beacon and the Somme Canal. Meanwhile the 10th Battalion was extending a protective flank along the canal. The 11th Battalion party was completely exhausted, so it took up a support position on the top of the Beacon while the 9th pushed further forward, establishing battalion head-quarters just at the foot of the Beacon.

That night the battalion advanced its positions 800 yards to a line passing through "Square Wood," encountering heavy machine-gun fire while doing so. Next day a quantity of enemy material was salvaged, and at 4.30 p.m. orders were received that as the enemy had withdrawn the 9th should continue to advance. Accordingly, in the morning of August 25th "A" and "B" Companies moved forward on the left along the Somme Canal, while "C" and "D" went towards "Olympia Wood."

"A" and "B" Companies, though hindered by a thick fog, established posts just south of Cappy, and "D" Company advanced towards the southern flank of "Olympia Wood," followed later by "C." Eventually a line was established running from the south-west corner of Cappy past the eastern edge of Olympia Wood. Patrols were then sent out by "A" Company. One, under Lieutenant Wrench, after passing through Cappy, saw on the far side some of the retiring enemy, upon whom it fired. After this, finding it was "in the air," and that other companies were held up at Olympia Wood, the patrol turned in that direction. It then ran out of Lewis-gun ammunition, and returned through Cappy to the rear of the village.

Another patrol, consisting of Corporal D. Howell and Privates Bayton, D. L. Suller and N. H. Mikalsen, went through the village, saw Germans retreating on the far side, and fired on them. Mikalsen was sent back with a request for reinforcements and more ammunition, but was killed on the way. The patrol remained in advance of Cappy all day till sundown, when it withdrew and rejoined the battalion.[5]

As there was some doubt at battalion headquarters as to the exact positions reported to have been reached by the different companies, the adjutant went forward to investigate the situation. He adjusted the front line so that it reached from the canal at a point where the village of Cappy began to a position about 300 yards south of the easterly corner of Olympia Wood.

At 4 a.m. on August 26th the battalion was relieved by the 10th, and moved back into the Chuignolles-Chuignes valley, just behind Froissy Beacon. The companies rested till 2.30 p.m., when they were ordered to go forward again to a position near "Earl's Wood" to act as support to the 10th. In the night, however, the battalion was relieved by a 2nd Division unit and went back to St. Germain Wood, where it arrived at 2.30 a.m. on the 27th, and had a much needed sleep. At 9.30 a.m. it moved further back to the Cérisy Valley, about two miles southwest of Cérisy Village, the men arriving dead-beat. There it remained for eleven days.

During the battle three supply tanks were allotted to the 3rd Brigade to bring forward supplies. A duplicate service of pack-trains was organised in case of failure of the tanks, but they were not required. A Comforts Fund stall was stationed at battalion headquarters, where all runners and other men reporting from the line while fighting was in progress were given a hot drink. The ranks of the battalion had become so depleted by this time that the total number engaged in the attack[6] was a little under 250. Its casualties were 4 officers and 76 other ranks. The captures amounted to 110 prisoners, 3 field-guns, 10 machine-guns, and a quantity of light railway material, those of the whole division being 20 field-guns, scores of machine-guns, and nearly 3000 prisoners—the greatest number of prisoners captured by any one British division in 24 consecutive hours during the whole war.

5 There is reason to believe that this and the party mentioned in the preceding paragraph went out originally as one patrol.
6 The Battle of Chuignes. Known in the battalion as Froissy Beacon or Cappy.

This victory was a most important one, and resulted in the 1st Division's capturing all the territory between the River Somme and Herleville to a depth of 1½ miles, and pushing back the enemy from quite a good habitable area to a region which had been devastated in earlier fighting. In addition, it rendered easy the capture of Bray by the 3rd Division on the night of the 23rd, with very few casualties. Sir John Monash described it as a smashing blow which far exceeded in its results any previous record in his experience, having regard to the numbers of troops engaged.

On August 30th the four-company organisation of the battalion was abandoned, and three companies, "X," "Y," "Z," were established, each having three platoons of three sections each. The end of the war was now in sight, and preparations were already in hand for the demobilisation of the A.I.F. A scheme for the educational training of officers and men during the period while they were waiting their turn for repatriation had been drawn up, and at Cérisy on August 30th the Bishop of Bathurst, the Right Reverend G. M. Long, a noted educationist, lectured to the brigade commanders and senior officers, explaining the plan. On the following day he addressed the officers and men of the 3rd Brigade on the subject. Bishop Long was afterwards put in charge of this scheme, with the rank of brigadier-general.

On September 7th the 3rd Brigade moved forward to the Mont St. Quentin area, the 9th Battalion reaching there at 3 p.m. and bivouacking a mile to the east of the village. Many took the opportunity of inspecting the site of the famous attack by the 2nd Division, which had captured the mount on September 1st. It seemed to most of them a miracle that this stronghold could have been attacked successfully, taking into account its great natural advantages and the wonderful field of fire which its defenders had. After three days here the battalion marched off on September 10th to Tincourt, 3½ miles further east, where it was quartered in huts.

An attack was now to be made on the enemy positions in front of the Hindenburg Line[7] by the Fourth Army, in conjunction with the Third Army on the left and the First French Army on the right. The rôle of the Australian Corps was to attack in the centre of the Fourth Army front, according to the scheme in the accompanying diagram:

---

[7] Known as the Hindenburg Outpost Line.

| | | | | | | |
|---|---|---|---|---|---|---|
| | | Battalions | 11 | 12 | 1st Objective | |
| | | | 9 | 10 | 2nd Objective | |
| | Brigade | 1 | | 3 | | |
| | Division | | 1 | | 4 | |
| Corps | III | | Australian | | | IX |
| Third Army | | Fourth Army | | | | 1st French Army |

    The 3rd Brigade was to advance on the village of Villeret, six miles east of Tincourt, and a couple of miles in front of the Hindenburg Line. The 11th and 12th Battalions were to attack the first objective (the Brown Line), the 9th and 10th passing through them to capture the second objective (the Red Line), and if that engagement progressed favourably, the Line of Exploitation (the Blue Line).

    Eight days were passed at Tincourt in support of the 1st Brigade, which was holding the front line. Defensive positions were prepared so as to prevent any possibility of a break-through by the enemy if he should make a strong counter-attack. Training was also continued here, and preparations made for the coming attack on the Hindenburg Outpost Line. The C.O. asked the intelligence officer, Lieutenant J. G. Earwaker, to have a large map made, and one was drawn on several sheets of map paper gummed together. This was used in lecturing to the troops and was afterwards lent to Colonel Neligan, of the 10th Battalion, for the same purpose. The strength of the 9th Battalion was:—

    With the battalion, 19 officers, 424 Other Ranks.
    Detached             15 ,,       189 ,,    ,,

    Total     ..  ..   34 ,,       613 ,,    ,,

    Just before midday on September 17th the battalion began to march off through Hamelet and Hervilly to the assembly point near Jeancourt, 4½ miles east of Tincourt. It rained very heavily, and the march through the mud in oppressive sultry heat was very trying. Several enemy aeroplanes were seen in front, flying low and bombing the ground over which the battalion would have to cross, but when it approached this danger area conditions became cloudy and misty. Only one bomb dropped near the 9th, but fortunately the battalion was in a sunken road at the time and no harm resulted.

## ATTACK ON VILLERET

By 2.30 a.m. on the 18th the battalion was at its assembly position, "X" and "Y" Companies in a sunken road near the battalion battle headquarters, and "Z" Company in a trench to the north-west. The assembly position did not afford much cover, but the troops were glad of the opportunity of resting after the heavy marching. At 4 a.m. a hot breakfast and a nip of rum were issued to all; this warmed up the wet troops.

"Zero" hour was 5.20 a.m. The barrage opened and the 11th and 12th Battalions advanced. The 9th was to follow the 11th, but, as that battalion had about 3000 yards to go to reach its objective, the 9th did not leave till 6.20 a.m. It passed through the 11th on the Brown Line, and formed up just in rear of the barrage, waiting for it to lift.

Two tanks were assisting the 3rd Brigade, but the one detailed to the 11th had not been able to keep pace with the advance. However, it reached the Brown Line soon after it had been captured, and, going a little further forward, rolled down the wire entanglements over which the 9th would have to go.

At 8.30 a.m. the barrage lifted and the 9th advanced to the attack, "X" Company on the right, "Y" on the left, with "Z" as "moppers-up" to both of them. A screen of riflemen went in front of each company, which advanced in lines of sections in file with 50 yards interval and distance. The creeping barrage, which lifted 100 yards in every four minutes, was well planned and excellently carried out, and the battalion maintained its direction; the intelligence officer, Lieutenant Earwaker, had been detailed to attend to this matter, being given no other duties in the attack.

It was difficult to advance, as the muddy ground was so sticky, and strong opposition was met with in places, but the tank gave splendid assistance, especially in clearing and taking the village of Villeret. The troops reached the Red Line at the appointed time, 9 a.m., and as soon as the barrage lifted—just before 10 a.m.—the battalion, which had been reorganised, went forward to the Line of Exploitation. By 10.30 it was digging in on this line, all of which was on high ground, and gave observation over the enemy territory for miles.

As soon as the 1st Brigade, on the left bank, advanced from the Red Line, its men met with determined opposition from an enemy strong-post known as "The Egg," and were held up. Noticing this, Lieutenant Meyers, commander of "Y"

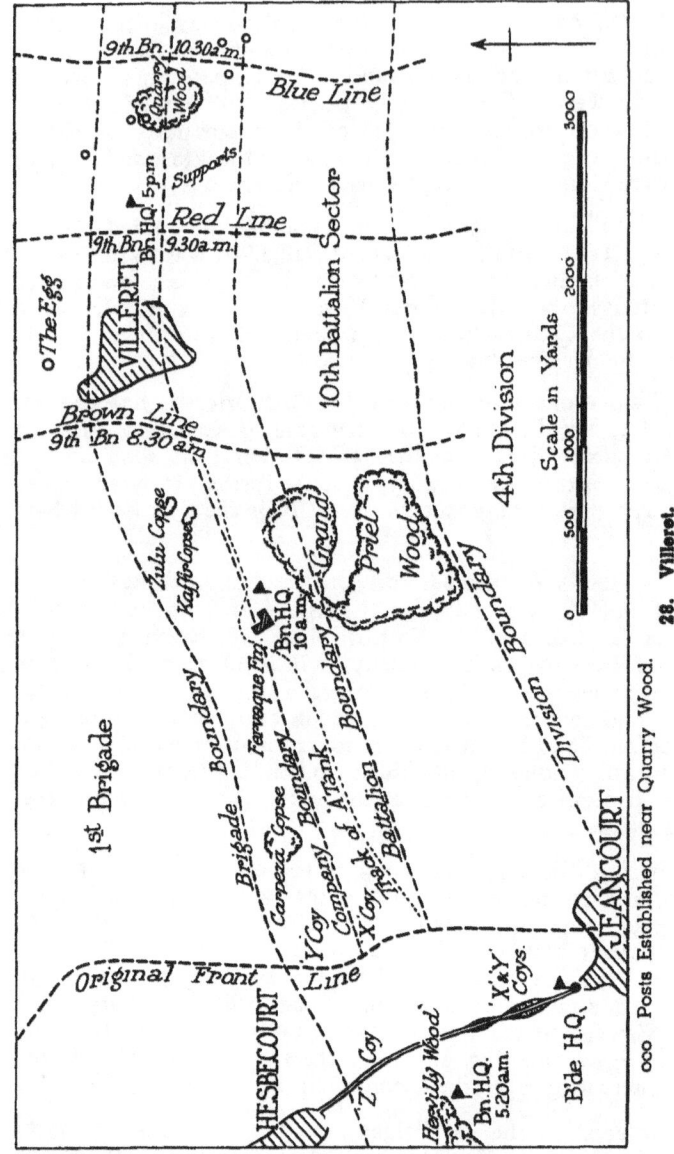

28. **Villeret.**

Company, sent Lieutenant Maddock with a platoon to assist them. Maddock enfiladed the enemy post with his Lewis guns, and, the opposition being thus subdued, the 1st Brigade went ahead.

The companies of the 9th, continuing their advance, came under what was practically point-blank fire from a battery of German field-guns. "Y" Company divided into two parties and, attacking the guns quickly from both sides, captured them. Maddock, however, was killed in the attempt. After this, "Y" Company met with very little opposition, and reached the Blue Line before 10 a.m. Brigade headquarters was surprised that the final objective had been reached so quickly, and sent up its intelligence officer to check the positions held. Later the divisional intelligence officer came, too, possibly to make a double check of the position, and he said that the divisional commander was delighted with the result of the operation.

The new line, about a mile distant from the Hindenburg Line, needed a great deal of repairing, but by 3 p.m. it was in good condition and was occupied by a series of posts.

During the final stage of the attack a patrol under Sergeant J. Bentley did excellent work in dispersing a party of the enemy who attempted to make a stand near "Quarry Wood," 1000 yards east of Villeret. For his leadership Bentley received the D.C.M.

Another party of only two Germans apparently attempted to make a stand. Sergeant Porter first tried to induce them to surrender, but when they refused to advance to him, he called out to Lieutenant Earwaker, "Can you speak German?"

"Why?" replied Earwaker.

"There are a couple of Germans here," answered Porter, "and they won't come out of the trench when I tell them to."

"Why don't you shoot them," continued the officer.

"I can't kill them in cold blood," exclaimed the sergeant.

Earwaker went over to the spot, and saw two of the enemy with a machine-gun between them. He told them to come out, but they did not stir. Then he pushed over the machine-gun so that they could not use it, and jumped into the trench, followed by another Australian. The Germans made signs that they wished to go into a dugout alongside of them to get something, but Earwaker, pulling out his revolver, told them to go back to our lines. At this they made their way without further demur in the direction indicated. Earwaker then investigated the dugout, which he found to contain a large supply of stick-bombs.

The casualties of the battalion were: Killed, 1 officer, 9 other ranks; wounded, 4 officers, 39 O.R.'s. 200 prisoners were captured as well as 8 howitzers, 3 field-guns and 40 machine-guns.

The result of the operation, known officially as the Battle of Epéhy, was an advance all along the line of the three armies engaged. The Australian Corps, which formed the spearhead, penetrated the enemy lines to a greater depth than any of the other troops engaged, advancing a total distance of three miles. The 9th was the only battalion on the whole Fourth Army front which reached the Line of Exploitation, and, as this proved to be its last battle, it was a fitting end to its long and honourable fighting career.

Lieutenant Meyers was awarded a second bar to his M.C. He was the only Queensland soldier having this distinction—indeed, there were only four officers in the whole A.I.F. who were awarded a second bar to that decoration. The cross itself, as has been mentioned before, was gained by Meyers at Polygon Wood in 1917, and the first bar in the advance on Lihons.

The front line was shelled heavily on the day after the attack, but the two succeeding days were quiet, and on September 21st, after garrisoning the line for three days, the 9th was relieved by the 11th and went back a short distance to act as support battalion.

An incident occurred on this day which illustrates the phrase "the fortune of war." An original member of the battalion, P. Cloherty, received news on the last night that the battalion was in the line that he had been granted long-service leave to Australia. While collecting his gear to go off he was blown to pieces by a shell which burst in the entrance to his dugout.

After two days in supports the 9th was relieved by an American battalion. As the new arrivals brought neither signallers nor signalling gear into the line, some of our gear and signallers were left with them. When Lieutenant Meyers was relieved the American company commander asked him to leave his equipment and a couple of signallers, and also a sergeant and a few men "to stiffen up his front line." Meyers did not

Plate xix.

39.—LIEUT. E. H. MEYERS, M.C. and two bars.

Plate xx.

40.—LIEUT.-COL. L. M. MULLEN, D.S.O.

detail any men to stay, but asked Sergeant McMaster and a few men, including two signallers, and they agreed to remain. However, some twenty-four hours later McMaster and his men reported back to their own lines, saying that they would stay no longer with the Americans, as they had not tasted any hot food during that time. This was, incidentally, a great tribute to the battalion and company cooks of the 9th, who were able on almost all occasions to get hot meals up to the troops in the front line. No American signallers arrived until the morning of the 24th, and their cooks must have been considerably later still, as the first hot meal they received was forty-eight hours after they had taken over, and that was sent up to them by the 9th Battalion cooks.

However, to return to the relief. This was completed by 9.20 p.m. and the battalion marched back to Tincourt Wood, being welcomed on its arrival by a hot meal and an issue of rum. But no sooner had the troops reached their destination than unwelcome news greeted ten or twelve of the N.C.O.'s, who were detailed to go back at once and act as advisers to the Americans in their first tour in the line. Those concerned, who had been looking forward to a well-earned rest, left on their 7-mile return walk uttering loud and bitter lamentations.

About this time the first draft left the battalion on "Anzac Leave." This was special long service leave to Australia, which was given to the men who had embarked during 1914, and of whom the vast majority had served at Anzac. They were granted two clear months' leave in Australia.

On the 25th orders were received that the 3rd Brigade was to go west to the Long area, between Amiens and the coast, for a long-promised rest, and next day the 9th entrained at Tincourt station in open trucks. The train moved off at 10 a.m., everyone on board being in the highest spirits, and arrived at Longpré at 3 p.m. From here it marched to Gorenflos, twelve miles to the north, where the billets were found to be good and very clean, equal to any that the battalion had had in France. The C.O. and his staff were billeted in the château, and in an annexe to this building accommodation was found for the company commanders.

The battalion strength now was:
With the battalion, 22 officers, 459 O.R.'s
Detached        ..   ..  10    ,,      99   ,,
Total           ..   ..  32    ,,     558   ,,

# CHAPTER XVI.

## THE END OF THE WAR AND OF THE BATTALION.

The 9th had not been long at Gorenflos when the C.O. was sent to England for a much-needed rest. He left the battalion on October 1st, and was succeeded by Major C. F. Ross, who was promoted to lieutenant-colonel.

Lieutenant-Colonel L. M. Mullen had sailed from Hobart as transport officer of the original 12th Battalion. He was promoted to captain at Anzac and to major in France, and on the 8th of December, 1916, he left the 12th Battalion to take command of the 9th, with the rank of lieutenant-colonel. He commanded the 9th through the mud and cold of Flers, the advance at The Maze, the repulse of the enemy at Lagnicourt, the capture of the edge of Polygon Wood in the Battle of the Menin Road, the last of the battalion's fighting in front of Hazebrouck, and the battles at Crepy Wood and Villeret. He also acted as brigade commander during the Second Battle of Bullecourt. A splendid C.O., he was specially noted as being "a fine sport" in both his personal dealings with all ranks and his great interest in all sporting activities. It was during his period in command that the 9th reached what was probably its peak of excellence. After finally leaving the 9th, he became O.C. the 1st Training Brigade at Sutton Veny, in England, and in February, 1919, he took command of No. 1 Command Depot at Perham Downs.

When the battalion settled down at Gorenflos, there was a general impression that the stay there would be an extended one, probably until the end of the coldest months, so everyone set out to make himself as comfortable as possible. There was every prospect of a very different winter to those of '15, '16, and '17; in fact, like the armies of ancient times, they were going into "winterquarters," as they thought.

Life became very pleasant. Much sport was indulged in, particularly football, and the officers were fortunate in being invited to play tennis on the *chateau* court, the owner, Madame de Bonnières, and her daughters, being most hospitable, and doing all they could to make life enjoyable for their guests. The battalion erected its own cinema and battalion baths and prepared a football ground, and here began the moulding of the Rugby Union team which achieved such distinction later in Belgium.

On October 11th Colonel Neligan, who was temporarily in charge of the brigade, ordered a brigade parade in honour of the Prime Minister of Australia, the Rt. Hon. W. M. Hughes, who was visiting the neighbourhood.

On the 29th the Rugby team went over to L'Etoile and played the 3rd Field Ambulance, winning by 26-5. Divisional rifle matches were held on October 30th and 31st, and on November 2nd brigade sports took place at Bussus, 9th Battalion men winning the 100 yards and 440 yards races. On November 3rd the sergeants met and defeated the officers at football.

An accident occurred at Gorenflos one day in the tailor's workroom. A brazier seemed to have gone out, and Tom Cherry, one of the tailors, before relighting it, poured on to it some petrol from a bottle. The petrol immediately took light, the bottle caught fire, and Cherry was badly burnt about the face and hands, being saved from worse injury only by the presence of mind of the corporal tailor, J. B. Kennedy, who promptly threw around him some of the clothing lying near by. About this time Captain F. Donaldson contracted pneumonia and was sent to hospital at Abbeville, where he died.

The beautiful dream of passing the winter in Gorenflos was dispelled when, on November 2nd, Major-General Glasgow, G.O.C. the 1st Division, came and inspected the battalion. He informed the C.O. afterwards that there was every possibility of an early move forward again, as the enemy, who had been in retreat, was making a rather determined stand in the Mormal Forest sector, near the Belgian border. Preparations to move had therefore to be made, and on November 5th they were in full swing, when a message was received ordering a postponement for twenty-four hours. During the next two days there were two more postponements, each for twenty-four hours, but by the 7th it was fairly definitely understood that the move was to be made next day.

At 4 p.m. on November 8th, to the great regret of all, the unit left Gorenflos, after a pleasant stay there of six weeks, and marched about eight miles to Pont Remy, where it entrained. There was a wait of seven hours before the train left, and

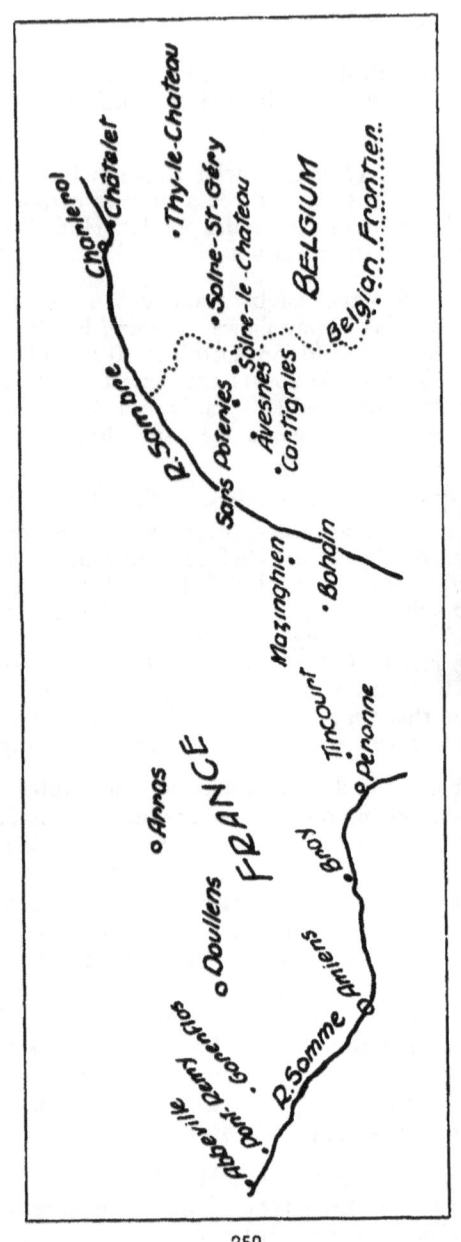

29. Gorenflos to Châtelet.

then followed a long, cold, tiresome journey to Tincourt, which was reached at 11 p.m. on the 10th.

Rain had fallen during the day, but this had stopped before the train arrived at Tincourt, where a sharp frost had set in. Consequently, the mud on the roads was partly frozen, and as the troops marched to their billets it crumpled under their feet like pastry. After the battalion had been comfortably settled down, the headquarters officers had a light meal seated round a brazier—and then, instead of going straight off to sleep or discussing the fighting towards which they were bound, they took the lead set by the padre, Captain McBain, and talked poetry until 2.30 a.m.

The next day was very cold, and in the morning there was heard the tooting of locomotive whistles in the distance, which indicated that something out of the ordinary had happened. Then rumours reached the village that an armistice had been signed; the war was over. Most of the officers and men had an idea that something of the sort was in the air, but they did not expect that the cessation of hostilities would come so soon, especially as they were awaiting orders to go up into the front line; some of them, in fact, had not even heard the word "armistice" before, and did not know what it meant. These rumours were confirmed by motor-transport drivers who passed through Tincourt.

All ranks took the news very quietly. There was no excitement whatever; the general feeling of the men seemed to be that as they had left a good "home" at Gorenflos, they should now be allowed to march straight into Germany. There was a good deal of speculation, however, as to what was going to happen to the different units of the A.I.F., and soon many rumours of all sorts were going the rounds of the village. Twice during the day the battalion was paraded for the purpose of moving off, and on each occasion the order was cancelled. At about 3 p.m., however, another parade was called, and after a short march the troops were put into motor-lorries and taken on to Mazinghien, a village which had been occupied until the day before by the retreating Germans. They reached there at 7.30 p.m. and then marched three kilometres to billets in two large farm-houses.

The next day was spent largely in cleaning the billets. The battalion pioneers had the unpleasant task of burying a number of horses which had been killed recently by shell-fire, and as many of these were round the farm occupied by battalion headquarters, the men dubbed it "Dead Horse Farm"; it had previously been used as a German unit headquarters. Several dead Germans were found lying among the horses, and had to be buried also.

The enemy had, prior to leaving, removed all stocks of food and clothing, and had informed the civilians that British troops would be taking over the area and would provide for their wants. Many French people who had been seized for labour drafts were now returning to their broken homes. They, as well as the people found in the village, were very timid, afraid even to speak, and when approached they cowered like beaten animals. The children were very frightened, and when spoken to they ran into the buildings and hid, like rabbits. The troops shared their rations, as far as they possibly could, with the people on whom they were billeted. In one case a family, when given some fresh meat, said that it was the first they had tasted in two years, and that for the past year they had lived practically on vegetables.

A number of released British prisoners of war, in a very bad way from want of food and exposure, were also met here. The Germans had taken all their clothing with the exception of a flannel shirt and a pair of trousers, and had issued them with old and worn German army boots; their main food for many months had been sugar-beet. These men were soon sent back to hospitals and convalescent camps.

There had been a good deal of shelling round about the village, and many of the buildings were in a very bad state. The farms were untilled, and there was a general air of desolation over the whole countryside; not a hoof of stock could be seen anywhere.

In November 13th there was a brigade parade, at which the brigadier, General Gordon Bennett, addressed the troops. The next day the battalion marched to Bohain, a fairly large town, in a good state of preservation, which was now the railhead of the advancing columns. Here again were witnessed many distressing scenes, as the people were practically starving, and as soon as Sergeant Hanlon had opened the battalion canteen the troops took a delight in purchasing what foodstuffs they could and distributing them to the hungry children, who soon made friends with the Australians. The first cooked meal of the 9th in Bohain was also equally divided between the civilians and the troops.

During the nine days' stay at Bohain the battalion carried out training, especially route-marching, to harden the men's feet for the big march into Germany, which was expected to take place in a few days' time. All ranks, even the canteen staff, had to take part in these marches. A good deal of trouble was also taken to smarten up the appearance of the troops, both in their uniforms and equipment and in their bearing, so that they would present a good appearance to the Germans.

While they were in this town both the 9th and 10th Battalions received a very liberal and unofficial rum issue, the persons responsible for the distribution being the transport sergeants of the two units, and not the headquarters, who had no knowledge of the issue nor of its source. It was not until about a week after the battalion had left the area that the persons concerned admitted that the spirit had been "souvenired" from the railhead, where it had been dumped in readiness for collection by the supply column of another division.

On the 22nd orders were received to proceed to a new area, and next day the 9th began (as was thought) its march to the Rhine, but actually returned to Mazinghien. On the 24th it marched on to Cartignies, and the following day to Sars Poteries, five miles north-east of Avesnes, this move being made in fairly good weather.

Shortly after the arrival of the battalion, the weather changed for the worse. The billets were very dirty, but the baths were fine, and the village was in a good state of preservation. The principal industry was a large glass-works, but most of the machinery had been removed or destroyed. The battalion was billeted in the glass-works, and many excellent specimens of the glass-workers' art drifted both to England and to Australia.

Early in the three-and-a-half weeks' stay here rumours arose that the Australians might not go into Germany, and everyone in the battalion was very disappointed. The King was in the neighbourhood, and on December 1st the battalion made a short route march to the Mauberge road to see the sovereign go past. On the same day orders were received that the 9th was to furnish a King's Guard, Lieutenant-Colonel A. M. Ross, of the Australian Corps staff, asking for the best physical types the battalion could produce.

Captain C. H. Ryan was appointed to command this guard, with Lieutenant H. N. Knowles second-in-command. Captain Ryan was afterwards created an M.V.O. in recognition of commanding the guard. The other members of the guard were as follows:—

| Number and Rank | Name | Company[1] | Number and Rank | Name | Company[1] |
|---|---|---|---|---|---|
| Sergeant | Whyte | A | Privates | | |
| Sergeant | Henley | B | 57707 | Tambling | A |
| Corporal | Clark | D | 139 | Taylor | A |
| " | Lewis | B | 53891 | Jerome | B |
| " | Rennick | B | 7276 | Johnson | B |
| L/Cpl. | Booth | B | 1155 | Kerr | B |
| " | Cox | B | 6792 | Pearson | B |
| Privates | | | 3752 | Wickham | B |
| 5030 | Bassingthwaite | A | 5442 | Brackenbury | C |
| 1995 | Blaney | A | 7211 | Brede | C |
| 3568 | Bugler | A | 53346 | Jones | C |
| 333 | Clear | A | 7755 | Plane | C |
| 3320 | Davidson | A | 4272 | Power | C |
| 756 | Dunne | A | 7311 | Rodney | C |
| 6021 | Frew | A | 50030 | Campbell | D |
| 2823 | Hack | A | 1634 | Eastwell | D |
| 5684 | Hopkins | A | 3058 | Havtin | D |
| 2732 | Keane | A | 6048 | Little | D |
| 53323 | Lowry | A | 6348 | Maddern | D |
| 7575 | Meyer | A | 3521 | McDonald | D |
| 577 | McFarlane | A | 6729 | O'Meara | D |
| 1832 | Phillips | A | 4638 | Petersen | D |
| 4754 | Platonoff | A | 6418 | Trede | D |
| 53360 | Reid | A | 5339 | Braithwaite | H.Q. |
| 6847 | Scott | A | 3876 | Porter | H.Q. |
| 2899 | Steadman | A | 4913 | Whittle | H.Q. |

1 The 3-company organisation adopted on August 30th had been abandoned by this time, and the regular four companies resumed.

Special pains were taken to fit out the men with the best possible uniforms for the occasion, and the result reflected great credit on Corporal J. Kennedy, the battalion tailor, and his staff, whose duty it was to equip the guard with special clothing.

Sergeant Whyte afterwards gave the following account of the four days on duty:—

"The guard was intensely trained for a short period before proceeding to take up duty. Captain Ryan was very strict, everything had to be right or it was a case of 'back to your company'; the number chosen was sixty men, but during training some of these were dropped out. The guard was sent by motor 'bus to Sebourg Chateau, a couple of miles north of Avesnes, where the King, the Prince of Wales and Prince Albert[2] were in residence.

"We relieved a guard of Princess Pat's Own (Canadians) who were on duty when we arrived on 4th December; our own guard was divided into two, and I had first tour of duty with two corporals and twenty men. The guard-room was at the main entrance to the chateau grounds and was, I think, the gatekeeper's house, the chateau being about one hundred yards back from the main road.

"The King and the two princes were away from the chateau when we took over, but were expected to return about 6 p.m., when every member

2 Now His Majesty King George VI.

of the guard was to be on parade for inspection by the royal party. His Majesty was late in arriving, and the Prince of Wales, coming in about half an hour before, advised Captain Ryan that as the King would be tired he thought an inspection would be better left until next day; the section not on duty then returned to billets while the others carried on with the job. When the King and Prince Albert returned, their car was preceded by a motor-car patrol, which gave us timely warning of their arrival, and the guard turned out and presented arms when the cars came through the gates.

"There were, I think, five posts, one man on the entrance to the grounds (guardroom), two men on the front of the chateau, one at the rear entrance to the chateau, and one on a gate which was a rear entrance to the grounds; the whole place was enclosed by a high stone wall, so it was simple enough to look after it.

"When taking the relief round the various posts about 10 p.m. on the first night, we found that Private Blaney had held up Inspector Quinn of Scotland Yard, who was on special duty with the royal party; the inspector was annoyed, but realised that Blaney was doing his duty, his instructions being that 'no one pass in or out by that door after dark.'

"The following morning about 9 o'clock the whole guard fell in and were inspected by the King and the two princes. His Majesty wore the uniform of a field-marshal, the Prince of Wales was in Guards' uniform, and Prince Albert in Air Force uniform. During the inspection they spoke to several of the members of the guard; the man on the right of the front rank had quite a talk with the Prince of Wales, who was impressed by his size; he was over six feet high and built in proportion.

"The tour of duty passed off without any untoward incident, although one little item might be recorded as showing the Prince of Wales' dislike of ceremonial at what he thought the wrong time for it. He was coming in from what would appear to be a private expedition, looking a bit muddy and carrying a few odds and ends (souvenirs); the sentry on the gate turned out the guard, who stood by to present arms as the Prince came in; the Prince apparently had other ideas, because he stood well back in the main road and waved the old army washout signal until it was realised that he meant the guard to turn in; this was done, and the Prince came in without any fuss.

"Our tour of duty ended on the 7th, when the royal party set off by car for another part of the line, while we returned to the battalion."

The selection of the 9th Battalion to supply this guard was a signal honour, as it was until 1937 the only occasion on which Australian troops had ever mounted guard over a royal residence when occupied by the sovereign, and it still is (1940) the only occasion on which an Australian battalion has ever supplied such a guard.

The most important event after this at Sars Poteries was a victory gained on the field of sport by the battalion Rugby team over the 2nd Battalion team, the N.S.W. men being defeated by 11 to 3. A great deal of football was played during the stay here, many of the matches being with other units, including some with "Tommies."

An unfortunate incident which occurred here was the death of two men, who were killed by the explosion of a large shell, or *minenwerfer* bomb, with whose nosecap they were tampering. They were buried in the local cemetery by Captain McBain.

On December 16th orders were received to proceed to a new area, and on the 17th the battalion marched out of Sars Poteries. The weather had continued bad, and on this day it was particularly vile, a bitterly cold sleety rain falling all the morning. Mounted officers were glad to discard their horses and march with the rest to keep warm. The route lay through Solre-le-Chateau, and warning had been received that the divisional commander would inspect the unit as it marched through that town.

Now in one of its last battles the 9th had captured a German "cooker" (field kitchen), together with a pair of horses to haul it. This proved most useful to the headquarters company, but it was in addition to the proper establishment and therefore should not rightly have been held. As on this move all the battalion transport would have to move with the unit, there was great danger that either General Glasgow or one of his staff would notice the extra unauthorised vehicle, which would mean the subsequent receipt by the C.O. of an enquiry containing the words, "please explain," followed by the surrender of the useful kitchen.

However, anyone who had been watching very early on that morning would have seen one German "cooker" and team with driver and brakesman minus their unit colour patches, making their way by devious back routes towards our destination. Had they been challenged they would have proved the most stupid "diggers" in the whole A.I.F.—they would have known nothing. As it happened, they got through safely, and the battalion marched past the general with flying colours and no complaints, not even a "please explain."

After passing through Solre-le-Chateau the battalion crossed the Belgian frontier and went on to Solre-St-Géry. On the next day, the 18th, it marched on again in most unfavourable conditions, sleety rain and a bitterly cold wind. Early in the afternoon it reached Thy-le-Chateau in much more moderate weather.

On the 19th the 9th again moved on and was once more lashed by bitterly cold rain all the morning. About 3 p.m. it reached Châtelet, a suburb of Charleroi, and itself containing about 12,000 inhabitants, with coal-mining as its chief industry. The population gave the battalion a wonderful reception. The billets here were the best occupied during the whole

Plate xxi.

41.—N.C.O.'s AND MEN OF THE 9th WITH DECORATIONS.
Taken at Chatelet, 25th March, 1919.
Left to right.—Back row: Cameron, F. Spearett, J. D. Allan, B. Kelly, F. Few, J. Skinner, ―――――.
Front row: W. Bath, A. Henley, E. O'Brien, R.S.M. S. Brand, R.Q.M.S. Gunderson, C.S.M. H. E. Thorley
(Aust. War Memorial Official Photograph. No. E 4983. Copyright.)

Plate xxii

42.—THE TUG-OF-WAR TEAM.
Taken May, 1918.
Left to right.—Back row: J. Bentley (?), Booker, McNalty, V. Noble, ———, ———,
Front row: ———, W. Malin, Sgt. W. Ramm, ———, W. Lake (?), F. L. White.
Sitting on ground: C.S.M. Todd.

43.—PRESENTATION OF COLOURS TO THE 9th/49th BATTALION, C.M.F.,
On 11th August, 1937, at Anzac Square, Brisbane. (See p. 282.)
Left to right.—9th BATTALION PARTY: Lieut. E. H. Meyers, O.C. (holding King's Colours), C.S.M. E. J. Gandy, Sgt. G. Walker, Lieut. W. C. Henzell (holding Regimental Colours), Sgt. A. J. Wagner. 9th/49th OFFICERS: Lieut. R. W. Swartz, Lieut. T. Willington.

war; quite a number of the troops were billeted with private families, while others were quartered in unoccupied shops and dwellings. Headquarters were in La Grande Rue. The Australians here formed part of the forces supporting the armies of occupation which took possession of the Rhine area.

On the 21st a civic reception was tendered to General Glasgow and the officers of the 3rd Brigade by the burgomaster and council in the hotel de ville (town hall). This was to welcome the Australian troops and to extend to them, on behalf of the Government of Belgium, the thanks of the people for their deliverance from the German invaders. Each battalion in the 3rd Brigade supplied a company to form a composite battalion, under the command of Lieutenant-Colonel Neligan, to take part in a triumphal march.

The day unfortunately turned out bleak and cold, and the troops had to parade in greatcoats. Just as the march was timed to begin from the bridge linking Châtelet with Châtelineau, snow commenced to fall, but this did not stop the people from turning out. The composite battalion, headed by a band, marched to the hotel de ville; and formed up in a hollow square, in the presence of a great crowd of onlookers, including children in hundreds waving flags.

While the troops were awaiting the arrival of General Glasgow, the snow began to fall more heavily, and several of the women present, anxious to protect the soldiers from the snow, soon had umbrellas up. This caused one very amusing incident. When arms were sloped just prior to the general's arrival, the corporal on the right flank of the 9th Battalion company tried to explain to an old lady that she would have to remove her umbrella, otherwise it might become damaged when arms were being presented. However, the lady could not understand English, and the corporal could not speak French, so the unequal contest was abandoned. The general arrived, the order for the general salute was given, a flash, and a bayonet was through the poor old lady's umbrella, but she was quite unconcerned when the corporal offered his apologies.

The burgomaster arrived soon after the divisional commander, and the battalion marched past to the accompaniment of great demonstrations with flags and cheering by the civilians, who would every now and then break into singing, "It's a long way to Tipperary," which most of them apparently believed to be the British national anthem.

After the martial display outside, the officers were entertained inside the hotel de ville. The city band was placed within the building near the council chamber, so as to provide music for the proceedings, especially to play the national anthems. It would persist in playing "God Save the King" at most inappropriate times.

General Glasgow was the guest of honour, and was first presented to all the notables and "near-notables" of the town. Then followed a number of speeches in French, thanking the Australians for their services. These were translated into English by an interpreter, and General Glasgow's reply, in English, was likewise translated into French. The toasts were drunk in splendid champagne of 1906 vintage, which had in some remarkable way been kept hidden from the Germans during the four years of occupation. The wine-glasses had been filled before the arrival of the guests, and were placed 4, 6, or 8 deep (the memory of those present fails on this point) almost the whole length of the long council table. After three or four of these had been drunk in rapid succession the glasses appeared to be 16, 24, or 32 deep. One officer remarked, after his second glass, "two more of those and a man would start to eat cobble-stones."

Very little was done during the next few days, but snow fell almost daily, and naturally the diggers took the opportunity of having snowball fights. On the first Sunday night, as the crowd was leaving the local cinema, snow was falling heavily, and the diggers began to snowball one another, with an occasional shot at some civilian. The townspeople were not too sure of themselves at first, as they had not been allowed to take part in any such pastime while the Germans had been in occupation, and they were a little afraid that if they snowballed the soldiers they would get into trouble. The small boys were the first to attack the Australians, and when the elders saw that the diggers were enjoying the fun, a general snow-battle commenced, which lasted until well after midnight. That night was responsible for a wonderful understanding between the Australian troops and the Belgian people, who looked on the diggers as a band of big brothers. It was also responsible for the civilians' taking a new attitude towards soldiers after what they had experienced during the preceding four years.

The inhabitants had been informed by the Germans before they left the area that Australian troops were coming into the towns around Charleroi, and would be billeted on them. This was the first intimation that these people had that there were Australian soldiers in the war, so they were naturally anxious to find out what they were like. One old couple admitted that they had turned up an atlas, and on finding the map of Australia, with pictures of an aboriginal, a kangaroo and an emu, they were highly indignant, as under the aboriginal was the title, "An Australian native." They thought that they were going to have black troops quartered in their houses. One can imagine their surprise when the different battalions marched in with their bands playing, all the soldiers were white men, and wonder of wonders, they all spoke English!

Even so, the townsfolk thought at first that the Australians were very wild men. Lieutenant Earwaker, who was billeting officer at Châtelet, found that the civilians refused to let the soldiers be billeted in their houses. He thereupon went to the prefect of police, who spoke English, and found him quite willing to help in the matter. The next morning he met the prefect and began by giving him half-a-dozen whiskies. Then they went to the first house, and the prefect asked the "madame" to take "deux hommes (two men)." She at once began to make excuses. "Mais, monsieur, ... (but, sir, ....)," when the prefect immediately cut in with, "Quatre hommes, alors (four men, then)." The lady at once capitulated. "Deux hommes, monsieur, deux hommes," she said, and the matter was thus arranged, and similarly at the other houses.

Great preparations were made to have a Christmas dinner quite out of the ordinary for all ranks, and these endeavours were quite successful, troops having their best Christmas dinner of the whole war.

In November Major-General Sir Talbot Hobbs (5th Division) had succeeded Lieutenant-General Monash as G.O.C. Australian Corps, and when the corps advanced into Belgium his headquarters were at Ham-sur-Heure, near Charleroi. During December the Prince of Wales was attached to Hobb's staff for a month as staff captain. On the 30th the Prince visited Châtelet, and the battalion gave him a wonderful reception. The civilians also turned out in force to welcome him, and seemed delighted that he should take such a keen interest in their welfare. He met the officers of the 3rd Brigade, and then proceeded into the local theatre, where he presented a number of decorations. The 9th furnished two particularly tall men as special guards at the theatre door, of whom Private L. O'Brien, of "C" Company, was one. The Prince then had a look round the billets and chatted with some of the men, including Privates Swain, of "B" Company, and Rooney, of H.Q. Company.

Thus ended the year 1918, which the battalion had begun on the Messines front. It suffered the misfortune of being badly gassed at Hollebeke, after which it assisted in the defence of Hazebrouck, and captured Le Waton. Then it went south to the Somme and participated in the last great series of victories, fighting at Crepy Wood, capturing Froissy Beacon and the edge of the village of Cappy, and finally capturing Villeret, and penetrating nearly to the Hindenburg Line. It then enjoyed a fine rest at Gorenflos, advanced once more to meet the enemy, but was anticipated by the Armistice, and ended the year by a triumphant entry into Belgium.

With the intention of creating a good impression, and also with a view to a little "window-dressing," the ceremonial side of training was indulged in soon after arrival at Châtelet. The headquarters guard mounting each afternoon was made quite an interesting ceremony. This also went a long way to convince any of the civilians who may not have been too kindly disposed to the Allied cause to realise that the occupying troops were still prepared to "carry on the good work." The changing of the guard was always an occasion for a large crowd of civilians to gather to watch the ceremony; and the manner in which the troops carried out the work gave the lie direct to all who considered that Australians could not be trained in ceremonial work. This ceremony was carried on for several weeks, but when demobilisation commenced in earnest it was impossible to furnish guards strong enough to keep up the procedure.

Apart from guard duties the men were occupied with drill in the mornings and sports and games in the afternoons. Leave was given to a party each week to visit Brussels for a few days. The troops, however, were not wholly dependent on this leave for their entertainment, as Charleroi, three or four miles away, with a number of adjacent villages (really small towns which were practically suburbs of Charleroi, and of which Châtelet was one) comprised a population of a couple of hundred thousand, and the delights of this "great city" were explored and enjoyed by many. A brigade race-course, complete with bookmakers, was organised, the racehorses being drawn from the ranks of the transport horses and mules—commonly called "donks."

The educational scheme, which had been planned some time before for the demobilisation period,[3] now came into force, and classes were formed in a number of subjects and

[3] See p. 241.

Plate xxiii.

44.—THE RUGBY TEAM. (See p. 261.)
Taken at Chatelet, 12th January, 1919.
Left to right.—Back row: Porte, Braithwaite, Barlow, Porter, Cpl. Keast.
Middle row: Ogilvie, Venn, Sgt. R. Kettle, C.S.M. E. O'Brien, E. C. Saunders, Wright, Harris.
Front row: Whaites, C.S.M. W. A. Porter, Sgt. L. Stuart (Capt.), Lieut. Leo. Alcock, Lieut. C. M. Wrench.
(Aust. War Memorial Official Photograph. No. E 4113. Copyright.)

45.—THE SOCCER TEAM. (See p. 261.)
Taken at Chatelet, 24th January, 1919.
Left to right.—Back row: A. Perrett, C.S.M. W. A. Porter, Lieut. Pickford, T. Douglas.
Middle row: A. Pedley (Capt.), J. Skinner, Lieut. Leo. Alcock, May, Wilkinson.
Front row: Palmer, H. Smith, Robinson, W. Knott.
(Aust. War Memorial Official Photograph. No. E 4227. Copyright.)

Plate xxiv.

46.—9th BATTALION OFFICERS.
Taken at Chatelet on 13th January, 1919.
Left to right.—Back row: Lieuts. Pickford, Dalzell, H. Harvey, Raff, Shaw, Forward, Partridge, Wrench.
Middle row: Lieuts. Martin, Knowles, Sheedy, Thomas, Alcock, Earwaker, Grinstone, Francis.
Front row: Lieut. Flinter, Capt. Grieve, Lieuts. Meyers, L. W. Butler, Lieut.-Col. Ross, Capts. Farmer, McNaught, Lieut. Bomford.

(Aust. War Memorial Official Photograph. No. E 4155, Copyright.)

occupations likely to be of use to men on re-entering civilian life. Many of the troops took advantage of this scheme, some with enthusiasm to make the best of their opportunities in this way, but some also in a spirit not so enthusiastic for the purpose in view of the authorities, but which may be indicated by the name of "Bon Military Enjoyment," which soon came into common use to represent the official title, Non-Military Employment. These activities in the 9th were in charge of Lieutenant Finter, who was appointed battalion education officer.

Teams were organised under the battalion sports officer, Lieutenant Leo Alcock, for Rugby Union and soccer football, in a divisional competition, and company teams were also formed for a battalion competition. The battalion Rugby team made a splendid beginning by two successive victories over the 2nd Battalion team, which was considered a "crack" one, containing a number of New South Wales interstate players. The 9th won the first game by 6 points to 3, and in the second they gained 23 points to their opponents' 6, the outstanding player in the 9th being "Rats" Flanagan, who is described as having played on the latter occasion "the game of his life." The captain of the 9th team, L. Stuart, also showed outstanding ability. The team eventually won the competition.

The following results of 9th Battalion Rugby matches are on record:—

January 1, against 1st Pioneers, won.
January 10, against 26th Battalion, won 8—0.
January 13, against 10th Battalion, won easily.
January 14, against 25th Battalion, won 14—3.
January 28, against Tunnellers, won.
February 15, against 3rd Battalion, won 14—6.
February 19, against Machine-gunners, drawn.

It will be noticed that two of these matches were against 2nd Division units.

Headquarters company proved the victor among the company teams.

The battalion soccer team also was very successful. The Belgian civilians took great interest in the football, and on most Sunday afternoons this team, with Corporal "Spokes" Pedley as captain, used to play a team of civilians; after losing five games on end the local team drew on a professional team in Brussels for four players to come to Châtelet and help them to beat the Australians. The first match was a real "humdinger," but again the 9th were the victors by 3 goals to 2. Still determined, the civilians arranged for a game on the following Sunday, and again the professionals were brought in; this proved to be one of the best matches seen on the Châtelet ground, the Belgians winning by 3 goals to 1. An attempt was made to arrange another game, but having beaten the Australians, the locals were content to rest on their laurels. The results of some of the soccer matches, which have been recorded, were:—

January 28, against Tunnellers, won.
February 15, against 5th Battalion, won 7—0.
February 22, against 3rd Battalion, won 1—0.
February 26, against 11th Battalion, won 4—0.
March 14, against 11th Battalion, drawn.

After the competition had been completed a game was arranged with a British artillery unit, and in this match the Black and Blues were beaten by 5 goals to 2, the Australians receiving a lesson as to how soccer really should be played, as the Englishmen were complete masters of ball control, and in most instances just "played" with their opponents.

There were many other forms of sport engaged in as well as football, and in each division of sport points were allowed towards the corps championship cup. This was eventually won by the 3rd Brigade, which finished with 19½ points, the runners-up having 19 points; as the 9th Battalion had contributed the greatest number of points for the winning formation, the custody of the cup was given to it.

The manner in which the 9th looked after its playing fields was a shining example to the units located in that area, and was a credit to Lieutenant Alcock, who was responsible for the care taken in this respect. The fields were always marked ready for playing, and no person was allowed even to cross them in case the playing surface should be cut up. This fact was often used as a joke against the unit, and when the Prime Minister of Australia visited Châtelet to address the troops, through some mistake on the part of the picquet that day the official party walked over the Rugby field. When it arrived at the place from which Mr. Hughes was to speak, General Glasgow jokingly told the Prime Minister that the 9th had bestowed an honour on him, as they had allowed him to cross their Rugby field, something which the general himself had never before been permitted to do. The honour was short lived, however, as the picquet was awake to its duties when the party was returning, and made it walk right round the field, much to the amusement of all concerned, especially of the diggers.

During January, 1919, the officers of the 9th were as follows:—C.O., Lieutenant-Colonel C. F. Ross; second-in-command, Major N. G. Armstrong (detached for duty at Leave Camp, Brussels); adjutant, Captain S. J. Chapman; assistant adjutant, Lieutenant A. L. Raff; quartermaster, Lieutenant T. J. Sheedy; transport officer, Lieutenant C. E. Pickford; medical officer, Captain J. W. Grieve; O.C., H.Q. Company, Lieutenant L. W. Butler; "A" Company, Captain F. J. Biggs; "B" Company, Captain T. W. Farmer; "C" Company, Captain J. F. McNaught; "D" Company, Lieutenant E. W. Martin; other officers, Lieutenants L. Alcock, Avery, A. H. Bonner, Dalziel, J. G. Earwaker, H. Finter, Fordham, T. Francis, Grinstone, R. L. Harper, F. R. Hayes, J. King, B. G. S. Mason, E. H. Meyers, H. J. Partridge, S. Shaw, Tennant, Thomas, C. O. Thompson, and C. M. Wrench. Captain W. G. Penrose had been O.C. of "D" Company until he left to go to a senior officers' school at Aldershot.

On January 29th a large draft of men of the 9th, under Lieutenant-Colonel Ross, and headed by the band, left for Charleroi, where it was joined by drafts from the other three battalions of the 3rd Brigade and certain divisional and corps details. At 9.30 next morning they left by train for Harfleur, which was reached on February 2nd, after a very slow and cold trip. The draft, amounting in all to over 1100, then crossed to England, and was quartered at No. 14 Camp, Longbridge Deverill. After the usual demobilisation leave it was expected that the detachment would be leaving England on the transport *Plassy*, but this arrangement was cancelled at the last moment and another few days of demobilisation leave were given, followed by a wait of a further fortnight in camp.

During most of this time there was a shortage of senior officers in the draft, which was handled by Colonel Ross and eleven subalterns; the latter used to say in jest that the draft was "run" by the colonel and eleven boys. However, ten days before embarkation Major Hogan, of the artillery, and Captain McNaught, of the 9th, joined the draft, which left in the *Suffolk*[4] on April 13th. After touching at Cape Town the *Suffolk* arrived at Adelaide and then went on to Melbourne, where the Queenslanders disembarked and entrained for Brisbane, which was reached at 6.30 p.m. on June 7th.

Lieutenant-Colonel C. F. Ross was one of the original subalterns of the battalion, and the only one of the original officers who was still with the 9th at the termination of hos-

---

[4] The *Suffolk* had been one of the transports in the First Convoy, which left Australia on the 1st of November, 1914.

tilities. He went into camp on 21st August, 1914, landed with the battalion at Anzac, and remained there until mid-October, 1915, when he became sick and was evacuated to hospital in England. Returning to the unit early in March, 1916, at Gebel Habeita, when it left for France, he was detailed to assist in transferring the 3rd Training Battalion from Tel-el-Kebir to Tidworth, in England, and remained on the training cadre there for a few months. It was thus mid-November, 1916, when he rejoined the 9th, in the Flers sector. He took part in the actions at The Maze, Lagnicourt, and Bullecourt, and at the end of June, 1917, succeeded Neligan as second-in-command of the 9th, being then promoted to major. After the Battle of the Menin Road he went to a senior officers' school at Aldershot, and returned to the battalion early in 1918.

Ross was wounded by a shell in June, 1918, at Moolenacker, and soon afterwards met with an accident, but he rejoined the battalion late in July in time to take part in the Battle of Lihons, where he was again wounded. He once more returned to the unit at Gorenflos early in October, and was immediately appointed to command the 9th and promoted to lieutenant-colonel. Ross was a man of few words, but these words were always to the point. He had a keen sense of humour, under fire was calm and cool as a cucumber, and set a fine example to officers and men, being well liked by everyone.

After the large draft had left Châtelet the 9th came to an end as a complete unit, and on February 5th the 9th and 10th were amalgamated to form one battalion under Lieutenant-Colonel Wilder-Neligan. The splendid old A.I.F. was now slowly melting away. It seems regrettable that arrangements were not made for a few of the older and more "historic" formations to return to Australia as complete units. The people at home could then have seen the wonderful efficiency and precision of movement that the troops had attained, and the return of these famous units as complete formations would have been of inestimable value as an example and inspiration to the citizen forces.

A week after the 9th and 10th had combined, Colonel Neligan arranged a big dinner and concert in the hotel de ville on February 12th. Over a thousand troops attended, and in addition civilians were admitted to the concert. Neligan also gave a dinner to the N.C.O.'s. The catering for these functions was carried out by the canteen staff, which also performed similar duties later on for a huge picnic which the new C.O. arranged for the troops at a spot three miles from Châtelet on April 21st.

Plate xxv.

47.—THE BAND.
Taken at Chatelet, 16th January, 1919.
Left to right.—Back row: C. Thompson (?), L. Emerson, Thwaites, T. McPherson, ———, McPherson, J. Perrett.
Middle row: Scott, F. Layton, Fretwell, Kettle, H. Layton, J. Butler, A. Beeston, A. McPherson.
Front row: E. Watts, Henry, C. Hamilton, Lieut. L. W. Butler, Lieut.-Col. C. F. Ross, McCorkill, G. Davis, H. Limpus.
Sitting on ground: Smith, Head.
(Aust. War Memorial Official Photograph, No. L 4154. Copyright.)

Plate xxvi.

48.—"BULLER." (See p. 275.)
(Photo lent by Miss M. Warham.)

49.—HOWITZER CAPTURED AT LIHONS.
Now at Water Street Drill Hall, Brisbane.
(See p. 234.)
(N.K.H. photo.)

50.—GUN CAPTURED AT POZIERES.
In Newstead Park, Brisbane. It is a 150 m.m. howitzer, which had been captured from Belgians by the Germans, and used by them at Pozieres, where it was recaptured by the 9th Battalion on 23rd July, 1916.
(N.K.H. photo.)

51.—MACHINE GUN, CAPTURED IN NELIGAN'S FLEURBAIX RAID.
Now at side of old Town Hall, Hamilton, Brisbane. The inscription reads:—Captured by 9th Battalion A.I.F. at Rouge de Bout, Flanders, 2/7/16.
(See p. 118.)
(N.K.H. photo.)

Further drafts now left for England, and on March 27th, after No. 22 Quota had gone, a single battalion, under Neligan, was formed from the remnants of the whole 3rd Brigade, each of the original battalions being represented by a single company. The 9th was No. 1 Company in this "3rd Brigade Group," as it was called, and soon after the formation of the group a parade of the 1st Division was held. A cup awarded for the best marching unit in the march past was won by the combined 9th and 10th Battalions, which marched under Captain Farmer.

On April 25th the 1st Division held a sports meeting, at which Private Dreghorn, of the 9th, won the divisional championship, with Corporal Pedley, also of the 9th, as runner-up. Cricket teams were now formed, but only a few games were played, as the teams could not be maintained owing to the number of men proceeding to England for demobilisation.

On May 5th the 3rd Brigade Group supplied a guard, which contained some 9th Battalion men, for the Duke of Connaught, uncle of the King, who was visiting the neighbourhood.

With the organisation of the Brigade Group a splendid band was formed, and several players who were due to be demobilised volunteered to remain behind in order that the band could be kept up. Warrant Officer Waldron, 10th Battalion, was bandmaster, and he worked hard to bring the band to a high standard. For a period it was attached to corps headquarters, where it was highly esteemed. It was afterwards arranged that the band should attend the Lyons Fair. During its visit to that city Mr. Hughes was there, and he adopted the band, insomuch as whenever he had to appear anywhere in an official capacity he arranged for the 3rd Brigade Band to be in attendance also.

The 3rd Brigade Group, from now on known officially as No. 56 Quota, left Châtelet on May 20th by road for Charleroi, where it was to entrain. The scenes along the streets will never be forgotten by those who took part in that march, and it showed clearly to every man the high place the battalion held in the hearts of the Belgian people of that area. Many of the men were looked upon as members of families, and the scenes at some of the partings were very touching. Hundreds of people also journeyed to Charleroi by tram in order to be at the station when the train left; many of these brought farewell gifts of chocolate, cigarettes and other "comforts" for the soldiers.

## LAST DAYS IN ENGLAND

The day before the departure there was much wine flowing. A man would call at a house to say good-bye, whereupon a bottle of wine would be brought up from the cellar, a process which was repeated at every call made, so that anyone who had several friends to whom he wished to bid farewell was likely to be somewhat "merry" by the time he had finished the last visit.

While the troops were marching from Châtelet to Charleroi, the canteen staff, under the direction of Captain S. J. Chapman, was engaged in placing cases of eatables, mostly fruit, in the railway trucks in which the men were to travel. The train was a long one of 43 trucks for the rank and file and four carriages for the officers. As it pulled out of Charleroi the band struck up "Good Byee," a popular song of that time, which all hands joined in singing. The civilians, some of them with tears streaming down their faces, cheered until the train was out of sight.

After a two days' trip Harfleur, at the mouth of the River Seine, was reached. Here the draft stayed two days at the Australian Base Depot, leaving on the afternoon of the 28th for Le Havre, to embark on the *Londonderry*, at 9.30 p.m. During the night it crossed the Channel, and arrived at Southampton at 6 a.m. on May 29th.

The Quota, now commonly known as "Neligan's Thousand," entrained for Heytesbury Camp, three miles southeast of Warminster, on Salisbury Plain. A staff of six N.C.O.'s under Captain Penrose now made all the necessary preparation for the last period of leave the troops were to have in the United Kingdom, and by working night and day they were able to arrange that the whole draft of about 1000 men commenced their leave on June 3rd.

On returning from leave the troops went to Sandhills Camp, Longbridge Deverill, a few miles south of Warminster, where boat rolls were prepared. The 9th Battalion men in No. 56 Quota were the last of the 9th to leave England as a definite unit of the battalion.

A cricket team was formed in the quota, and played a few matches, meeting the Y.M.C.A. at Bath on July 9th, the Gloucester Band at Bristol on the 10th, and the Military Depôt at Bristol on the 11th, the quota team winning all three matches.

On July 18th the quota marched out from Sandhills Camp and entrained at Warminster, large crowds gathering along the line of march and also at the station to bid farewell. Reaching Devonport in the evening, it embarked on H.M.A.T. *Takada,* which sailed next day, Saturday, July 19th. This was the official day in England for celebrating the signing of the peace treaty. In harbour at Plymouth[5] were a number of ships of the Grand Fleet, which had just returned from service in the North Sea, and at 7.30 a.m. the whole of the ships broke flags as though by the pressing of a button. The *Takada* pulled out from the wharf at 9 o'clock and anchored out in the harbour until noon, when the ship began its voyage to Australia, passing through a line of warships gaily dressed and firing the peace-day salute.

Neligan was in command of all troops on the ship. The 9th Battalion officers on board were Captain T. W. Farmer (O.C. No. 1 Company), W. G. Penrose (adjutant), S. J. Chapman, J. W. Grieve (M.O.), and Lieutenants R. H. Penman, W. Chataway, C. M. Wrench, B. G. S. Mason, F. R. Hayes, E. Gordon, and E. W. Martin. The R.S.M. was Steve Brand, the C.S.M. Sergeant Mat. Baillie, and the C.Q.M.S. Vic. Savage. Besides the quota from Longbridge Deverill, there were on the ship about 500 men collected from various places, who had come direct from London to Devonport, and most of the colour patches of the A.I.F. were represented on the ship.

The trip home in the *Takada* was more in the nature of a pleasure cruise, with only a period of physical training during the morning and the necessary cleaning fatigues. The second day out a good entertainment committee was formed, each detachment having a representative. Aboard the ship was a band of 45 men, an orchestra, a concert party, and a complete cinema outfit; a different type of entertainment was arranged for each night in the week, and the afternoons were devoted to card tournaments and athletic sports. A "Diggers' Parliament" was held every Tuesday night, debating teams being arranged and subjects allotted for each meeting. The team introducing the subject was known as the "government," and what amused the diggers most in all these debates was that on every occasion the "government was defeated on a popular vote." On these nights all the vantage points on the well deck were occupied long before the time set down for the opening of "parliament," which could not take place until after officers' mess was over, as all the officers, and also some nurses on board, were keenly interested in the proceedings.

One night was devoted to an election, parties were formed, and about a dozen candidates mounted the hustings to seek

[5] Plymouth and Devonport are two adjoining towns, really forming one town, on the one harbour, Plymouth Sound.

election. After they had completed their speeches they had to answer questions from members of the audience. A vote was then taken, two of the candidates—Sergeant Somerville, of the Tunnellers, from Victoria, and Corporal R. G. Ginn, 9th Battalion—tying for first place. The first and second prizes, given by the ship's captain (Captain Smith-Lawson) and Colonel Neligan, were divided between the two winners.

When the *Takada* arrived at Colombo a sports day was arranged ashore, in front of the barracks. Some good performances were put up by the different contestants, in spite of the fact that they had been three weeks in a crowded troopship. The championship was won by Private Dreghorn, 9th Battalion, but unfortunately Queensland did not get the credit of Dreghorn's win, since, as he was disembarking at Melbourne, he had been allotted to the Victorian quota for the voyage.

After a pleasant run to Fremantle, the 11th Battalion quota left the ship, this being the final break up of the old 3rd Brigade, whose units had weathered some very hard and trying times together. Adelaide saw the departure of the 10th Battalion company, and on arrival at Port Melbourne the remainder of the brigade broke up, the 9th Battalion men disembarking and leaving by train for Brisbane almost as soon as they got ashore. Melbourne also was the place of parting from Colonel Neligan, who had endeared himself to all the units on the ship. When the troops left the wharf, cheers were given for him, and he remained standing on the boat deck until the trains were out of sight.

Brisbane was reached on 9th September, 1919, just over five years from the time when the battalion had come into existence. After the formalities of passing through the Customs and the hospital at Kangaroo Point had been completed, the last portion of the 9th Battalion scattered to the four winds, thus ending the glorious associations of that gallant old unit, and breaking up a wonderful band of comrades.

# CHAPTER XVII.

### ET CAETERA.

Besides those whose main duty it was to fight, there were numerous members of the battalion whose work was not fighting, but who were quite as necessary as the riflemen and bombers, since without them the battalion could not have carried on its duties.

The orderly room was the office of the battalion, where the records were kept and orders issued, and the clerical work was carried on. This section was in charge of an officer, the adjutant, who had under him the R.S.M., an N.C.O., and a couple of clerks. In 1914 the establishment provided for only an N.C.O. as clerk, but in 1915 a sergeant and a clerk was allowed, and in 1917 an additional clerk. Towards the end of the war another officer was added as assistant adjutant.

Captain T. V. Brown was the original adjutant, followed by E. C. Plant, M. Wilder-Neligan, W. A. Collin, C. H. Ruddle, Frank Page, C. D. Monteath, E. H. Meyers, and S. J. Chapman, the latter being a younger brother of Lieutenant (later Major) D. K. Chapman, an officer of the original battalion, who was the first man to land at Anzac. When in the later stages of the war an assistant adjutant was appointed, Lieutenants T. Goward and A. L. Raff successively occupied that position. The original R.S.M. was E. Addy, and among his successors were J. M. Perrier, A. R. Knightley, C. H. Ruddle, S. Corfield, E. Kelsall, and S. Brand. The first orderly room sergeant was R. H. Verry, and M. Wilder acted as orderly room N.C.O. on board the *Omrah*.[1]

In the eyes of some of the men the paying of the troops was the most important work of the orderly room. The Australian private was paid the sum of six shillings per day, of which one shilling was "deferred" until demobilisation, when the lump sum was handed over to him. Of the remaining five shillings, a soldier could choose to draw either one or two shillings a day for his own needs, the remainder being allotted to his next of kin or other person whom he nominated.[2]

---

[1] An attempt has been made to compile lists of those who held particular offices in the battalion, but it has been found impossible in many cases to draw up complete lists through lack of information.

[2] A soldier who had no dependants could draw the whole of the five shillings if he so wished.

This allotment was paid regularly to the soldier's nominee, while the soldier received his portion at intervals, which were fairly regular when he was out of the line, but when the battalion was in the line a man might have to go for some time without an issue of pay. As a rule he was not allowed to draw the whole of the pay which was due, so that he could have a fairly good credit to draw on when he went on leave.

The battalion was only paid once while on the *Omrah*, and consequently when it arrived in Egypt a considerable amount of back-pay was due to each man. Some of this was allowed to be drawn soon after arrival at Mena. "What a binge!" was one man's remark on recalling this occasion.

Pay was only issued twice at Anzac, ten shillings on each occasion, so that on arrival at Sarpi, after leaving the Peninsula, everyone had a large balance in his pay-book, and was once more allowed to draw some of it. There was very little opportunity of spending it here, however, and most of it disappeared (for a large number of the men) in gambling.

Certain offences were punished by fines, which were drawn from the balance in the offender's pay-book, and in certain instances expenditure could be incurred, which was liquidated from the pay-book balance; the chief item of this nature was cablegrams to Australia.

The pay-book contained particulars of the soldier for identification purposes, and it, together with the identity disc worn round the neck, was if possible recovered when a man was killed, so that they could be handed in at the orderly room.

Originally the company commander drew money from the adjutant and paid his company. Later a special sergeant was attached to battalion headquarters to attend to all matters regarding the pay of the battalion. Sergeant C. C. Campbell was pay sergeant of the 9th for a long time.

The quartermaster's department was in control of all supplies, ammunition, food, clothing, and everything else required for the working of the battalion. An officer was in charge of this, the quartermaster, assisted by a regimental quartermaster-sergeant and a storeman who held the rank of private. Each company also had a quartermaster-sergeant, assisted by a private. Major W. C. Harvey was the original quartermaster, but Captain S. L. McIntyre occupied the position for the greater part of the battalion's fighting career. McIntyre had been on the staff of the 3rd Brigade, and was appointed quartermaster of the 9th at Serapeum after the battalion returned to Egypt from Gallipoli. After October, 1918, Lieutenant T. W. Cameron was quartermaster. The first Q.M.S. was W. Aggett, who afterwards received a commission. Aggett was succeeded by H. Bull.

A considerable amount of supplies and gear had to be carried when the battalion was on the move, and for this the battalion transport was responsible. When the battalion was in the line it had nightly to carry, as far forward as vehicles could go, stores, ammunition, food, and water. During the Gallipoli operations the transport had necessarily to stay behind in Egypt, but when the 9th went to the Western Front this section functioned once more. Normally, when the battalion was in the line the transport was left some distance in rear. The original transport officer was Captain H. W. Lee, later occupants of the post being Lieutenants W. S. Mactaggart, T. W. Cameron (afterwards quartermaster), Gordon, Pickford, and Warner. The first transport sergeant was Mactaggart, and others were A. W. Farmer and Chalmers.

The duty of the battalion signallers was to maintain all the internal communications in the battalion; that is, between battalion headquarters and the various companies and other subdivisions of the battalion. The maintenance of communication with brigade headquarters and other formations outside the battalion was the responsibility of the divisional signal company. In the later stages of the war wireless stations were established at battalion headquarters and sometimes even at company headquarters, but these were staffed and maintained by the wireless section of the divisional signal company.

At Anzac the battalion signallers at first employed flags, heliograph, and lamps; later, telephones were lent by the divisional signal company and staffed by the battalion personnel. In France, telephones became a regular part of the battalion signallers' equipment, and henceforth the main means of communication between the different headquarters was by telephone and by runners, the latter being men specially detailed for carrying written messages by hand. The work of the signallers and runners during a battle was of a most dangerous nature, as they had to leave the cover of the trenches whenever necessary to maintain communications, no matter how heavy the bombardment or intense the rifle and machine-gun fire at the time. Even when no actual engagement was going on they often had to go into the open, risking any bombardment or small arms fire in which the enemy might decide to indulge.

The battalion signal section consisted of an officer, a sergeant, a corporal and 15 privates, besides the battalion runners, who also were under the command of the signal officer. Lieutenant W. J. Williams was the original signal officer, and others were Lieutenants P. Adsett, Frank Page (later adjutant), and B. Nicholls, the latter occupying the position for a long time.

There was a regular postal service in each battalion, a special man being told off to attend to it. All letters and parcels received were delivered to the addressees, even when they were in the front line, provided that it was possible to reach them. Letters written by members of the battalion were left unsealed, censored by an officer—the padre came in for a good deal of this duty—stamped "passed by censor," and forwarded to their destination without the need of a postage stamp. The first battalion postal orderly was Corporal E. Keid, but Lance-Corporal H. H. McBow occupied that position during most of the battalion's active career.

Each battalion had a regimental medical officer, who was assisted by a corporal and four privates of the A.A.M.C. attached for water duties; as well as by a corporal and a lance-corporal as medical orderlies, a corporal and six other ranks as a regimental sanitary detachment, and 16 stretcher-bearers selected from the battalion personnel. Of the stretcher-bearers four were attached to each company.

Dr. A. Graham Butler, a well-known Brisbane physician, was the original medical officer. He left the battalion while it was at Gebel Habeita in February, 1916, being succeeded by Captain A. McKillop. When McKillop was wounded at Rouge de Bout in April, 1916, Captain Norman M. Gibson was detached from the 3rd Field Ambulance to act in his place, and remained with the battalion until October, 1916, when McKillop returned from hospital. Captains Appleyard, R. Aspinall, Field, Rae, and J. W. Grieve were the later M.O.'s. Jock Grieve, a brother of Captain Bob Grieve, V.C., 37th Battalion, was very popular with the troops. A good Australian Rules footballer, he would often go out among "the boys" and "have a kick." The stretcher-bearers were a fine body of men, who have been specially mentioned in connection with the Landing at Anzac and the Battle of Pozières. Dr. Butler's first medical orderly was Corporal A. Kirby, who was killed on 8th May, 1915; the most noteworthy of his stretcher-bearers was Corporal H. Mahaffey, who was killed at Flers. Later members of the medical officer's personnel included Corporals

R. Mills and King, who in turn succeeded to Kirby's position, Corporal Bull and Private J. J. Kelly. The men who looked after and sterilised the drinking water, and the sanitary squad, although their work was of necessity for the most part "behind the scenes," deserve the highest praise for their consistent carrying out of very necessary duties without the incentive given by coming under the public eye.

Every battalion had attached to it a chaplain, commonly known as "the padre."[3] While at Enoggera the 9th had no chaplain, but the Rev. E. N. Merrington (Presbyterian) acted in that capacity during the voyage on the *Omrah*. Neither had it a chaplain during the stay at Mena and Lemnos, but one joined the battalion soon after the Landing, and later the Rev. Gordon Robertson (Congregational), of Sydney, was attached, but he left in September, 1915, sick with enteric fever. The Rev. W. Ashley-Brown (Anglican) became chaplain on December 28th, 1915, at Lemnos, but did not remain very long. The Rev. J. Lundie (Presbyterian) was padre at Gebel Habeita and for a while in France, and after him came the Rev. — Gibson. At the beginning of 1917 the Rev. — Milne was the padre, but in February of that year he was transferred to England and replaced by the Rev. — Macaulay, who was followed by the last of the 9th's chaplains, the Rev. S. McBain.

The cooks, otherwise called the "babbling brooks," filled a most important position in the unit, as an army has been said by a certain great authority to "march on its stomach." It was a great credit to the 9th Battalion cooks that on almost all occasions they succeeded in sending hot meals up to the front-line troops. The original sergeant cook was J. R. Irvine, who could not be kept out of the line on the day of the Landing.[4] Later on Sergeant Souter occupied that position, and after him Sergeant Coles, promoted from "A" Company, made a very efficient sergeant cook for a considerable period. During the first stay at Lemnos the cooks worked under great difficulties, owing to a combination of green wood brought from Alexandria, much wet weather, and constant high winds.

A battalion canteen was opened in December, 1915, at Sarpi Camp, Lemnos, but this was not kept going permanently as a regular organisation. During most of the time in France a canteen was in operation; at Fleurbaix there was one in the front line, to which supplies had to be carried up at night. A permanent canteen was opened early in January, 1917, when the battalion was at Dernancourt, an amount of

[3] From the Spanish padre, fa her.
[4] See p. 55.

two thousand francs being handed over from regimental funds to provide the initial capital. Sergeant E. M. Hanlon was placed in charge of it, and he carried on until well after the Armistice.

Supplies for the canteen were obtained from the British Expeditionary Force Canteens, which had wholesale and retail depots at or near each rail-head. A large amount of business was done, especially when the troops were in forward areas where there were no counter-attractions to draw their money, as was the case in the back areas. Notwithstanding the reasonable prices charged, the original 2000 francs capital rapidly multiplied, as running expenses were nil, and fairly large sums were paid into regimental funds. In addition to alcoholic drinks, cigarettes and tobacco, which were sold at less than half the prices charged in England, were always in great demand, as was also anything edible in tins, while the amount of chocolate consumed was enormous.

The canteen's peak period was in the early part of 1918, when it took over premises in a derelict double-fronted shop at Neuve Eglise and had a branch at Kemmel, the two establishments having between them about £400 worth of stock. Near the Neuve Eglise shop was a large stock of "dead marines" which, a humorist stated, rivalled Mont des Cats in size; the battalion pioneers had eventually to be called in to dispose of them by smashing them up. After the last German advance in March, 1918, supplies were very spasmodic, and at times it was difficult to get anything at all.

The Australian Comforts Fund was a civilian organisation established during the war for raising money and distributing free to the troops such "comforts" as hot coffee and cocoa, tinned fruit, cigarettes and additional clothing. Everything given by the Comforts Fund was absolutely free of charge to the recipient. Stalls were established by the Fund's officers behind the lines—not very far behind—and a hot drink at one of these was very often the first relief received by a "walking wounded" case making his painful way back out of the line. At least once, during the Battle of Chuignes, a branch of the Australian Comforts Fund was established at battalion headquarters.[5] Those who spent the terrible winter of 1916-17 in the Flers sector will always gratefully remember the Comforts Fund's post on the Longueval Road near Delville Wood. The troops had always the highest praise for the work of the Fund and its officials.

5 See page 240.

The canteen and the Comforts Fund were of great importance even from the strictly military point of view, especially as the Australians, being the highest paid troops participating in the war, made heavy purchases of "extras," and this abundance and variety of food and drink, together with adequate smoking material and much warm clothing, contributed a good deal to their well-being.

About April, 1918, a corporal tailor, J. B. Kennedy, was appointed, and was sent to the nucleus battalion at Morbecque. He continued his work until after the Armistice. In October, 1918, at Gorenflos, he had a section of five men working under him, and when the battalion was at Châtelet in 1919 the number was increased to six or seven. While at Gorenflos they carried on their work in a long shed divided into four rooms, the sergeant bootmaker, sergeant armourer, and postal orderly occupying the other three. As previously mentioned, he and his staff fitted out with uniforms the royal guard detailed from the battalion in December, 1918, to guard the château near Avesnes, where the King was residing.

The original armourer-sergeant was J. W. Moore, who unfortunately was injured by the explosion of a spirit-stove on the *Omrah* and died at Mena Hospital early in January, 1915. He was succeeded by Sergeant E. Finlay.

While the 9th was at Mena a sergeant bootmaker, J. McGreehin, was on the strength of the battalion. Two bootmakers, Sergeant Hopper and a private, were appointed in August, 1916, while the 9th was at Bonneville, and these men continued to function to the end of the battalion's career.

The battalion pioneers, comprising carpenters and other tradesmen, also carried out most important work, including the burial of the dead.

Band instruments were provided for the original battalion by public subscription, and the band carried on from the Enoggera period right up to the end. During the first stay at Lemnos Sergeant Thompson was the band sergeant. Later the battalion had also a pipe band, under A. Macpherson.

"C" Company of the original battalion had a mascot, a bull-terrier, named "Buller." Mrs. J. W. Kendrick, of Red Hill, Brisbane, gave him to her son Ben when he went into camp in August, 1914, so he could well claim to be an "original." He did not land with the covering party at Anzac, but was brought on to the beach there soon afterwards (it is said that he was seen there on the evening of the first day), and he remained at Anzac for three months until he distinguished himself by receiving a wound in the ear. "Buller," although originally "C" Company's mascot, came to be regarded as belonging more or less to the whole battalion, and was with the 9th nearly all the time from August, 1914, until 1918, when he was sent over to England. He did not return to Australia, and in 1932 he died in a military dogs' home near London, aged 19 years.

Gambling, though many regretted its prevalence, played a large part as one of the favourite amusements of a great number of the battalion's members in their moments of leisure, the games most in vogue being two-up, crown and anchor, poker, bridge, and housie, the latter being known in civilian life under the name of "lotto."

The original battalion comprised 32 officers and 1005 other ranks, making a total of 1037. 26 detachments of reinforcements for the 9th left Australia between December, 1914, and October, 1917, numbering 4364 of all ranks, of which 59 were officers. Everyone in these reinforcements did not join the 9th, some being diverted to other units, some falling sick after embarkation; conversely, there were many men added to the battalion at various times who had not left Australia as definite reinforcements for it, and after October, 1917, all new recruits embarked as "General Reinforcements," to be used for any unit as need should arise. The total number of men who belonged to the 9th at one time or another amounted to about 8000.

The casualties of the battalion were as follows:—

|  | Officers. | O.R.'s. | Total. |
|---|---|---|---|
| Killed in action | 32 | 746 | 778 |
| Died of wounds, etc (1) | 11 | 233 | 244 |
| Wounded | 79 | 2014 | 2093 |
| Gassed | 21 | 308 | 329 |
| Prisoners of war | 1 | 8 | 9 (2) |
| Total battle casualties | 144 | 3309 | 3453 |
| Died of disease, etc. | 2 | 70 | 72 |
| Total | 146 | 3379 | 3525 |

(1) Including 2 officers and 9 O.R.'s died of gas poisoning.
(2) Seven were captured at Anzac and two in France.

## BATTLE CASUALTIES IN THE TWO THEATRES OF WAR.

|  | Gallipoli. | France. | Total. |
|---|---|---|---|
| Killed in action, and died of wounds and gassing | 236 | 786 | 1022 |
| Wounded, gassed and prisoners | 397 | 2034 | 2431 |
| Total battle casualties | 633 | 2820 | 3453 |

From April 25th to 30th, 1915, the 9th sustained 515 casualties. These were the heaviest casualties of any battalion except the 7th, at the Anzac Landing, the 7th Battalion having received 541.

The following honours and decorations were awarded to members of the 9th:

### BRITISH.

| | | | |
|---|---|---|---|
| V.C. | 1 | Albert Medal | 1 |
| C.B. | 1 | D.C.M. | 35 |
| C.M.G. | 1 | M.M. | 158 |
| D.S.O. | 5 | 1 bar to M.M. | 10 |
| M.V.O., 4th Class | 1 | 2 bars to M.M. | 1 |
| M.C. | 36 | M.S.M. | 4 |
| 1 bar to M.C. | 2 | M.I.D. | 52 |
| 2 bars to M. C. | 1 | Hon. Mentions | 20 |
| | | Congratulatory Mentions | 5 |

### FOREIGN.

| | |
|---|---|
| Medaille Militaire | 1 |
| Croix de Guerre | 3 |
| Medaille d'Honneur avec Glaives (en Vermeil) | 1 |

There was, however, one decoration awarded not of an official but of a private nature, which is unique, and will now be mentioned. When the battalion finally left the Peninsula, on November 16th, 1915, there were only 63 officers and men of the original members who had remained with the unit without a break since April 25th.

When the 9th had been six months at Anzac the suggestion was made in the battalion that some form of memento might be arranged for those who had remained there during the whole of that period. The suggestion was passed on to some friends at home in Queensland and was taken up with enthusiasm by Miss M. Butler, of Kilcoy, who set to work and collected funds. A medal was designed and struck by Hardy Bros., of Brisbane, and was sent to 6 officers and 88 other ranks of the battalion who had spent six consecutive months in the front line at Anzac between April 25th and November 16th, 1915. Besides the original members of the unit, about 500 reinforcements had joined the battalion during the first few weeks at Gallipoli, so out of the 1500, 94 per cent. had become casualties through death, wounds, or sickness. Many of the wounded and sick of course returned to Anzac after recovery, but the special medal was sent only to those with an unbroken six months' stay. However, by the time the medals were made and sent overseas, the infantry divisions were in France, and by then many of those eligible to receive them had already made the supreme sacrifice. In such cases the medals were eventually sent to the next of kin.

The following were the recipients of this medal:—

Lieutenant P. Adsett
,, W. Aggett
,, G. R. Harrington
,, A. R. Knightley
,, A. Warren
,, N. L. Weynand
C.S.M. E. A. B. Lynch
,, J. L. Saunders
Sergeant R. Brennan
,, R. Colvin
,, S. A. McKenzie
,, W. Morgan
,, G. H. Page
Corporal J. Keaney
,, J. McGlynn
,, N. T. Scrivener
,, W. Thrupp
,, J. Wynd
L./Cpl. J. W. Giles
,, G. R. Gray
,, E. F. Little
,, J. Melrose
,, A. Villiers
,, G. Walker
,, F. H. Whitnell
Bugler A. Wardell
Private J. G. Allen
,, H. Baker

Private R. Baker
,, E. A. Bale
,, C. J. Bangs
,, G. Bartlett
,, A. Brown
,, D. Buckley
,, J. Chandler
,, W. Chandler
,, R. Chatters
,, C. Cooper
,, A. G. Edwards
,, J. Ffelan
,, F. J. Finneran
,, W. J. Frawley
,, C. H. Godebye
,, J. Greenfield
,, B. B. Grimish
,, A. Grumont
,, H. S. Hadland
,, H. F. Harley
,, M. Harty
,, G. Higgerson
,, H. Holding
,, C. Holdway
,, B. Hooper
,, J. W. Hunter
,, G. E. Jamieson
,, W. Jarrett

| | | | |
|---|---|---|---|
| Private | J. B. Jeffries | Private | W. O'Brien |
| ,, | E. A. Keid | ,, | O. R. Patterson |
| ,, | P. Kelly | ,, | J. Pirie |
| ,, | J. F. Kerr | ,, | W. J. Rider |
| ,, | E. J. Lamming | ,, | H. Sales |
| ,, | T. Lewis | ,, | H. Sanderson |
| ,, | N. W. Liddle | ,, | H. Sibbald |
| ,, | G. Little | ,, | E. Smith |
| ,, | S. F. Lucas | ,, | C. Stubbs |
| ,, | P. Macaleff | ,, | A. R. Summers |
| ,, | H. McFarlane | ,, | G. H. Taylor |
| ,, | L. Mackay | ,, | F. Thomas |
| ,, | D. McKenzie | ,, | J. Thompson |
| ,, | C. McMillan | ,, | L. Thompson |
| ,, | J. C. Milne | ,, | J. Trennant |
| ,, | J. J. Mole | ,, | G. Tyler |
| ,, | H. Morris | ,, | J. Wiltshire |
| ,, | P. Morrison | ,, | E. Wreford |
| ,, | T. H. Neale | ,, | C. Young |

## COMMANDING OFFICERS OF THE 9th BATTALION.

Lieutenant-Colonel H. W. Lee
,, ,, J. C. Robertson
,, ,, L. M. Mullen
,, ,, J. Newman
,, ,, C. F. Ross

The following officers were in temporary command of the battalion at various times:—

Major A. G. Salisbury
Major R. H. Walsh
Major J. A. Milne
Major Shaw (10th Battalion)
Major W. M. Young
Major M. Wilder-Neligan
Major H. James
Major McPherson (12th Battalion)

## THE BATTLES OF THE 9th BATTALION.

Landing at Anzac.
Defence of Anzac. The Turkish counter-attack of May 19th, 1915. Defensive only.
Pozières.
Mouquet Farm. Only a partial success.
The Maze (Le Barque).
Lagnicourt. Counter-attack.

Bullecourt II.
Menin Road (Polygon Wood).
Meteren. An advance was made, but the main object failed.
Le Waton.
Lihons (Crepy Wood).
Froissy Beacon (Chuignes).
Villeret.

Of these thirteen engagements, eleven were successes, and in each one the battalion made an advance, except in the Battle of the Defence of Anzac, which was purely a defensive action.

The Battle Honours of the battalion are:—

The Landing at Anzac, The Defence of Anzac, Pozières, The Somme, 1916-1918, Bullecourt, Menin Road, Amiens, The Hindenburg Line, Ypres, 1917, Hazebrouck.

# CHAPTER XVIII.

**POSTSCRIPT.**

Although the 9th Battalion, A.I.F., came to an end officially at the conclusion of the Great War, yet it is still alive, its soul goes marching on. Its former members combined themselves into the 9th Battalion A.I.F. Association, and every year, in August, is held a reunion dinner at which officers and men meet once more and fight their battles over again.

The committee of the Association also meets at intervals throughout the year, and it has carried out certain tasks, for example, the Battalion Memorial. After a great deal of arduous organising work sufficient funds were raised, and the Memorial was erected in the crypt beneath the Queensland War Memorial in Anzac Square, Brisbane. Designed and executed by Mr. W. Leslie Bowles, the Queensland-born sculptor, it was completed at a cost of over £500, and was unveiled on August 18th, 1937, by the Governor-General, Brigadier-General Lord Gowrie, V.C., G.C.M.G., C.B., D.S.O.

A tablet over four feet square of grey Buchan marble carries at either end a bronze statue of an Australian soldier, one in the uniform and equipment of Gallipoli, the other as he appeared in France. Between them is a brass tablet inscribed with the record of the battalion's service, over it being a bronze bas-relief depicting the Landing at Anzac, and beneath it the grouped arms of an infantry battalion in bronze.

Another work the Association set out to do was the recording of the deeds of the battalion in a permanent form, and the result is this history.

The 9th Battalion was on actual military duty once more in 1937 in the person of Mr. D. L. Suller, the honorary secretary of the Association, who was selected as one of the special contingent of Australian troops sent to London for the coronation of His Majesty King George VI. and who, with the other members of this contingent, mounted guard at Buckingham and St. James' Palaces on May 10th/11th, 1937.

Finally, the 9th still lives in its daughter battalions carrying the same number, the 9th/49th in the Commonwealth Military Forces, and the 2nd/9th Battalion of the 6th Division A.I.F., which will continue the traditions made and sustained by the original 9th.

To the militia unit were handed over the colours of the 9th Battalion A.I.F. on August 11th, 1937, in Anzac Square, Brisbane, Brigadier-General J. Campbell Robertson commanding the parade. The ceremony is shown in the illustration on Plate XXII., under which are given the names of the persons appearing in the colour-parties. Two of these, Lieutenant W. C. Henzell and C.Q.M.S. E. J. Gandy, have since passed to the Great Beyond.

In addition to the Memorial, there are in Brisbane certain other visible and tangible evidences of the battalion's deeds. In Newstead Park is a 150-m.m. Belgian howitzer, which, captured by the Germans, was recaptured by the 9th at Pozières on 23rd July, 1916. In front of the School of Arts at Bulimba can be seen the machine-gun taken by Lance-Corporal Miller and Private Vance near Merris on 20th June, 1918, and beside the former Hamilton Town Hall, now the School of Arts in that suburb, stands the machine-gun which was captured during Neligan's Raid at Fleurbaix on 2nd July, 1916. There are also guns at the drill-halls at Albion and at Water Street, Brisbane, reputed to have been captured by the 9th; the latter is said to be one of the 4.5-inch howitzers captured at Lihons.

As this book goes to press we are in the dark shades of another great international conflict and the members of the old 9th are again playing their part. Some of them, who are members of the Australian permanent forces, are already serving in the new war, on administrative, training and garrison duty, others have responded to the call to the colours, while others again are assisting as members of a reserve.

# GLOSSARY

# Glossary

| | |
|---|---|
| A.A.M.C. | Australian Army Medical Corps. |
| A.F.A. | Australian Field Artillery. |
| A.I.F. | Australian Imperial Force. |
| Anzac. | This word has three meanings. (a) The Australian and New Zealand Army Corps. (b) The area in Gallipoli occupied by the Australians, New Zealanders and other troops, and having Anzac Beach as its base. (c) A soldier who served in that area. |
| A.S.C. | Army Service Corps, the arm of the service responsible for bringing up supplies from the base to the troops. |
| Barrage. | Shells bursting in a line so as to form a barrier. Creeping barrage. A barrage which advances slowly towards the enemy. |
| Boche. | A German, the usual French wartime term. |
| C.B. | Companion of the Order of the Bath. |
| C.C.S. | Casualty clearing station, a military hospital some distance back from the line, which receives casualties from the advanced or main dressing stations (field ambulances), gives them any temporary attention required, and passes them on to a base hospital, or in cases of slight injury returns them to their unit. |
| C. de G. | Croix de Guerre (War Cross), a French and Belgian military decoration. |
| C.M.G. | Companion of the Order of St. Michael and St. George. |
| C.O. | Commanding officer of a battalion or other unit. |
| Communication sap, or trench. | A trench leading from the rear to the front line, or forming a means of communication between one trench and another. |
| "Cooker." | A portable field "kitchen" or cooking range on wheels |
| C.Q.M.S. | Company Quartermaster-Sergeant. |
| C.S.M. | Company Sergeant-major. |
| D.A.D.M.S. | Deputy-Assistant-Director of Medical Services. |
| D.C.M. | Distinguished Conduct Medal. |
| "Digger." | An Australian or New Zealand soldier. |
| D.S.O. | Companion of the Distinguished Service Order. |
| "Dud." | A shell which has failed to explode. |
| Enfilading. | Firing at a line of men or trenches from the flank. |
| Estaminet. | A small public-house. |
| Formation. | A certain number of men organised in a body for military purposes. The largest formation was the army, and the smallest, in the infantry, was the section. |
| Fritz. | A German. (See Hun.) |
| G.H.Q. | General Headquarters. |
| G.O.C. | General Officer Commanding an army, a corps, a division, or a brigade. |
| G.S.Waggon. | General Service Waggon, a four-wheeled vehicle used for transport purposes. |
| Gyppo. | A native of Egypt (A.I.F. slang). |
| H.E. | High explosive. |
| H.M.A.T. | His Majesty's Australian Transport. |
| H.M.T. | His Majesty's Transport. |
| H.Q. | Headquarters. |

## GLOSSARY (Continued)

Hun. — A German. Also called a Fritz, Fritzer, Squarehead, Squid, Boche (the usual French term), and Jerry (used by the "Tommies").

M.C. — Military Cross.

M.E.F. — Mediterranean Expeditionary Force.

M.I.D. — Mentioned in Despatches.

M.M. — Military Medal.

M.O. — Medical Officer.

Mop up. — To make a search of trenches and dugouts in order to find and capture any of the enemy who may have escaped an attacking force.

M.S.M. — Meritorious Service Medal.

M.V.O. — Member of the Royal Victorian Order.

N.C.O. — Non-commissioned officer.

No-Man's Land. — The unoccupied territory between the front lines of two opposing forces. It varied in width from twenty or thirty to several hundred yards.

O.C. — Officer commanding a formation smaller than a battalion.

O.R.'s. — Other ranks, all those other than commissioned officers.

Parados. — A small earthwork behind a trench, corresponding to the parapet, which was in front.

Pill-box. — A strong-post or shelter above the surface of the ground, built of concrete.

Possy. — A place or position.

Q.M.S. — Quartermaster-Sergeant.

R.A.P. — Regimental Aid Post. The position occupied by the R.M.O. and his staff, where the first and most urgent treatment was given to casualties, and whence they were sent back to the C.C.S., unless the injury was slight.

R.M.O. — Regimental Medical Officer.

R.Q.M.S. — Regimental Quartermaster-Sergeant.

R.S.M. — Regimental Sergeant-Major.

Spr. — Sapper.

Squarehead. — A German (See Hun).

Squid. — A German (See Hun).

Tour in the line. — A period spent by a unit in the front line.

Very light. — A flare fired from a special wide-bore pistol.

Whizbang. — A German shell of 77-m.m. (about 3 inches) diameter.

W.O. — Warrant Officer, a grade between commissioned officers and N.C.O.'s.

# INDEX

# INDEX

This index does not include names given in the lists of the participants in Neligan's Fleurbaix Raid (P. 114), the Royal Guard (P. 254) and the recipients of the special Anzac Medal (P. 278), nor the names mentioned in the preface. Brigades of the 1st Division, battalions of the 3rd Brigade, and companies of the 9th Battalion have not been indexed.

Certain localities of a valley-like nature were called sometimes valley and sometimes gully. These are indexed under the name which seems to have been that most commonly used. Mc is entered as if spelt Mac, Mt. as Mont, and St. as Saint. Battles are given under the heading "Battle of", and the various battalions, brigades, divisions, corps and armies under the headings here mentioned.

Some names may be inserted twice (with references to different pages) on account of difficulty in identifying the person concerned, especially when a man has been promoted to higher rank or when the original authority gave an incorrect initial.

It is possible also that mistakes may have occurred in some names, owing to difficulties met with in checking them. For any involuntary errors of this kind the author expresses his regret and makes his apologies.

---

*Abbassia*, H.M.T. ............... 92
Abbeville (Map 12, 29) .... 149, 249
Abeele (Map 1) ............... 186
Accroche Wood ............... 231
Adams, Lieut. ............... 164, 167
Addy, Lieut. E. .......... 5, 68, 269
Aden ......................... 12
Adjutant ................. 269, 270
Adsett, Lieut. (now Major) P. (Plate II.) 4, 5, 69, 88, 100, 272.
Aeroplanes .. 29, 31, 172, 204, 211, 242
Affringues (Map 1) ........... 185
Aggett, Lieut. W. ... 5, 68, 130, 134, 271
A.I.F. ......................... 2
Albany ....................... 7-9
Albert (Map 2), 122, 132, 135, 137, 144, 159, 162, 184.
Albert Medal ................. 227
Albert, Prince (now H.M. the King), 254-255.
Alcock, Lieut. Leo (Plate XVI., XXIII., XXIV.), 261-263.
Alexandria (Map 3) 15, 23, 24, 96, 103, 104.
Allah Gully (Map 9) ........... 54
Allan, J. D. (Plate XXI.) .... 177, 214
Allan, W. ..................... 82
Allan, W. F. ............... 214-215
Allonville (Map 2) ........... 231
Amalgamation of battalions and companies 241, 254, 264.
Ambulance, 1st Field, 200, 2nd Field, 82, 3rd Field, 182, 249, 272.

Amiens (Map 2, 12, 29), 154, 181, 203, 204, 231.
Anderson Knoll (Map 8, 9) .... 35, 36
Andrews, Capt. ................. 94
*Anglo-Egyptian*, H.M.A.T. .......... 5
Anzac (Map 6, 7, 8), 34-93, 270, 275; Anzac anniversary, 110, 211, 265; the name "Anzac", 22.
Anzac Cove (Anzac Beach) (Map 8, 9), 34, 63, 92.
Anzac Landing (Plate VIII., Map 8, 9), 34-57, 61-64, 73, 92, 137, 281.
Anzac Ridge (Map 16) 186, 192, 193, 195.
Appleyard, Capt. ............... 272
Arabic ............. 18, 41, 112, 119
Arabs .................. 67, 70, 99
Archer, Sgt. C. ................. 236
Argoueves (Map 2) ............. 203
Ari Burnu (Map 8, 9), 34, 35, 40, 41 Ari Burnu, Little (Map 9), 34, 35, 44.
Armenians ..................... 73
Armentieres (Map 1) ........... 109
Armistice to bury dead, 71-73; at end of war, 251.
Armourer ..................... 275
Armstrong, G. ................. 236
Armstrong, Major N. G., 125, 128, 134, 233, 235, 263.

# INDEX (Continued)

Army, Second, 109, 205; Third, 202, 241-242; Fourth, 153, 156, 231, 241-242; Fifth, 153, 156, 167, 202; Reserve, 121.
Army Medical Corps (Plate V., XI.), 4, 5, 78, 82, 177, 272; 33rd A.A.M.C. 4
Army Service Corps ............ 5, 66
Arras (Map 12, 29) ............ 167
Arrell, Capt. W. L. ............... 100
Artillery (Plate V.), 4, 53, 66, 71, 79, 172, 187, 189. 1st B'de. A.F.A., 200. 7th B'ty. A.F.A. (Plate V.), 68, 70, 78. 9th B'ty. A.F.A., 78. 14th B'ty. A.F.A., 4. Royal Horse Artillery, 183.
Artillery Road (Map 9) .......... 92
*Ascanias*, H.M.A.T. ............... 12
Ashley-Brown, The Rev. W. ...... 273
Asia Minor (Map 6) ............. 36
*Askold*, The ................ 12, 28
Aspinall, Capt. W. R. ...... 145, 272
Aspinall-Oglander, Brig.-Gen. C. F. .. 84, 92, 93.
Atkins, P'te. J. R., D.C.M. ...... 182
Audruicq (Map 1) .............. 149
Auger Wood (Map 26) ...... 234-235
Australian Comforts Fund, 132, 240, 274, 275.
Australian Imperial Force .......... 2
Auton, T. ....................... 214
Avery, Lieut. (Plate XVI.) .. 210, 263
Avesnes (Map 12, 29) ...... 253-256
"A5" (Plate III.) ·.. 5-15, 269, 270, 275

Bac St. Maur (Map 1, 13) .. 119, 203
Bailey, Lieut. D. McG. W. ...... 196
Bailey, Lieut. (Plate XVI.) ...... 220
Bailey, Sgt. L. H. ........... 83, 102
Baillie, Sgt. Matt. ............... 267
Baizieux (Map 2) ............... 122
Baker, Major (British Army) ...... 159
Bale, Cpl. ...................... 133
Band (Plate XXV.), 4, 159, 263, 265, 275.
Bank Trench (Map 18) ·.. 161, 163-165
Bapaume (Map 2, 12) .. 123, 174, 181
Barbed wire (See Wire).
Barclay, Lieut. ................. 227
Barcroft, Lieut. (Plate XVI.) ...... 219
Barley Trench .................. 161
Barlow, P'te. (Plate XXIII.)
Barnett, Lieut. ........ 163, 166, 167
Barque, Le (Map 2, 18) .... 161-168
Barrages (See Bombardment).
Barry, Sgt. H. A. ............... 120
Bartlett, E. Ashmead ............. 37
Baths, Bathing, 21, 66, 96, 111, 229, 248
Bathurst, Bishop of .............. 241
Battalion, 1st, 177, 217. 2nd, 92, 152, 168, 177, 191, 197, 255, 261. 3rd, 110, 177, 212, 261, 262. 4th, 61, 138, 177, 178. 5th, 131, 173, 180, 216, 218, 219, 223, 233, 262. 6th, 8, 54. 7th, 131, 148, 163-165, 277. 8th, 61, 131, 193. 13th, 237. 15th, 3, 58. 16th, 200. 17th, 170. 20th, 172. 24th, 143. 25th, 100, 261. 26th, 261. 28th, 188, 190. 29th, 198. 31st, 102. 36th, 88. 41st, 88. 47th, 192. 49th, 99-100, 135. 50th, 137. 9th/49th, 281-282. 2nd/9th, 281-282. Nucleus, 134, 138, 142, 206.

Battle of Amiens, 231; Le Barque (Map 18), 162-168; Broodseinde (Map 1, 16), 192-193; Bullecourt I., 170; Bullecourt II. (Map 2, 20), 175-180; Chuignes (Map 2, 27), 237-240, 274; Crepy Wood (Map 26), 232-236, 282; Defence of Anzac, 69-71; Epehy (Map 2), 242-246; Froissy Beacon (Map 27), 237-241, 274; Fromelles, 228; Krithia, 67; Lagnicourt (Map 2, 19), 170-173; Landing at Anzac (Plate VIII., Map 8, 9), 34-57, 61-64, 73, 137, 281; Le Barque (Map 18), 162-168; Le Waton (Map 22, 25), 223-228; Lihons (Map 2, 26), 232-236, 282; Lone Pine (Map 9), 87; The Maze (Map 18), 161-168; Menin Road Ridge ("Polygon Wood") (Map 16, 21), 186-192; Meteren (Map 23), 207-211; Mouquet Farm (Map 1, 15), 137-143; Passchendaele (Map 16), 193, 194; Polygon Wood (Map 16, 21), 186-192; Pozieres (Map 1, 15), 123-135, 282); The Somme, 123-143, 187, 202; Villeret (Map 28), 242-246; Ypres III. (Map 16), 186-194.
Battle Honours ................. 280
Bavarian Division, 4th .......... 220
Bavarian Regiment, 173rd ........ 156
Bayenghem-les-Eperlecques (Map 1), 148
Bayenghem-lez-Seninghem (Map 1) .. 185
Bayonet Charge ............. 29, 235
Bayonet Trench (Map 18), 161, 162, 164, 168.
Bayonvillers (Map 2) ............ 231
Bayton, P'te. .................... 240
Bazentin-le-Grand (Map 17), 154-155, 157-159, 168.
Bazentin-le-Petit (Map 2, 17), 159, 161, 181.
Beach Fatigue Party .......... 69, 79
"Beachy Bill" .................... 66
*Beagle*, H.M.S. ............... 38, 43
Bean, Dr. C. E. W., 41, 47, 54, 114, 189
"Bearded 9th," The (Plate IX.) ... 95
Beaumetz-lez-Cambrai ............ 189
Beaumont Hamel ................ 153
Beauval (Map 2) ........... 121, 144
Becourt Wood (Map 2) ...... 132, 137
Bedwell, Sgt. E. K. .............. 61
Beer .............. 10-11, 28, 159, 199
"Beery 9th," The (Plate IX.) .... 95
Beeston, A. (Plate XXV.).
Bendigo Camp .................. 168
Bennett, Maj.-Gen. H. Gordon, C.M.G., D.S.O., 174, 185, 218, 252.
Benson, Capt. C. E., 55, 68, 86, 115, 117-120.
Bentley, Sgt. J. ................. 245
Bentley, J. (Plate XXII.).).
Bernafay Wood (Map 17), 150, 152, 153
Berteaucourt (Map 2) ...... 135, 136
Berthen (Map 1) ................ 121
Besika Bay (Map 6) .............. 36
Best, Sgt. ...................... 170
Bethune ........................ 111
Biggs, Capt. F. J. (Plate XVI), 125-126, 134, 219, 263.
Bikanir Camel Corps ............. 99
Billets, 106, 112, 205, 249, 251, 256-257, 259.
Billets shelled ..... 109-110, 206, 213

## INDEX (Continued)

Birdwood, Lt.-Gen. R. W. (Plate IX.), 22, 29, 32, 57, 64, 72, 76, 77, 80, 82, 84, 89, 91, 103, 107, 113, 121, 135, 137, 181, 184, 185, 194, 198, 199, 222.
Blackburn, Lieut. (now Lieut.-Col.), A.S., V.C. .................... 130
Blackman, P'te. C. T. ........... 118
Black Watch Avenue (Map 15), 124, 126, 127.
Blair, Lieut. A. B. ....... 127, 134
Blaney, P'te. ................... 255
Blaringhem (Map 1) ...... 218, 222
"Blighty" leave ........... 113, 144
Blue Cut (Map 18) .... 161, 165, 166
Blue Line (Map 21, 26, 28), 187, 190, 232, 234, 237, 242, 245.
Bluett, Lieut. C. W. C., M.C., 194, 196
Boase, Lieut. (now Colonel) A. J. (Plate II., VIII.), 4, 5, 13, 47, 48, 50, 51, 61.
Bohain (Map 29) .......... 252-253
Bois de Crepey (Map 26) 232-234, 236, 237.
Bois St. Germain (Map 27) .. 237, 240
Bolton's Hill .................... 50
Bolton's Ridge (Map 9), 35, 45, 49, 50, 54, 55, 56, 64, 65, 66, 69.
Bombardment (Plate XVII.), 66, 109, 110, 112, 113, 127, 130, 132, 137-143, 187-190, 201, 204, 206, 213, 233, 238, 243.
Bombs, 82, 113, 125, 128, 130, 178, 179, 227.
Bomford, Lieut. (Plate XXIV.).
Bonner, Lieut. A. H. ............ 263
Bonneville (Map 2) ........ 121, 136
de Bonnieres, Mme. ............ 248
Booker, P'te. (Plate XXII.).
Bootmakers .............. 136, 275
Boots ....... 73, 76, 101, 107, 144
Boore (Plate XVII., Map 1, 22), 206, 221, 222.
Borre South .............. 212, 216
Bostock, J. D. .................. 40
Boulogne (Map 12) .... 149, 158, 198
Boursies (Map 2) ........ 168, 169
Bowles, Leslie W. ............... 281
Bowman, V. A. ........... 134, 155
Boxing ................... 159, 222
Boyd, "Scotty" ................. 155
Boylan, Capt. J. S., M.C., .... 171-172
Boyle, P'te. C. H., D.C.M. ...... 167
Bradshaw, H. ................... 214
Braithwaite, General W. P. ...... 72
Braithwaite, P'te. (Plate XXIII.).
Brand, Major (later Maj.-Gen.) C. H., 37, 47, 48, 51.
Brand, W.O. Steve (Plate XXI.), 267, 269.
Brandhoek (Map 1) ............ 146
Bray (Map 2, 29), .... 183, 237, 241
Brennan, Capt. R. G. ........... 134
Bresle (Map 2) ........... 159, 168
Brickfields at Albert, 132, 135, 137, 144
Bridges, Maj.-Gen. W. T. ...... 1, 57
Bridges' Road (Map 9) .......... 60
Brigade, Infantry, 12th .......... 154
Brigade, Light Horse, 2nd ...... 79, 80
Brigade Group, 3rd ............. 265
Brisbane ...... 1-5, 263, 268, 281-282
Brockman, Major (later Brig.-Gen.), E. A. Drake ................... 43
Bronfay Farm .................. 183
Broodseinde Ridge (Map 1, 16) .. 192
Brown, C.S.M. J. ............... 210

Brown, P. ...................... 120
Brown, Lieut. C. O. ............ 217
Brown, Lieut. ....... 145, 147, 179
Brown, Lieut. R. W., M.C. ..... 182
Brown, Capt. T. V. (Plate II.), 4, 5, 269.
Brown, The Rev. W. Ashley- .... 273
Browne, Sgt. P. G. ............. 126
Brown Line (Map 28) ...... 242, 243
Brown's Dip (Map 9) ............ 53
Bruce, Cpl. W. ................. 140
Bruns, W. B. ................... 74
Brussels (Map 12) .... 260, 261, 263
Bryson, Lieut. J. H. ............ 200
Buire (Map 2) .................. 154
Buire-sous-Corbie .............. 149
Bulair (Map 6) .............. 62, 91
Bull, R.Q.M.S. H. J., D.C.M., 182, 271, 273.
Bullecourt (Map 2, 20), 170, 174-180
"Buller" (Plate XXVI.) ......... 275
Bully-beef ........ 66, 73, 87, 98
Busseboom (Map 1) ....... 145, 148
Bussus (Map 2) ................ 249
Butler, Lt.-Col. A. Graham, D.S.O. (Plate II., VII.), 4, 5, 8, 41, 42, 60, 68, 78, 95, 101-102, 182, 272.
Butler, J. (Plate XXV.).
Butler, Lieut. L. W., M.C., D.C.M. (Plate XXIV., XXV), 120, 194, 196, 233, 263.
Butler, Miss M. ................ 277

Caestre (Map 1, 22) ............ 203
Cairo (Map 3), 15, 17, 18, 23, 100, 101
Calais (Map 12) ................ 149
Camels .................... 99, 102
Cameron, — (Plate XXI.).
Cameron Highlanders ........... 203
Cameron, Lieut. ........... 166, 167
Cameron, Lieut. T. W. (Plate XVI.), 191, 271.
Camp 165 ..................... 183
Campamare (Map 1) ............ 198
Campbell, Sgt. C. C. ............ 270
Canadian Corps, 146, 175, 194, 195, 197, 230, 231, 254.
Canaples (Map 2) .............. 121
Canteens, 80, 94, 95, 99, 216, 252, 264, 266, 273-274, 275.
Capetown ...................... 263
Cappy (Plate XVII., Map 2, 27), 239-240.
Cardonette (Map 2) ........ 154, 231
Carroll, Capt. C. J. .. 97, 102, 155, 177
Carroll, Sgt. W. H. ............. 120
Cartignies (Map 29) ............ 253
Casualties (Plate VIII.), 61, 92, 276-277
Casualty Corner (Map 15) ...... 123
Catelet, Le (Map 2) ............ 231
Cauchan, P'te. A. C. ............ 220
Caven, H. ..................... 236
Caves of Naours ........... 121-122
Cerisy (Map 2) ............ 240-241
Chalmers, Sgt. ................. 271
Chambers, Lieut. R. W. L. (Plate II., VIII.), 4, 5, 20, 50, 52, 61, 128, 134, 139, 143.
Chandler, P'te. ................. 163
Chandler, Stretcher-bearer ...... 132
Chaplains ........... 132-133, 272, 273
Chapman, Lieut. (later Major) Duncan K. (Plate II., VI.), 4, 5, 40, 100, 269.

## INDEX (Continued)

Chapman, Capt. S. J., M.C. (Plate XVI.), 155, 182, 186, 263, 266, 267, 269
Charleroi (Map 12, 29), 256, 258, 260, 263, 265, 266.
Charlton, Harry ................ 155
Charlton, P'te. ................ 162
Chataway, Lieut. V. M., M.C. .... 267
Chateau Belge (Map 16) .... 148, 194
"Chateau" of Meteren ...... 209, 212
Chateau Segard (Map 16) .... 186, 187
Chateau Wood ................ 188
Chatelet (Map 29) ..... 256-265, 275
Chatelineau ................... 257
Chemin-des-Dames ............. 174
Cherry, T. .................... 249
Cheshire, Lieut. F. L. ......... 134
Chester, Lieut. E. J. ...... 193, 233
Chinese Labour Corps ....... 197-198
Christmas billies, 96; Day, 96, 156, 199, 200, 259; dinner, 156, 159, 259; Eve, 18-19.
Chuignes (Map 2, 27), 237, 238, 240
Chuignolles (Map 2, 27) .... 237, 240
Church Parade ......... 30, 69, 103
Cigarettes, 132, 143, 189, 236, 265, 274
Clark, J. ..................... 236
Clarke's Gully (Map 9) ...... 44, 68
Clay, Lieut. .................. 192
Cleveland, V. ................. 236
Clogstoun, Major H. O. ........ 17
Cloherty, P. .................. 246
Clytte, La (Map 1) ........... 203
Cocos Island .................. 10
Coe, Scout-Sgt. F. C. .......... 40
Coisy (Map 2) ................ 231
Coles, E. ..................... 40
Coles, Sgt. ................... 273
Collin, Capt. W. A., 94, 99, 132, 134, 143, 144, 164-166, 269.
*Colne* H.M.S. .............. 38, 43
Colombo .................. 11-12, 268
Colour-patches ............ 31-32, 116
Colours (Plate XXII.) ......... 282
Comforts .......... 94, 96, 99, 275
Comforts Fund, Australian, 132, 240, 274-275.
Commanding Officers ............ 279
Commune, La .................. 148
Companies amalgamated ..... 241, 253
Connaught, H.R.H. the Duke of .. 265
Connaught Lines ............... 145
Conscription referendum ..... 149, 198
Contalmaison (Map 2, 15), 122, 123, 168.
Convoy, The First ........ 6-15, 263
Cooee Gully (Map 9) ........... 82
Cooks .. 66, 154, 170, 206, 247, 273
"Cookers" ................. 168, 256
Cooper, T. .................... 74
Corfield, W.O. S. ...... 136, 157, 269
Cork, Lieut. ............. 221, 236
Cornford, H. G. ............... 74
Corps, Australian, 199, 230, 237, 241-242, 246, 259. Australian and New Zealand Army (Anzac) 21-22, 24, 35, 45, 63, 86. 1st Anzac, 114, 121, 199. 2nd Anzac, 199. Canadian, 146, 175, 194, 195, 197, 230, 231, 254, III., 230, 242. VIII., 80. IX., 242. XV., 205, XXII., 199.
Costin, Lieut. J. W. (Plate II., VIII.), 4, 5, 51, 52, 61.
Courte Croix (Map 22) ......... 212
Covering Force ............. 35-37
Crater Dugouts ........... 200, 202

Crawford, Capt. A. J. P. ........ 76
Creedon, D. B. ............... 81-82
Crepy (Crepey) Wood (Map 26), 232-234, 237.
Cricket .............. 221, 265, 266
Cunningham, P'te. J. ...... 118, 120
Cup, The (Map 9) .. 46-47, 50-52, 56
Cuppy, T. .................... 236

Dagg, E. .................. 214-215
Daisy Patch, The (Map 9), ..... 47
Dalle (Map 1) ................ 198
Dalziel, Lieut. (Plate XXIV.) .... 263
Darchy, F. E. ................ 116
Dardanelles, The (Map 6, 7), 24, 28-31, 34-36; 48, 49, 68.
Darling Downs Regiment .......... 4
Darnell, Lieut. (11th Bn.) ...... 69
Dearden, Lieut. E., M.C. ....... 202
Dearden, P'te. V., D.C.M. ...... 182
Decorations (Plate XVIII., XXI.), 78, 86, 95, 120, 128, 130, 132, 133, 167, 182, 184, 194, 215, 227, 229, 235, 236, 245, 246, 253, 277-279.
de Kennebeke Siding ........... 198
De Lisle, General Sir Beauvoir ..... 205
Demicourt (Map 2) ............ 168
Demobilisation ....... 241, 260, 269
Denham, The Hon. D. F. ........ 1
Dernancourt (Map 2) .. 154, 159, 273
de Robeck, Vice-Admiral J. M. .. 45, 80
Despair, Valley of (Map 9)....... 81
Deuchar, Sgt. .................130
Devine, Lieut. P. .......... 134, 196
Devonport ..................... 267
Devonshire Lines ......... 145, 186
Dewar, Lieut. W. J. (Plate IV.), 68, 86
Dexter, The Rev. — ............ 84
Dibble, F. .................... 74
Dickebusch (Map 1) .... 192, 201-202
Dijon (Map 11) ............... 105
Dillon, P'te. B. J. ............ 120
Disease (See Illness).
Division, 2nd, 175, 181, 187, 190, 192, 231, 240, 241, 261. 3rd, 19, 192, 200, 231, 241. 4th, 154, 170, 231, 242. 5th, 116, 181, 228, 231. 1st British, 125, 135. 7th British, 175, 177, 179-180. 9th British, 223, 228, 229. 17th British, 203. 29th British, 30, 35, 62. New Zealand, 192.
Divisional Signal Company ....... 271
Dominion Camp ............ 148, 194
Donaldson, Capt. F. (Plate XVI.) .. 249
Dougall, Capt. J. M. (Plate II.), 4, 5, 49, 50, 60, 64, 100.
Doudeauville (Map 1) .......... 198
Douglas, T. (Plate XXIII.).
Doullens (Map 2, 12, 29) .. 121, 144
Downes, F. H. (Plate VII.) ...... 61
Drake Brockman, Major (later Brig.-Gen.) E. A. .................... 43
Dreghorn, P'te. ........... 265, 268
Drying room .................. 157
Duckboards (Plate XV.) ........ 152

Earl's Wood (Map 27) .......... 240
Earwaker, Lieut. J. G. (Plate XXIV.), 242, 245-246, 259, 263.

# INDEX (Continued)

Eaucourt L'Abbaye (Map 2, 17), .. 161
Educational Training .... 241, 260-261
"Egg," The (Map 28) ...... 243-245
Egypt (Map 3), 13-23, 62, 85, 96-104, 113, 158, 270.
Elliott, Lt.-Col. C. H. ...... 170-172
Embarkation, 5, 23, 92, 96, 103-104, 267
Emden, S.M.S. (Plate IV.) ........ 10
Emerson, L. (Plate XXV.).
Enfilade ................ 70, 196
Engineers, 3rd Field Company ..... 70
Enoggera (Plate III.) ............ 1-5
Enos (Map 6) ................ 62
Entertainments, 38, 95, 137, 145, 146, 159-161, 264, 267-268.
Enver Pasha ................ 58, 63
Equipment ............ 3-4, 31, 37
Esplanade Sap ............ 194, 197
Estaires (Map 1) .............. 203
Estaminets ................ 149, 205
Etaples (Map 12) .... 111, 149, 158
L'Etoile (Map 2) ............ 249
European Expeditionary Force ...... 2
Evacuation of Anzac ............ 92
Ewe Farm (Map 25) ............ 225
Excelsior Band ................ 4
Expeditionary Force Canteens ...... 274
Exploitation, Line of .... 242-244, 246

Fabeck Graben ........ 138, 140-142
Factory Corner (Map 17) ....... 155
Fahy, The Rev. — .......... 84, 110
Farmer, Sgt. A. W. ............ 271
Farmer, Capt. T. W. (Plate XXIV.), 239, 263, 265, 267.
Fatigues, 27, 65, 69, 102-103, 111-112, 146, 148.
Ferguson, Rt. Hon. Sir Ronald C. Munro 4
Few, F. (Plate XXI.).
Field Ambulance, 1st, 200. 2nd, 82. 3rd, 182, 249, 272.
Field Artillery (See Artillery).
Field, Capt. .................. 272
Field Company Engineers, 3rd ...... 70
Finlay, Sgt. E. ................ 275
Finter, Lieut. H., M.C. (Plate XVI., XXIV.), 194, 261, 263.
Fisher, Capt. J. L. (Plate II., VIII.), 4, 5, 27, 50, 61.
Fisher, W. A. ................ 40
Flammenwerfer (Flame-thrower) (Plate XIII.) ................ 177-178
Flanagan, "Rats" .............. 261
Flanders, 106-121, 144-149, 184-203, 205-230.
Flares ................ 90, 112, 204
Flers (Map 2, 17), 152-157, 159, 272, 274.
Flesselles (Map 2) .......... 203-204
Fletre (Map 1, 22) ............ 206
Fleurbaix Area (Map 1, 13), 111-120, 273.
Flies .................... 79, 85
Flynn, Lieut. H. M. ............ 191
Foch, Marshal F. .............. 230
Fog ..... 156, 161-165, 168, 211-212
Folkestone .................. 158
Food containers ............. 153
Football (Plate XXIII.), 200, 248, 249, 255, 261-262, 272.
Foot-inspections ........... 107, 122
Foote, Lieut. L. H. ............ 192
Forceville (Map 2) ............ 122

Ford, Lieut. .................. 134
Ford, P'te. .................. 156
Fordham, Lieut. ................ 263
Forrister, H. .................. 74
Fortescue, Capt. (now Lt.-Col.) C., D.S.O., M.C., V.D. (Plate II., VIII.), 4, 5, 42, 48, 51, 52, 60, 61, 78, 100.
Forward, Lieut. (Plate XVI., XXIV.).
Foster, S. C. .................. 19
Fothergill, Lieut. A. E. .......... 110
400 Plateau (Map 8, 9), 35, 45, 46, 49-53, 56, 64.
Fourth Avenue (Map 15) ........ 139
Francis, Lieut. T. (Plate XXIV.) .. 263
Franvillers (Map 2) ............ 154
Franz Ferdinand, Archduke ...... 83
Fraser, Lieut. (Plate XVI.).
Fraser, Sgt. "Sandy" ........ 109, 113
Fremantle .................. 268
Fremicourt (Map 2) ........ 169, 174
French Troops, 28, 30, 36, 104, 206-207, 241-242.
French 321st Regiment ...... 206-207
Fricourt (Map 2), 149, 153, 154, 159
Froissy Beacon (Map 27) .... 237-240
Fusilier Wood (Map 16) ........ 201
Fusiliers, 17th Lancashire ........ 109

Gaba Tepe (Plate X., Map 7, 8), 34-36, 40, 45, 50, 63, 65, 66, 71, 72, 74, 81.
Gable Farm .............. 199, 200
Gallipoli (Map 6) ........ 34-93, 103
Gambling ............ 236, 270, 276
Gandy, C.S.M. E. J. (Plate XXII.), 282
Gap Trench (Map 17) ........ 155
Gapaard Farm (Map 16) .. 198-199, 200
Gardiner, A. .................. 74
Garenne Wood (Map 27) ........ 238
Gas, 78, 84, 90, 107-108, 112, 121, 122, 201, 212, 228, 276-277.
Gas alarms .............. 108, 111
Gas helmets .............. 107, 121
Gebel Habeita (Plate X., XI., Map 3, 10), 98-102.
Gellibrand, Lt.-Col. (now Maj.-Gen.), J., 96.
George V., H.M. King ...... 253-255
George VI., H.M. King .. 254-255, 281
German Officer's Ridge (Map 9) .. 49
Gibraltar (Map 15) .......... 139
Gibson, The Rev. — .......... 273
Gibson, Capt. N. M. 120, 134, 145, 149, 272.
Gibson, P'te. .................. 55
Gilvarry, F. J. .................. 19
Ginger Cut (Map 18) .......... 166
Ginn, Cpl. R. G. .............. 268
Gird Trench (Map 18) ...... 161, 162
Glasgow, Maj.-Gen., The Hon. Sir T. W., 249, 256-258, 262.
Glencorse Wood (Map 21) .. 187, 188
Godewaersvelde (Map 1, 11), 106, 121
Godley, Maj.-Gen. Sir A. J. ........ 57
Goeben, S.M.S. ................ 66
Gordon Bennett, Maj.-Gen. H., C.M.G., D.S.O., 174, 185, 218, 252.
Gordon, Sgt. D. W. ............ 236
Gordon, Lieut. E. (Plate XVI.), 267, 271
Gordon, Capt. M. L. (Gordon Highlanders), 179.
Gordon Highlanders .......... 179-180

# INDEX (Continued)

Gorenflos (Map 2, 29), 247-249, 251, 275.
Gough, Gen. Sir Hubert ..... 121, 135
Goulburn, Sgt. G. ............. 221
Goward, Lieut. T. (Plate XVI.), .. 269
Gower, Lieut. H. R., 202-203, 211-215, 233.
Gowrie, H. E. Lord .............. 281
Graham, Sgt. T. A. ............... 44
Graham, Stretcher-bearer .......... 132
Graham, P'te. ................... 156
*Grampian*, H.M.T. ................ 96
Granatenwerfer ............. 178, 180
Grandal (Map 1) ................. 198
Gray, Lieut. J. L. (Plate XI.) .... 100
Greaves, Sgt. W., D.C.M. ......... 182
Green, Sgt. G. W. ................ 236
Green, Cpl. ...................... 164
Green Line (Map 21) ........ 187, 190
Grey, P'te. R. G. ................. 83
Grieve, Capt. J. W. (Plate XXIV.), 227, 263, 267, 272.
Griffiths, L./Cpl. ................. 162
Grimish, Cpl. B. .................. 236
Grinstone, Lieut. (Plate XXIV.) ... 263
Guard Division, 3rd (German) ..... 173
Guard Grenadier Regiment, 5th (German), 166.
Guards, 11-12, 184, 253-255, 260, 265, 281.
Gueudecourt (Map 2, 17) ......... 161
Gunderson, R.Q.M.S. (Plate XXI.).
Gun Ridge (Map 8, 9), 35, 36, 45, 54, 64.
Guns captured by 9th Battalion (Plate XVIII., XXVI.), 47, 118, 129, 220, 282.

Haig, F.M. Sir D., 111, 114, 135, 156, 174, 186.
"Hairy 9th," The (Plate IX.) ...... 95
Haines, P'te. C. J. ............... 149
Halfway House (Map 16) .......... 193
Halifax Camp .............. 148, 197
Halloy-les-Pernois (Map 2) ....... 121
Hamel (Map 2) .................. 231
Hamelet (Map 2) ................. 242
Hamilton, A. S. .................. 74
Hamilton, Sir Ian, 29, 57, 63, 64, 72, 76, 80.
*Hampshire*, H.M.S. ............. 11, 14
Ham-sur-Heure ................... 259
Hanlon, Sgt. E. M. .......... 252, 274
Hansen, L. ....................... 40
Haplincourt (Map 2) .............. 174
Harbonnieres (Map 2) ....... 231, 232
Harfleur ................... 263, 266
Harman, L./Cpl. .................. 51
Harper, Lieut. R. L. .............. 263
Harrington, Lieut. G. R. ....... 68, 91
Harris, P'te. (Plate XXIII.).
Harrison, Cpl. P. W., 46, 47, 49, 51, 56
Harris Ridge (Map 9) ............. 74
Hart, Staff Nurse J. M. ............ 5
Harvey, Lieut. H. (Plate XXIV.).
Harvey, Lieut. H. C. (Plate II., VIII.), 4, 5, 61.
Harvey, L. ....................... 236
Harvey, Major (now Lt.-Col.) W. C. (Plate II.), 4, 5, 270.
Hatton, Lt.-Col. N. G., M.C., M.M., 25
Havre, Le ........................ 266
Hayes, Lieut. F. R. ......... 263, 267

Haymen, Lieut. F. G. (Plate II.), 4, 5, 51-53, 61.
Hayward, J. ..................... 218
Hazebrouck (Map 1, 12, 22), 121, 203, 205, 216, 217.
Head, P'te. (Plate XXV.).
Heaton, Sgt. C. R., D.C.M., 18, 55, 79, 86, 133-134.
Heliopolis (Map 3) ......... 100, 113
Helles, Cape (Map 6), 34, 35, 67, 75, 80, 85, 92.
Hell Fire Corner ................. 59
Hell Spit (Map 8, 9) .............. 44
Hellmuth, T. A. .................. 40
Henderson, J. C. ................. 40
Henencourt (Map 2) .............. 182
Henley, Sgt. A. (Plate XXI).
Henzell, Lieut. W. C., M.C. (Plate XVI., XXII.), 178-179, 182, 193, 201, 228, 282.
Herimez (Map 1) ................. 198
Herissart (Map 2), 122, 136-137, 144
Herleville (Map 2) ........... 237, 241
Hermies (Map 2) ................. 168
Hervilly (Map 2) ................. 242
Hessian Wood ................... 202
Heuringhen (Map 1) .............. 230
Heytesbury Camp ................ 266
High Wood (Map 17) ........ 155, 163
Hill 60 (Map 16) .......... 146-148, 200
Hilton, Lieut. .............. 166, 167
Hindenburg Line, 167, 168, 170, 172-180, 241-246.
Hinton, Capt. A. C. (Plate II., VIII.), 4, 5, 100.
Hobbs, Lt.-Gen. Sir J. J. Talbot .... 259
Hodgson, Sgt. 126-127, 159, 164, 165
Hogan, Major ................... 263
Holdway, C. (Plate IX.) ........... 40
Hollebeke (Map 1, 16), 200, 202-203
Holly Ridge (Map 9) ....... 80, 81, 86
Holm, Cpl. C. .............. 214-215
Hondeghem (Map 1) .. 205, 218, 222
Hooge (Map 1, 16) ............... 193
Hopper, Sgt. .............. 136, 275
Horner, L./Cpl. .................. 133
*Hororata*, H.M.A.T. .............. 8
Howard, T. ..................... 215
Howell, Cpl. D. ................. 240
Hughes, Major (now Lt.-Col.) F. A. . 70
Hughes, The Hon. W. M., 249, 262, 265
Hun's Walk ..................... 199
*Hussar*, H.M.S. .................. 26
Huts, Nissen .................... 154

*Ibuki*, The ................... 8-11
Illness, 26, 85, 87-89, 99, 152-153, 159
Imbros (Map 6), 37, 72, 79, 84, 85
"Imshee" Battery ................ 112
Indian Mountain Battery ...... 53, 71
Intelligence Officer ...... 186, 242, 243
*Ionian*, H.M.T. ............. 23-25, 31
Irvine, Sgt. J. R. ............ 55, 273

Jabber Trench .................. 189
Jackson, Capt. I. (Plate II., VIII.), 4, 5, 44, 49, 61.
James, Major H., M.C. .. 194-198, 279
James, P'te. .................... 164
Jamieson, Sgt. W. .......... 118, 210

INDEX (Continued)

Jarrett, W. .................. 40
Jeancourt (Map 2, 28) ........ 242
Joffre, Marshal J. J. C. ......... 174
Johnson, A. C. ............... 236
Johnston's Jolly (Map 9), 46, 49, 51, 52
Jones, —— .................. 26
Jones, Capt. L. A. (Plate II., VIII.), 4, 5, 61, 83.
Jones, P'te. (now W.O.) W. K. (Plate VII.).
Jordan, Lieut. S. R. .......... 68, 81

Kapa Tepe ................... 34
Keast, Cpl. (Plate XXIII.).
Keid, Cpl. E. ................ 272
Kelly, B. (Plate XXI.).
Kelly, P'te. J. J. ............. 273
Kelsall, E. .................. 269
Kemal, Mustapha ........... 58, 87
Kemmel (Map 1, 16), 198, 200, 212, 274.
Kendrick, B. H. (Plate IX.) .. 40, 275
Kendrick, D. ................. 40
Kendrick, Mrs. J. W. .......... 275
de Kennebeke Siding .......... 198
Kennedy, Cpl. J. B. .. 249, 254, 275
Kenyon, Sgt. J. E., D.C.M., M.M., 56, 74-75, 78, 118, 120, 133-134.
Ker, Lieut. H. G. (Plate II., VIII.), 4, 5, 61, 86.
Kerr, C. A. .................. 236
Kettle, Sgt. R. (Plate XXIII.).
Kettle, —— (Plate XXV.).
Keys, Staff Nurse C. M. (Mrs. C. M. Pennefather) ............... 5
King, H.M. the, George V., 253-255, George VI., 254-255, 281.
King, Lieut. J. ........... 153, 263
King, Cpl. ................... 273
King, P'te. G. B. ............. 81
King, P'te. ................... 162
King's Royal Rifle Corps ....... 155
Kirby, Cpl. A. ............ 68, 272
Kitchener, F. M. Lord, 11, 13, 24, 91
Klite-Hil (Map 22) ........... 217
Knife-Edge, The (Plate X., Map 9), 80, 82.
Knight, P'te. R. P. ............ 217
Knightley, Major A. R., M.C. (Plate VII., XI.), 54, 55, 58, 68, 86, 87, 99, 102, 124, 134, 139, 141, 165-166, 177, 180-182, 184, 192, 269.
Knott, W. (Plate XXIII.).
Knowles, Lieut. H. N., M.C. & Bar (Plate XVI., XXIV.), 193, 213, 214, 236, 253.
Koch, Lieut. (Plate XVI.) ........ 22
Kreule, La (Map. 1), 218, 222-223, 229
K. Trench (Map 15) .. 123, 138-140
Kum Kale (Map 6) ............ 36

La Clytte (Map 1) ............ 203
La Commune ................. 148
Landing at Anzac (Plate VIII., Map 8, 9), 34-57, 61-64, 73, 92, 137, 281.
Lagnicourt (Map 2, 19) .... 169-173
Laies "River" (Map 13, 14) ..... 119
La Kreule (Map 1), 218, 222-223, 229
Lancashire Fusiliers, 17th ........ 109

La Neuville-Corbie ............ 231
Larsson, L./Cpl. .............. 131
Lart (Map 1) ................. 185
La Sablon (Map 1) ............ 230
Latimer, P'te. G. E. ............ 82
Latimer, W. E. ................ 40
Laventie (Map 1, 13) .......... 203
La Vicogne (Map 2) ........... 135
Lawrance, Capt. S. N., D.S.O. (Plate XVI.), 124, 127, 134.
Leak, P'te. J., V.C. ........... 128
Leane, Capt. (later Brig.-Gen.) R. L. 86
Leane's Trench ................ 86
Leave of absence, 17-18, 113, 144, 247
Le Barque (Map 2, 18) .... 161-168
Le Catelet (Map 2) ............ 231
Ledingham (Map 1) ....... 197-198
Lee, G. F. ................... 81
Lee, Col. G. L. ................ 4
Lee, Lt.-Col. H. W. (Plate II.), 2-6, 12, 25, 279.
Lee, Capt. H. W. (Plate II.), 4, 5, 271
Legge Valley (Map 8, 9) ......... 50
Le Havre .................... 266
Lemnos (Map 5, 6), 25-33, 37, 62, 91, 94-96.
L'Etoile (Map 2) .............. 249
Le Waton (Map 22, 25) .... 223-228
Lewis, C. .................... 215
Lewis Guns .. 102, 136, 168, 201-202
Leyton, P'te. (Plate XXV.).
Light Horse, 67, 73. 6th L.H., 85. 7th L.H., 85. 2nd L.H. Brigade, 79, 80.
Lihons (Plate XXVI., Map 2, 26), 232, 234, 237, 282.
Lihu Wood (Map 26) .......... 236
Lille (Map 12) ................ 217
Little Ari Burnu (Map 9) .. 34, 35, 44
De Lisle, General Sir Beauvoir .... 205
Logan and Albert Regiment ........ 4
Londonderry, S.S. ............. 266
Lone Pine (Map 8, 9), 46, 48, 49, 52, 54, 56, 57, 66, 82, 87.
Long (Map 2) ............ 231, 247
Long, Brig.-Gen. The Rt. Rev. G. M., 241
Longbridge Deverill ........ 263, 266
Longpre (Map 2) .......... 231, 247
Loutit, Lieut. (later Lt.-Col.) N. M., 48-50.
Louverval ................... 173
Lowe, P'te. .................. 126
Lucas, L./Cpl. S. T. ........... 119
Luc Wood (Map 27) ........... 238
Lukin, Lieut. J. M. ........ 130, 134
Lumbres (Map 1, 12) ...... 184-185
Lundie, The Rev. J. ...... 110, 723
Lynch, L./Cpl. .............. 58-59
Lyons (Map 11) .......... 105, 265

Macaulay, The Rev. —— ........ 273
McBain, The Rev. S. .. 251, 256, 273
McBow, L./Cpl. H. H. ......... 272
McCann, Capt. (later Lt.-Col.) W. F. J., 233-234.
McCorkindale, P'te. (Plate XXV.).
McDonald, J. .................. 74
McGreehin, Sgt. J. ............ 275
Machine-guns (Plate XVIII., XXVI.), 5, 51, 52, 61, 69, 80, 115, 118, 209-210, 220, 282.
Machine-gun Battalion ......... 261
McIntyre, Capt. S. L. (Plate XVI.) 270
Mackay ...................... 2

INDEX (Continued)

M'Kay's Hill (Map 9) ........ 44, 46
McKenzie, Lieut. R. McN. C. .. 40, 191
McKenzie, P'te. .............. 74, 221
McKenzie, S. A. ................... 40
McKillop, Capt. A., D.S.O., 110, 149, 272.
MacLagan, Brig.-Gen. (now Maj.-Gen.) E. G. Sinclair-, 4, 6, 17, 19, 33, 44, 47, 48, 50, 65, 71, 74, 83, 86, 88, 99, 111, 113, 121, 135.
MacLagan's Ridge (Map 9) ....... 35
MacLaurin's Hill (Map 9) ........ 60
McMaster, Sgt. ............. 207, 247
McNalty, — (Plate XXII.).
McNaught, Capt. J. F. (Plate XVI., XXIV.), 134, 165-166, 196, 213, 215, 263.
Macpherson, A. (Plate XXV.) .... 275
Macpherson, T. (Plate XXV.).
McPherson, Major H. A. .... 201, 279
Mactaggart, Lieut. W. S. .... 179, 271
Maddock, Lieut. ................. 245
Mahaffey, Cpl. H. ............... 272
Mahoney, P'te. D. ............... 120
Mailly-Maillet (Map 2) ........... 182
Mails, 14, 28, 30, 31, 67, 97, 135, 272
*Malda*, H.M.T. .... 31-33, 37, 38, 88
Malin, Sgt. W. W., M.M. (Plate XXII), 162.
Mal Tepe (Map 7) ............... 35
Malt Trench (Map 18) .. 161, 166, 167
Mametz (Map 2) ........... 151, 157
Manchester Regiment ............ 174
Manchester Territorials ........... 15
Mango Farm ............... 228-229
Maps .............. 62, 186, 242
Marching, 4, 102, 107, 136, 150, 168, 197, 231.
Maricourt Wood (Map 19) ....... 171
Marines, Royal .............. 59, 60
Markham, R. C. ................. 236
Marmora, Sea of (Map 6) ........ 49
Marseilles (Map 11) ............. 104
Martin, Cpl. ..................... 164
Martin, Lieut. E. W. (Plate XXIV.), 263, 267.
Mason, Lieut. B. G. S., M.M. & 2 Bars, 263, 267.
Matthews, C. .................... 81
Matthews, N. .................... 19
Maxwell, Bugler H. F. ........... 47
May, P'te. (Plate XXIII.).
Maze, The (Plate XIII., Map 18), 161-168.
Mazinghien (Map 29) ...... 251-253
Meals, 26, 153, 157, 168, 207, 236, 247
Medical Officer .................. 272
Mediterranean Expeditionary Force, 63, 92
Melbourne ............. 6-7, 263, 268
Melbourne, Capt. A. C. V. (Plate II., VIII.), 4, 5, 11, 52, 61, 78.
*Melbourne*, H.M.A.S. ........ 8-12
Memorial, 9th Battalion (Plate I.) .. 281
Mena Camp (Plate V., Map 3, 4), 15-23, 270.
Merris (Map 1, 22, 25), 106, 205, 219-222, 229.
Merrington, The Rev. E. N. ...... 273
Messines (Map 1, 16) .. 198-200, 203
Meteren (Map 1, 22, 23), 106, 205, 206, 207-212, 213, 223-225, 228
Meteren, Attack on, April 23-24, 1918 (Map 23), 207-211.
Meteren Baths Raid ......... 212-215
Meteren-Becque (Map 22, 23, 25) .. 206

Meyers, Lieut. E. H. W., M.C. & 2 Bars (Plate XVI., XIX., XXII., XXIV.), 188, 194, 225, 235-236, 243, 246-247, 263, 269.
Michin, W. ..................... 236
Mikalsen, N. H. ................. 240
Miller, L./Cpl. ............. 220, 282
Mills, Cpl. R. ................... 273
Mills hand grenade .... 113, 136, 227
Millward, Sgt. W. ................ 19
Milne, Capt. (later Lt.-Col.) J. A., D.S.O. (Plate II., VIII.), 4, 5, 29, 44, 46, 49-52, 61, 88, 279.
Milne, The Rev. —. ............. 273
Minenwerfer .................... 147
Mines, Mining ...... 76-77, 146, 181
*Minotaur*, H.M.S. .............. 8-10
Molloy, Cpl. .................... 162
Monash, Lt.-Gen. Sir John, 21, 76, 230, 241, 259.
Montauban (Map 2, 17), 150, 151, 168, 169.
Mont des Cats (Map 1) ......... 121
Monteath, Capt. C. D., M.C. (Plate XVI.), 125-128, 134, 143, 196, 233, 269.
Mont St. Quentin (Map 2) ...... 241
Moolenacker (Map 22, 25) ....... 228
Moore, Sgt. J. W. ........... 19, 275
Moore, Maj.-Gen. The Hon. Sir Newton J., 181.
Morbecque (Map 1) ........ 206, 275
Morchies (Map 2, 19) .. 170, 171, 173
Morcourt (Map 2) .............. 237
Moreton Regiment ................ 4
Morgan, Lieut. W. .............. 236
Morrison, P. .................... 74
Morse, Lieut. C. ................. 68
Moulle (Map 1) ................. 148
Mouquet Farm (Map 2, 15), 137-143, 146.
Mud (Plate XIII., XV.), 137, 146, 148, 149-155.
Mudros (Map 5) ............ 25-31
Mudros Harbour (Map 5) .... 25-33, 37
Mullen, Lt.-Col. L. M., D.S.O., V.D. (Plate XVI., XX.), 155, 174, 181, 191, 194, 200, 201, 213, 234, 242, 248, 279.
Munster Alley (Map 15) ......... 125
Murray, Lieut.-Gen. (later General) Sir A. J., 97.
Murray, Lieut.-Col. H. W. ........ 184
Murrumbidgee Camp ............ 203
Mustapha Kemal ............. 58, 87
Mutiny .................... 197-198

Naours (Map 2) ........... 121-122
Neligan, Lt.-Col. M. Wilder-, C.M.G., D.S.O. & Bar, D.C.M., C. de G. (Plate V., XIV.), 2, 13, 50, 57, 68, 74, 75, 78, 86, 89, 90, 95, 99, 102, 114-120, 154, 159 162, 165, 174, 177, 181, 182, 183-184, 229, 242, 249, 257, 264, 265-268, 269, 279, 282.
Neligan's Raid at Anzac, 74-75; at Fleurbaix (Plate XXVI., Map 14), 114-120.
Nelson, N. ..................... 236
Neuf-Fosse Canal ............... 218
Neuve Eglise (Map 1), 120, 198, 200, 274

## INDEX (Continued)

Neuville-Corbie, La .............. 231
Newbolt, Sgt. ........ ........ 164
New Carlton Camp (Map 17) ... 155
Newman, Lt.-Col. J. ........ 203, 279
New Zealand convoy, 7, 8. New Zealand troops, 8, 9, 21, 42, 58, 62, 63, 67.
Nicholls, Lieut. B. (Plate XVI.) .. 272
Nissen huts .................... 154
Nivelle, General R. ............. 174
Noble, V. (Plate XXII.).
No-Man's Land ............. 112, 116
Non-Military Employment .... 260-261
Nonne Bosschen (Map 21) ........ 189
Noreuil (Map 2, 19), 170, 173, 175, 180
Norman, Cpl. P. ................ 227
Norman, P'te. ................... 159
Norris, Lieut. H. L., M.C. .... 177, 194
Nucleus Battalion, 134, 138, 142, 186, 206, 231.
Nurses .................... 6, 267

Oat Lane (Map 18) .... 161, 163, 166
O'Brien, C.S.M. E. (Plate XXI., XXIII.).
O'Brien, P'te. L. ............... 259
O'Callaghan, J. .................. 81
Ogilvie, P'te. (Plate XXIII.).
Oglander, Brig.-Gen. C. F. Aspinall-, 84, 92, 93.
O. G. Lines, Old German Lines (Map 15, 20), 123-128, 130-133, 175-180.
Olive Grove (Map 7) .......... 66, 82
Oliver, Lieut. C. C. .............. 90
Olympia Wood (Map 27) .... 239-240
Oman, J. ........................ 68
Omrah, H.M.A.T. (Plate II., III.), 5-15, 269, 270, 275.
One Blanket Hill ................ 158
O'Neill, K. ................. 196-197
Oosttaverne (Map 1, 16) ........ 200
Oost Houck (Map 1) ............ 148
Oratunga Sap ................... 81
Orvieto, H.M.A.T. ............... 14
Osterley, R.M.S. .................. 9
Ottawa Camp ................... 186
Ouderdom (Map 1) ........ 148, 186
Oultersteene (Map 1, 22) ........ 120
Owen's Gully (Map 9) .. 46-48, 50-52
Oxley Regiment ................ 2, 4
Oxley Regiment Band .............. 4

Padres (See Chaplains).
Page, Capt. F., M.C., M.M., 109, 134, 194, 269, 272.
Palmer, P'te. (Plate XXIII.).
Parados ....................... 111
Parapet ........................ 65
Paris (Map 11) ................ 105
Park Lane (Map 15) ....... 139, 143
Partridge, Lieut. H. J. (Plate XXIV.), 263
Passchendaele Ridge (Map 16), 193-195
Paten, Staff Nurse E. M. ........... 5
Pattison, Lieut. W. B. (Plate VIII.), 4, 5, 61.
Pay ................. 28, 31, 269-270
Payne, P'te. .................... 60
Peck, Capt. (later Lt.-Col.) J. H. ... 49
Pedley, Cpl. A. (Plate XXIII.), 261, 265

Penman, Lieut. R. H. ............ 267
Penrose, Capt. (later Lt.-Col.) W. G., 233, 263, 266, 267.
Perham Downs ............ 158, 248
Periscopes ................. 69, 147
Perrett, A. (Plate XXIII.).
Perrier, Lieut. J. M. .. 68, 80, 86, 269
Petillon (Map 13, 14) ...... 111-120
Pettigrew, Lieut. H. J. .......... 143
P.H. gas helmets .......... 108, 121
Philomel, H.M.S. .................. 8
Phincboom (Map 22) ........... 206
Phipps, C.S.M. G. T. ........... 110
Pickford, Lieut. C. E. (Plate XXIII., XXIV.), 263, 271.
Pill-boxes ................. 189, 190
Pine Ridge (Map 8, 9) ...... 54, 69
Pinkenba ........................ 5
Pioneer Battalion, 1st ...... 200, 261
Pioneers, Battalion .......... 157, 275
Pitceathly, A. .................. 207
Plant, Capt. (now Brigadier) E. C. P., O.B.E., D.S.O. (Plate V.), 48, 49, 61, 70, 74, 78, 88, 89, 100, 269.
Plassy, H.M.T. ................. 263
Plate-Becque ................... 221
Plugge's Plateau (Map 9), 34, 41, 42, 45, 46, 48.
Plumer, General Sir H. C. O., 109-111, 121, 185, 187, 188, 218.
Plymouth ...................... 267
Pollard, W.O. .................... 3
Pollock, W. ..................... 40
Polygon Wood (Map 1, 16, 21), 190, 191
Polygone de Zonnebeke (Map 21) .. 191
Pommiers Camp ................ 151
Pont Noyelles (Map 2) .......... 231
Pont Remy (Map 2, 29), 149, 231, 249
Poperinghe (Map 1) ............ 144
Poppy Valley (Map 9) ........... 70
Port Curtis Regiment ............. 4
Porte, —— (Plate XXIII.).
Porter, Sgt. W. A., D.C.M. (Plate XXIII.), 179-180, 182, 195, 245.
Porter, P'te. (Plate XXIII.).
Port Melbourne ................ 268
Port Said (Map 3) .......... 13-15
Portuguese Troops ......... 203, 217
"Possies" .................. 12, 90
Postal orderly ................. 272
Potsdam Group ................ 202
Pozieres (Plate XXVI., Map 2, 15), 123-135, 138, 143, 183.
Pozieres Trench (Map 15), 124-125, 127, 129, 130, 133.
Pradelles (Map 1, 22), 213, 222, 228-229.
Preston, Sgt. H., 117-119, 139-140, 171, 223.
Price Weir, Lt.-Col. S. ...... 88, 103
Prince Albert (now H.M. King George VI.), 254-255.
Prince of Wales, H.R.H. the, 103, 254-255, 259.
Prisk, Lieut. (now Brigadier) R. C. G. 54, 56.
Prisoners (Plate IV.), 11-12, 14, 81-82, 118-120, 153, 156, 172, 202, 211, 214, 220, 223, 231, 235, 240, 252, 276-277.
Proven (Map 1) ................ 144
Proyart (Map 2) ............... 237
Pumfrey, Lieut. B. L. (Plate XVI.).
Pyramids (Map 4) ........ 16-18, 20
Pyramus, H.M.S. ............... 8, 9

## INDEX (Continued)

"Quarry, The" (Map 15), 138, 140, 143
Quarry Wood (Map 28) ........ 245
Quartermaster ............. 270-271
Quartermaster-sergeant ........ 270-271
Queant (Map 2) ............. 170
Queen, H.M.S. ............. 37-39, 57
Queen Elizabeth, H.M.S. ............ 27
Queensland Point (Map 9) ........ 44
Quentin, Mont St. (Map 2) ...... 241
Querrieu (Map 2) ............. 231
Quinn, Inspector ................ 255
Quinn's Post (Map 9) ........ 76-77
Quota No. 56 ............. 265-267

Rae, Capt. (Plate XVI.) ........ 272
Raff, Lieut. A. L., M.C. (Plate XVI., XXIV.), 219-220, 263, 269.
Rafferty, Lieut.-Col. R. A. .... 143, 201
Raid, Neligan's at Fleurbaix (Plate XXVI., Map 14), 114-120, 282; Neligan's on Twin Trenches, 74-75; on Meteren Baths, 212-215.
Ramillies Camp .................. 200
Ramkema, Capt. J. P., M.C., 115, 117-120, 128, 134, 179-180.
Ramm, Sgt. W. (Plate XXII.).
Rations, 28, 31, 32, 37, 65, 66, 73, 79, 87, 89, 98, 99, 113-114, 122, 157, 162, 205-206.
Rattlesnake, H.M.S. .......... 74, 79
Rawlinson, General Lord ............ 231
Razorback, The (Map 9) ........ 46
Red Line (Map 21, 26, 28), 187, 189, 190, 232, 236-238, 242, 243.
Red Sea ................... 12-13
Referendum for conscription .. 149, 198
Regiment, Light Horse, 6th, 85; 7th, 85.
Regimental Medical Officer ........ 272
Regimental Quartermaster-Sergeant, 270-271.
Regimental Sergeant-Major ........ 269
Reinforcements, 3, 22, 31, 67, 74, 80, 94, 97, 100, 101, 113, 135, 154, 157, 158, 159, 194, 237, 276, 278.
Renescure (Map 1) .............. 197
Reninghelst (Map 1) ........... 145
Rest Wood ................ 137
Rhone, River (Map 11) ......... 105
Ribemont (Map 2) ........ 181-183
Richards, Sgt. E. M. ............ 200
Richardson, P'te. ............... 181
Rider, B. .................... 40
Rifle-grenades ........ 136, 147, 226
Rigby, Lieut. W. J. (Plate II., VIII.), 4, 5, 61.
Roache, J. ................. 236
de Robeck, Vice-Admiral J. M. .. 45, 80
Roberts, Lieut. J. P. (Plate II., VIII.), 4, 5, 61.
Robertson, Lt.-Col. (now Brig.-Gen.) J. C., C.B., C.M.G., D.S.O., V.D. (Plate II., VIII., XII.), 4, 5, 41, 43, 61, 75, 84, 88, 94, 95, 97, 103, 134, 141, 147, 154, 279, 282.
Robertson, The Rev. Gordon ...... 273
Robertson, P'te. ........... 220, 221
Robertson, Major S. B. (Plate II., VIII.), 4, 5, 43, 61.
Robey, P'te. G., D.C.M. ... 56, 74, 78
Robinson, P'te. (Plate XXIII.).
Rockets .............'........ 90, 119
Rooney, P'te. .................. 259
Ross, Lt.-Col. A. M. ...... 6, 72, 253

Ross, Lt.-Col. C. F., M.C. (Plate II., XI., XVIII., XXIV., XXV.), 4, 5, 44, 60, 81, 84, 86, 155, 177, 179, 182, 183, 185, 207, 210, 211, 218, 233, 234, 236, 248, 263-264, 279.
Ross, L./Cpl. .................. 126
Rouge Croix (Map 1, 22), 186, 206, 217
Rouge de Bout (Map 1, 13) ...... 109
Royal Guard ............ 253-255, 281
Royal Horse Artillery ............ 183
Royal Marines ............. 59, 60
Royal Naval Division .......... 30, 67
Royal Scots .................. 203
Ruddle, Lieut. C. H. 97, 133, 134, 269
Rue du Bois (Map 1, 13, 14), 109, 115
Rum .. 29, 148, 151, 201, 210, 253
"Rum Hollow" ................ 148
"Rum-jars" .................. 147
Runners .. 133, 196-197, 240, 271-272
Russell, Lieut. S. H., M.M. (Plate XVI.), 223, 228.
Russell's Top (Map 9) .......... 84
Ryan, Capt. C. H., M.V.O., M.C., 253-255.
Ryan, Lieut. (Plate XVI.)
Ryder, Capt. J. F. (Plate II., VIII.), 4, 5, 43, 48-50, 61.
Rye Trench (Map 18), 161, 166, 167
Ryrie, Maj.-Gen. Sir G. de L. ...... 88

Sablon, La (Map 1) ............. 230
Sailly-sur-la-Lys (Map 1, 13), 109-111, 113, 203.
St. Germain Wood (Map 27) .. 237, 240
St. Omer (Map 1) ........ 216, 230
St. Pierre Divion .............. 153
St. Pol ..................... 121
St. Roch railway station ..... 203, 204
St. Sylvestre Cappel (Map 1) .... 213
Salisbury .................. 158
Salisbury Plain .......... 13, 158, 266
Salisbury, Lt.-Col. A. G., C.M.G., D.S.O. & Bar, Legion d'Honneur (Plate II., VI., VIII., XI.), 4, 5, 20, 40, 43, 45, 47, 48, 50-54, 59, 61, 70-72, 75, 78, 80, 88, 96, 98, 100, 103, 126, 134, 137, 279.
Salisbury, Lieut. R. B., M.C. (Plate XVI.), 194.
Samer (Map 1) ................ 198
Sami Bey, Colonel .............. 64
Sanders, General Liman von .... 58, 63
Sandhills Camp ................ 266
Sanitary squad ........... 272-273
Sari Bair .................... 35
Saros, Gulf of (Map 6) .... 36, 62, 91
Sarpi Camp (Plate XI., Map 5), 94-96, 97, 270, 273.
Sars Poteries (Map 29) ... 253, 255-256
Saunders, E. C. (Plate XXIII.).
Saunders, C.S.M. J. L. ........... 143
Sausage Valley (Map 15), 122-124, 138
Savage, C.Q.M.S. Vic. ........... 267
Saxonia, H.M.T. ............ 103-104
Scott, P'te. (Plate XXV.).
Scougall, Lieut. F. B. ....... 68,191
Scouts ........ 109, 124, 145, 155
Scrivener, Lieut. N. T., M.C. ...... 164
Scrubby Knoll (Map 8) ... 35, 36, 52
Scully, Vin .................. 155
Sebourg Chateau ........... 253-255
Semple, P'te. (Plate XXV.).
Sequieres (Map 1) ............. 198

# INDEX (Continued)

Serapeum (Map 3, 10), 98, 100, 102-103, 271.
Sercus (Map 1) ............ 216, 218
Sergeant-Major ................ 269
Shaw, Major (10th Battalion) .. 88, 279
Shaw, Lieut. S. (Plate XVI., XXIV.), 263.
Sheedy, Lieut. T. J. (Plate XXIV.), 263
Sheepskin vests ................ 151
Shell Green (Plate XI., Map 9), 79, 80, 84.
Shelter Wood Camp ............ 168
Shield, Lieut. H. M. ........... 170
Short, J. W. (Plate IX.).
Shrapnel Green (Map 9) ........ 65
Shrapnel Gully (Map 8, 9), 45, 56, 59, 65, 69, 79.
Shrewsbury, Lieut. W. A. .. 163-165, 171
Shropshire, H.M.A.T. ........... 12
Sickness (see Illness).
Siegfried Line ................ 167
Signallers (Plate XVII.), 26, 133, 246-247, 271-272.
Silt Spur (Map 9) .......... 80, 82
Sinclair, Sgt. J. ............. 5, 59
Sinclair-MacLagan (see Maclagan).
Sizer, Cpl. H. ................. 72
Skeen, Lieut.-Col. A. ........... 72
Skinner, J. (Plate, XXI., XXIII.).
Slaughter, Cpl. ................ 132
Smith, Lieut. ................. 236
Smith, Lieut. (10th Battalion) .... 185
Smith, C. ..................... 120
Smith, P'te. Hugh (Plate XXIII.) .. 119
Smith-Lawson, Capt. ............ 268
Smoke Trench (Map 17) .... 155, 156
Sniper's Ridge (Map 9) .... 80-84, 90
Snow ...... 154, 158, 159, 257, 258
Soissons ..................... 167
Solre-le-Chateau (Map 29) ...... 256
Solre-St.-Gery (Map 29) ........ 256
Somerville, Sgt. ............... 268
Somme Area (Map 2), 121-144, 149-184, 203-205, 231-247.
Somme Canal (Map 27) ...... 237, 239
Somme River (Map 12, 27, 29), 237, 241
Souter, Sgt. .................. 273
Souterrains at Naours ....... 121-122
Southampton ................. 266
South Borre ............. 212, 216
Spearett, F. (Plate XXI.).
Spoil Bank (Map 16) ...... 200, 203
Sports 9, 95, 111, 146, 159, 181, 182, 185, 194, 200, 216, 218, 221, 222, 248, 249, 255, 260-262, 265.
Square Wood (Map 27) .......... 239
Squids ....................... 213
Staffordshire Regiment ......... 124
Staple (Map 1) ............ 184, 185
Star of England, H.M.A.T. ........ 5
"Starvonia," H.M.T. ............ 104
Steadman, P'te. ............... 200
Steele, Lieut. A., D.C.M., 5, 52, 53, 68, 69, 78.
Steele's Post (Map 9) ........... 60
Steenbecque (Map 1) ........... 184
Steenvoorde (Map 1) ...... 148, 192
Steenwerck (Map 1) ....... 114, 203
Stenhouse, Lieut. (Plate XVI.) .... 193
Strazeele (Map 1, 22) .. 106, 213, 222
Street, Lieut. L. W. ......... 58, 60
Stretcher-bearers, 56, 68, 82, 132, 167, 272-273.
Stuart, Sgt. L. (Plate XXIII.) .... 261
Suez (Map 3) ............. 13-14

Suez Canal (Map 10), 14-15, 92, 98, 102-103.
Suffolk, H.M.T. ................ 263
Sugar-loaf, The (Map 13, 14) .... 115
Suller, D. L. ......... 213, 240, 281
Sullivan, P'te. W. J. ............ 81
Sutton, Sgt. .................. 220
Sutton Veny .................. 248
Suvla Bay (Map 6, 7), 34, 62, 86, 87, 91, 92.
Swain, Lieut. (now Major) H. L. .. 100
Swain, P'te. .................. 259
Swartz, Lieut. R. W. (Plate XXII.).
Swayn, L./Cpl. ................ 131
Switch Trench (Map 17) .... 125, 155
Sydney, H.M.A.S. ............. 8-10

Tailor, Battalion ...... 249, 253, 275
Takada, H.M.A.T. .......... 267-268
Talikna Point (Map 5) .......... 31
Talmas (Map 2) ............... 144
Tamblyn, J. .................... 7
Tanks .......... 151, 231, 240, 243
Tasmania Post (Map 9) .......... 86
Taylor, G. R. ................. 236
Tel-el-Kebir (Map 3) ......... 96-98
Tennant, Lieut. ............... 263
Therma ....................... 96
Thienshouk (Map 1) ........... 186
Thiepval (Map 2) .............. 123
Thomas, Lieut. G. (Plate II., VIII.), 4, 5, 21, 30, 46-48, 50, 51, 53, 61
Thomas, Lieut. (Plate XXIV.) .... 263
Thomas, L. .................... 40
Thompson, Lieut. C. O. ......... 263
Thompson, Lieut. .............. 134
Thompson, Sgt. ............... 275
Thorley, C.S.M. H. E. (Plate XXI.).
Thursby, Rear-Admiral ...... 38, 57
Thwaites, P'te. (Plate XXV.).
Thy-le-Chateau (Map 29) ....... 256
Tidworth ..................... 158
Tidyman, N. M. ............... 236
Tiger's Tooth ............... 19-21
Tincourt (Map 2, 29), 241-242, 247, 251.
Todd, C.S.M. (Plate XXII.) ..... 236
Torpedo-boat wrecked ........... 29
Tournai Camp ............ 201-202
Townsend, Cpl. ............... 134
Townsville ................. 2, 183
Training, 2-3, 6, 13, 17, 19-22, 27, 31, 80, 158, 168, 216.
Transport, Battalion ....... 191, 271
Transports (see Troopships).
Trenches (Plate VII., XI.), 65, 75, 89, 98, 111-112, 152.
Trench feet .......... 150, 153, 157
Trench mortars ........... 112, 147
Triumph, H.M.S. ............... 74
Troopships, 5-15, 23-25, 31-33, 92, 96, 103-104, 263, 266, 267-268.
Troop-trains ....... 105-106, 121, 149
Tug-of-war team (Plate XXII.) ... 200
Tunn, Lieut. J. P., Albert Medal (Plate XVIII.), 227.
Tunnellers .......... 261, 262, 268
Turkey Knoll (Map 9) ....... 80, 82
Twin Trenches (Map 9) ...... 74-75
Twomey, P'te. ................ 159
Tyne Cottage (Map 16) .... 195-197
Tyrrell, H. J. ................. 68

# INDEX (Continued)

U.S.A. .............. 221, 246-247

Vadencourt (Map 2) ............ 137
Vaire (Map 2) ................ 237
Vance, P'te. .............. 220, 282
Vauchelles-les-Quesnoy .......... 149
Vaughan, Lieut. G. (12th Battalion) 185
Vaulx-Vraucourt (Map 2, 19), 170, 175
Vauvillers (Map 2) .... 232, 236-237
Venn, P'te. (Plate XXIII.).
Verbranden Road (Map 16) ...... 148
Verry, R. H. ................. 269
Versailles (Map 11) ........... 105
Very lights .............. 112, 219
Vicogne, La (Map 2) ........... 135
Victoria Cross ........ 128, 130, 227
Victoria Gully (Map 9) ... 44, 49, 53
Vieux-Berquin (Map 22) .... 185-186
Villeret (Map 2, 28) ...... 242-245
Villers-Bretonneux (Map 2) ....... 88
Villers-sous-Ailly (Map 2) ....... 231
Vowles, Capt. A. S., D.S.O. ...... 143

Wagner, A. J. (Plate XXII.) ...... 133
Waldron, W. O. ................ 265
Wales, H.R.H. the Prince of, 103, 254-255, 259.
Walker, Sgt. G. (Plate XXII.) .... 235
Walker, Lt.-Gen. Sir H. B., 110, 113, 146, 216.
Walker, Lieut. H. M. ............ 233
Wallon-Cappel (Map 1) ......... 218
Walsh, Major R. H. .. 81, 83, 88, 279
Walsh, Lieut. ................. 185
Wambeek (Map 16) ............ 200
Ward, P'te. .................. 220
Warloy (Map 2) .......... 135, 144
Warminster .................. 266
Warneminde, Lieut. C. J. ........ 201
Warner, Lieut. A. .............. 271
Warren, Capt. A. ........ 31, 81, 116
Water, 28, 65, 78, 79, 98-99, 136, 151
Waterlow, Lieut. J. B. ........... 40
Waton, Le (Map 22, 25) .... 223-228
Watten (Map 1) ............... 148
Wavrons (Map 1) .............. 198
Webster, P'te. Eric .............. 26
Weir, Lieut.-Col. S. Price .... 88, 103
Weir Ridge (Map 9) ............ 69
Wemyss, Rear-Admiral Wester, 26, 45, 92
Westhoek Ridge (Plate XV., Map 16, 21), 186, 187, 193, 195.

Wet Pond .................... 202
Weynand, Lieut. N. L. ..... 68, 91, 134
Whaites, P'te. (Plate XXIII.).
Wheat Trench (Map 18), 161, 163, 166, 167.
Wheatley, Lieut. A. R. ....... 196, 210
White, Lt.-Gen. Sir C. B. B. .... 1, 110
White, Capt. R. M., M.C., 128, 129, 134, 165, 166.
White, P'te. .................. 74
White's Gully (Map 9) .......... 46
Whyte, Sgt. F. L. (Plate XXII.), 225, 254.
Wide Bay Regiment ........... 2, 4
Wilder-Neligan, Lt.-Col. M. (see Neligan)
Wilkinson, P'te. (Plate XXIII.).
Williams, Staff Nurse B. M. ........ 5
Williams, Lieut. W. J. (Plate II., VIII.), 4, 5, 74, 78, 272.
Williams, Stretcher-bearer, V. H., 56-57, 59.
Willington, Lieut. T. (Plate XXII.).
Wilson, C'pl. ................. 218
Wilson, J. ................... 236
Wilson, L. S. H. (Plate IX.).
Wilson, Lieut. (Plate XVI.).
Wire, Wiring, 63, 75, 111, 116-117, 207, 222.
Wire Gully (Map 9) ............ 49
Wismes (Map 1) .............. 198
Wittkopp, Lieut. C. A., 130, 134, 172, 192.
Wizernes (Map 1) ......... 198, 230
Wrench, Lieut. C. M., M.C. (Plate XXIII., XXIV.), 181, 206, 225, 234, 239, 263, 267.
Wright, P'te. (Plate XXIII.).
Wulverghem (Map 1, 16), 197, 199, 200

Yellow Cut (Plate XIII., Map 18), 161, 163, 165, 166.
Young, Capt. H. T., M.C., 114, 116-118, 120.
Young, Lieut. J. (Plate XVI.), 200, 206
Young, J. .................... 235
Young, Major W. McK. G., 4, 5, 50, 71, 81, 96, 103, 130, 134, 279.
Ypres (Map 1, 12, 16), 144, 146, 188, 194, 197.
Ypres Area (see Flanders).
Ypres-Comines Canal (Map 16) ... 201

Zeitoun ...................... 97

www.ingramcontent.com/pod-product-compliance
Lightning Source LLC
Chambersburg PA
CBHW021831220426
43663CB00005B/202